Navigating Souths

SERIES EDITOR

Riché Richardson, Cornell University

FOUNDING EDITOR

Jon Smith, Simon Fraser University

ADVISORY BOARD

Houston A. Baker Jr., Vanderbilt University

Leigh Anne Duck, The University of Mississippi

Jennifer Greeson, The University of Virginia

Trudier Harris, The University of Alabama

John T. Matthews, Boston University

Tara McPherson, The University of Southern California

Claudia Milian, Duke University

Navigating Souths

TRANSDISCIPLINARY
EXPLORATIONS
OF A U.S. REGION

EDITED BY
Michele Grigsby Coffey
AND Jodi Skipper

The University of
Georgia Press
ATHENS

Paperback edition, 2020
© 2017 by the University of Georgia Press
Athens, Georgia 30602
www.ugapress.org
All rights reserved
Set in 10/13 Kepler Standard by Graphic Composition, Inc.

Most University of Georgia Press titles are
available from popular e-book vendors.

Printed digitally

Library of Congress Cataloging-in-Publication Data

Names: Coffey, Michele Grigsby, editor. | Skipper, Jodi, editor.
Title: Navigating Souths : transdisciplinary explorations of a U.S. region / edited by Michele Grigsby Coffey and Jodi Skipper.
Other titles: New southern studies.
Description: Athens : The University of Georgia Press, [2017] | Series: The new southern studies | Includes bibliographical references and index.
Identifiers: LCCN 2016055853 | ISBN 9780820351070 (hardback : alk. paper) | ISBN 9780820351087 (ebook)
Subjects: LCSH: Southern States—Civilization—Study and teaching (Higher)—United States. | Interdisciplinary approach in education—United States.
Classification: LCC F208.5 .N38 2017 | DDC 975.007/1—dc23
LC record available at https://loc.gov.2016055853

Paperback ISBN 978-0-8203-5877-2

CONTENTS

ACKNOWLEDGMENTS vii

Introduction 1
MICHELE GRIGSBY COFFEY AND JODI SKIPPER

PART 1. Laying the Groundwork

Reimagining Southern Studies
Time and Space, Bodies and Spirits 21
CHARLES REAGAN WILSON

PART 2. Reframing Norms

Deconstructing the Bible Belt 57
JOHN HAYES

Katrina Babies
Reproducing Deviance in the Future Unknown 72
ALIX CHAPMAN

PART 3. Engaging Politics

Southern Inhospitality
Latino Immigrant Attrition and Resistance in the South 87
GWENDOLYN FERRETI

Public History, Diversity, and Higher Education
Three Case Studies on the African American Past 101
JODI SKIPPER, KATHRYN GREEN, AND RICO D. CHAPMAN

Where Do We Go from Here?
The Implications of Black Intellectual History in the Modern South 123
ROBERT GREENE II

South Unbound
A Case Study in Ron Rash's Appalachian Fiction 135
DANIEL CROSS TURNER

PART 4. Southern Studies in Practice

Interlocality and Interdisciplinarity
Learning from Existing Models of the Global South 153
KIRSTEN DELLINGER, JEFFREY T. JACKSON,
KATIE B. MCKEE, AND ANNETTE TREFZER

Finding Strength in Southern Studies Pedagogy
*Cultivating Individual Resilience through a
Representative Narrative* 167
MICHELE GRIGSBY COFFEY

Southern Transformations
Three Documentary Films by Anne Lewis 182
ANNE LEWIS AND LEIGH ANNE DUCK

Surviving the Economic Apocalypse
*Capitalism, Consumption, and the Indian Imaginary
in Karen Russell's* Swamplandia! 201
MELANIE BENSON TAYLOR

Last (Un)Fair Deal Going Down
*Blues Tourism and Racial Politics in
Clarksdale, Mississippi* 214
KATHRYN RADISHOFSKI

The Politics of Hillbilly Horror 227
EMILY SATTERWHITE

PART 5. Drives and Desires

For They Know Not What They Do
*Southern Studies Centers, Normativity, and
Fantasies of White Redemption* 249
JON SMITH

BIBLIOGRAPHY 265

CONTRIBUTORS 293

INDEX 299

ACKNOWLEDGMENTS

This collection materialized from our vision of bringing together scholars, practitioners, and activists in various disciplines working in and on the U.S. South. We are grateful to many individuals who made that effort possible. Our first thanks are to Ted Ownby and Charles Reagan Wilson for their early generosity in supporting the Transforming New South Identities Symposium, which shaped our approach to this book and enriched our understanding of southern studies as academic practice. We are also grateful to Walter Biggins, our editor at the University of Georgia Press, for having faith in the symposium and book project from the beginning and for sending the manuscript to discerning readers whose comments and vision strengthened this book.

We would also like to express our gratitude to Elaine Abadie, Barbara Harris Combs, Jeffrey T. Jackson, Katie McKee, and Ted Ownby, who collaborated with us as members of the steering committee for the Transforming New South Identities Symposium held at the University of Mississippi in 2014; to all of the University of Mississippi faculty who suggested participants; and to Robert Brinkmeyer, Deirdre Cooper Owens, Barbara Harris Combs, Simone Delerme, Kirsten Dellinger, Leigh Anne Duck, Robbie Ethridge, John J. Green, Darren E. Grem, Ross Haenfler, Andy Harper, Jeffrey T. Jackson, Willa M. Johnson, Katie McKee, Ted Ownby, and Zandria Robinson for answering our call to serve as symposium facilitators, discussants, and peer reviewers. Thanks also to Becca Walton for her thoughtful and judicious assistance in symposium planning. We are also particularly appreciative of the generous funding from the Center for the Study of Southern Culture's Endowment for the Future of the South, which made the symposium possible.

This book grew out of papers presented at the Transforming New South Identities Symposium. We are especially indebted to those who daringly came together for the symposium in 2014, including Martyn Bone, Zac Henson, Sabrina Pendergrass, Tom Okie, and Susan O'Donovan, whose works are not published in this volume but who participated in the symposium's peer review process. Their critiques are visible in the works of their peers. We also wish to express our appreciation to the authors whose essays are included here. It was a privilege to observe and participate in your scholarly and creative processes.

Finally, we are thankful for the generous mentorship of Marjorie Spruill, who always made time to talk us through particularly complex steps in editing a collection.

Navigating Souths

Introduction

MICHELE GRIGSBY COFFEY
AND JODI SKIPPER

This book began with conversations in a living room in Oxford, Mississippi, in 2011. As a historian and an anthropologist who both study the South, we were at roughly the same place in our academic careers. We had each worked outside of and within the academy in multiple southern states and were each beginning our first year as faculty at the University of Mississippi's Center for the Study of Southern Culture. We had many conversations about our personal academic projects, as well as broader political, social, cultural, and economic issues impacting the region we choose to study. Although we are both outspoken and anticipated, perhaps welcomed, hotly contested disputes, we were surprised to discover that the most spirited moments in our energizing debates did not stem from differences in opinion but were instead rooted in disciplinary differences, in the basic ways in which we framed and verbalized our work. For example, we both prioritized community engagement as one of our academic goals, yet we spent a great deal of time arguing about whether we should identify ourselves as activist-scholars, public scholars, or perhaps something else entirely. We found through our conflicts on the matter that such determinations were not solely personal decisions but were influenced by what we perceived as acceptable in each of our fields or even individual departments. In some cases, the labeling of oneself as an activist might be applauded; in others such a label could mean setting oneself apart.[1]

Such conversations are obviously one of the privileges of academia, yet we could not trivialize them as unimportant. They were manifestations of what ultimately proved to be larger, often political, vocabulary differences that would emerge especially when we engaged the theoretical debates taking place not only in our disciplines but more importantly in what we came to know as southern studies. After all, we were not just a historian and an anthropologist. We also had joint appointments in the Center for the Study of Southern Culture (CSSC) and therefore should arguably be engaging a shared literature with a reasonably clear understanding of other disciplinary engagements in southern studies. However, we quickly realized, as scholars who study the South, that our incapacity to speak across our home disciplines impeded our ability to collaborate with maximum benefit. We began to wonder how such issues might be reflected in larger transdisciplinary dialogues around southern studies research.

Defining southern studies is challenging for there is no one definition that suffices in all fields or circumstances. Indeed, some will argue that such an exercise will inevitably be a moot one, as such a conceptual framework is as fluid as the region it proposes to investigate. Scholars in history, literature, and, to a lesser extent, other disciplines have often discussed the relationships between the historical, social, and cultural forces that have helped to shape the U.S. South. However, most of these debates have taken place within specific academic disciplines, with few attempts to cross-engage. Recent anthologies explicitly attempting to consider humanities and social science approaches connect scholars through particular lenses of study. Examples include Jennifer Jansen Wallach's *Dethroning the Deceitful Pork Chop: Rethinking African American Foodways from Slavery to Obama* (2015); William Reynolds's *Critical Studies of Southern Place: A Reader* (2014); Khyati Y. Joshi and Jigna Desai's *Asian Americans in Dixie: Race and Migration in the South* (2013); John T. Edge, Elizabeth Englehardt, and Ted Ownby's *The Larder: Food Studies Methods from the American South* (2013); Brian Ward, Martyn Bone, and William Link's *The American South and the Atlantic World* (2013); and Jessica Adams, Michael P. Bibler, and Cécile Accilien's *Just Below South: Intercultural Performance in the Caribbean and the U.S. South* (2007).[2]

We see these more anthologies as necessary and positive steps toward more multidisciplinary analyses of specific topics in the field of southern studies.[3] However, we are not acting in response to those works. We are more specifically responding to John Lowe's call for a "firm interdisciplinary grounding" in southern studies as expressed in *Bridging Southern Cultures: An Interdisciplinary Approach* (2005). We are particularly attracted by Lowe's appeal to "fertiliz[e] interchange with colleagues from other disciplines" to most effectively "explore new questions and issues."[4] *Navigating Souths: Transdisciplinary Explorations of a U.S. Region* answers that call, yet, for us, bridging southern studies is less about seeking firmness and more about understanding the fluidity of its boundaries. Ours is not an attempt to define southern studies but to present research as sites through which readers can think through the practicality, or perhaps impracticality, of southern studies as a transdisciplinary study. At a very basic level, this requires a collective awareness and understanding of southern studies practice and theory. We also believe that it requires recognition of how diverse perspectives complicate perceptions of an exceptional or quintessentially southern region. We seek to affirm this recognition with the pluralized "Souths" in our title.

Through this collection, using broader and more collective transdisciplinary languages, we seek to explore shared, complex platforms from which those who conceive of the U.S. South through various conceptual frameworks might find greater common ground on which to establish clearer theoretical and methodological communication. This book is one trial in that experiment, which began with the Transforming New South Identities Symposium, which we organized through the Center for the Study of Southern Culture at the University of Mississippi.

The Transforming New South Identities Symposium

We began planning for the Transforming New South Identities Symposium by asking CSSC core and affiliated faculty to suggest individuals for participation. The resultant list was massive and broadly interdisciplinary. It also contained the names of scholars who were at various stages of their careers, from graduate students to full professors as well as independent scholar-activists. We organized an interdisciplinary steering committee to help narrow participation to a productive and fundable level. Of the invited scholars, fifteen chose to participate. Participants represented nine disciplines, including geography, literature, anthropology, history, documentary filmmaking, sociology, and American studies. Through the exchange of pre-circulated, original papers, sharing of experiences, and discussion of research strategies, participants explored the project theme, transcending southern identities, as a way to examine how southern studies scholars move across their various disciplines to interpret the social dynamics within the region, as well as how southern studies offers a framework for those who work in the South to place their projects within regional and global contexts. Aside from divergences between and within academic disciplines, we recognized that many scholars were doing work in and on the U.S. South without specifically connecting to a southern studies field. This meant that scholars not traditionally associated with disciplines more largely represented in formal southern studies debates could be overlooked or not be recognized. As a result, we sought to bring such scholars into these conversations as vital voices necessary to understand the limitations of the field as it is currently practiced.

The three-day symposium was organized into three main parts: peer review sessions, research-focused workshops, and roundtables focusing on the field as a whole. Each participant was expected to take part in a peer review process, designed to prepare participants for a more concentrated symposium workshop and possible submission to an edited collection. Contrary to the standard peer review process for academic journals, our process was not anonymous. Reviewers and authors spent reflective and productive time with each other, in groups of three to four people, which included no more than two authors working on related projects. Our goal was to inspire conversations and interdisciplinary exchanges, as well as encourage long-term partnerships. Individual authors were placed in groups based on thematic interests rather than specializations, and center-affiliated faculty members in disciplines other than those of the authors were selected as facilitators. Participants were asked not only to discuss their paper projects but also to prioritize disciplinary differences, including theory, methodologies, and data. It was our hope that such interactions might inspire more integrative, transdisciplinary approaches within individual works.

Participants were then shuffled into workshop groups, paired with different authors, who again did not share specializations. Workshop participants were asked to consider how their work might be expanded to speak to larger, interdisciplinary audiences; how their experiences working in and on the South might influence research outcomes; how that experience might be better used to strengthen the work; and where their work fit within existing dialogues of southern studies. As part of this process, a designated former or present University of Mississippi faculty facilitator guided in-depth discussions of the pre-circulated papers in relationship to these questions.

The symposium concluded with two roundtables facilitated by faculty who were either currently affiliated with the CSSC or who had been affiliated with the center in the past. In these roundtables, participants, facilitators, and invited affiliated faculty and graduate students engaged first in a pedagogical conversation on teaching southern studies. The second roundtable focused on conversations designed to create basic platforms for transdisciplinary dialogues. General feedback describing the symposium as "invigorating and thought-provoking with just the right mix of intense, high-level intellectual exchange and relaxing, easy camaraderie," "an enriching opportunity," "extremely helpful and rewarding," and "productive and enriching" was encouraging.

Following the symposium, contributors of papers were invited to revise their work for this book. For these revisions, we more specifically asked that contributors address the primary goals of the book by elaborating on the transdisciplinary elements of their work, reflecting on the ways in which their work might stimulate additional transdisciplinary conversations in southern studies, and/or explore ways in which others might continue these sorts of transdisciplinary dialogues. It was our hope that the subsequent work would speak to those outside of the contributors' specific disciplines, as well as to those employed outside of academia. In addition, we asked that those whose projects lent themselves to such theorizing analyze the challenges to doing transdisciplinary work in the current academic environment or provide readers with greater insights into potential models for their own work. Our requests were broadly interpreted and, we think, evocatively reflect diversity in disciplinary lines and research stages, as well as differing individual comfort, anxiety, and familiarity with approaching such issues.

The resulting book is designed to introduce readers to contemporary intellectual debates in research, theory, and methods in southern studies, including the variety of ideas that underlie the articulation of the very construct of "southern studies." As such, it 1) approaches key research issues related to the study of the South, as introduced by scholars in several academic fields; 2) considers the applicability and relevance of different methods of acquiring, interpreting, and presenting knowledge on the U.S. South; 3) considers southern studies as a geopolitical frame and as a distinct intellectual project; and 4) explores the ways scholars have conceptualized and theorized the South and how its communities are imagined. It is our hope that this book will inspire additional critical discussion about what constitutes evidence, how to analyze data, and what are useful strategies for writing, presenting, and using research on the U.S. South.

Part 1: Laying the Groundwork

Because theory and practice overlap and inform the chapters of this book, we begin by theoretically grounding readers. Part 1 provides a foundation for the present state of southern studies scholarship through Charles Reagan Wilson's historiography of southern studies and responses to the gaps that he identified within the scholarship he surveyed. His featured lecture at the Transforming New South Identities symposium translates into a remarkable essay examining academic imaginings of the South as a U.S. region, liminal space, and global world, by privileging the analytical categories of time, space, bodies, and spirits. Considering, imagining, and theorizing the U.S. South within regional, national, and global contexts is not new. However, few scholars have the skill or experience to historiographically frame approaches to studying the U.S. South with the depth and artistry of Wilson, former director of the CSSC. His "Reimagining Southern Studies: Time and Space, Bodies and Spirits" surveys scholarly answers to Houston Baker Jr. and Dana D. Nelson's 2001 call for a "new Southern studies."[5] Wilson's assertion—that "not every historian will engage with cultural studies, nor will every cultural studies scholar want to hear the voices from contemporary ethnography, but the generous engagement with each other's work offers the best long range hope for a new Southern Studies"—sets the tone for a basic memorandum of understanding from which this book grew.[6] Here Wilson challenges scholars in and of the South to engage our more recent historiography through a comprehensive assessment of the field. We see his genealogy as a point of reflection for those already familiar with scholarship on the U.S. South and a necessary foundation for those new to such discussions.

Part 2: Reframing Norms

Several scholars in this work build on the existing frameworks presented in Wilson's essay by exploring new questions and issues designed to help readers think more critically about studying the South through ideological, as well as more concrete, theoretical constructions.[7] In his essay, Wilson contends that "innovative works in southern religious studies that draw on theory—a major concern for a new southern studies—have not worked their way into recent discussions of interdisciplinary approaches to the South."[8] Speaking to this concern, John Hayes reminds us that ideological constructions generally associated with the U.S. South should be historicized in their more appropriate contexts. In "Deconstructing the Bible Belt," he identifies more contemporary interpretations of the Bible Belt as imprecise representations of what was actually a distinct era in the South's regional history. Hayes argues that the Bible Belt is also misrepresented as a uniquely southern concept by showing how characteristics of the Bible Belt become apparent across the nation. Likewise, he contends that there is nothing distinctly southern about religious nationalism. Hayes's work challenges the reader not only to rethink particular images traditionally correlated with the U.S. South but also to deconstruct them through specific historical moments and across broader regional spaces.

Through ethnography and personal narratives, Alix Chapman's "Katrina Babies: Reproducing Deviance in the Future Unknown" goes beyond what Wilson's survey presents as a centering of African Americans in current discourses on "the South" by rendering queer people of color narratives necessary to studies on the U.S. South. Chapman's work highlights Lowe's recognition of the potential contributions of program studies by intersecting southern and African diaspora studies with queer theory in a critique of heteronormative notions of family, kinship, and social reproduction in post–Hurricane Katrina New Orleans. Here Chapman presents queer theory as a lens through which to analyze how particular forms of race, class, and sexuality are alienated from more privileged notions of reproduction, amid systemic oppression. Through their voices Chapman gives us a glimpse into the real and symbolic roadblocks that black queer subjects face in their attempts to reproduce families and have futures.

Chapman presents his intervention as one queer studies scholar who works in and on the U.S. South. His work not only confronts the scarcity of queer theory as a tool in southern studies research, it also subtly challenges scholars who perceive engaging both queer theory and the experiences of queer persons of color as optional. Chapman examines that which is essential to the survival of the community in which he works and moves. Similarly, we see works like Chapman's as essential to the survival of any southern studies seeking a firmer interdisciplinary grounding. That survival is dependent upon an understanding of the genealogy and contemporary state of queer theory, to better equip scholars in their critiques of intersecting oppressions.[9]

Part 3: Engaging Politics

Part 3 aims to complicate perceptions of southern studies as an apolitical field of research. It is quite the opposite due to the intensely political spaces in which many of us operate and the multiplicity of ways in which southern studies research often directly relates to the political tensions and problems in the region.[10] Although many scholars of the South recognize these present and pressing connections, efforts to engage personally and examine institutional motives and modes of production are uncommon. The essays in part 3 call into question whether a larger transition from theory to practice is not only timely but also necessary.

In "Southern Inhospitality: Latino Immigrant Attrition and Resistance in the South," Gwendolyn Ferreti uses activist ethnographic research to assess responses on the ground to the passage and implementation of Alabama's HB56, which greatly curtailed the rights of undocumented immigrants in that state and became one of the harshest anti-immigration laws in the United States. Ferreti argues that such laws, with comparable versions in other parts of the U.S. South, represent a shift from an African American–focused "white supremacist racial binary" to a "new lens of xenophobic hyper-nativism."[11] Simultaneously, even in the face of these exclusionary efforts, Ferreti contends that some Latinos not only assume a southern but also an activist southern identity. Ferreti's context for HB56 and its effects are highlighted by her voice as an activist scholar, as a witness to and participant in this new immigrant activism. Like scholars of southern Native Americans and other scholars of the Latino experience, Ferreti recognizes that the traditional racial binary of black and white is both unsatisfying and problematic in southern studies research. Yet what is most distinguished about her research is its direct consideration of a new relationship of southern studies to social activism, especially in the contemporary South, which Wilson cites in his essay as inadequately addressed.[12] Ferreti's social activism as a concerned citizen and scholar parallels the Alabama undocumented immigrant community's resistance struggles in defense of the South as their place. As an activist scholar, Ferreti takes this placement for granted, as necessary not only to understand issues in culture and identity but also to understand the personal experiences of contemporary southerners. Wilson presents the problem "that much of the literature on social activism in the South is not taken into account by those of us who intentionally do southern studies of any sort."[13] Ferreti's work reconceptualizes that concern by prioritizing scholarship in action, beyond more one-dimensional literature assessments. Such an approach is necessary to understand public policies and their real effects on contemporary communities in the U.S. South.

The authors of "Public History, Diversity, and Higher Education: Three Case Studies on the African American Past" make clear that the institutional politics surrounding southern studies extend outside of southern studies centers themselves. Rico Chapman, Kathryn Green, and Jodi Skipper recently formed an interdisciplinary faculty working group from three Mississippi universities after meeting at a conference on African diaspora heritage tourism in February 2015. Through their collaboration, they hope to better understand diversification in southern studies scholarship through the lens of public history. In their essay, Chapman and Green, both historians, and Skipper, an anthropologist, assess their institutional foundations as well as methodological approaches to community-based public history work. This chapter has implications for profiling diversity in southern studies scholarship, which makes it a direct response to Jon Smith's classed, raced, and gendered critique of southern studies practice and practitioners in the collection's final essay.

In the next essay of part 3, Robert Greene II continues the analysis of history within southern studies, suggesting a fresh frame for post-1965 southern intellectual history through the rise of "New South Democrats," the inclusion of Southern conservatives, and the roles of African American historians and political progressives. "Where Do We Go from Here? The Implications of Black Intellectual History in the Modern South" is relevant and thought-provoking not only in its goal of creating a model for historically analyzing the U.S. South from the Voting Rights Act to the first election of President Barack Obama, but also in its discussion of the South's ambiguous role as a place of opportunity and a place rife with potential pitfalls. Greene further complicates notions of the region and its relationship to the rest of the country, exploring the South as at times a politically useful Other but also a partisan stronghold of occasional political advantage. As a public intellectual with a distinguished online presence, Greene is also uniquely positioned to speak to a much larger interdisciplinary audience. Through his writing for the blog of the Society for U.S. Intellectual History, Greene draws an audience into historical analyses with timely political, social, and cultural analyses. Greene also assesses this experience, operating as a historian in a public sphere in a way that is useful for those thinking through what it means to be an effective public intellectual, one who in this case is reaching a broad and ambiguous audience seeking to intellectualize the political South.

Greene's work raises many important issues, but we were particularly drawn to it as his position as a graduate student engaging in such public forums raised pedagogical concerns for us. While it is increasingly common for scholars to debate the risks of public engagement within the context of tenure or lack thereof, graduate students like Greene are more regularly being called upon to publish or are voluntarily posting their ideas publicly, particularly ideas about politically charged topics. They do so without the benefit of secured employment and without the assistance of institutional training as most of us who are educating graduate students remain wary of such work ourselves. The vulnerability and bravery of students like Greene should inspire us to develop methodologies and best practices that would better serve this ever-increasing number of graduate students who are prolific, political, and publicly exposed.[14]

In "South Unbound: A Case Study in Ron Rash's Appalachian Fiction" Daniel Turner approaches the power of work that spans division between social sciences and the humanities by negotiating a largely literary interpretation through sociological contexts. Turner uses the undead—zombies—in the work of popular fiction writer Ron Rash as a lens through which to examine the instability of regional, national, and global boundaries in the modern Appalachian South. Turner calls attention to real contemporary Appalachian "zombies" produced by methamphetamine addiction in particular. Through his focus on the western North Carolina Piedmont, Turner highlights the region's embeddedness in global economic and cultural forces and argues that "understanding the South, in no uncertain terms, matter[s], and this form of interdisciplinary southern studies must matter still."[15] Fundamentally, Turner challenges his readers to recognize, even in fiction, the power of southern studies to impact the politics of the region it studies.

Part 4: Southern Studies in Practice

The chapters in this section most specifically answer John Lowe's call for scholars to cultivate a rich exchange with others outside one's own discipline, through the authors' resourceful consideration of interdisciplinary work as methodology and process, thereby providing diverse models for transdisciplinary scholarship as case studies. This section is composed of collaborative working groups, as well as individual scholars who prefer transdisciplinary approaches in their particular research projects.

The authors of the first piece in this section have been purposefully collaborating as an interdisciplinary faculty working group at the University of Mississippi for several years, seeking to bridge disciplinary divides between English, sociology, and southern studies through the lens of the global South. In "Interlocality and Interdisciplinarity: Learning from Existing Models of the Global South," Kirsten Dellinger, Jeffrey T. Jackson, Katie B. McKee, and

Annette Trefzer describe how their group has helped them to jointly create and individually pursue a global South methodology. In this coauthored piece they describe how their global South not only manifested itself as an interdisciplinary theoretical concept but also as a working tool, strengthening their individual abilities to conceptualize the region in which they work and research. In the process, they provide useful theoretical discussions, practical insights into collaborative, scholarly relationships, and discerning critiques of the applications of the concept of the global South.

"Finding Strength in Southern Studies Pedagogy: Cultivating Individual Resilience through a Representative Narrative" is a response to the concerns raised during the teaching roundtable at the Transforming New South Identities Symposium. Drawing from her background in both curriculum development and specialization in the history of racialized southern politics, Michele Grigsby Coffey writes reflexively about her time teaching southern studies in Mississippi. Further, she uses her essay to argue the benefits of incorporating educational psychology and critical pedagogy as part of a transdisciplinary approach to southern studies. Coffey contends that southern studies courses can be intentionally structured in ways that could improve learning and behavioral outcomes for all students who are attracted to the study of the South, including those who are particularly invested in white supremacist ideology. Grounding her assertions in psychological findings, Coffey asserts that these improved outcomes can be achieved by focusing on the development of what she terms the "intellectual intergenerational self," a complex understanding of one's self in relationship to diverse multicultural experiences through the lens of southern studies courses.[16]

Chapter 10 is an analysis of three of Anne Lewis's best-known documentaries, *Anne Braden: Southern Patriot*, *Morristown: In the Air and Sun*, and *Justice in the Coalfields*, written as a dialogue between Lewis—via her writings for the Transforming New South Identities Symposium—and Leigh Anne Duck's extensive research and engagement with Lewis's work. "Southern Transformations: Three Documentary Films by Anne Lewis" explores the contradictions posed by the symposium's theme. Building on the conception of "New South" as a southern industrial marketing campaign first promoted by white men like Henry Grady in the late nineteenth century, Lewis contends that the modern incarnation of the New South as economically productive and racially tolerant is as problematically nonexistent in the present as it was nonexistent when Grady coined the phrase. Duck's theoretical underpinnings contextualize "Lewis's work in relation to documentary theory and history," while framing Lewis's personal manifesto on southern documentary filmmaking.[17] Lewis's voice projects cinema vérité as her inspiration to "provoke the truth" through her films, in which she interjects an analysis of both a sustained pattern of white supremacy and worker exploitation in the southern Appalachian region. Her intimacy with film subjects and her subject matter closes up the distance frequently found in documentary films. Her conclusion that "black lives matter!" is consistent with her declaration that "every southern documentary film is about race except for those set in Appalachia, which are about class and sometimes race too." This is one small note in a conscious body of work striving to make the intersections and nuances of race and class identity and social transformations accessible through film.[18]

Even without working groups or discursive dialogue, several contributors not only assumed transdisciplinary approaches as integral to their work but necessary and preferential to disciplinarily approaching their arguments. Melanie Benson Taylor straddles what she describes as the "seemingly disparate worlds" of American and southern literature and Native American studies.[19] Through the trope of "playing Indian," she explores the complex relationship between the political economy and perceptions and portrayals of southern Indians in her essay "Surviving the Economic Apocalypse: Capitalism, Consumption, and the Indian Imaginary in Karen Russell's *Swamplandia!*" Through her analysis of Russell's fictional Bigtree family, a "faux-indigenous" family who operates an alligator-wrestling theme park in southern Florida, Taylor explores what she termed in her abstract for her symposium paper "the pageants of authenticity, ascent and belonging that underwrite and undo the American narrative." Albeit through the lens of a fictional account, Taylor's work is comparable to Kathryn Radishofski's recognition of the racial power dynamics at play in the Mississippi Delta and the United States at large. Taylor argues that her work serves as a reminder of the hegemonic relationships present as those with supremacy seek "to inhabit stories instead, ones that claim community and power while denying the dollars and cents that always underwrite such possessions."[20] And she poetically concludes that the "historical memory" of southern bodies and the capitalist realities that surround them represent both that which is most dangerous in the region and simultaneously that which is coveted by its inhabitants.[21]

In "Last (Un)fair Deal Going Down: Blues Tourism and Racial Politics in Clarksdale, Mississippi," Kathryn Radishofski examines the racial politics at play in the heritage tourism of this popular "blues history destination" in the Mississippi Delta. Radishofski, an ethnomusicologist, brings national and global discourses to bear on race, heritage tourism, cultural representations of the past, and music to bear on the activities of the largely white cadre of civic leaders and entrepreneurs helming the blues tourism industry in Clarksdale. This transdisciplinary study links the presentation and performance of blues in a space with a long and lasting history of racial intolerance and conflict as well as a modern reconciliation campaign and a national impulse to popularly brand American society "post-racial" and celebrate and commodify African American heritage and identity. She argues that the racial ideologies at play in this multifaceted economic and artistic exchange exemplify the perpetuation of racial inequality as white consumers and tourism managers shape the spaces and enjoy the socio-economic benefit from the performances.

In "The Politics of Hillbilly Horror," Emily Satterwhite begins by recognizing interdisciplinarity in "scholarship about rural-set horror films" across the humanities and the social sciences as "a form of collaboration that is both inherent in southern studies and a model for future work in southern studies" (227 in this volume). What Satterwhite uniquely addresses are the limitations of those cross-disciplinary collaborations, specifically scholarly readings of the hillbilly horror genre as promoting or progressively "challenging hegemony," especially through white working-class-conscious depictions of political discontent over "structural problems" within the larger American society (227). Satterwhite incorporates "methods and insights from the field of reception studies" to get to underappreciated "actual viewers' interpretations of, and investments in, hillbilly horror films" (228). This additional line of evidence is fruitful as it provides evidence of "a third set of responses heretofore unanticipated by close readings of the films themselves" (229). Satterwhite not only proves the potential value of incorporating nontraditional methodologies in scholarly research. She also offers a new lens through which scholars can assess southern white male reactionaries. This is not only significant to historical analyses but to more recent efforts to profile such demographics on a national scale.

Drives and Desires

We end the book with a chapter by Jon Smith, a key voice in new southern studies scholarship. In "For They Know Not What They Do: Southern Studies Centers, Normativity, and Fantasies of White Redemption," Smith examines the political practicality and potential for southern studies as a field, calling on those of us who are especially in leadership positions to examine that which drives the collective decision making of southern studies institutions. Smith approaches this institutionalization of southern studies, steering from more traditional assessments of scholarship to a direct engagement of southern studies scholars as political actors and public content promoters. We see in Smith's piece the potential to stimulate conversation and open doors to institutional assessments of southern studies centers and associated institutions, a desire repeatedly expressed throughout the symposium process. Smith's chapter is crucial to considerations of the purpose and meaning of southern studies. Yet it is our hope that such assessments can go beyond literary criticism, web page analysis, and anecdotal experience to understanding and profiling the motivations of all southern studies scholars, students, and the communities in which, and with whom, they work. Some of the contributors to this book have sought to do this, just as some scholars outside of the field have modeled.

Smith argues that "we may have entered an era in which the chief fault line in southern studies no longer lies between literary scholars and historians" but between "'progressive' and 'more traditional' scholars and students."[22] We trust that this edited collection of essays demonstrates that to be the case. As we began this project, we were driven by the fact that what Smith presents as a binary is in fact an amorphous, complex, racialized, gendered, and classed playing field that will continue to be undervalued and misinterpreted if platforms for transdisciplinary exchanges tend to be perceived as burdensome or unnecessary by the majority of scholars in the field. As Smith reiterates, several scholars have made calls for such collaboration, yet, outside of academic texts, we as a field have not created enough productive spaces for communication to help understand and bridge our disciplinary gaps.

Smith characterizes subliminal and overt desires of southern studies scholars, with critiques of more recent academic assessments of the field, and he selectively samples the contradictory roles that some of these scholars play primarily within southern studies centers. As editors, we affirm that the fault does not lie in the hands of one or two individuals or their associated institutions. As Smith contends, the crux is our "moral obligation to understand how our desires and drives shape—and distort—our scholarship."[23] That work begins with a shared awareness, sense of academic responsibility, and the willingness to make choices that at times are painful.

Processing the Collection

We wish it were possible to include many more contributors, disciplines, and topics in our symposium conversations, as well as in this book. No one volume can cover all, yet the diversity of scholars and methods represented here has both practical value for research and pedagogy as well as broad theoretical implications for southern studies scholarship. It represents a remarkable array of individuals, and we are proud to have brought these scholars together. We organized the Transforming New South Identities symposium to create a physical space in which a relatively small number of those studying the U.S. South could engage in greater transdisciplinary conversation. *Navigating Souths* is our attempt to bring that physical space into print. Not only are contributors continuing the symposium work, but they are also creating a space through which more multidirectional and transdisciplinary work can be done and applications of critical theory in southern studies can be explored. We believe that the best and most necessary future southern studies will intentionally incorporate and engage unfamiliar voices, while challenging those more experienced in southern studies dialogues to critically reflect on the practical uses of their work to impact southern communities.

As the authors in this book make clear, that work is and will be most likely to engage the people in the region we study. Those studying the South are increasingly called on to address the political circumstances that intersect their work. As is apparent from Greene's essay, it is not necessary for one to seek a role as a public intellectual. We are increasingly commissioned, as members of the public come looking for what they see as our insights and expertise. And this is true at a time when a growing number of us are employed in contingent positions or are underfunded, even after we have secured tenure-track positions. Even as many of our institutions are calling for us to engage in greater transdisciplinary research, the programs in which we operate are being defunded, and tenure-track faculty lines are being reduced. Some of us who study the South recognize the present political implications of our work and are willing to assume the responsibility of undertaking such endeavors. However, we are doing so in increasingly difficult personal and professional circumstances.

It was very clear when we started contacting scholars that there is an intense desire for increased collaboration across disciplines, far greater than we achieved with our one symposium or this book. However, finding ways to accomplish even this collaboration has proven difficult. In order for all of us who are working on and in the South to do our best transdisciplinary work, we cannot solely count on the support of academic funding or disciplinary institutions. We were very fortunate to have the CSSC support our initial symposium with funding through the Endowment for the Future of the South. We also had the support of the staff as we organized the practicalities of the symposium itself. We know that such good financial and organizational fortune is rare. We did not even have it uniformly. When one symposium participant suggested forming a professional organization so that we could gather with other scholars more regularly, we hit a stumbling block. Many of us had limited or no conference funding. Among those of us who did have institutional support, many were junior scholars who had to reserve our meager funding for the one conference at which we needed to present each year in order to maintain our careers.

The model that we used is well worth considering, but it was not without limitations. The symposium and resulting book ultimately alienated two populations who we were particularly determined to include in the process: activists and contingent faculty. The process of writing, revision, and peer review inherently privileges those who have the time and resources to undertake it. We did not find a way to successfully overcome that obstacle. However, in many ways, the best part of this process was getting to see the ways in which other scholars work. Even in our relationship with each other, we got to analyze how sources and ideas moved across disciplines and scholars' essays through our conversations and emails and even our Facebook pages. The result was that we got to see when they moved the easiest, with the least resistance and cost to the originator.

Because we considered southern studies broadly, the authors in this book are not tied to a particular historical, cultural moment or line of analysis. Instead, many of our contributors connect their works to larger frames or debates, inviting engagement from a variety of scholars for whom such forms of examination are important. When conceiving of this project, we encouraged participants to think about how their work fit within the existing dialogues of southern studies scholarship, if they were in fact familiar to them; how an interdisciplinary collaborative experience might strengthen their individual work; and ultimately to expand their work to speak to larger, interdisciplinary audiences. Outside of these considerations, we expected that the resulting multi-linear approaches would reflect each individual's course in her or his own right, and we assumed that each would pursue her or his own theoretical track. That being understood, we did not expect contributors to fully survey the complete body of research in their respective or incorporated disciplines. Such gaps are inevitable in any transdisciplinary venture, and it is our hope that this collection will result in larger conversations about potential strategies to bridge these gaps more effectively in the future. In order for those conversations to be productive in the current economic and institutional environments, we scholars will have to be freer in sharing our knowledge and more humble in asking for that knowledge to be shared. The sad and empowering truth is that disciplinary biases and pride are what chiefly keep us from greater transdisciplinarity. Most basically we need the humility to acknowledge that each discipline may not hold most, or even many, of the answers we seek.

Notes

1. For examples of the limitations and possibilities of activist scholarship, see Hale, introduction to *Engaging Contradictions*, 1–28; Working Group on Evaluating Public History Scholarship, "Tenure, Promotion, and the Publicly Engaged Academic Historian."

2. The impact of two recent works that only engaged humanities scholars is also clearly evident in several of the essays in this book. See Anderson, Hagood, and Turner, eds., *Undead Souths*; Bone, Ward, and Link, eds., *Creating and Consuming the American South*.

3. See especially two new edited collections released in 2016: Bates, ed., *We Will Always Be Here*, and Romine and Greeson, eds., *Keywords for Southern Studies*.

4. Lowe, *Bridging Southern Cultures*, 5, 16.

5. Baker and Nelson, eds., "Preface: Violence, the Body, and 'the South,'" 231–32. As readers engage this section, we encourage them to keep in mind that, much as Wilson himself concludes in his essay, we do not advocate conceiving of a single trajectory of southern studies, either in the past or forward. Yet we respected any contributor's decision to frame works in this way. We again endorse plurality, attempting not to reduce discussions of southern studies to unilinear progressions. It is, however, important for any reader unfamiliar with the field prior to engaging this collection to be aware that the contributions of those who identify themselves as "new southern studies" scholars have been crucial in southern studies scholarship in the past fifteen years. Therefore, while we do not intend to define southern studies in such a way as to imply that an "old" southern studies has somehow given way or is giving way to a "new," the inclusion of this term is necessary to any attempt at grounding new readers in southern studies. See especially Bone, *The Postsouthern Sense of Place in Contemporary Fiction*; Bone, Ward, and Link, eds., *Creating and Consuming the American South*; Duck, *The Nation's Region*; Greeson, *Our South*; Romine, *The Real South*; Jon Smith, *Finding Purple America*; Smith and Cohn, eds., *Look Away!* Although we believe it is important to move the field forward multidirectionally, we are honored that this collection is part of the University of Georgia Press's New Southern Studies series.

6. Wilson, "Reimagining Southern Studies," 52 (this volume).

7. Although our editorial choices make it seem as though the contributors whose essays follow Wilson's were directly responding to his calls, it is important to note that without exception they were already in the process of doing such work when he articulated his vision as the opening remarks to our symposium.

8. Wilson, "Reimagining Southern Studies," 46 (this volume).

9. Here we specifically relate to the concept of intersectionality as it relates to sociological circles in the late 1960s and early 1970s, the third-wave feminist movement, and black feminist thought. There would be no intersectional analyses without those efforts. Through our work and this process, we have found that some southern studies scholars consider and address intersectional approaches (combining race, gender, and class) without giving credit to movements like the black feminist and queer Combahee River Collective, which, after they began meeting in 1974, presented a statement on intersectional oppression. See Barbara Smith, ed., *Home Girls*, the pioneering black feminist and lesbian activists' anthology, which includes "The Combahee River Collective Statement." For further readings on black women and intersectional oppression, see Angela Davis, *Women, Race and Class*; Crenshaw, "Demarginalizing the Intersection of Race and Sex." Crenshaw coined the term "intersectional" in the latter essay. See also Hull, Bell-Scott, and Smith, eds., *All the Women Are White*.

10. For example, in 2013, Dan Jones, University of Mississippi chancellor at the time, hired two consultants to review "the university's environment on race and related issues" after 2012 anti-Obama election-night student protests brought these issues to the surface. Part of the review by consultants Ed Ayers and Christy Coleman included discussions with groups invited to meet with them "because of particular work being done by each, or because of concerns previously expressed" by the group. Southern studies faculty members were included in these discussions. The consultants' work followed recommendations from the university's Sensitivity and Respect Committee,

which raised issues "concerning [university] building names and symbols," on which those present southern studies faculty members commented "that [the] University should rename several of its streets, especially Confederate Way and Rebel Drive," that they "find the name 'Ole Miss' problematic, preferring to use 'The University of Mississippi' instead," and "that some resented the fact that "olemiss.edu" was used for the email system versus 'UMiss.edu.'" They elaborated that "they viewed the email address as a signal to the outside world that the university is a place that embraces notions of the old south and its historically exclusionary practices." Ayers and Coleman, "Three Recommendations to the University of Mississippi."

More recently, University of North Carolina at Chapel Hill "faculty members who specialize in the study of the American South" publicly supported student movements to remove the statue of a confederate soldier, known as Silent Sam, saying that "their argument that the monument to Confederate soldiers was an integral part of the white supremacy campaign that swept the South in the late 19th and early 20th centuries is historically sound." Englehardt et al., "Letter: Activists Correctly Call Silent Sam Racist."

11. Ferreti, "Southern Inhospitality," 93 (this volume).

12. For a comparable full-length study on the effects of Latino immigration in the South, see activist anthropologist Angela Stuesse's *Scratching out a Living: Latinos, Race, and Work in the Deep South*.

13. Wilson, "Reimagining Southern Studies," 49–50 (this volume).

14. Sarah Madsen Hardy and Marisa Milanese recently examined the importance of teaching even undergrads how to ethically engage in scholarly public writing, in a useful piece that includes an analysis of their own classroom techniques. Hardy and Milanese, "Teaching Students to Be Public Intellectuals.

15. Turner, "South Unbound," 137 (this volume).

16. Coffey, "Finding Strength in Southern Studies Pedagogy," 172 (this volume).

17. Lewis and Duck, "Southern Transformations," 182 (this volume).

18. Ibid., 198, 197, 183 (this volume).

19. Taylor, "Surviving the Economic Apocalypse," 203 (this volume).

20. Taylor, 207 (this volume).

21. With respect to Taylor's transdisciplinary approach, we include her chapter in this section yet recognize her contribution to centering southeastern Indians, even as cultural performance, within the canon of southern studies. She is doing the work Wilson advocates through his reference to Trefzer's call for "cross-fertilization" in program studies. See Wilson, "Reimagining Southern Studies," 29 (this volume).

22. Smith, "For They Know Not What They Do," 254 (this volume).

23. Ibid., 253 (this volume).

PART 1

Laying the Groundwork

Reimagining Southern Studies

Time and Space, Bodies and Spirits

CHARLES REAGAN WILSON

In Salmon Rushdie's short story "In the South," which appeared in the *New Yorker* in 2009, we meet characters called Senior and Junior, described as "two very old men," just as they are waking up one morning. They begin at once to speak, with words that were not new to them. "These were ritual speeches," Rushdie writes, "obeisances to the new day, offered in call-and-response format." "'Be thankful we are men of the south,' Junior said, stretching and yawning. 'Southerners we are, in the south of our city in the south of our country in the south of our continent. God be praised. We are warm, slow, and sensual guys, not like the cold fishes of the north.'" Senior disagreed. "'In the first place,' Senior said, 'the south is a fiction, existing only because men have agreed to call it that. Suppose men had imagined the earth the other way up! We would be the northerners then. The universe does not understand up and down; neither does a dog. To a dog, there is no north or south. In this regard, the points of the compass are like money, which has value only because men say that it does. And in the second place you're not that warm a character, and a woman would laugh to hear you call yourself sensual. But you are slow—that is beyond a doubt.'"[1]

Junior's speech seems that of a southern traditionalist indeed, celebrating the South as a real place, producing a distinctive, appealing character type, contrasted with people of the North, and his mentioning God seems to place southerners under God's blessing. We might see this as part of a long tradition contrasting the North and South in North America. Remember Thomas Jefferson in 1785 contrasting people in the northern and southern colonies: "In the north they are cool, sober, labouring, persevering, independant, jealous to their own liberties, and just to those of others, interested, chicaning, superstitious and hypocritical in their religion." By contrast, he said, "In the south they are fiery, voluptuary, indolent, unsteady, independent, zealous for their own liberties, but trampling on those of others, generous, candid, without attachment or pretentions to any religion but that of the heart."[2]

These generalizations became conventional wisdom in the nineteenth century as Americans in general affirmed the stereotypes of southern cavalier and northern Yankee.

But Rushdie's story is not about the U.S. South but southern India, and it's not the Christian Bible but the ancient texts in Sanskrit that he mentions. Senior, in contrast to Junior, in any event, has an entirely different attitude toward his South. As students of the Global South, we are like Senior, aware that "the South" is a construction and that language is crucial to its invention. Yet the particularities of the Indian South figure importantly in Rushdie's story, beyond social construction. A tsunami in the end brings an environmentally specific and very tangible death from the Indian Ocean. And the city of Mumbai, where the story is set, is a metaphor, as Rushdie writes, "that city which was neither of the north nor of the south but a frontierville, the greatest, most wondrous, and most dreadful of all such places, the megalopolis of the borderlands, the place of in-between."[3]

Recent work looking at the U.S. South develops the related idea of the American South as not only a region within the United States but also a "place of in-between" the northern world and a broader southern world. The latter encompasses, most directly, the plantation regions of the Caribbean and Latin America. The South, from one angle, is the northernmost extension of the plantation system of South America and the Caribbean. More broadly, scholars increasingly see the U.S. South as a place with connections to geographical areas outside the power centers of world capitalism, yet the South is part of the global North as well. Study of globalization's impact on the South and, more broadly, the Global South is in any event among the most prominent features of efforts to define a new southern studies since the beginning of the new millennium.[4]

The study of the U.S. South is at a creative moment. Southern studies is redefining itself, drawing from a complex web of theoretical and methodological developments that have enabled its proponents to reposition the study of the South beyond traditional categories. Commentators, to be sure, periodically assert that the study of regions is out of date, given national homogenization, a new context of globalization that seems to deny the importance of local differences, and new forms of communication that seem to deny the importance of regionalism's emphasis on space across time. Regions like the South, however, continue to be dynamic fields, mediating the global, the national, and the local. The U.S. South has undergone significant changes that make for a different context for its study.

Literary scholars and historians have been among the leading academic interpreters of the South, and developments in these fields suggest much about the reimagining of southern studies. The Vanderbilt Agrarians, authors of the 1930 symposium in print *I'll Take My Stand*, not only defended the agrarian

South against change but also, as critics, helped to establish major categories for the study not only of southern literature but also, more broadly, southern culture. Fred Hobson and Michael Kreyling point to Louis Rubin Jr. as a "neo-Agrarian" whose 1953 co-edited *Southern Renascence* defined the study of modern southern literature.[5] The book outlined a canon of writers and suggested key terms of study. Another Rubin co-edited text, *South: Modern Southern Literature in Its Cultural Setting* (1961), marked the emergence of the concept of "southern sense of place" as a pervasive descriptor of a distinctive southern literature (thanks to an article by that title by Frederick Hoffman). Kreyling is particularly judgmental of Rubin for "inventing" a "southern" literature that failed to incorporate African Americans and women into the canon of southern writing.[6]

Houston Baker Jr. and Dana D. Nelson edited a special issue of *American Literature* in June 2001 that built on the work of Kreyling, Hobson, and others who had begun the sharp revision of the terms for the study of southern literature. In that special issue Baker and Nelson explicitly called for "a new Southern studies, an emerging collective already producing a robust body of work in current American Studies scholarship." As examples of the "new Southern studies" they cited several then-recent books, including those by Patricia Yaeger, Richard Gray, and Anne Goodwyn Jones and Susan Donaldson, all of which, they wrote, "reconfigure our familiar notions of Good (or desperately bad) Old Southern White Men telling stories on the porch, protecting white women, and being friends to the Negro."[7] As they suggested, nothing has been more fundamental to reenvisioning the study of the South than the inclusion of African Americans and women as formative figures in the southern cultural imagination. I would argue that inclusion was actually far along in 2001, but it has surely escalated in work since then. Baker and Nelson called the emerging new approaches to the South at the turn of the twenty-first century a paradigm shift, with the potential to complicate "old borders and terrains" and "to construct and survey a new scholarly map of 'the South.'"[8]

This essay surveys this "new scholarly map of 'the South'" that has come into shape a decade or so after the Baker-Nelson call. And what of the cartographer who aspires to map new southern studies efforts? One reviewer of my most recent book noted that I was "unrelentingly self-conscious" about my scholarship in that book. I don't know if he meant that as a compliment, but I took it as such. In putting together a survey of recent work on the interdisciplinary study of the South, I do so from my particular perspective. I was trained not in southern history but in U.S. intellectual and cultural history and in American studies at the University of Texas. I had the good fortune to teach in an American studies program at the University of Würzburg in Germany for my first teaching position. Like most American studies programs in

Europe in those days, it was overwhelmingly oriented toward literature, and Wurzburg turned out to be a hotbed of theoretical interest in postmodernism under the Americanist Gerhard Hoffman. So that impelled me to read southern literature extensively for the first time and to think about postmodernism. I remember many jovial evenings in German pubs debating postmodernism's influence on southern writers, raising glasses to "prost" each other, using the German toast. In fact, when I left, my friends gave me a beer stein, on top of which is engraved, "To Charles, the Prostmodern Texan."

In the summer of 1980, I became a fellow in a National Endowment for the Humanities Summer Seminar on the South in Chapel Hill with sociologist John Shelton Reed. There I learned what Reed now cheerfully calls "southern studies classic," including much social science literature I had not explored. Next in this possibly self-indulgent story, I ended up at the University of Mississippi, in the early days of the Center for the Study of Southern Culture, with the excitement of developing the *Encyclopedia of Southern Culture*, which compelled me to read and think about the many disciplines that were studying the South. In the early years of the twenty-first century, we developed *The New Encyclopedia of Southern Culture*—notice the use of "new"—and we tried intentionally to formulate our volumes to make use of the emerging scholarship on new southern studies.

I review all this to acknowledge that I am someone who has long thought about southern studies in terms of scholarship and curriculum, and my purpose is to argue that we need to broaden our focus beyond any one approach to studying the South. Finding a new southern studies should involve understanding the many perspectives scholars have on the South and rubbing them together productively. Southern cultural studies has produced great work in the last decade and its proponents have thought most directly about a new southern studies, raising *essential* issues to think about. Notice I used the word "essential," a word scholars seldom would use in talking about the South itself, but it seems to me that Baker and Nelson's call for a new southern studies has resulted in work that is sometimes now referred to as *the* new southern studies, suggesting that there is such a thing and that we can know it. My purpose is to broaden the focus of those of us, including myself, who consciously embrace the search for a new southern studies and appreciate southern cultural studies. I will review some seminal recent works and urge us to bring as many scholars as possible into our conversations. Some of you will know some of what I say, but I doubt we have all been able to keep up with work in disciplines other than our own. I cannot, but I offer this survey to contribute to the cause. My purpose is not to critique the limitations of scholarly works but to suggest what it is they have to offer our search for a new southern studies.

Other scholars quickly emerged after Baker and Nelson addressed the need for reimagining the study of the South with new questions and approaches. Tara McPherson, author of *Reconstructing Dixie: Race, Gender, and Nostalgia in the Imagined South* (2003), praised practitioners of southern studies for their focus on region and place as "ground[ing] contemporary theory's generalizations and abstractions, allowing one to test the claims of theory in a site-specific frame" (8). But she suggested that "Southern studies, for its part could also profit from an encounter with contemporary critical theory" (9), to provide greater complexity to the idea of the South. Her call to arms was her conclusion that "we need a reconstruction of southern studies, a study of the South that can shake us free from those tired old clichés of southernness, taking up the work of cultural studies and poststructuralist theory without abandoning an appreciation of the specificities of place" (10). McPherson referred to "the many versions of the South that circulate throughout U.S. history and culture," saying that "one has always to see them as fundamentally connected to, and defined in relation to, the non-South," and called "to position the South in a wider context" (2). She argued, "In an era of increasing globalization, the region circulates as an alternative to the nation-state, shifting in meaning and content" (2). She referred to "our cultural schizophrenia about the South," saying that "the region remains at once the site of the trauma of slavery and also the mythic location of a vast nostalgia industry. In many ways, Americans can't seem to get enough of the horrors of slavery, and yet we remain unable to connect this past to the romanticized history of the plantation" (2). McPherson explored the structures of feeling through explicit engagement with the emotion of "feeling southern." "Mapping the emotional registers of southernness" through popular culture, she said, "can help us to access the latent feelings supporting seemingly straightforward ways of being southern" (5).

An important part of McPherson's argument was, of course, that reconstructing Dixie is indeed possible, as she explored texts that help us "spin feeling southern differently, encouraging a kind of affective mobility that moves beyond nostalgia, guilt, and white racial melancholia toward forms of reparation" (6). McPherson evoked an important part of the emerging new southern studies in the early years of the new millennium: the political project of reenvisioning southern representations aimed at a more progressive region. She sees this change as possibly helping southern scholars "to reconstruct the South's history of commonality across racial lines" (6), and she calls for "new models of cross-racial alliance that also recognize the dangers laced through dreams of union" (7). McPherson drew from the language of film studies in establishing a distinctive interdisciplinary perspective, suggesting a model for understanding race in southern narratives, namely "a lenticular logic of racial visibility" (7), meaning "copresent" images, in this case black figures and white figures, appearing as separate and not intertwined. By looking at all figures in the southern landscape through the same frame, she hoped to offer insights into "what it means to be southern and progressive" (8).

McPherson's book had been well in process when Baker and Nelson's manifesto for a new southern studies appeared, but Michael Kreyling responded more directly to the essay with an analysis of works that might contribute to the reimagining of southern studies, also using the term "paradigm shift" and noting that the study of southern literature had evolved into "southern studies." He saw this field struggling to absorb several "'new' discourses," especially memory studies and interest in globalization. He concluded that a new southern studies "surrenders its traditional claim to regional and historical distinctiveness, finds a common language in public debates over globalization of identities, and takes its chances in the dangerous, new, postmodern land where construction replaces essence."[9] Another seminal text in the reinvigorated interdisciplinary study of the South was Kathryn McKee and Annette Trefzer's special 2006 issue of *American Literature*, "Global Contexts, Local Literatures: The New Southern Studies." They emphasized the fundamental point of "the region's fascinating multiplicity and its participation in hemispheric and global contexts," which have remained key descriptors for a new southern studies. They concluded that the South of the new paradigm "emerges as an in-between space, a process, an agenda, an itinerary, a discourse, an idea, [and] a relational concept in a global context." In a resonant image, they saw "a shape-shifting South" with fluid boundaries.[10]

The titles of two influential collections of essays reference classic southern texts but take off from them. *South to a New Place: Region, Literature, Culture* (2002) consciously invokes African American writer Albert Murray's *South to a Very Old Place* (1971), a key volume in asserting the post–Jim Crow claim by southern blacks on southern culture, while *Look Away! The U.S. South in New World Studies* (2004) echoes the song "Dixie" and its association with white Confederate identity but indeed "looks away" from that nineteenth-century South by positioning the region in a global world. These volumes offered fresh perspectives on familiar literary works but also examined wide-ranging texts that went beyond literary productions. They broadened the canon of traditional literary studies and provided historical and cultural context. The titles of other scholarly books of the last decade also suggest transformations, as in *Redefining Southern Culture* and *Bridging Southern Cultures*.[11]

The extensive use of the term "new" suggests how anxious we all are to see new directions in southern studies, to quote the title of the University of North Carolina Press book series. That series has published studies of lynching and mass culture, women writers and the South's visual culture, Memphis as a site of globalization, and the persistence of slavery-generated commodification of bodies in modern popular culture. The University of Georgia Press's New Southern Studies series likewise is a key forum, producing studies on, among other topics, gender and blackness, "grounded globalism," the economics of southern identity seen in literature, and literary modernism's regional-national connections. Issues of authenticity and nostalgia are recurring concerns from the beginning of discussions of a new southern studies.

Scott Romine's *The Real South: Southern Narrative in the Age of Cultural Reproduction* (2008) positions itself in the mainstream of southern cultural studies, wrestling with how to understand the South in an age "increasingly dominated by mass media, global corporations, and the logic of commodification." Consumption and product branding define identities in general, more than memory and tradition, creating an age of "reproductions, counterfeits, and simulacra."[12] Concern for the issue of authenticity in the contemporary era recurs through the book and through the new southern cultural studies. The "real" South is not defined by cultural traits as much as it is by "a set of anxious, transient, even artificial intersections, sutures, or common surfaces" between the fluid concepts of the imaginary and the real.[13] One of the things I love about new southern studies is the range of materials studied. Romine is fascinated with the "fantastic" narrative forms he observes in the South, and he analyzes the Julie Dash film *Daughters of the Dust*, the Tara Club Estates housing development in Georgia, the reporting of Tony Horwitz and V. S. Naipaul, reality television, fiction of the civil rights movement, and most deliciously, the menu of Mama Dip's Kitchen in Chapel Hill. He reminds us of the continued centrality of fiction to the new southern studies, suggesting that idealized narratives of the southern past have actually driven its economic and social transformations. Romine sees efforts to find authentic, "real South" inventions as actually helping to camouflage how they make dramatic changes seem manageable for a region that prizes tradition. As Leigh Anne Duck noted in a review of the book, "proliferating versions of commodified southernness constitute not debased substitutions for a previous 'real South' but heterogeneous efforts at creating more small-scale Souths, which help the residents of a deterritorialized world construct senses of self and social space."[14] Romine's "South" becomes "a site of negotiation and mutual navigation," suggesting the contested and reconfigured spatial aspects that fit comfortably with other efforts to reimagine the South.[15]

Jon Smith is one of our most incisive and provocative advocates for a new southern studies. His book *Finding Purple America: The South and the Future of American Cultural Studies* (2013) argues that both old southern studies, as he calls it, and American studies are fundamentally antimodern. Smith searches for a humane way to live in neither premodern southern fantasy nor a futuristic American fantasy. As usual, Smith's work is well versed in theory, including postcolonial, cultural studies, Lacanian psychology, branding theory, and fashion theory. He unpacks structures of feeling, dealing with such topics as anxiety, authenticity, community, loss, and melancholy. Consumerism, political and religious conservatism, and civil rights are all queried, and the range of his cultural analysis engages me, moving from Faulkner's work to hipster fashion, *American Idol*, Johnny Cash, and Neko Case. Most engaging and revealing is the last chapter, "In the Garden," where he tells us of his purposes and pleasures of constructing his backyard garden in Birmingham, Alabama. He quotes Miwon Kwon's *One Place after Another*, where she calls for "imagining a new model of belonging-in-transcience," which would avoid "both the nostalgic desire for a retrieval of rooted, place-bound identities on the one hand, and the antinostalgic embrace of a nomadic fluidity of subjectivity, identity, and spatiality on the other." Kwon suggests that it is not "a matter of choosing sides—between models of nomadism and sedentariness, between space and place, between digital interfaces and the handshake. Rather, we need to be able to think the range of the seeming contradictions and our contradictory desires for them together." She urges readers to understand "seeming oppositions as *sustaining* relations."[16] Smith takes this message to heart, writing of his garden with a poetic turn that suggests his investment in that place. "Even ten years ago, most critics of southern culture . . . would have discussed my garden labors, if pressed, as evidence of my southern 'sense of place,' my 'attachment to the land,' and so on" (134). Others might have seen his efforts as "tragically 'post-southern': removed from the land of my ancestors, thrust into a world of postmodern space." Many postmodern geographers, he observes, "would have simply ignored the site, and potentially all Birmingham's parks as well" (134). Smith ends the book with his placement on issues of spatialization. "I've argued that the current spatializations of time—blue states for the future, red states for the past—and of ethics and authenticity are symptomatic of a national and transnational process of Othering and self-definition . . . which goes back a very long time" (134). He spends much time on the alt-country works of Neko Case "because they disrupt these spatializations of a divided American and global jihad-versus-McWorld psyche" (134). Smith gives us a very personal AND theoretically informed take on the South in the nation, offering an explicit new model for southern studies to continue distancing itself from fantasies of exceptionalism. He wants to live in the moment, in the here and now, embracing hybridities that would disrupt binaries of urban and rural, national and regional. "Yet rocking up here in the dirty South of my backyard garden above my modern, affordable, integrated Hispanic-South Asian-Lebanese-black-white neighborhood," he writes, he takes in the view and observes, "I do it swaying gently in what both is and is not a southern—global southern—porch swing" (135). Smith thus manages to redeem the porch swing as a meaningful contemporary image, when part of his reimagined southern context.

Smith's book is as much or more about American studies as southern studies. John Lowe agrees that new southern studies needs "the firm interdisciplinary grounding that has been developed in recent years by American studies," but he adds black studies and women's studies programs as well, pointing to the need to position a new southern studies not only in terms of American studies but also program studies.[17] Annette Trefzer, in an article on "Indian Literature" in *The New Encyclopedia of Southern Culture*, suggests how including southeastern Indians more intentionally within the canon of southern studies can productively broaden the latter, and her insights indicate more generally the value of cross-fertilization, not only among academic disciplines and the larger American studies movement but also program studies, such as Indian studies and southern studies. Trefzer argues that "the study of southern American Indian literature necessitates dialogue and intellectual exchange between Native American and southern studies not in the sense of colonizing incorporation of one into the other, but in a much needed recognition of the way native contributions to the southern canon—many of them predating European contact and inspiring 'southern' writers—can creatively and productively reshape our understanding of the South's geography, history, and literature."[18] The inclusion of southern Native Americans as specifically southern writers pushes back the timeline of southern history to include the oral tales of southeastern tribes. Rubbing the Native American perspective against the frontier white experience of the early nineteenth century deepens the understanding of the significance of that era in the formation of the entity called "the South."

If including Native American literature in the study of southern literature can expand the contours of southern history, it can also expand the traditional sense of place that has been under contention. Southeastern tribes that were forcibly removed from the South continued their relationship with southern culture even on reservation lands in the Indian Territory and later the state of Oklahoma. Robbie Ethridge's work on Native southerners has led historians to make the Native story a specifically southern story in the eighteenth and nineteenth centuries, and the new journal *Native South* furthers this project. Contemporary Native writers like LeeAnne Howe think of themselves as southerners and imaginatively engage with the region. She narrates her story in the documentary film *Indian Country Diaries*, in which she goes to Cherokee, North Carolina, the reservation site of her father's people. Much of the film shows the Cherokee beauty pageant and a Cherokee High School football game—conveying how the tribe embraces key southern performative rituals, as well as exploring issues of education, health care, and spirituality of place. At the same time, Howe insists that including her people as "southerners," making their story of removal and modern developments central to southern history, not marginal, should force rethinking meanings of the South itself.[19]

Much of the energy for a new southern studies has thus come from literary studies and cultural studies, but fresh interdisciplinary work on the South has appeared in other disciplines as well. As I am arguing, a new southern studies should be inclusive enough to reflect the breadth of such scholarship. Recent ethnographic studies challenge the dominance of cultural studies in interpreting southern cultural patterns. Celeste Ray's edited book *Southern Heritage on Display: Public Ritual and Ethnic Diversity within Southern Regionalism* (2003) gathers essays by scholars who "look at how people identity themselves through popular religiosity, musical spectacles, ethnic festivals and celebrations, exhibitions of material culture, and particular dress, and what they communicate about themselves verbally and non-verbally in public gatherings" (4). This event-based fieldwork shares with others in southern studies a focus on the contested or oppositional nature of identity and power within a specifically southern context. Ray, who is an anthropologist, draws from theory, not the postmodernism of much of the new southern studies but rather the ritual theory of social science. Ray emphasizes how performance of ritual can produce a *communitas*, a sense of unity even in an otherwise divided society. At the same time, cultural celebrations can show what divides some members of a community from others who may have different memories of the same selected past. The ethnographic approach of Ray and her colleagues provides a model that differs from that of many of the works explicitly identified with a new southern studies but surely merits inclusion in the field. Like literary scholars and historians, she agrees that the South is "not a cultural monolith but a complex creation of multiple traditions" (7). Her usage of the word "creole" to describe southern cultural identity reverberates with others in a new southern studies, by giving a rich specificity to understanding this "blending of cultures after long exposure, coexistence, and interaction of two or more social groups" in the region (7).

Sociologists have also made important contributions to a new southern studies. Wanda Rushing's study of Memphis as a site of globalization challenges the conventional wisdom that globalization diminishes the significance of place. Although rejecting the idea of southern exceptionalism, Rushing argues that cultural and economic distinctiveness persists in local places because global processes work themselves out in communities with particular histories and cultures. Her findings in Memphis reflect broad southern patterns, with a sense of place coming from particular embodiments of social relations and social processes more than simply from landscape. Rushing's eclectic approach combines sociological theory (especially theories of space-time compression), literary narratives, thick description, and a new historical sociology, which represents an alternative to the variables-oriented paradigm that dominates social science research. Rushing thus contributes a fresh perspective to her academic discipline as well as to the interdisciplinary study of the South.[20]

One of Rushing's former students, Zandria Robinson, has published another notable sociological study, *This Ain't Chicago: Race, Class, and Regional Identity in the Post-Soul South* (2014), which reveals the reimagined South of African Americans through examining the black southern identity in the post–civil rights movement era. Baker and Nelson's essay on a new southern studies called for the positioning of African Americans more centrally as shapers of southern culture, and Robinson's book answers that call. Robinson sees black southern identity as a "strategically negotiated accomplishment" (19), suggesting that black and white southerners in everyday life, cultural elites constructing ideologies, and corporations selling southern consumer goods all accomplish specific versions of the South that suit their purposes. The book puts forward the concept of "country cosmopolitanism," meaning that African Americans she has studied see themselves as having a specific regional African American worldview, rooted not just in issues of race, class, and gender but also in a regional worldview that blends rural and urban features and creates belief in what respondents label a "better blackness," based in southern experiences, than African American identities in other parts of the United States. One of the contributions of the study is to link race, class, and gender to African American regionality. The respondents in the study recognize unflinchingly the survival of older racism in the newest South but downplay emotional reactions when confronted with it, believing their southern black culture gives them knowledge on handling whites. The respondents hold fast to traditional notions of masculine and feminine but modernize those ideas to fit contemporary realities of work and family. The respondents' understandings of country cosmopolitanism draw class lines with northern African Americans, seeing the South as a site for African American political success, creating a strong middle class that also functions as the center of "down home" blackness. The study's methodology brings together popular culture representations of the black South with respondents who detail their everyday experiences that have produced the country cosmopolitan outlook. Robinson employs an urban ethnographic model, using a participant-observer ethnography to capture the everyday experiences of informants in a variety of settings and presenting a range of people, of differing ages, social groups, social classes, genders, and occupations. The author is part of the story, coming from Memphis, the study's locale, and interacts with informants, using their quotations and life stories well to capture the nuances and diverse experiences within country cosmopolitanism. The methodology also includes examination of films about the black South and the music of hip-hop, the analysis of which provides a larger representation of the South as a whole to place beside the respondents' everyday experiences. *This Ain't Chicago* (2014) makes the case for Memphis as "the geographical and epistemological center of a post-soul southern blues" (62). The author argues for the blues as the ongoing language of black southern identity, with contemporary Memphis hip-hop performers claiming that language. The performance of the country cosmopolitan identity is a recurring concern throughout the book, seen in both everyday life and in the films and music of the region's African American culture.

Historians have used the terminology of a new southern studies less frequently than literary scholars, but they have produced studies that surely contribute to this developing field, with its focus on the multiplicities of the South, theoretically grounded works, and explorations of new topics and materials for study. Historians often resist theory and criticize cultural studies for overuse of jargon, but the interest in multiplicities and constructionism has shaped recent revisionist accounts. Ted Ownby, director of the Center for the Study of Southern Culture, surveyed the "most notable developments" in southern historical writing over the last decade, and his list provides a useful guide to disciplinary work that is contributing to a new southern studies. "Perhaps nothing in the past decade or so has been as influential," he writes, "as the argument that concepts, ideas, arguments, assumptions about race, blackness, whiteness, gender, nation, region, and lots of other ideas are constructions" that people use to "support existing social relations, to try to make them seem natural or normal, or to subvert or at least complicate those social relations."[21] He also lists the Global South; gender studies and women's studies; respectability and uplift; Indians; the slave trade; memory; civil rights scholarship (local studies and white southerners' responses); the environment; and the end of social history, cultural history, and maybe political history as separate fields. These trends suggest a reinvigorated study of southern history that should be brought into discussions of a new southern studies.[22]

Jack Temple Kirby's *Mockingbird Song: Ecological Landscapes of the South* (2000) draws from agronomy, archaeology, geology, sociology, and literature to enhance his model historical narrative about what he calls the poetics and politics of the southern environment. Anchored in the materiality of the southern environment, he argues, unlike many recent studies of the South that I urge us to consider as a new southern studies, for a regional distinctiveness rooted, in this case, in environmental realities. The South is generally warmer, wetter, weedier, snakier, and more insect-infested and disease-prone than other regions of the country. Exhibiting violent cycles of growth, abandonment, dereliction, resettlement, and reconfiguration, this relationship has the sometimes melodious, sometimes cacophonous vocalization of the South's iconic avian, the mockingbird. He uses writers Marjorie Kinnan Rawlings and Zora Neale Hurston as central figures in his story, but he ends up focusing on scientists, specifically the ecologist Eugene Odum in his sweeping panorama of the region's landscapes. His epilogue, "Postmodern Landscapes," is a witty and speculative piece.[23] "I am persuaded that differing elevations and geologic morphologies yield differing sensibilities and musical styles," he writes, and he goes on to analyze the Coen brothers' *O Brother, Where Art Thou?*, suggesting that the Coen brothers and musical director T-Bone Burnett were engaged here in a playful homogenization of upland and lowland white Souths, in which the South, "always a singular idea despite its irreconcilable varieties, is effectively leveled."[24]

Kirby is only one example of the influence of postmodernism on southern historians. Perhaps the change has been less dramatic in history than in the study of literature because the leading modernist historian of the South, C. Vann Woodward, had early moved away from the W. J. Cash metanarrative of the singular "mind of the South" to deconstruct the South's white power establishment and its white supremacist strictures. Woodward, for example, showed that Jim Crow legal segregation was historically contingent and not the immutable system its advocates suggested, becoming an important argument for the civil rights movement.[25] The editors of a seminal collection of essays, *Jumpin' Jim Crow: Southern Politics from the Civil War to Civil Rights* (2000), point out their contributors see white supremacy "as a precarious balancing act, pulled in all directions by class, gender, and racial tensions." Stressing "the contingent nature of Jim Crow by seeing it as dependent on individual actions through time helps to denaturalize white supremacy" (Dailey, Gilmore, and Simon, 4). Woodward wrote the preface for the book, and here he points out that "what distinguishes the new history is not only its inclusion of subjects that the old history neglected, but the new questions it raises and the way it treats the traditional subjects" (ix). He mentions in that regard "the roles played and leadership provided by a race, a gender, or a class, that had heretofore been treated by historians not as participants, but as helpless spectators or victims."[26] Moreover, the volume broadens our understanding of politics in dramatic new ways, complicating white electoral politics in finding "contestation in the creation and interpretation of law, in the rhetoric and structure of political parties, and in governmental agencies and the court" (4). Other contributors to the volume borrow from cultural studies, anthropology, and feminist theory and see the political in such unlikely spaces as the household, the overflowing aisles of a dime store, and in confrontations on the street. In the end, "politics" here sweeps "from the polling station to the front porch, and bridges the distance between public and private contests for power and dignity" (4). Using this broadened understanding of what constitutes political behavior, the volume uncovers extensive resistance to segregation, undermining "the traditional periodization of postwar southern history at the same time that it strips Jim Crow of the sense of inevitability and invulnerability traditionally ascribed to it" (5). The authors, moreover, position African American southerners, white dissidents, and women at the center of southern history, and thereby help to "rewrite the history of the 'backward' South—that miasma of reactionary politics, poverty, and violence—and focus instead on those portions of the South that served as an incubator for one of the most extraordinary social justice movements in the history of the United States" (5).

Edward Ayers's synthesis of late-nineteenth-century history, *The Promise of the New South: Life after Reconstruction* (1992), written well before recent talk of a new paradigm, reflects postmodernist influences, with its multiplicity of voices existing in a contested terrain. Ayers lets people speak for themselves, from their own perspective, and he admits that he did not try "to maintain the narrative illusion of a seamless story."[27] Ayers's book was a poststructuralist account, one that opened new subjects that had often not been treated seriously before in such a synthesis, including treatment of country music, blues, and Pentecostal religion. The title of Ayers's essay "What We Talk about When We Talk about the South" in itself suggested the importance of narrative in understanding the South. He writes, "The categories in which we place things have everything to do with what we take those things to be" and articulates the southern historian's central concerns, urging scholars "to talk first of concrete things—poverty and power, specific people with specific interests."[28] Ayers and other contemporary southern historians continue Woodward's focus on understanding power, but they present their material in very different ways, investigating issues of cultural centers, borders, and margins, social diversity, and contingent cultural similarities as well as differences between the South and the North. In Ayers's essay "The Inevitable Future of the South," he adopts a playful air, with a sixteen-year-old narrator in the year 2076 who lives on land that had once been known as "the South." Ayers's narrator is a Scottish-Ghanaian-Honduran-Korean-Cherokee schoolboy who lives in the later twenty-first century, with Ayers suggesting that the year 2076 was thirty-three years after what he calls the Great Consolidation, when the southern states ceded their political control to a centralized authority in Atlanta. He intended his ruminations here to suggest a postmodern ethos, with his focus on the South's future giving a historian like him the leeway to speculate in ways that his more sober historical writing would not.[29]

Reimagined southern studies can be seen in revised concepts and new ones that have become central analytical categories, and I want to talk briefly about four of these: time, space, bodies, and spirits. The formative figures in creating a canon of southern writers and themes that we contest so thoroughly now saw the sense of the past in the present as a key foundation for southern literature, a distinctive sense of time within an American culture that always seemed more oriented toward the future than the past, and the reconfiguring of chronology and the relationship among the southern past, present, and future are key expressions of a reimagined southern studies. Leigh Ann Duck's *The Nation's Region: Southern Modernism, Segregation, and*

U.S. Nationalism (2006) offers a sophisticated analysis of "chronotypes" that helped to maintain a segregated regional society in a nation rooted in liberal ideologies. Looking at southern modernist writers, Duck shows how they explored the temporal disjunctures between the nation and the South. The nation seemed to embody "the progressive linear time of the capitalist market and workplace," while the South represented in imagination "the cyclical or contemplative time of tradition and ritual."[30] The architects of Jim Crow had used what Duck calls "a two-pronged temporal strategy," picturing African Americans as backward and destined for premodern behavior characterized as "slow time."[31] At the same time, segregationists portrayed southern society more generally as one shaped by traditional, face-to-face relationships beyond easy reform. Race relations thus involved immutable interpersonal relationships, not simply structural patterns. Modernist writers Faulkner, Caldwell, Hurston, and others depicted moments in which the region's and the nation's multiple temporal forms convulsively intersected, thus undermining the traditionalist belief in unchanging time. Duck shows how the belief in southern backwardness unraveled as southern white apologists for a South static in time faced such mid-twentieth-century changes as urbanization and industrialization, as well as the pervasive presence of the mass media, consumerism, and evolving experiences in race relations.

Duck fully contextualizes the historical interwar moment. Historians deal centrally with time in other ways, and recent works are shifting historiographical interest to different time periods than those that traditionally dominated southern historical narratives. Southern historians, for example, used to give only glancing attention to the colonial era, traditionally focusing overwhelmingly on the era of southern opposition to the nation, roughly from the early 1820s to the 1960s, when changes in race relations and economic development seemed to terminate what had been seen as a distinctive way of life. Recent historians, and other scholars, are reconfiguring southern chronology, though, exploring the South's diversity in the colonial era and in recent times. They suggest that the defensive mentality against an imagined monolithic North of the mid-nineteenth century and the twentieth was a moment in time in the region's life, between periods of diversity that better reflect the South's position in the world. John Giggie's book *After Redemption: Transformation of African American Religion in the Delta, 1875–1915* (2007) studied African American religion in the Mississippi and Arkansas Delta from the end of Reconstruction to World War I. Generally seen as the low point in African American life, Giggie finds a vibrant religiosity based around dreams and visions and new experiences of opportunities emerging from a modernizing society that enabled black Deltans to define identities beyond the confines of Jim Crow segregation. Jacquelyn Dowd Hall and others have dramatically reimagined the chronology of civil rights, arguing for the long civil rights movement and crediting progressive labor and Communist front efforts in the South of the 1930s as the beginnings of the civil rights movement.[32]

Finally, in terms of time, comes scholarship deconstructing the collective public memories of the South. Historian Fitzhugh Brundage argues in *The Southern Past* (2005) that "black and white southerners have been locked in an ongoing struggle over the past since at least the Civil War" (11). Historians have shown how ideas of the past were constructed, reflecting power differentials between white southerners and black southerners, resulting in a southern public landscape that gave legitimacy and reinforced the seeming normalcy of the southern white cultural memory of past time. Brundage concludes that "the enduring presence of white memory in the South's public spaces and black resistance to it, in short, is a central theme of the southern past" (7), referencing the old conventional wisdom of U. B. Phillips that white supremacy was the central theme of southern history. Scholars of southern memory are showing how one important aspect of a new southern studies—the essential political project of changing southern society through deconstructing older supports of traditionalism—is seen in the reimagining of the southern public landscape in the contemporary period, as the memory of the civil rights movement is increasingly entering the center of southern public life with at least a dozen civil rights museums, scores of markers to local and national civil rights leaders, and the Martin Luther King Jr. holiday and memorial in Washington, D.C. Communities surely do not devote enough resources to such projects, but it is historically notable that the state of Mississippi, for example, is funding a state civil rights museum at a high level, as is happening in other states and cities. As Brundage says, "For individuals and groups alike, memory provides a genealogy of social identity" (4), and past public time—as represented by collective southern memory—looks very different now than a generation ago.

New explorations of time in understanding the U.S. South have been matched by efforts to reconfigure the concept of space as it relates to the global, national, regional, and local. The traditional narrative of "the South" portrayed the region as a unified metaphysical space positioned primarily against "the North" and downplayed subregional spaces within the greater South. No term has been more interrogated by the new southern studies than a particularly southern expression of space, which is the distinctive southern sense of place. The Southern Agrarians talked of this concept, and Louis Rubin's anthologies of southern writing that helped create a southern canon put the term "sense of place" into common academic usage. Eudora Welty famously showed how "one place comprehended can make us understand other places better."[33] But literary critic Patricia Yaeger has undercut the traditional grounding of sense of place in the South. As I have previously written, "Looking for a 'phrenology of place,' she does not find it in a special rootedness in the region but rather in the images that suggest fragmentation, decay, and melancholy. She finds that southern women writers often portray landscapes that swallow up whole women, children, and African Americans."[34] This is a long way from the Mayberry warm and fuzzy feelings of place in the traditional view. Yaeger does come to affirm the centrality of place to southern writers, but she concludes that their landscapes were always haunted by the specters of racial segregation and disorder of place.[35]

Martyn Bone has offered a most sustained analysis of a "postsouthern" sense of place, well rooted in literary understanding but with a broader "historical-geographical materialist" approach that emphasizes the processes for the production of place in general. Southern scholars have been so intent on undercutting the idea of a unique sense of place in the South that they sometimes underplay the pervasiveness of sense of place in most societies. What differentiates a sense of place are the particular ingredients that shapers of cultural representations draw from in articulating places and, as Bone suggests, the relationship of local places to large economic forces. Bone faults traditional southern literary criticism for seeing "place" as only a literary poetic image, an abstraction, pointing to the Agrarians' interest in the 1930s in issues of real property and trying to find radical ways to preserve small proprietors in the face of growing corporate power. Bone cites David Harvey's work on the "spatial fix" of late capitalism, whereby excess capital and labor are rerouted into "the production of new spaces within which capitalist production can proceed."[36] Harvey's argument provides a new grounding for a post-southern sense of place. Harvey specifically mentions the U.S. South as one such space that is continuing even in contemporary times to represent a distinctive place, based in the socioeconomic realities of uneven geographic distribution. Appalachian coal regions are a good example. As multinational coal companies strip-mine local mountain communities, the people who have lived there, still live there, and want to make their futures there invest in their sense of place their time, money, and energies to oppose the coal companies' ruination of their places. Edward Soja's call for a "reassertion of space in critical social theory" provides an important grounding for a reimagined southern studies.[37] The online journal *Southern Spaces* offers a lively exploration of the spatial anchoring of a new southern studies, making effective use of the spatial dimensions of the Internet in illuminating spatial issues related to the South. Its linkages to other web sites, its use of diverse electronic media, and its critical regionalist approach that echoes the work of David Harvey, Deborah Massey, and other theorists of space create a lively forum for a new southern studies.[38]

"Routes" are indeed challenging "roots" as a key descriptor for the U.S. South. Historians explore the Atlantic South. The transnational movement of goods, ideas, and peoples is a tangible reality in the twenty-first-century

South, and southern studies scholars increasingly examine implications of globalization for a regional society. One of the first volumes to explore globalization and the South was anthropologist James Peacock's somewhat idiosyncratic *Grounded Globalism*. It shows how the global and the southern sometimes clash but just as often overlap and intertwine. Like other scholars of globalization and the South, Peacock argues that awareness of the South's positioning in global networks takes the focus away from the traditional North-South spatial connection. The South is now defined not by opposition to the nation but by its integration with the world. He makes a clever contribution to the discussion of southern sense of place, insisting that the "transcendent ethics that ignore place have fostered destruction of the earth."[39] Alternative ethics, such as nurturing the local environment and its web of communal relations, value the earth. Like Kentucky poet Wendell Berry, Peacock sees southern place as a part of global ecology but one grounded in a long valuation of place. Berry defines regionalism as "local life aware of itself."[40] Peacock's book seems an engaging meditation by a native southerner, whose extensive global fieldwork and his outreach with international studies at a leading southern university gives him a particular participant-observer perspective on globalization.[41]

Robert H. Brinkmeyer Jr.'s *The Fourth Ghost: White Southern Writers and European Fascism, 1930–1950* (2009) is a seminal literary study in our survey because it manages to reposition southern writers of the 1920–50 era as sharp participants in an international dialogue on European and southern fascism, offering a particular contribution to the ongoing effort to wrench southern literary studies from an outdated focus on the Agrarians as singular shapers of a provincial southern canon. He shows that such writers as William Faulkner, Thomas Wolfe, Katherine Anne Porter, Robert Penn Warren, and W. J. Cash were well aware of European political and cultural currents, especially with fears that the region's obsessions with orthodoxies represented a nascent totalitarianism about to blossom into full racist bloom. Brinkmeyer spatially refocused the writers of the Southern Literary Renaissance from a North–South axis to an East–West positioning, as he shows the writers' extensive engagement with the European interwar context.[42]

Another literary study, Thadious M. Davis's *Southscapes: Geographies of Race, Region, and Literature* (2011), draws from a wealth of spatial theory in arguing that African American writers in the South reconstituted racial exclusion under segregation and its legacies as creative space, rather than simply a site of trauma and resistance. The experience of these writers provided a spatial and racial perspective from which they could imagine and represent the subject matter and aesthetic interests that they defined. Segregation imposed trauma and pain on African Americans, but the book argues that black writers from the Deep South used "their spatial location to imagine, create, and define new and unproscribed subjectivities" (4). They made geographical claims on the South as a place and violated Jim Crow's boundaries to challenge racial exclusion. This oppressive South was an inhibiting space, but it was "nonetheless a landscape of desire and want that fed dreams, resistance, creativity, and revolution during the era of segregation" (341). She establishes the African American claims on a southern identity, identifying the desire among southern blacks to own that identity.

Davis's term "southscape" points to the South as a "social, political, cultural, and economic construct but one with the geographic 'fact of the land,'" emphasizing the materiality of the region as well as its symbolic power. The term recognizes how the relationship between society and the environment reveals how the "shape of the land" affects "raced human beings" (2). She uses the concept to expand geographical imagination about the South, drawing from Edward Soja's concept of "Thirdspace," which Davis defines as a "flexible term that attempts to capture what is actually a constantly shifting and changing milieu of ideas, events, appearances, and meanings" (2). This "spatial imaginary" applied to the South expands the boundaries of regional discourse by extending to race matters within a regional context. Davis explores issues of "political and power dynamics of the South," trying to understand "the persistent conceptual power of the South as a spatial object and ideological landscape where matters of race are simultaneously opaque and transparent" (2). Davis places "African Americans at the center of current discourses on 'The South' and 'Southern Literature' as categories of critical inquiry, literary analysis, and theoretical positioning," wanting readers to see black writers "as central to any full analysis of writing within the southern region and its local and global contexts" (2).

Globalization has affected southern studies through seeing connections between the U.S. South and other places around the world, including South Africa (whose apartheid connects to Jim Crow), Italy (with the United States and Italy both having comparable souths), and Britain (whose Celtic connections with the South have fostered a surprising number of studies in music, literature, religion, and ethnic identity). Of special interest is exploration of the Global South, which encourages scholars to probe the boundaries of nation and imagine space in new configurations. Global southern studies situates the U.S. South within a hemispheric context. The U.S. South's positioning within a circum-Caribbean region imaginatively repositions the U.S. South as "North" to parts further south yet a southern site at the same time because of its shared postcolonial plantation experience.[43] Geographer Bonham Richardson defines the circum-Caribbean region as an area "with Little Rock at the northwest corner and French Guiana at the southeast, and incorporating the eastern rim of Central America as well as the Bahamas."[44] Immanuel Wallerstein similarly identified "the creation of a new peripheral region... the extended Caribbean, stretching from northeast Brazil to Maryland" during the emergence of the modern capitalist world system.⁴⁵ But my favorite definer of the circum-Caribbean region is Gabriel García Márquez who, in 1999, in a discussion with Carlos Fuentes, William Styron, and Bill Clinton, claimed "the Caribbean is a vast 'historical and cultural space extending from the north of Brazil to the Mississippi delta.'" Clinton was said to have cheerfully proclaimed his own Caribbean identity.⁴⁶

Matthew Guterl's recent study of southern slave owners places them in the context of a Caribbean plantation world with surprising connections, drawing from Faulkner's character Thomas Sutpen in introducing his argument. Like recent literary scholars, Guterl highlights Faulkner's continuing relevancy for understanding the hemispheric South. In *Absalom, Absalom!* Quentin tells of Sutpen going as a poor mountain man to the West Indies, a place his teacher once said was where a poor man went to become rich. Guterl in *American Mediterranean* (2008) sees Sutpen as "an archetype of the Old South" at a particular moment in time, in the early nineteenth century, a symbol of a slaveholding history (4). Sutpen looked back to an earlier time when Mississippi planters had vibrant connections with Guadeloupe and Haiti, establishing social networks and well-traveled routes. The antebellum southern planter saw himself carrying his European heritage, which he identified as "civilization," to his particular place in the New World, one bound to his fellow slave owners "by shared tradition, by culture, and by the informal, border-crossing practices of translation, mediation, and appropriation" (4). Guterl sees the antebellum slave owner embodying a particular model of the creole. His creolism was "a deliberate performance, and not just a sociological or biological process—a performance of consanguinity, of assumed sameness, of knowledge production across borders" (4). Southern slave owners were "hemispheric and cosmopolitan" (5), bound to other members of the hemisphere's master class, who might speak Spanish, French, Dutch, and English. The southern slave owners were different from their Caribbean fellows, developing a proslavery argument that drew from scientific racism, wrestling with the complex tensions between republican national ideals and a separate southern nationalism. Despite their distinctiveness, their American Mediterranean ethos made them aware of a common history of racial bondage and "the postemancipation 'labor problem' [that] were pan-American concerns" (9). Guterl is a historian looking at the slaveholders late in the history of American slavery, recognizing that by the time of the Civil War, southern slave owners with ties to the Caribbean feared that rising nationalism and democratic ideals portended the inevitable end of slavery, post-emancipation labor problems, increasing loss of their power, and "the threat of a looming apocalypse" (7).

Attention to space has helped ground the reimagining of the South, and a concern for bodies has similarly brought attention away from the traditional centrality of the "mind of the South" in understanding southern identity. The interest in the mind of the South has not disappeared, of course. Witness Jim Cobb's recent *Away Down South: A History of the Southern Identity* (2005), which focuses on ideas of the South. Other scholars argue that attention to ideas about the South has diverted critical attention, as Jay Watson says, "from the body of work that has always served as the South's material ground. For if the southern way of life was built upon ideas, it has in an even more fundamental sense been built upon, and by, southern bodies."[47] The new southern studies sees a need to view southern ideologies "grounded in the activity and sentient experiences of southern bodies, and in the cultural values associated with them."[48]

Literary critics working in gender studies have been leaders in "rematerializing the study of the South through close attention to the way ideas about identity, difference, and power work themselves out, in, on, and through southern bodies."[49] As Anne Goodwyn Jones and Susan Donaldson have written in *Haunted Bodies: Gender and Southern Texts* (1997), "surely no bodies ever appeared more haunted by society. From the body of the white southern lady, praised for the absence of desire, to the body of the black lynching victim, accused of excessive desire, southern sexuality has long been haunted by stories designating hierarchical relationships among race, class, and gender."[50] Racial violence has been a key topic for historical and cultural investigation in the last decade, with broken black bodies the focus for study, amid suggestions of the South's role for the nation in controlling black bodies, from the plantation's regulated and sometimes violent discipline to the contemporary "economics and politics of the prison-industrial complex."[51] Amy Louise Wood's *Lynching and Spectacle: Witnessing Racial Violence in America, 1890–1940* (2007) crosses disciplinary lines through close analysis of the local contexts of lynching, with their gory details, and the visual representations related to lynching, from lynching photographs to films that portrayed lynching and helped turn national attitudes against the practice and even embarrassed southern elites into change.[52]

Katherine Henninger's *Ordering the Facade: Photography and Contemporary Southern Women's Writing* (2007) develops another aspect of the scholarly attention to the body through the idea of the South's visual culture, reflecting a new emphasis on understanding the body's senses, in this case sight, as a way to understand the construction of the South itself. Henninger draws from feminist theories of photography and the visual and feminist criticisms of southern culture and literature. Questioning the traditional assumption that the South was predominantly an oral culture of storytellers, singers, lawyers, and preachers, Henninger asserts the importance of the visual to southern culture. In this culture, visual signs—the shape of a lip, a skin's shade, external sex characteristics, the carriage of one's body, the condition of one's clothing—determine "place" and may once have literally meant the difference between life and death. "Whether employed to help essentialize and fetishize the image of the white southern lady," Henninger writes, "or to naturalize racist anthropology or sexual stereotypes of 'white trash' women, nineteenth and early twentieth century photography played a key role in creating a hegemonic 'South.'"[53] Photography was also, though, a part of "strategies of resistance" to this version of the South and in the construction of differently imagined communities of "southernness." Henninger goes on to show how contemporary southern women writers create fictional photographs in their works, representations of diverse images that challenge those representations that supported the racial, class, and gendered assumptions of the older South.

The study of music in the South has long been a foundational aspect of southern studies, and recent works illustrate perspectives that depart from traditional scholarship and point to the continuing significance of the aural dimension of southern culture. Conventional wisdom long emphasized the concept of musical authenticity in terms of such forms of music as blues and country, with folk versions retaining racial distinctions and isolation from mainstream American popular sounds. Revisionist studies easily fit into a new southern studies, which challenges assumptions of authenticity. Delta bluesman Robert Johnson may be the ultimate icon for a primitive southern folk culture whose music was local and traditional, but music critic Elijah Wald argues in *Escaping the Delta: Robert Johnson and the Invention of the Blues* (2004) that Johnson was an ambitious young performer, well grounded in American popular music and a variety of blues styles beyond the Delta. Not the troubled loner who consorted with the devil to gain his genius, Wald's Johnson was a professional entertainer who longed for the celebrity he saw in urban blues performers like Leroy Carr.[54] Adam Gussow goes beyond Johnson to argue for the blues as a form of cultural criticism, "contesting the narrative of black abjection imposed by the white South,"[55] affirming life without obscuring the horrors to which whites subjected Africans Americans. Gussow sees the origins of the blues in relation to the breaking of black bodies in spectacle lynchings, with what he calls the "blues subject" emerging from this violence. One of the exciting aspects of his work is his drawing from a wide range of texts, including novels, autobiographies, and poems, in addition to lyrics and music, arguing for "a conception of blues textuality that understands blues literature and blues orature to be an expressive continuum rather than a self-evident binary."[56] If creolization is a major theme in a new southern studies, then Glenn Eskew gives us an innovative portrait of popular composer and performer Johnny Mercer as a hybrid musical figure who emerged out of the black and white folk culture of coastal Georgia, combined that influence with his absorption of blues and jazz recordings by black and white musicians, and then through his recordings and productions of other musicians commodified those sounds of a biracial culture beyond a regional culture into a national and global context.[57] Books by Cecilia Tichi, Curtis Ellison, and Barbara Ching, among others, are similarly repositioning country music into broader contexts than their folk origins.[58] Ching's study of "hard country" music argues that this style associated with such performers as George Jones and Merle Haggard is an intentional burlesque that represents a countercultural force in the South and nation, theorizing her argument of "hard country's incurable unease" through Pierre Bourdieu's discussion of ways that cultural hierarchies legitimate class divisions.[59]

The book on music that perhaps best signifies a new approach to sounds of the South is Karl Miller's *Segregating Sound: Inventing Folk and Popular Music in the Age of Jim Crow* (2010). Miller explores a central issue in American history, racial segregation, but he offers an original and sustained analysis of music's role in that. He offers a new chronology: southern states passed new, rigid segregation laws in the 1890s, but musical segregation did not really solidify until the 1920s, when cultural changes in the music industry and the academic world led to rigid commercial identification of "race" (black) and "hillbilly" (white) music genres. Miller convincingly shows how black and white performers in the South that produced so much of the commercial music after 1920 had earlier not limited their repertoires to racialized musical forms, but rather had drawn from wide-ranging and eclectic forms of local and national music. Their ability to perform in many styles maximized these performers' marketability, and the spread of Tin Pan Alley mass musical culture offered them new musical opportunities, along with the localized music around them. He moves beyond looking at African American music as a reflection only of African origins and a distinctive black historical experience to argue that it is not the distinctiveness of black (or white) music that is most significant but rather their interaction in a broader musical culture. Miller's work challenges folklorists, as he historicizes the works of early folklorists in creating the still-dominant paradigm for interpreting much American music in ethnically and regionally essentialist ways. Miller shows a talent for broad interpretive analysis in a rather sweeping narrative that goes from the development of a "minstrel paradigm" in the nineteenth century to the "folkloric paradigm" in the early twentieth century.[60] Overall, the study shows how Americans, including southerners, used music to construct more complex and even contradictory identities than the neat separation into racial and regional styles has suggested.

One aspect of sexuality, LGBT studies, has proven a productive focus for the South's body of work. John Howard's study of homosexuality in Mississippi examines the spatiality and mobile networks of same-sex culture in a rural

South that was previously omitted from national narratives of LGBT culture. Similarly, Gary Richards's study of sexual otherness in southern fiction demonstrates the centrality of issues of sexuality to the Southern Literary Renaissance. Howard and Richards both probe sexuality's relationship to class, race, and southern identity. Benjamin Wise's recent biography of William Alexander Percy is a revelation in reimagining someone who seemed an outdated literary figure, associated with defense of the South's sharecropping system more than anything else. Wise's close study reveals Percy's hidden sexual life that was not that hidden, tying him to an international gay culture that Wise manages convincingly to place next to Percy's commitment to localism in small town Mississippi. He shows Percy's openness to an unconventional sexuality, for Mississippi society did not lead him to engage his conventional racial attitudes.[61]

Food is an essential material ingredient nurturing southern bodies, and the study of southern foodways has recently entered a productive new phase of scholarly work. The Southern Foodways Alliance was founded in 1998 at the University of Mississippi, with its early work emphasizing celebration and preservation of southern food, but its commitment to its academic mission has steadily increased, with a postdoctoral fellow for two years, a new tenure track joint appointment professorship in the university's southern studies program, an extensive documentary film project, and an award-winning oral history project that is an archive for research on southern cultural issues of not only food but other topics. The first book in a new Southern Foodways Alliance book series, Studies in History and Culture, at the University of Georgia Press is a collection of essays, *The Larder: Food Studies from the American South* (2013), which consciously defines the field as an academic area of research. The editors organized their articles by methodology, choosing from "a range of disciplines, including history, geography, social sciences, American studies, gender studies, literary theory, visual and aural studies, cultural studies, and technology studies." Their aim is "to place those essays in a context that catalyzes conversations about best methodological practices."[62] The volume explicitly engages the work of two of our leading southern cultural studies figures, Tara McPherson and Scott Romine, on the issues of authenticity and nostalgia. Andrew Warnes, in an article entitled "Edgeland *Terroir*: Authenticity and Invention in New Southern Foodways Strategy," argues that food scholars should relate "their ethnographic enterprise to the critique of authenticity, and to think about which of its findings hit home and which fall short."[63]

Ted Ownby's conclusion to the volume notes that the contributors to *The Larder* "show little interest in the nostalgia that characterizes, whether subtly or directly, a good deal of writing about food."[64] Writing explicitly from the perspective of a southern studies scholar, Ownby is struck that few of the essays are even "centrally concerned with issues of southern identity." "In part," he says, "we want to study all of life, without always asking for the 'southern' parts, however defined."[65] He concludes that food scholars are not "searching for a central theme in southern food history," distancing the new southern foodways from an older scholarly paradigm.[66] With this configuration, the southern signifier seems to float free of cornbread and fried chicken, raptured in the skies above the frying pan.

The field has already produced a striking text for our broadened new southern studies. Elizabeth S. S. Englehardt's *A Mess of Greens: Southern Gender and Southern Food* (2011) opens up issues of gender and southern food through five stories she tells, watershed "moments in the southern food story" (15). We meet moonshining women, observe the struggle between biscuit and cornbread for respectability, see young women in canning clubs that provided surprising empowerment for them, feel the blight of pellagra in mill towns before World War I, and read about the importance of cookbooks and curb markets as venues for a certain community feeling. Acknowledging that southern women always functioned "against the backdrop of unequal social hierarchies or race, class, gender, and region, the mess of greens, nonetheless, was a story of possibility and promise if we wish to listen to it. Food. People. Places. Shared stories" (191). Englehardt's book is a solid historical work, studying southern foodways at a key moment in time, when domestic messages about women and food competed in the early twentieth century with the invention of the female consumer of kitchen products. But Englehardt is trained in American studies, taught in the American studies program at the University of Texas, and is now a southern studies professor at the University of North Carolina at Chapel Hill, and she reminds us that "food studies emerged in American studies research because both explore material culture, historical changes, and literary discourses and give us traction" (15) on issues of food and gender. Her methodology pairs "a feminist theoretical approach (that looks at race, class and gender in individuals and institutions) with an American studies methodology (that uses a flexible interdisciplinary definition of texts)" (15). In writing about cookbooks and curb markets, she says the term "mess" is appropriate, suggesting "the disorderly, collective, and communal spaces" they occupied (167).

If a focus on the body literally grounds a reimagined southern studies, a concern for spirituality reflects the perceived importance to the region's people of transcendence in constructing ideas of the South. Religion is surely an enduring prop for southern culture and for ideological expressions of the South itself. Although evangelical Protestantism only emerged at the end of the colonial era South, this religious tradition became one of the central institutional embodiments of the southern way of life. Much work has elaborated on this dominant popular religiosity, wherein God figured too often for whites as a spiritual force for the status quo. Similarly, much work has outlined how evangelical Protestantism's stress on freedom and equality has fostered very different traditions among African Americans and working-class white people, offering empowerment for the disenfranchised. Civil rights leader and later U.S. congressman John Lewis wrote in his 1998 autobiography that "there remains in the South an inherent sense of purpose, of belief, of people pulling together and actually effecting change." He affirmed, "There is still a *spirit* in the South, a spirit that was not and *is* not felt in the same way in the North."[67] Lewis thus constructs a South of the spirit beyond the mind of the South and beyond the materiality of the body. I noted in my recent collection of essays *Flashes of a Southern Spirit* that the new southern studies has not focused enough on issues of religion, despite the continuing centrality in the South of its predominant evangelical Protestantism and despite the region's evolving religious context through the growth in the last decade of such "new" religions to the South as Latin American Catholicism, Islam, Buddhism, and Hinduism.[68]

Moreover, innovative works in southern religious studies that draw on theory—a major concern for a new southern studies—have not worked their way into recent discussions of interdisciplinary approaches to the South. Donald Mathews's landmark study of the religious roots of lynching in the South draws on the work of a wide variety of theorists, such as Victor Turner on ritual, Mary Douglas on purity, and Rene Girard on religious violence. Mathews's article appeared in the online *Journal of Southern Religion*, which regularly publishes wide-ranging reviews of films as well as texts that cross academic boundaries. Paul Harvey's exploration of religious interracialism between white southerners and black southerners provides a rich source for understanding the South's "creolization" in spirituality. Harvey's recent book *Moses, Jesus, and the Trickster in the Evangelical South* (2012) brings together literature, music, and folklore with traditional churchly documents in unexpected and fresh ways. Black and white southerners used Moses and Jesus in differing ways, but they were "not capacious enough" to give voice to all of southern religious experience.[69] The region's moral ambiguities made a binary of good and evil too simple, and Harvey's bringing of the trickster figure into southern religious historiography is a wonderful insight. He sees the same moral ambiguity in the fourth of his iconic figures, the biblical Absalom, who he explores in not only Faulkner's *Absalom, Absalom!* but also Toni Morrison's *Beloved* and Edward P. Jones's *The Known World*. Harvey's book connects the pious faith of missionaries and revivalists with the low-down religion of blues musicians and Johnny Cash, thus offering innovative takes on three centuries of southern evangelicalism, including the "countercultures that circled the edges."[70] In general, recent work in southern religious study, as Harvey notes, "has pushed toward understanding pluralism, to 'decentering the narrative,' to incorporating the stories and religious traditions of those historically ignored in the dominant consensus historiography, and to examining alternative religious traditions."[71] Historians have urged an understanding of early southern religious history that does not assume that evangelicalism would emerge triumphant and that places Catholicism front and center as an actor in southern religious history. All of these trends will be useful to include in a broadened and inclusive new southern studies.[72]

Much of the interdisciplinary reimagining of southern studies can fit in the perspective of critical regionalism. In a book with that title, *Critical Regionalism* (2007), Douglas Reichart Powell argues that regions are "categorically different from other conceptualizations of place, like home, community, city, state, and nation, in that region must refer not to a specific site, but to a larger network of sites; region is always a relational term" (4). He argues that "when we talk about a region, we are talking not about a stable, boundaried, autonomous place but a cultural history, the cumulative, generative effect of the interplay among the various, competing definitions of that region" (5). The usefulness of this concept for a broadened understanding of new southern studies is that it places all our disciplinary and programmatic conceptions of region side by side, bringing them into conversation with each other, to try to figure out how they are part of a process that not only deconstructs regions but creates regions as well. As Powell notes, critical regionalism "involves tracing a path across the disciplines as well as the dimensions of the place under consideration. It is about being aware that writing about a region creates and sustains a definition of that region" (7). To complicate matters, Powell notes that critical scholarly study of regions "have clustered not only around academic subfields but also around the regions themselves" (6). In scholarly, programmatic, curricular, or institutional aspects, New England studies, Appalachian studies, southern studies, and western studies engage often parallel but sometimes collaborative projects. Multiple definitions of place in these endeavors occur, "sometimes convivially and sometimes antagonistically" (5). Powell sees in the study of regions "a shifting emphasis away from the products of regional culture, the definitions of regions themselves, and all their representative artifacts, to the processes by which ideas about regions come into being and become influential" (7), so that the core idea of critical regionalism is that "a region is not a thing so much as a cultural history" (6). Regions are not the backdrop of social, cultural, political, and economic forces but the result of those activities.

A key term in the new southern studies is "southern imaginary." Baker and Nelson wrote in 2001 of "the U.S. social, political, racial, economic, ethical, and everyday-life imaginary written as 'regionalism.'"[73] Kathryn McKee and Deborah Barker in *American Cinema and the Southern Imaginary* (2010) explore the topic in more depth, looking specifically at how it can inform analysis of films about the South. Arguing that the southern imaginary "is integral to the history and development of American cinema," they see the term as useful because of "its evocative, overdetermined, and contradictory impulses and its many critical and theoretical resonances" (2). The essays in the collection flesh out the southern imaginary "as an amorphous and sometimes conflicting collection of images, ideas, attitudes, practices, linguistic accents, histories, and fantasies about a shifting geographic region and time" (2). They see the "southern imaginary" as a "multifaceted, multivalent concept that informs our understanding of U.S. culture, especially in relation to ideas about race, gender, and region" (3).

Allen Tullos also makes central use of the concept "southern imaginary" in *Alabama Getaway: The Political Imaginary and the Heart of Dixie* (2011), a major work in new southern studies. It looks at Alabama as an ideological construct, one appearing natural and normative, but he shows how it has been maintained and perpetuated with results that have left the state with deep-seated social and economic problems. The book is noteworthy for its solid grounding in social theory. Theorists in critical justice theory and critical regionalism inform his application of theory to the case study of modern Alabama history and culture. Tullos has a fertile imagination for concepts and uses them well. His version of the "southern imaginary" is a specifically political one, defining the "political imaginary" as "the public shape of power, representation, and possibility" (1). The state government coined the term "Heart of Dixie" in the 1940s as a promotional concept (5–7), but Tullos shows how it has survived into the twenty-first century as "a retrograde political imaginary, mapped by a constellation of pernicious habits, that remains tenacious, dynamic, and at odds with efforts to extend social justice, and subject to wincing reconfirmation with any morning's headlines" (1–2). He charts the state's political imaginary with a devastating depth of research, including legislative acts, words of public figures, rumors, jokes, statistics, journalistic accounts, blog entries, art, and music. His main concern is with representations of Alabama and what he calls the "debilitating habits of judgment and feeling" (5), adapted from theorist Judith Butler, and his book shows how culture can frame and limit possibilities for a range of people in southern society. The book points to how a new southern studies can contribute to pushing along social justice efforts, as it charts the inequalities and intolerance that govern public life in the state and region. He coins the term "terrortory" to characterize the legacy of violence and intimidation of the Deep South's past (2), lays out the injustices in the state's criminal justice system, reveals the corruption and inefficiencies of a state with a dysfunctional constitution, and deplores the tax inequities that are stark in exploitation of the majority of people to the advantage of a few. After detailing the situation, Tullos asks, like an Old Testament prophet, "How many ways can you say 'disparity' so that the injustice becomes clear?" (4). The book crosses genre lines from a study of cultural ways to public policy, expressing strong judgments on the need for change. It offers hope for change through Tullos's examination of the reform efforts of black Alabamians and white allies.

Inherent in much of the cultural studies of new southern studies is the commitment to reinventing the South. Tara McPherson, for example, probes social structures in the South that were surely structures of dominance, but she sees cultural expression in the South opening "the space for imagining other ways of being southern" than those of the dominant culture that scholars have long mined.[74] Patricia Yaeger admits the politics at work in such an approach, noting that critical regionalism can "represent an act of progressive political intervention," which "challenges any symptomatic nostalgia for lost objects."[75] Jon Smith positions his book *Finding Purple America* as an effort to get past what he sees as fruitless political divisions in the modern United States.

Reinventing the South has special meanings in terms of social activism, and a question for us to consider is how any new southern studies relates to social activism, especially in the contemporary South. At a February 2004 symposium entitled "The U.S. South in Global Contexts," held at the University of Mississippi, sociologist Barbara Ellen Smith argued that "globalization is dialectically producing, on the ground in the South, place-based forms of social activism and resistance struggles in defense of place."[76] In her "Place and the Past in the Global South," published in 2006, she cites as examples the opposition to mountaintop removal in Appalachia, community development projects in the West Virginia coalfields, anti–factory closing protests in East Tennessee, and the campaigns against Walmart in northern Mississippi and elsewhere in the South. She notes that these struggles "create place by invoking selective constructs of what a specific place represents" (693). Smith gives us a concrete sense of place, with particular meanings for progressive reform. "*Place* in these diverse struggles," she writes, "becomes a symbol of all that is worth fighting for: continuity of human connection and mutual commitment, environmental stewardship, the integrity of moral rather than material priorities." Social activists in the South rarely create "a South," and certainly do not "defend a static geographic place," because their concerns are "far more specific, concrete, and personal: the ten blocks of a neighborhood, a watershed or hollow, a rural community." Although "the South" is too large a concept to be engaged in these projects, she concludes, nonetheless, that "these struggles are in the South and of the South—shaped by the framework of Southern history and politics, influenced by the contours of its social relations and cultural life." In effect, on the ground, "these struggles *are* the South, in the sense that even as they resist the prescriptions of the powerful, they imagine and construct the region's future" (693).

A problem is that much of the literature on social activism in the South is not taken into account by those of us who intentionally do southern studies of any sort. Much of it is in labor history, immigration history, or ethnic studies, not necessarily dealing with issues of culture and identity. Mary Frederickson's book *Looking South: Race, Gender, and the Transformation of Labor from Reconstruction to Globalization* (2011) examines what she calls "two paradigm shifts in the region's workforce," one after Emancipation and freedom for the enslaved and the other at the end of the twentieth century as a result of deindustrialization and globalization (247). Frederickson's argument is that "the labor systems" the South pioneered as it industrialized in the late nineteenth century "became the model for U.S. industrial [development] in the twentieth century" and the paradigm for the exportation of American industry abroad, beginning after World War II (248). She also argues that in the twenty-first century, the model of industrial expansion and production that began in the late nineteenth century and triumphed nationally in the late twentieth century has become the norm for global capitalist development. "The Global South is heir to the New South," Frederickson writes, "with the powerful triptych of anti-unionism, low wages, and state-supported industry firmly in place" (248). Frederickson, like other scholars, sees the South having a legacy of activism that can create hope for the future. She notes occasions when collective actions triumphed over southern individualism "as workers sought to join unions to change the system and gain the respect and dignity they deserved" (249). She also sees hope in "the dream of interracial solidarity, realized most completely by workers in unions with black and white members," insisting that this outlook remains "a powerful vision" (249). Frederickson has a resonant image, suggesting that today the South is "seen as the gateway to a land of new opportunity for immigrants coming to the United States, especially those from Mexico and Central and South America" (249). She hopes that new southern studies will have ethnographic initiatives that will explore and analyze their roles in the newest South, looking at their labor struggles within the context of social relations shaped by the older southern context and looking at issues of their roles in the South's changing culture and identity (248–49).

The reimagined southern studies has long moved away from essentialist views of the South, and scholars are less likely to be interested in the region's exceptionalism than its connections to other places, broadening from a North–South axis to a transnational one that its immigrants are a part of. A contribution of a new southern studies to American studies is to insist that generalizations about "American" take into account the southern experience. In this time of flux, scholars increasingly use the term "hybridity" to describe the region and its continuing, broad interest to observers. The creolization process that began in the colonial period with its mixture of ethnicities and cultures is taking on new embodiments in the twenty-first century. In the globalized world, North and South and East and West increasingly meet and reconfigure themselves in the process. The U.S. South has been a site of exchange, a test case of cultural processes, over almost four centuries. The reimagining of southern studies will surely have understanding of the dynamics of this process, both historically and in the contemporary era, as one of its top research agendas.[77]

It is good for us to affirm also Barbara Ladd's observation that while "the *theorizing* of place is problematic," "the *experience* of place remains dynamic and vital."[78] As Richard Gray has noted, "Change has brought an even more acute self-consciousness and an even greater pluralism than ever before. The South is still a concept active in the everyday lives and exchanges of communities; it is still there as a determining part of their mental maps and speech acts."[79] But the context in which southerners and others think about the South is drastically changing in a wired world of apparently limitless communication possibilities. Black and white southerners, in any event, continue to visit regional historical sites of the Civil War and the civil rights movement, they argue over display of the Confederate flag, they maintain religious values and practice them far more enthusiastically than in most other parts of the nation and the Western world, and they vote in ways that create new twists on older political demographics. Yet the new Latino population that will have a major long-range impact on the South has little reason to be interested in such traditional issues. New cultural blendings are undoubtedly underway, and as scholars we need to have our antennae up for evidence of new complexities of the southern past, present, and future. Meanwhile images of Our Lady of Guadeloupe are becoming widespread on the southern landscape, with processions of Our Lady's feast day in December typically parading around town squares, past the Confederate monument that once symbolized the southern public space. Perhaps soon in southern towns and cities, after the procession, Latino Catholics will gather for traditional tacos, made now with southern barbecued pork, but with a tomato sauce in one part of the South and a mustard-based sauce in another, offering a new creolization for analysis by southern studies.[80]

In closing, I return to my perspective. I have offered one scholar's views on the need for a broadened southern studies that takes seriously the potential for cross-disciplinary exchange. My thematic framework, on "time and space, bodies and spirits," offers a way to bring new texts together, despite sometimes differing disciplinary vocabularies and academic territoriality. Scholars in specific disciplines may feel some key recent works in their fields should have been included, and I likely would understand that concern, as many valuable books could not be covered. I selected texts based on my thematic interests and my perceptions of their contribution to multidisciplinary conversation, more than for their importance to specific academic disciplines. My hope is that this essay will stimulate other overviews of recent southern studies works.

We can see ways a new southern studies has reimagined the South through the work of differing disciplines and interdisciplinary projects, all of which have infused southern studies with a new energy and creativity. In thinking about, not *the* new southern studies, but *a* new southern studies, we should broaden our conversation, reading the work of disciplines studying the South and keeping in mind how knowing of other projects can enrich our own work. Leigh Anne Duck, in her review of Scott Romine's *The Real South* in the *Journal of Southern History*, expressed almost off-handedly what I see as a new southern studies. Praising Romine's book as one rooted in aesthetic concerns, she noted that it also "examines conflicts over the meaning of southern history as well as the potential for contemporary southern culture to provide or express collective meaning."[81] She suggests that although its methods and materials differ significantly from those of W. Fitzhugh Brundage's *The Southern Past* and James C. Cobb's *Away Down South*, Romine's book "could be read alongside such works for a mutually invigorating dialogue." Similarly, "where Romine's understanding of style would benefit any analysis of contemporary regional culture," she adds that his consideration of artificial geographies having real people in them "could usefully be augmented by empirical research on those residents' lives."[82] Not every historian will engage with cultural studies, nor will every cultural studies scholar want to hear the voices from contemporary ethnography, but the generous engagement with each other's work offers the best long-range hope for a new southern studies that continues to enlighten not just academics but broader constituencies interested in the South's future in a globalized world.

Notes

1. Rushdie, "In the South."
2. Boyd, *Papers of Thomas Jefferson*, 468.
3. Rushdie, "In the South."
4. S. W. Jones and Monteith, eds., *South to a New Place*; Smith and Cohn, eds., *Look Away!*; Cobb and Stueck eds., *Globalization and the American South*; Peacock, Watson, and Matthews, eds., *The American South in a Global World*.
5. Rubin and Jacobs, eds., *Southern Renascence*.
6. Hobson, *The Southern Writer in the Postmodern World*; Kreyling, *Inventing Southern Literature*, xi, xiii, 33–55.
7. Baker and Nelson, eds., "Preface," 231–2.
8. Ibid., 243.
9. Kreyling, "Toward 'A New Southern Studies'," 4, 16.
10. McKee and Trefzer, "Preface: Global Contexts, Local Literatures," 677, 681, 682.
11. S. W. Jones and Monteith, eds., *South to a New Place*; Smith and Cohn, eds., *Look Away!*; Cobb, *Redefining Southern Culture*; Lowe, ed., *Bridging Southern Cultures*.
12. Romine, *The Real South*, 2.

13. Ibid.
14. Duck, review of *The Real South*.
15. Romine, *The Real South*, 236–37.
16. Quoted in Smith, *Finding Purple America*, 127.
17. Lowe, *Bridging Southern Cultures*, 5.
18. Trefzer, "Indian Literature," 95.
19. Ethridge, *From Chicaza to Chickasaw*; *Indian Country Diaries*.
20. Rushing, *Memphis and the Paradox of Place*.
21. Ownby, "Director's Column," 2.
22. Ibid., 2–3.
23. Kirby, *Mockingbird Song*, 312–30.
24. Ibid., 314.
25. Woodward, *The Strange Career of Jim Crow*.
26. Ibid.
27. Ayers, *The Promise of the New South*, ix.
28. Ayers, "What We Talk about When We Talk about the South," 80.
29. Ayers, *The Promise of the New South*, 14; Ayers, "The Inevitable Future of the South."
30. Duck, *The Nation's Region*, 8.
31. Ibid., 6.
32. See "Part I: The Colonial South," in Boles, ed., *A Companion to the American South*, 3–82; Peacock, *Grounded Globalism*; Giggie, *After Redemption*; J. Hall, "The Long Civil Rights Movement and the Political Uses of the Past," 1233–63.
33. Welty, *The Eye of the Story*, 128.
34. Charles Reagan Wilson, "Sense of Place," 254.
35. Patricia Yaeger, *Dirt and Desire*.
36. Harvey, *The Condition of Postmodernity*, quoted in Bone, *The Postsouthern Sense of Place in Contemporary Fiction*, 49.
37. Soja, *Postmodern Geographies*.
38. Bone, *The Postsouthern Sense of Place in Contemporary Fiction*, 42.
39. Peacock, "Grounded Globalism," 109.
40. Berry, "The Regional Motive," 65.
41. Peacock, *Grounded Globalism*.
42. Brinkmeyer, *The Fourth Ghost*.
43. For an anthology that frames the U.S. South and the Caribbean as a "regional interculture," see Adams, Bibler, and Accilien, *Just Below South*. Inspired by Joseph Roach's *Cities of the Dead: Circum-Atlantic Performance* (New York: Columbia University Press, 1996), it frames the intercultural region of the circum-Caribbean through the lenses of performances (e.g., music and language) and identities.
44. Richardson, "The South and the Caribbean," ix.
45. Wallerstein, *The Modern World-System II*, 167.
46. Smith and Cohn, *Look Away!* 7. See also Doyle, *Nations Divided*; Taylor, *Circling Dixie*.
47. Watson, "Body," 30.
48. Ibid. See also Watson, *Reading for the Body*.

49. Watson, "The Body," 31.
50. Jones and Donaldson, eds., *Haunted Bodies*, 1.
51. Baker and Nelson, "Preface," 233.
52. Wood, *Lynching and Spectacle*.
53. Henninger, *Ordering the Facade*, 8
54. Wald, *Escaping the Delta*.
55. Gussow, *Seems Like Murder Here*, 2.
56. Ibid., 10.
57. Eskew, *Johnny Mercer*.
58. Tichi, *High Lonesome*; Ellison, *Country Music Culture*; Ching, *Wrong's What I Do Best*.
59. Ching, *Wrong's What I Do Best*, 23.
60. Miller, *Segregating Sound*, 217.
61. Howard, *Men Like That*; Richards, *Lovers and Beloveds*; Wise, *William Alexander Percy*.
62. Edge, Englehardt, and Ownby, eds., *The Larder*, 4.
63. Ibid., 350.
64. Ibid., 364.
65. Ibid., 369.
66. Ibid.
67. Lewis and D'Orso, *Walking with the Wind*, 207.
68. Charles Reagan Wilson, *Flashes of a Southern Spirit*. For an example of a study of a religion new to the South, see Jeff Wilson, *Dixie Dharma*.
69. Harvey, *Moses, Jesus, and the Trickster in the Evangelical South*, 26.
70. Ibid., 27, 28.
71. Ibid., 4.
72. Mathews, "The Southern Rite of Human Sacrifice"; Paul Harvey, *Freedom's Coming*.
73. Baker and Nelson, "Preface," 235.
74. McPherson, *Reconstructing Dixie*, 11.
75. Yaeger, ed., *The Geography of Identity*, 17.
76. Barbara Ellen Smith, "Place and the Past in the Global South," 693.
77. Lassiter and Crespino, eds., *Myth of Southern Exceptionalism*; Shafer and Johnston, *End of Southern Exceptionalism*; S. W. Jones and Monteith, *South to a New Place*; Cohn and Smith, *Look Away!* The latter two explore the U.S. South as a place of cultural exchange and hybridity.
78. Ladd, "Dismantling the Monolith," 34.
79. Gray, "Inventing Communities, Imagining Places," xx.
80. Ibid. See also Tweed, "Our Lady of Guadalupe Visits the Confederate Memorial," 72–93.
81. Duck, review of *The Real South*, 802.
82. Ibid.

PART 2

Reframing Norms

Deconstructing the Bible Belt

JOHN HAYES

The Bible Belt is, arguably, the most widespread and vivid image of the American South. The phrase "Bible Belt" immediately conjures up sharp, distinct associations: it's a place where it's hard to get a drink and transgressive to dance, where strangers ask you what church you go to, where roadside signs beckon with urgent summons like "Have You Been Redeemed by the Blood of Jesus Christ?" and "You Can Become a Child of God Today." In journalism and social commentary, the phrase functions often as shorthand to invoke a place where basic tenets of evolutionary science are rejected, where defense of the patriarchal family is a galvanizing cultural issue, where the politics of militant nationalism, corporate deregulation, nativism, and weak environmental regulation hold especial (if not unique) sway. The titles of well-received works of academic scholarship likewise invoke (and thus substantiate) this popular imagery: Christine Heyrman's Bancroft Prize–winning *Southern Cross: The Beginnings of the Bible Belt* (1997) and Darren Dochuk's Dunning Prize–winning *From Bible Belt to Sunbelt: Plain-Folk Religion, Grassroots Politics, and the Rise of Evangelical Conservatism* (2011), among others.

Indeed, more broadly, the leading scholarship in southern religious history has fortified such imagery, lending academic credence to popular conception. In the 1960s the pioneering scholar Samuel Hill theorized that evangelical Protestantism so dominated religious life in the region that it constituted a "southern church" and that "substantially the same syndrome of belief, practice, and emphasis" that had coalesced around 1800 still defined the South.[1] Hill's work portrayed a coherent region with remarkable religious homogeneity. His model came to so strongly define the field that in the 1990s, scholars who wanted to break new ground had to confront and challenge it. "An overly simple and static use of the concept of evangelicalism hides the diversity of southern religious life," Paul Harvey argued in a 1997 book.[2] Donald Mathews critiqued the "myth of [the South's] evangelical homogeneity" in a 1998 essay.[3] And in a 1998 forum Beth Barton Schweiger argued that "the question remains whether the very term 'southern religion,' which imposes a singular unity and purpose and mind, serves at all."[4]

But the political dominance of the Republican Party during the years after the 2000 elections brought the coherent, homogenous model back. In a 2005 collection, Charles Reagan Wilson wrote of the "long cultural hegemony of evangelical Protestants," of how Baptists, Methodists, and Presbyterians were so all-encompassing that they effectively constituted "the Southern Church."[5] The new element was not the region or the religion itself, but rather regional religion's political mobilization. Wilson argued that George W. Bush stood as the "avatar" of this new mobilization "in the white evangelical belt."[6] In the same collection, Samuel Hill reaffirmed his original model, although now extending its chronology into the early 2000s: "for close to two centuries, a regional version of evangelical Protestantism prevailed as the pacesetter for the religious life of the people."[7] In the concluding pages of a sweeping 2005 narrative of religious change over two centuries, Paul Harvey argued that "white southern evangelicals still live in the 'solid South,' but one that is solidly conservative Republican."[8] The qualification of "white" showed a recognition that "the South" could not accurately be shorthand for "white people," that the religious life of southern African Americans had informed different political and cultural expressions, but still the image of the Bible Belt remained: a coherent region, defined by a homogenous religion, with very definite political/cultural implications. A 2004 political meme coined a new phrase but expressed the same basic sense. As the twenty-first century dawned, the South was a red state "Jesusland," the Bible Belt all over again.

The Bible Belt is a historical artifact, a concept whose origins are revealing of both its currency and its limitations. The phrase first appeared in the pages of H. L. Mencken's *American Mercury* in October 1924.[9] In its first appearance (not unlike the "Jesusland" meme if one looks closely) Mencken applied the phrase to a wide swath of the United States, encompassing South and Midwest. But on the heels of his coverage of the trial of high school teacher John T. Scopes the following year in Dayton, Tennessee, for violating the state's new anti-evolution law (the "Scopes Monkey Trial" in Mencken's coinage), the phrase "Bible Belt" became much more closely associated with the South. The acerbic, urbane Mencken, perhaps the most influential journalist and editor of the 1920s, was then in the midst of broadcasting a highly critical portrait of the region. In his 1917 essay "The Sahara of the Bozart" he had first laid out the basic features of this portrait: the states of the former Confederacy, home to "a civilization of manifold excellences" in the colonial and antebellum eras, had experienced a massive cultural catastrophe.[10] By the late nineteenth and early twentieth centuries, the once-noble region had become "almost as sterile, artistically, intellectually, culturally, as the Sahara Desert."[11] Mencken theorized several explanations for the dramatic decline, but he came throughout the 1920s to focus on a single one: where there was once an aristocratic civilization, a "Baptist and Methodist barbarism" had come to reign. The New South was home "to the Methodist parson turned Savonarola," a stifled social landscape where "every village is bossed by a Baptist dervish."[12] Into the mid-1930s, Mencken continued to argue that "the essential difficulty in the South is still a religious one."[13] Rejecting the rational empiricism of modern science, the recreational fun of alcohol and dancing, women's suffrage, and the social equality of blacks and immigrants, Baptist-Methodist Christianity dominated the region and stifled impulses toward cultured civilization. It also made the South the nation's strange, retrograde stepchild. Mencken's portrait gained wide currency and was followed by echoes and reiterations. Colleen McDannell notes that "northern cultural modernists configured their progressive beliefs as the polar opposite of southern evangelical Protestantism in order to draw a clear line between two American 'worlds.'"[14] The South imagined as cultural other—religious, superstitious, reactionary—thus played a critical role in the self-understanding of modernists—secular, scientific, progressive—as the vanguard of the national future.

Mencken's portrait of a regional Bible Belt wasn't concocted out of nothing, and it didn't have substance merely as an imaginary other. Baptist and Methodist churches did dominate the religious scene of the New South. Howard Odum's map of membership in Baptist and Methodist churches in his influential 1936 *Southern Regions of the United States* used the 1926 Census of Religious Bodies to sketch the outlines of a distinct region with uncanny precision.

On the main streets of the innumerable new towns that sprouted across the New South, sturdy brick "First" Baptist and Methodist churches occupied central spaces. Baptists and Methodists funded and operated prominent colleges and leading hospitals, and their clergy were social leaders with great prestige and widespread influence. Massive revival meetings were such familiar events that newspapers printed statistics on each year's converts, while the composing of gospel songs was so pervasive that the region was home to over a dozen gospel-song publishing houses. A theological vision of life dominated to such an extent that that observant daughter of the Bible Belt, Flannery O'Connor (1925–1964), quipped that "the Southerner, who isn't convinced of it, is very much afraid that he may have been formed in the image and likeness of God."[15]

This does not mean that there was religious unanimity under the Baptist-Methodist umbrella. As the example of O'Connor suggests, Catholics were spread throughout the region, concentrated especially in southern Louisiana, southern Florida, and the larger cities. Older Protestant groups—the Episcopalians, Presbyterians, and Lutherans—were a presence throughout the region, and in some cities and towns, their elaborate, imposing churches

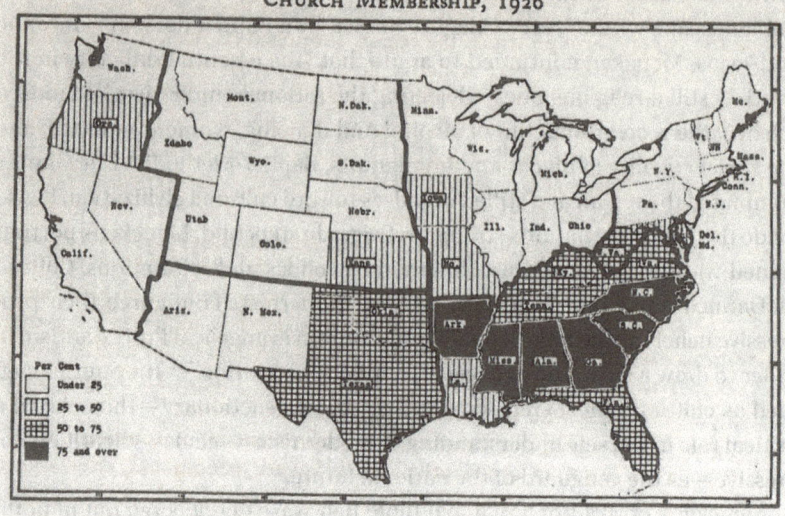

PHOTO 1. The Bible Belt at its zenith. From *Southern Regions of the United States* by Howard Odum. Copyright © 1936 by the University of North Carolina Press, renewed 1964 by Anna K. Odum. Used by permission of the publisher.

could easily suggest to a visitor that they, not the newer Baptists and Methodists, were religiously dominant. Groups that originated contemporaneously with the Baptists and Methodists—most notably the Disciples of Christ and their offshoot the Church of Christ—appeared throughout the region, especially in the western areas, and by the 1920s a variety of Holiness-Pentecostal groups were gaining adherents in urban and rural areas: the Church of God, the Church of God in Christ, the Assemblies of God, the Nazarenes, and others. In tight-knit clusters, Jews appeared in towns and cities throughout the region. And, notably, many people throughout the region did not formally belong to religious institutions. As another map in Odum's *Southern Regions* showed, membership in religious institutions as of the 1926 census displayed no clear regional pattern. The population of Rhode Island and Connecticut was just as "religious"—with 71.8 percent and 68.1 percent of residents belonging to religious institutions—as South and North Carolina, with 72.3 percent and 69.6 percent.[16] Indeed, the most "religious" state was Mormon Utah, with 92.3 percent of the population being religious members.[17]

So the New South was neither a religious monolith nor unusually religious in the formal sense. Different groups embodied alternate, sometimes rival claims about the essence of genuine religion, and a notable percentage of the population did not formally participate in religious life. Still, with these caveats and qualifications, Baptists and Methodists fit a familiar historical rule: a group can wield cultural power in a society far beyond its actual numbers—it can enjoy cultural hegemony. Insofar as other groups had to define themselves against the Baptists and Methodists, insofar as the Baptists' and Methodists' moral vision gained the force of law and manners, and insofar as the public spaces of the New South showed the Baptists' and Methodists' shaping hand, these two groups displayed remarkable cultural power in the region.

But was there something distinctly "southern" in this dominant religion? The voluminous, rapidly expanding scholarship in American religious studies has explored the complicated milieu of late-nineteenth and early-twentieth-century national and transatlantic evangelicalism, revealing (often by inference or implication) that New South Baptists and Methodists were participating in these broad currents. The Chicago-based evangelist Dwight Moody and his song leader Ira Sankey pioneered the genre of the gospel hymn, while the New York Methodist Fanny Crosby penned some of the genre's most popular songs. Iowa-born Billy Sunday was the nation's most prominent revivalist in the early twentieth century, modeling the urban revival in dramatic, theatrical style, while Los Angeles–based evangelist Aimee Semple McPherson brought Hollywood flair to the Pentecostal cause. From Los Angeles in the 1910s came the pamphlet series *The Fundamentals*, seeking to codify the essentials of Protestant Christianity over and against liberalism (or modernism), providing a rallying point for the new cause of fundamentalism. The Women's Christian Temperance Union and the Anti-Saloon League were national groups whose efforts met ultimate success in the Eighteenth Amendment, enacted in the Prohibition Act sponsored by U.S. representative Andrew Volstead of Minnesota. At the most basic but perhaps least tangible level, respectability and domesticity were dominant tropes in evangelical culture, informing such varied endeavors as settlement house work with the urban working class (pioneered by Jane Addams in Chicago), the YMCA for rural migrants to the city (founded in London), imperial endeavors justified as "uplift" for backward peoples (on vivid display in places as varied as the Philippines and South Africa), and a post-slavery racism that imagined "colored" people as incapable of attaining respectability (as in the Hollywood epic *The Birth of a Nation*) or needing the guiding hand of a superior race to even approximate it (Rudyard Kipling's "The White Man's Burden").

The Baptist-Methodist Christianity that was culturally dominant in the New South, then, was not a unifying force that pulled a place together in differentiation from other places outside, but rather a widely diffused concatenation of beliefs, practices, impulses, and extensions without a definite center. It permeated an extensive geography with indefinite borders. Within the United States, religious differences that seemed to delineate a region were differences of degree, not kind. This religious culture was stronger in the South—both in relative number of adherents and in cultural power—but it was not distinctly or uniquely "southern."

A critical reason why it was stronger was the lack of new competing voices in substantive numbers. The regional economy that emerged from the Civil War—with low wages, limited capital, costly credit, and per capita income well below the national average—was an unappealing magnet for immigrants. The vast majority of the approximately twenty-eight million immigrants who came to the United States in 1880–1930 bypassed the South. The region participated very little in this massive demographic phenomenon that transformed the nation. The New South thus received only tiny numbers of the Catholic, Orthodox, and Jewish immigrants who brought their European forms of these religions with them—and who became the numerically dominant group in many places throughout the nation.

Noting the regional economy that emerged in the post–Civil War South, and the demographic transformation it did not foster, suggests that the region's religious differentiation (of degree) was also a post–Civil War phenomenon. Just as the southern economy had not always been the "Nation's No. 1 Economic Problem" (as Franklin Roosevelt famously phrased it in 1938), so too had the South not always been the nation's Bible Belt, a place where Protestant Christianity of the Baptist-Methodist type was unusually strong.[18] Indeed, late in the antebellum period and into the Civil War and Reconstruction, many northern Protestants viewed the region as a place of deficient Christianity, a place where genuine religion had been perverted by the institution and experience of slavery. Few offered a more trenchant and piercing critique than the nation's most prominent black abolitionist, the Methodist exhorter and former slave Frederick Douglass. In the appendix to his 1845 *Narrative*, he wrote:

> What I have said respecting and against religion, I mean strictly to apply to the *slaveholding religion* of this land [emphasis in original], and with no reference whatever to Christianity proper; for, between the Christianity of this land, and the Christianity of Christ, I recognize the widest possible difference.... To be the friend of the one, is of necessity to be the enemy of the other. I love the pure, peaceable, and impartial Christianity of Christ: I therefore hate the corrupt, slaveholding, women-whipping, cradle-plundering, partial and hypocritical Christianity of this land.[19]

Though Douglass was in the vanguard of activism, he was hardly speaking in a vacuum. Just as he was publishing these words, the Baptists and Methodists were experiencing major regional ruptures. When northern Baptists insisted that a conventionally sponsored missionary could not be a slave owner, and northern Methodists insisted the same of a bishop, Baptists and Methodists in slave-owning states organized their own separate organizations, the Southern Baptist Convention and the Methodist Episcopal Church, South. Such ruptures showed the ascendancy of an antislavery (if not abolitionist) spirit in northern evangelical Protestantism, and they provided concrete, institutional form to the northern Protestant sense that there was something wrong in the Christianity of the South.

This sense continued into and was even accentuated by the Civil War. What began as a Unitarian abolitionist's poem became the "Battle Hymn of the Republic," the Union's most prominent anthem. In the colossal violence of the war, the Union was playing a messianic role, fighting to end slavery and thereby open up a new day of genuine religion for the wayward South:

> Mine eyes have seen the coming of the glory of the Lord
> He is trampling out the vintage where the grapes of wrath are stored
> He hath loosed the fateful lightning of His terrible swift sword
> His truth is marching on....
> I have seen Him in the watch-fires of a hundred circling camps
> They have builded him an altar in the evening dews and damps.[20]

A significant number of northern Protestants—"carpetbaggers" and missionaries alike—were informed by such visions as they labored to reconstruct the former Confederacy with a free labor economy and an authentic Christianity. For the many workers sent south from New York by the American Missionary Association, for the organizers of new denominationally funded colleges, and for other teachers and missionaries, reforming the Christianity of the former slaves was a critical part of this regional reconstruction. In their vision, the experience of slavery had deprived slaves of genuine Christianity; what slaves practiced was a hodge-podge of fragments they had appropriated from the slave owners' Christianity, mixed with pieces and remnants of African religions. The Charleston-born free black and African Methodist Episcopal (AME) bishop Daniel Payne, who returned to the region in May 1865 after thirty years in the North, imagined a massive task ahead as he observed "extravagances" and "strange delusions" in the worship of allegedly Christian slaves.[21] "We need a host of Christian reformers like St. Paul," he insisted, "who will not only speak against these evils, but who will also resist them.... The time is at hand when the ministry of the AME Church must drive out this heathenish mode of worship."[22]

Though some white religious leaders in the region repudiated visions of rebuilding and instead fostered religious devotion to a sacralized Lost Cause, other regional religious leaders joined northern Protestants in viewing the defeat of the Confederacy and the end of slavery as the beginning of a new day for Christianity in the region. In his 1880 sermon "The New South: Gratitude, Amendment, Hope," white Methodist bishop and educator Atticus Haygood applauded the new order. "I am grateful that slavery no longer exists.... It is better for our industries and our business, as proved by the crops that free labor makes. But by eminence it is better for our social and ethical development. We will now begin to take our right place among both the conservative and aggressive forces of the civilized and Christian world."[23] In an 1892 address, black Baptist leader J. W. E. Bowen likewise envisioned a close connection between the new economy and Christian morality: "Contemporaneously with the New South, the New Negro has appeared upon the scene, the Negro born of schools and colleges, and bent more on acquiring a home, amassing wealth, and the improvement of the social conditions of his home, than the support of the grog shop, the gambling hall, and other institutions of idleness."[24] In this emergent vision, the economic incentives of the postslavery order rewarded Christian morality—or at least the austere, temperate, self-controlled, fun-shunning morality that the Baptists and Methodists had preached since their earliest appearance in the region in the mid- to late-eighteenth century. In the New South this moral vision would foster proper bourgeois citizens; Baptist-Methodist morality would point the way forward for an emergent, ascendant middle class. The fruits of this vision were on clear display a generation later for theologian Reinhold Niebuhr, who toured the Mississippi Delta in the mid-thirties and observed that "the organized church . . . is as middle class in the south as anywhere else."[25]

Leaders like Haygood and Bowen understood that the new order of the New South presented Baptists and Methodists with an opportunity they had not had before: to set the cultural tone for the region. Although by the 1830s Baptists and Methodists had attracted a probable majority of the white population and over a fourth of the black population, they had done so by accommodating to the existing order rather than by refashioning it according to their own visions.[26] White Baptists and Methodists reshaped their message for the patriarchal household (slaveholding or not), while slaves reshaped Baptist-Methodist Christianity to articulate their own longings, in creative synthesis with fragments of African tradition. The public culture of the antebellum South was dominated by a distinctly un-Baptist, un-Methodist character, a competitive, honor-bound white patriarch whose emblematic behavior W. J. Cash memorably evoked: "To stand on his head in a bar, to toss down a pint of raw whisky at a gulp, to fiddle and dance all night, to bite off the nose or gouge out the eye of a favorite enemy, to fight harder and love harder than the next man, to be known eventually far and wide as a hell of a fellow—such would be his focus."[27] Baptists and Methodists may have gained numerical primacy by the antebellum period, but they did not enjoy cultural hegemony. Indeed, a quick glance at the religious affiliation of Confederate leaders (political and military) shows that the antebellum elite was overwhelmingly

Episcopalian and Presbyterian, with Baptists and Methodists no more numerous than Catholics.[28]

The implicit argument of prominent books like Heyrman's *Southern Cross* and John Boles's *The Great Revival: Beginnings of the Bible Belt* (the full title of the 1996 revised edition of the 1972 book) and the influential, explicit argument of religious historian Samuel Hill—that the beginnings of the Bible Belt are to be found in the early nineteenth century—needs to be reset. The appearance of Baptists and Methodists in significant numbers, and even their numerical primacy, should not be conflated with cultural hegemony. When this is clarified, the Bible Belt (understood not as exotic national Other but rather as a place of special Baptist-Methodist strength, of numerical primacy *and* cultural hegemony) has its beginnings in the intense, turbulent years of Reconstruction.

The Bible Belt—the real-world religious milieu that provided fodder for Mencken's portrait, even as that portrait is now heavily qualified—was thus a contingent historical development, not a perennial regional characteristic. It emerged after the dramatic transformation wrought by the Civil War, as an unfolding market revolution, an ascendant middle class, and a new relative poverty (and thus minimal immigration) became defining features of the social order called the New South. The ruptures in regional history need to be weighed if religion is to be properly understood. At the same time, religion needs to be rigorously historicized. For scholars who are personally religious, this can be an uncomfortable proposition: one's worship, the object of one's deepest devotion—isn't it troubling if this is viewed as contingent? It's one thing to see religion in changing contexts, another to see religion itself as a changing phenomenon, contextual in its meaning(s). Doesn't this make religion all too human?

This problem is particularly acute when the religion at issue is "evangelicalism" or "evangelical Protestantism," as Baptist-Methodist Christianity is often categorized. As a historical phenomenon, evangelicalism is unusually resilient, a highly adaptable form or style of Christianity. Looking just at regional history in thumbnail sketch, are the austere, exclusivist, leveling "evangelicals" of Rhys Isaac's *The Transformation of Virginia*, the hierarchical, paternalistic, Confederacy-sacralizing "evangelicals" of Drew Faust's *The Creation of Confederate Nationalism*, the feminized, anti-competitive, reforming "evangelicals" of Ted Ownby's *Subduing Satan*, and the servant-heart, service economy "evangelicals" of Bethany Moreton's *To Serve God and Wal-Mart* all participants in a common phenomenon? If so, if the term is to have descriptive meaning, the malleability of evangelicals—a malleability that is imaginatively obscured when "evangelical" becomes shorthand—has to be persistently emphasized.

Scholars who self-identify as evangelical bring a special problem to the table. Their form of Christianity is, at least at the conscious level of its own vision, radically ahistorical and anti-tradition. Martin Marty writes that "the Evangelicals are the pioneer religious moderns, with their pietist *ecclesiola in ecclesia*," their perennially "new community" with its presentist "code-words."[29] With this modernist vision, evangelical scholars can too easily project the timelessness, the eternal now of their religious ethos back into the past, fostering a sense of static changelessness to the religion at the heart of the Bible Belt trope. And in the cultural politics of the contemporary United States, scholars who do not identify as evangelical, but who may very much see evangelicals as political opponents, can too readily take them at their word. In the wake of the 2004 elections, for example, when the dominant media analysis held that "evangelical voters" with their concern for "moral values" had been the deciding factor in Republican victories, when the red-state Jesusland meme was in full circulation, I heard a chorus of aggrieved, distressed musings and laments from self-identified liberal and progressive academics, bemoaning the evangelicals who had seized the reins of national power. Right on the heels of the election, at the annual Southern Historical Association meeting, then-president Wayne Flynt's address, an account of how poor white evangelicals came to endorse the reformist policies of the Democrats' New Deal, provoked a heated debate and rebuttal, ending with one scholar insisting, "But these people voted for Bush."[30] The radically ahistorical nature of such a claim suggests that in contemporary cultural politics, the old trope—of religious Other in a deviant region—has significant power. Like the cultural modernists of the 1920s, contemporary liberals or progressives can find great utility (if not always constant comfort) in imagining their opponents as geographically distinct. The liberal/progressive version of nationalism—the basic optimism that time is on the side of liberal politics—retains power if conservative/reactionary forces are consigned to a retrograde region with a static religion.

The malleability of evangelicals and another dramatic wave of regional transformation come sharply into view when one traces the genealogy of evangelicals' role in contemporary cultural politics. In 1925, just as Mencken's Bible Belt portrait was crystallizing, the fundamentalist movement was experiencing a wave of defeats: in its public image, in its drive to control the seminaries, in its attempt to gain the upper hand in the denominational machinery. Liberals won the struggle, becoming the dominant face of American Protestantism, while the fundamentalists seemed to go underground. By the time of World War II, a younger cohort of fundamentalists was pushing for greater cultural engagement, for a softening of the hard, pre-millennial edge that fundamentalism had taken. In a 1944 meeting in St. Louis, they organized a new group, the National Association of Evangelicals (NAE). They began to self-identify as "evangelical" or "neo-evangelical," in distinction from both fundamentalists and liberals. With this usage, "evangelical" began to shift from a simple synonym for "Protestant" or a historian or religion scholar's category for conversionist Protestant groups, to a badge of distinct identity itself. Evangelicals eagerly drew on the idioms of modern psychology and consumerism, imaging authentic Christianity as a "personal relationship with Jesus," beckoning each individual to make a personal "decision for Christ." Barely five years after the NAE's founding, neo-evangelical Billy Graham was gaining national publicity for massive rallies in Los Angeles, and a dozen years later, neo-evangelicals were beginning to challenge the liberals' *Christian Century* with their new *Christianity Today*, published in suburban Chicago. In 1972 *Life* gave front-page coverage to Explo '72, a massive neo-evangelical youth rally in Dallas, and the coverage was prescient: in the subsequent decade neo-evangelicals began to displace liberals as the dominant face of American Protestantism. In 2001 a neo-evangelical Texan entered the White House, and a 2007 Pew survey revealed that 26.3 percent of Americans self-identified as evangelical (with Catholics in second place at 23.9 percent).[31] In 2015, the nation's fourteen largest religious institutions (each with a weekly attendance over twenty thousand) were all evangelical "megachurches."[32]

Americans living in the South have been part of this national phenomenon of rapid evangelical ascendancy. Walker Percy's 1980 novel *The Second Coming* captured this evangelical flowering as the widower Will Barrett ruminates on his daughter and her husband: "Leslie and Jason were born-again Christians and had no use for anything, liturgy or sacrament, which got in the way of a personal encounter with Jesus Christ."[33] For many, self-identifying as evangelical has meant leaving long-established Baptist or Methodist churches—now dismissed as merely formal, as outward "religion," not heartfelt, personal "relationship"—and participating in the life of a new, nondenominational church or parachurch organization. Such a departure typically has intense personal meaning, but this is badly lost when the familiar categories suggest a move from "evangelical" Baptist-Methodist to self-identifying evangelical. At the same time, also confusing matters, some of the well-established Baptist and Methodist churches have transformed themselves, becoming active participants in neo-evangelical culture. Little in their worship style, ethos, or public presentation may differentiate them from a nondenominational church, but they very likely may inhabit the same building or piece of real estate that First Baptist or First Methodist once did over one hundred years ago. Blurring categories even more, the map of the fourteen largest evangelical megachurches spills over familiar regional boundaries: Texas (four), Arizona (two), Georgia, Oklahoma, Illinois, South Carolina, Alabama, California, Kentucky, Nevada. Of these, the two largest Southern Baptist–affiliated are in Texas (Fellowship Church) and California (Saddleback Church).[34]

Such blurred boundaries are testament to the dramatic changes that have swept what was once "the Nation's No. 1 Economic Problem," once the nation's "Bible Belt." The cumulative effect of New Deal programs, of the massive expansion of the defense state during and after World War II, of aggressive industrial recruitment by southern state legislators, was a wholesale regional transformation. The mechanization of agriculture began a huge rural exodus, with millions leaving the region altogether for industrial jobs in the North and West. Military bases, defense plants, and new capital-intensive industries brought rising per capita income, and the region's demography displayed a decisive shift: for the first time since the Civil War, in-migration began to supplant out-migration. In a 1963 essay, Flannery O'Connor quipped that when a Wisconsin friend of hers recently moved to Atlanta, the Massachusetts-born realtor commended one suburban location by saying, "You'll like this neighborhood. There's not a Southerner for two miles."[35] Flows of people and capital made seemingly clear regional boundaries fuzzy.

Accompanying these changes, also blurring lines, was the region's participation in the resurgent nationalism of the post–World War II period. In the mid-fifties, for example, the phrase "under God" was officially added to the Pledge of Allegiance, and "In God We Trust" was declared the official national motto. The astute critic Will Herberg discerned that what was going on in this resurgent nationalism was not just the Cold War image of a religious United States in contrast to an antireligious Soviet Union, but a religion of the United States itself, a sacralization of America. In his 1955 *Protestant, Catholic, Jew* he argued that "by every realistic criterion the American Way of Life is the operative faith of the American people."[36] More recently the decade and a half since September 2001 has witnessed a new flowering of such nationalism, with Ground Zero in New York City becoming a sacred site, "In God We Trust" appearing on license plates and bumper stickers, and "God Bless America" becoming the automatic closing line of political speeches. There is bipartisan agreement that the affairs of state—politics—are the arena of deepest meaning, and political categories—liberal, conservative, et cetera—are the markers of one's deepest identity.

It is in the context of this modern nationalism that a potent political force, the Religious Right, is to be understood. One image is unusually revealing of what is and is not at work in the Religious Right: in a photograph from the late 1970s, Jerry Falwell stands in front of his Thomas Road Baptist Church in Lynchburg, Virginia. He is smiling, and cradled in his arm is an album by the Life Action Singers. On the cover a girl stands in an old schoolhouse, reverently pledging allegiance to a massive U.S. flag. The album is advertised as "a musical expression of the American spirit," and its title is *America, You're Too Young to Die!*

The object of devotion, the locus of ultimate meaning, is the nation. The nation deserves our deepest allegiance, our worshipful reverence, and it is for

PHOTO 2. Jerry Falwell, circa 1970s. It's all here (well, everything except Jesus). Photo by Dennis Brack/Black Star.

the salvation of the nation that the Religious Right is mobilized through its vision of patriarchal, heterosexual nuclear households and public spaces like schools, courthouses, and parks proclaiming the religiousness of America.

In popular conception and scholarly analysis, the Religious Right is too often conflated with neo-evangelicalism. The confusion has some basis in actuality: Baptist and Methodist churches of the older "evangelical" type like Thomas Road can serve as institutional hosts for the Religious Right, and so can newer neo-evangelical churches. The evangelical form is, again, malleable. But the Religious Right is diffuse too, gestating in think tanks and nonprofit foundations, in organizations like the American Family Association, Christian Broadcasting Network, Eagle Forum, Family Research Council, and Focus on the Family, whose geography (Mississippi, Virginia, Illinois, the District of Columbia, Colorado), like that of megachurches, displays no discernible regional pattern. It draws adherents from a diverse constituency—older evangelical groups, neo-evangelicals, Catholics, African American Protestants, and many whose religion is simply America—around a clear vision of the sacralized nation. Like the nationalism of which it is a species, institutional bases are only part of it; in its full manifestations it is amorphously powerful.

Properly categorizing ascendant religious forces in today's United States, tracing their genealogy to the post–World War II years, while at the same time weighing the structural transformations that have reshaped the South, reveals that the Bible Belt began to end in the 1940s. Historians, religious studies scholars, and others scholars of the region need to firmly inject history into analyses of religion, even as they also need greater categorical precision to express the changing religious forms that have often accompanied dramatic regional ruptures. Although religion necessarily involves passion and devotion—whether the sacred object is a god, a nation, or something else—hefty doses of scholarly detachment are critical if those who study the South are to step outside contemporary cultural politics and interpret religion in context.

Notes

1. Hill, *Southern Churches in Crisis*, 23, 67.
2. P. Harvey, *Redeeming the South*, 1.
3. Mathews, "We Have Left Undone Those Things Which We Ought to Have Done," 306.
4. Mathews, Hill, Schweiger, and Boles, "Forum: Southern Religion," 162.
5. Charles Reagan Wilson and Silk, eds., *Religion and Public Life in the South*, 9.
6. Ibid., 18, 197.
7. Ibid., 159.
8. P. Harvey, *Freedom's Coming*, 256.
9. Mencken, "Americana," 171. In the term's first appearance, Iowa was part of the (as yet undefined) "Bible Belt," and Kansas was satirized in the next entry for its "Christian rectitude."
10. Mencken, *Prejudices*, 157, 158.
11. Ibid., 158.
12. Ibid., 160; Mencken, "Editorial."
13. Quoted in Hobson, *Serpent in Eden*, 180.
14. McDannell, *Picturing Faith*, 84.
15. O'Connor, *Mystery and Manners*, 44–45.
16. Odum, *Southern Regions of the United States*, 144.
17. Ibid.
18. Carlton and Coclanis, eds. *Confronting Southern Poverty in the Great Depression*, 42.
19. Douglass, *Narrative of the Life of Frederick Douglass*, 81.
20. Julia Ward Howe, "Battle Hymn of the Republic."
21. Daniel Payne in P. Harvey, *Through the Storm, through the Night*, 163–64.
22. Ibid.
23. Haygood, *The New South*, 12.
24. Quoted in Washington, *Frustrated Fellowship*, 197.
25. Sparks, *Religion in Mississippi*, 186.
26. Heyrman, *Southern Cross*, 265. Heyrman distinguishes between members and adherents. With their exclusivist, voluntary ethos, Baptists and Methodists set a high bar for membership. But many whites and blacks regularly sought out evangelical worship without becoming members. Thus, *adherents* as a percentage of the regional population is a more meaningful gauge of the Baptists' and Methodists' numerical strength.

27. Cash, *The Mind of the South*, 52.
28. Wakelyn, *Biographical Dictionary of the Confederacy*, 529–33.
29. Marty, "The Revival of Evangelicalism and Southern Religion," 15, 18.
30. Email, Paul Harvey to John Hayes, December 2004.
31. *Religious Landscape Study*.
32. "Databases of Megachurches in the U.S."
33. Percy, *The Second Coming*, 145.
34. *Religious Landscape Study*.
35. O'Connor, *Mystery and Manners*, 57.
36. Herberg, *Protestant, Catholic, Jew*, 75.

Katrina Babies

Reproducing Deviance in the Future Unknown

ALIX CHAPMAN

> They don't know
> we are becoming powerful.
> Every time we kiss
> we confirm the new world coming.
>
> Essex Hemphill, "American Wedding"

In the year following the levee breaks, news reports began covering an increase in the number of birth rates in New Orleans. Local and national journalists found that the city's birth rate increased 39 percent from May 2005 to May 2006, with one hospital seeing a 25 percent increase in births nine to twelve months after Katrina.[1] Some parents reported that these births simply reflected the difficulty in accessing contraception and medical practitioners, whereas others said that they had made "a conscious decision to conceive as a way to foster hope for the future in the wake of Katrina's wrath."[2] Local obstetricians and gynecologists took these births as signs of a renaissance in the city of New Orleans, and local obstetricians and gynecologists cited the desires that prompted them as a "stress reliever" and as a way that couples could "fill the time."[3]

In August 2006, a white family of seven from the New Orleans Metairie suburb was interviewed and depicted in a CBS broadcast titled "Katrina Brides and Babies."[4] The broadcast described how in the absence of physical reconstruction, in the wake of Mother Nature's destruction, rebirth is possible through human nature. The program described the Metairie family's contribution to a new generation of New Orleanians and paralleled the new births to a recent growth in the city's wedding industry. In the face of concerns about ongoing infrastructural inadequacy and worries about the city's and region's future, mass media expressed optimism and hope in such reports, and reporters, doctors, and parents referred to "evacuation babies" and more commonly "Katrina babies." My research counters this media narrative by offering a different lens through which to see the reproduction and meaning of life, specifically the experiences of queer people of color.

The focus of this chapter is not dominant culture's recursive need to emphasize the biological reproduction of white middle-class families, although that deserves address. I am more interested in defining other social formations and modes of reproduction and futurity prompted by Katrina, how it "pushed people toward reevaluating what was important—family, connections with people and moving forward."[5] For those who cannot rely on biological reproduction or who are just not seen as "productive" to the formation of communities and the nation, I argue that Katrina babies become "family" in a nonbiological sense, as discursive subjects who have been pushed out by processes of dispossession and displacement.

I link the black queer subject as a particular icon of vulnerability and risk within the context of Katrina babies and to a broader trope representing those who are most often seen as pariahs. Widely said to be a burden on the wider public, these subjects include refugees, ghettoized youths, so-called welfare babies and anchor babies (the latter born in the United States to undocumented immigrant mothers), and all undocumented immigrants. My focus is not only ostracized LGBTQ populations but also single mothers, sex workers, black poor people, and working-class populations displaced from New Orleans.

In black queer vernacular, "the kids" (or "the children") refers to LGBTQ youths and young adults, but the term is not necessarily linked to age as much as to their position within structures of power and oppression.[6] Within that context, I appropriate the term "Katrina babies" to represent black queer subjects, removing it from sole use as a figure signaling the reproduction of white middle-class heteronormativity in the wake of disaster. The babies to whom I refer are diasporic subjects, birthed out of ephemeral relationships. They may not be widely seen as appropriate contributors to a new New Orleans, the nation, or dominant social order, but they are productive.

This chapter explores how and why a framework focused on black queer diasporas complicates the hegemony of white heteronormative kinship and examines the conditions of social reproduction that characterize black queer subjectivity and kinship, looking at black subjects who do not meet heteropatriarchal expectations. This includes those who may be heterosexual but who are marginalized by heteronormative models, such as the nuclear family. Their lives can inform us about nonlinear, nonbiological modes of reproduction available to marginalized populations, despite sexual orientation.

Transdisciplinary Intersections

In previous writing I have argued about the difficulties of defining a history of black queer people and other marginalized subjects, as figures that have been historically erased from traditional archives and discourses of heritage.⁷ Here I offer a transdisciplinary analysis of these marginalizing forces, the ways they interlock, and alternative notions of kinship and reproduction.

My aim is to push forward a discussion of desire prompted by anthropologist Gloria Wekker's investigations of sexuality in the African diasporas. She states that instead of being "God-given, context-free, and eternal," "sexuality in a particular setting is something that people shape collectively on the basis of their cultural archives and changing political and economic circumstances," and "furthermore . . . there is a politics to passion."⁸

My Katrina babies appear at the intersections of queer theory, African diaspora, and southern studies. We cannot take for granted the political implications of asserting identities in New Orleans or the South at large. There is no monolithic South, yet the boundaries and bodies that inhabit it can be as naturalized as the processes of biological reproduction I reference in the microcosm of Katrina babies. Discourses of southern heritage and its legacy rest on the effects of crisis, Confederate defeat in the Civil War, even as these discourses serve in the maintenance of that heritage. Not unlike New Orleans, the South as a whole maintains its status as a stronghold of white supremacy through investment in heteronormativity and the gender binary. This has recently been evident in southern conservative discussions of states' rights and recent pushes for anti-LGBT laws in Tennessee, Texas, North Carolina, and Mississippi. It is also a matter of systemic and structural oppression at the level of social institutions such as the church and state and the ideologies they reproduce and disseminate. My goal is to investigate how black and queer subjects find themselves kicked and pushed out of closets into structural positions of vulnerability and survival.

Here queer theory is useful as it offers a means of deconstructing epistemologies of gender and sex through processes of knowledge production primarily at the level of discourse and performativity. Discourse produces what we consider natural in that we perceive the world and produce meaningful understanding through a network of associations.⁹ Judith Butler's notion of performativity established gender not as a biological fact but rather complex sets of discursive practices that are not universally true but understood in context.¹⁰ These discursive practices are contingent on repetition and their ability to produce and anchor meaning. In this gender is not unlike kinship, which queer studies scholar Elizabeth Freeman theorizes through Bourdieu's notion of "habitus," stating, "Kinship consists of relationships renewed, and their very renewal is what is relational at all."¹¹ These social formations are renewed through their very extension across the temporal circumstances of rupture and trauma. The extension and reproduction of their value through caring and exchange make them relational.

Katrina babies are conceived through new social formations, diaspora, and personal and ontological change where none was expected. The experiences of Katrina babies reveal that marginalized populations can engage in an alternative mode of reproduction, one that innately subverts dominant culture's dependence on biological reproduction and allows queer people of color to socially reproduce outside of white, heteronormative frames of kinship. Southern studies can benefit from analyzing these counternarratives as challenges to more traditional performances of southern heritage, rooted in white, heteronormative discourses of safety and family values and gendered notions of family and modes of reproduction (as are evident in southern conservative discussions of LGBTQ rights).

Over the last ten years, I have heard of Katrina babies referenced as unexpected births that happened during the storm due to stress and shifts in barometric pressure, and more generally to mean anyone who experienced Hurricane Katrina at a very young age.[12] I am interested in the notion of Katrina babies as a set of reproductive social relationships and desires, that—going back to Wekker—are the product of "changing political and economic circumstances."[13] By examining these, I begin to define a form of reproductive futurity that is grounded in material struggles to survive current forms of crisis, a set of practices that incorporate notions of contact, caregiving, and renewal.

There is a futurism to disaster capitalism in that crisis is used as a driving force for new modes of market production and infrastructure.[14] There is optimism toward the capacities of disaster and those who govern the flows of life and death to galvanize populations and rejuvenate neocolonial projects.[15] I see no future in which black queer subjects do not find themselves mediating these forces.

Black feminist scholars have complicated the study of kinship and reproduction through their investigation of the roots and routes of African diasporas transnationally and intra-nationally.[16] Historically, any notion of black families or kinship structures has been defined against the figure of the white heteropatriarchal nuclear family.[17] Black people's gendered subjectivity and sexuality, regardless of orientation, is recursively pathologized and invalidated by consequence of their abilities to self-determine kinship and reproduction.[18] Extended families and other alternative kinship systems have been central to black people's survival from slavery onward. Anthropology of the African diaspora allows us to find continuities in the ways of performance, oral history, and other cultural archives.[19] Integrating queer theory allows us to consider the performance of diaspora kinship as it is reproduced through lived discursive practices. A focus on black queer subjectivity and kinship allows us to glean the social practices of sexual and gender minorities but also delineate the racialized boundaries of kinship and social reproduction more broadly.

This project is motivated by recent academic debates concerning the future and the figure of the child. In Lee Edelman's *No Future* he argues that society invests in reproducing a child whose "future" furthers dominant social orders and at the cost of today's adult problems, such as homophobia, war, and poverty.[20] Edelman's brand of anti-relational and anti-normative critique assumes that society is optimistic about all its children. By embracing conservative notions of queerness as a threat to the heteronormative family structure, we destroy those children's futures. Black and queer of color scholars such as Jose Muñoz have countered this critique, arguing, "All queers are not the stealth-universal-white-gay-man ... all children are not the privileged white babies to whom contemporary society caters."[21] In "For 'the Children' Dancing the Beloved Community," Jafari Allen writes not on behalf of Edelman's anti-queer child but "Dorothy's, or in more recent Black gay parlance, same-gender-loving—gay, bisexual, lesbian, trans, queer—people of color. These children's temporal, spatial, and relational orientations and on the ground politics are certainly distinct from the gay world divorced of relationality, politics, and reality that Lee Edelman theorizes."[22] Allen's and Muñoz's works call for the voices of the "children" that mainstream media and a certain section of queer academic discourse have not brought into a discussion of kinship or reproduction. Likewise, I situate the voices of Katrina babies in their relational and political present.

This research is part of a longitudinal study of displacement and the reproduction of blackness in New Orleans and among its diaspora starting in 2007. The interviews and oral narratives presented here were peripheral to the primary context of my research on New Orleans's Bounce music scene. I began to use methodologies of co-performance, in which researchers use performance to further ethnographic engagement in fieldwork and analysis.[23] D. Soyini Madison has described co-performance as when "you not only do what subjects do, but you are intellectually and relationally invested in their symbol-making practices as you experience with them a range of yearnings and desires."[24] Given my access to my respondents' lives, I needed a methodological frame that would account for my experiences and observations. In order to achieve this goal, I used cultural biography, a method that combines ethnography and life history interviews, to intervene in the discourse of Katrina babies as figures of blind optimism and often heteronormative notions of reproductive futurism. This allowed for a self-reflexive critique of my own experiences as a black queer scholar working within a community in which I move between positions of insider and outsider.[25]

Crisis and Black Queer Becoming: Ana's Story

Our rendezvous was a gas station somewhere in Tulsa, Oklahoma. I had just spent a few days visiting family in the area when a friend called to ask if I could help a young woman who had been displaced and was trying to get back home to New Orleans. Before I knew it, my mother and I were waiting in a parking lot, getting the car serviced, when another car pulled up. Out came Ana, a nineteen-year-old woman of Afro-Cuban descent with chestnut skin, a few tattoos, and a smile on her face.[26] My mother asked, "Where are all your things?" To which Ana replied, "This is it," shrugging a small duffle bag on her shoulder. Ana's flight from her family had been prompted by a mixture of resistance to her father's traditional gender values, tensions around her budding queerness, and the freedom and community she longed for back in New Orleans. "When you think about it in the scope of life you're just some random guy I felt safe enough [with] to ride [with] for eleven hours from Oklahoma to New Orleans," Ana confided years later while I interviewed her about our adventure. "I was very excited, and I felt like I had gotten over on them, not really lied but stretched the truth a little bit.... I remember the ride down we talked a lot. I feel like I told you my life story and you told me yours." Even at Ana's young age she could write a book about the complications her family had experienced in multiple migrations and displacements between Cuba, Louisiana, and Oklahoma.

Ana went on to say, "I remember your mom. I really liked how much she was worried; I wouldn't say 'concerned' but just a doting mother. To me we were just talking, and she was very polite, but then she was like 'What size shoes do you wear? You know I have some sandals in my car you want to try them on. I don't want to make you uncomfortable but they're really great.' Things just kept coming out. It was incredible. I don't know if this is her own survival coming out, but she had lots of snacks and lots of advice but not advice. She was like, 'Stay aware ... you'll be safe with this ... make sure you do that ... you don't want to be in that town when it gets too late.' It wasn't overbearing or over-protective. It was good to see that much emotion[al] interchange between adults."

What my mother did not know was that our helping Ana was not simply a matter of her displacement due to the mass migration of people after Hurricane Katrina but also Ana's displacement from her family due to homophobia among her relatives. Our meeting Ana was prompted by a loose network of associations connected to being black but also Ana's and my status as queer people. In a loose, amorphous sense, we were family. Although Ana had not acquired the material amenities to stabilize and endure the compounded effects of disaster, she had already begun to develop her own survival strategies, daring to hope in a queer and uncertain future.

I usually teased my mother for her over-preparedness. The oldest daughter of eight, she didn't have indoor plumbing till she was thirteen, and throughout her life she had learned to make plans within plans. I knew this was partly a survival strategy in response to the economic conditions in which she was raised but also practices that had mediated gendered and racialized oppression for generations.

Ana and I drove eleven hours through the night. We got to know each other and talked about our similar yet differing relationships with our families. Although we came from very different class positions, geographies, and gendered experiences, it was telling how much we had in common and shared despite those differences. The common denominator was our awareness of a cultural archive in which we could relate to each other despite our differences.

The next morning I dropped off Ana at a friend's house, and she soon reconnected with her mother, who had separated from her husband and moved back to New Orleans's Eighth Ward. In the years following, I would occasionally run into Ana, and she would update me on her family, which was still split between Louisiana and Oklahoma. Within a few years her mother died of health complications. Whenever I see Ana, she always says, "I'll never forget you and your mom and how you helped me get back home; that was our underground railroad."

The exchanges between Ana, my mother, and me rest on notions of kinship and caring that are key to thinking about black queer cultural labor. My mother, Ana, and I are connected within a black queer critique that focuses on one's relative proximity to power rather than one's identity and our relative exclusion to notions of family and reproduction based on white nuclear bonds. These encounters are not about identity alone but also recognition of the structural positions in which black and queer people find themselves and work together to overcome.

My mother realized that Ana would need to be ready to face the challenges of pervasive and ongoing systems of oppression, even if she was not aware of Ana's queerness. She knew that there was no safe space awaiting Ana, and her intervention indicates the necessity of those survival skills to those who continuously find themselves in precarious spaces. My mother's contact with Ana facilitated preparation for her uncertain future, on which, I argue, her social reproduction is dependent. Ana was able to receive this "advice but not advice" because the message was addressed with respect and great care. My mother took on the role of mother in a fictive kinship with Ana. Ana neither requested advice from my mother, nor did she likely see it as necessary. My mother, as a marginalized woman, knew that Ana would need a tool kit to help her survive and mediate her marginalization. Ana became my mother's Katrina baby.

In this narrative the fictive and biological relationships between mother and child are tested by the circumstances of crisis, the specter of the white middle-class nuclear family, and the historical negation of black parenthood as problematic, as represented in the infamous Moynihan report, *The Negro Family*.[27] The West is and has always been pessimistic about any future for the black family. Nonetheless, women and their children endure, and their endurance is the reproduction of their care amid the complex set of circumstances that is the West. Looking back on my mother's preparedness in helping Ana, I am reminded of all the bottles of water and clothing, not to mention her care and giving. Those provisions she had stocked are material manifestations of an inner orientation toward continued sociality and efforts at securing the future.

This cycle of contact, caregiving, and renewal is a mode of production. It is discursively reproduced in notions of black exceptionalism, where black youth are told to be two, three times, and even more prepared than their peers, not necessarily to achieve "success," but to have a life at all. These forms of social reproduction are performative and reflected in the black queer term "the life"—in which "the life" is not a given state of being but something that must be acquired and reconstituted, through kinship networks, self-making, and performances of desire and autonomy.

Crisis and Black Queer Becoming: Tasha's Story

"When I first came back [to New Orleans] actually," New Orleans resident Tasha explained in the back of a Seventh Ward bar,[28]

> I had to adjust myself for the simple fact that during Hurricane Katrina I stayed.... I stayed, and I didn't evacuate. I stayed where I was in New Orleans East, and there it was like twenty feet of water, and I actually stayed through it all. I was at a friend's house, a group of my friends. We really didn't pay attention to the storm and didn't think the storm was going to be as bad as it was.... it was the aftereffect when down here in New Orleans the levee busted and we were right by the levee, and if we was to peep our head out the window, you could see the water just rushing and just hitting houses and stuff. It was like the movie *Titanic*, and when the ship was sinking the water was just hitting through everything.

Tasha's experience and recognition of the breaking levees, not Hurricane Katrina directly, as the source of devastation is significant as it implicates the state. Tasha's interview, which goes on to describe the days and weeks after Katrina, directly references the role of queer kinship, defined by a preexisting network of friends from New Orleans clubs and the city's music scene. She describes how members of this social network survived the flood and its aftermath:

> [Three days later] there were people riding 'round on boats, basically telling you to get what you need to survive... whatever we could get out of the store we took and brought back to this hotel... everybody broke the windows, the

> whole hotel was full ... and then after that we wind up finding a truck, and they brought the truck back to the hotel where we were, and they loaded the truck with not just us, they picked up other people and tried to help other people, actually a Heineken truck, and there was twenty-seven of us ... so they picked up other people, ... one person had a dog, they had like maybe five or six kids, two older people, one had an oxygen tank and ... we just left there and we tried to drive and head towards Baton Rouge.

Here Tasha recounts a kind of solidarity, kinship, and caretaking that cannot be provided by dominant social institutions such as the church, economic system, or state.

I argue that kinship in this context falls within a mode of social relation defined by black gay scholar Samuel Delany as "contact." The circumstances of rescue and the help of strangers within a public sphere that is urban and contingent apply to this notion. Network and contact are not binary oppositions but constitute differences of scale, high and low. This is significant in that "more ordinary sorts of contact yield their payoff in moments of crisis," Delany writes.[29] Contact is more often marked as dangerous as it can exist outside dominant social institutions, thus necessitating discipline and regulation. This is evident in Tasha and her friends' attempts to evacuate:

> When we got into St. Charles Parish they tried to make a turn with the truck, and the truck caused traffic [to back up] ... the police stopped the truck and all twenty-seven of us were arrested for looting, and we were on the Channel 4 news.... Of course, the cops were, like, 'This is a bunch of gay people' and basically laughing and clowning about it. They tried handling us badly, pushing some of us, guns to our faces, cause we were looting, that's what they said, when we were trying to survive.

The discourse of criminality constructed in the days following Hurricane Katrina often represented white families as survivors "finding" bare necessities while blacks were portrayed as "looters."[30] The confluence of media representations and political rhetoric describing these "criminal activities" was used to stigmatize evacuees as they resettled and to justify the negligence of the Federal Emergency Management Agency (FEMA) and local and federal agents who were authorized to shoot to kill.[31] Although these tactics are most often cited in response to those who were left in the city, Tasha's experience reveals a general approach to black evacuees throughout the region.

> We sat in jail for two weeks ... they took the children and sent them away from their parents. They sent the children to some kind of child care. They didn't keep the children at the jail. They took all of us, the older people, and put us all in orange.... When we got to court the judge couldn't believe that those cops had arrested us for looting when we had to do what we had to do to survive, and

the judge was like, "This is stupid, I had to steal a boat to ride my family from one place to another. Get all of these people out of my courtroom; all of these people are free to go."

Tasha's narrative points to the experiential field and function of contact as a generative yet contingent mode of social reproduction and, as I show, survival. Her story provides a small window into the lives of post-Katrina evacuees who necessarily disidentified with heteronormative notions of progress and reproduction regarding their survival. The affinities and circumstances that brought together those twenty-seven people were determined by corporeal possibilities set within a terrain of scarcity. This coming together was shaped by the dispossessive force of the state—both the breaking of the levees and police violence—and the media that construe black survival as a threat. Violence is engendered in their actions partly because of the ways black people's attempts at survival are repeatedly understood through a racial-historical narrative in which blackness is conflated with threat. Despite this, as apparent in the judge's dismissal, shared experiences of trauma and crisis can provoke action and exchange in ways that defy the organizing principles of the racial state. When I asked Tasha what happened after she got out, she said, "Well, first my grandmother died, then my mother got sick, then I came home and I took care of her.... I started entertaining more and competing in pageants. It was a Sunday afternoon, and I was talking to my mother, and I told her, 'I wanna basically just become a woman,' and my mama was like, "If you gonna be a woman you need to be the best at whatever you be," and she told me, "I'm behind you 100 percent." Tasha's formation of a trans-subjectivity is born of a process that is relative, one in which she becomes a different kind of subject. This is constituted by the ways she has extended her life across hard times and hard places while negotiating self-understandings of gender. To better understand this, it is helpful to bring Delany's notion of contact into conversation with discussions of temporality and futurity.[32] Through this analysis I hope to pinpoint those ephemeral embodied forms of care in the present that create potential futures for those like Tasha and Ana.

Contact and Caring

For Katrina babies, contact and caring—nonbiological forms of social reproduction—are key to their survival. Delany's notion of contact applies as it describes the importance of embodied encounters, both sexual and platonic, to this process. Contact presumes a corporeal relationship in a public context of unknowns, as in moments of disaster when bodies are most vulnerable. Contact is the very thing that conservative, racist, homophobic, classist, and misogynistic rhetoricians fear as can be seen in their phobic statements about physical proximity to others. It is the fear of an encounter that transforms or leads to irrevocable change. For example, homophobic rhetoric that conflates homosexuality and gender nonconformity with pedophilia, drug abuse, and rape (particularly among men) relies on notions of debasement that cannot be recovered from. Blackness and queerness are not productive to dominant frames of family and future but represent incoherence that might destroy nuclear bonds or one's sense of self. Therein lie the potential of black queer sociality as a site of reproduction that is simultaneously designated nonproductive within a dominant frame.

I expand Delany's notion of contact to articulate a self-reflexive and ontological becoming, as in Tasha's experience of gender transitioning. Her shifting personhood occurs in the midst of recovery, investment in black queer cultural forms like pageantry, and caring for her mother. These forms of cultural labor function not unlike parenting as documented in Jenny Livingston's 1980s depiction of House and Ball culture in *Paris Is Burning*, a documentary depicting 1980s black and Latino queer communities in New York City.[33] In this film, contestants representing particular "houses" (or kinship or social groups) perform in drag balls for prizes and titles. These houses serve as surrogate families for youth participants, with house "mothers" and "fathers" playing key parental roles. Interviewees discuss the efficacy of queer kinship in this structure of performance, in helping queer people of color to deal with poverty, racism, homophobia, and transphobia. In the film, becoming a house "mother" to queer youth has nothing to do with blood ties or biological age but instead with assessing need and giving care.

These potentialities (for whatever growth and self-determination we choose) are available to us all and offer forms of endurance through hard times, but they are not valued in a capitalist and heteronormative worldview. It may sound far-fetched, but how many of us have experienced relationships, if not our own subjectivity, as fluid and changeable out of a sense of necessity? Black queer sociality is a provisional cultural labor that offers a different yet valuable way for us to think about the broader public's ability to reproduce fragile relationships while remaining aware of those forces that could end them.

For the Kids

The travails of my Katrina babies, not the white icons of normative nuclear bonds but those discursively produced as threats to it, are linked to a political and economic terrain whose temporal structure is more chronic then acute. Black lives continuously experience mundane forms of dispossession brought on by post-Katrina infrastructural neglect and state violence by way of a punitive criminal justice system and neoliberal privatization in education, health care, and housing. To learn to endure, those like Ana, Tasha, my mother, and I must continuously mediate recursive assaults and roadblocks that require care and faith in the possibilities of contact as a form of personal renewal and social change. Our experiences and the conditions that brought us together are driven by a need for contact and support shaped by uncertain movements across uncertain times and spaces.

In this chapter, I have chosen the time of Hurricane Katrina to discuss my interlocutors' experiences of evacuation and return. I have used personal narratives to intervene in the discourse of Katrina babies as figures of blind optimism and biological notions of reproductive futurism. I have situated these discussions of the lived experiences and voices of black queer subjects, arguing that their lives can inform about nonlinear, nonbiological modes of reproduction available to marginalized populations despite sexual orientation broadly.

Beautifully articulated in black gay poet Essex Hemphill's "American Wedding," "Every time we kiss we confirm the new world coming." Each point of contact, whether a fleeting kiss or a helping hand, is productive of a future, new possibilities, and new life if we have the audacity to self-determine their value. I have used ethnographic engagement to produce dialogue within the spaces and movements of black queer subjects as they struggle to survive, find home, and find themselves. This method has led me to see the broader significance of "the children" or "the kids" within black queer vernacular. I have come to the conclusion that this research is itself one of Katrina's babies as it has been made through the dialogic relationship of disaster and my own desire toward some future. My kids are all over these pages, which are imbued with years of fluid sociality, contact, and care. I mean for my seeds and their episteme to take root, grow, and thrive no matter how rocky the terrain and no matter that future unknown.

Notes

1. Szabo, "New Orleans Births Soar"; Simmons, "Baby Boom Adds Life to Rebirth of New Orleans."
2. Simmons, "Baby Boom Adds Life to Rebirth of New Orleans."
3. Szabo, "New Orleans Births Soar."
4. "Katrina Brides and Babies."
5. Janet Ross quoted in Simmons, "Baby Boom Adds Life to Rebirth of New Orleans."
6. See, for example, Livingston, *Paris is Burning*; Allen, "For 'the Children' Dancing the Beloved Community"; E. Johnson, "Mother Knows Best," 251.
7. Chapman, "The Punk Show."
8. Wekker, *The Politics of Passion*, 67.
9. See Foucault, *The History of Sexuality*.
10. Butler, *Gender Trouble*; Sedgwick, Koseofsky, and Frank, *Touching Feeling*.

11. Freeman, *Queer Belongings*, 308.

12. Rechdahl, "Boy Born a Day before Hurricane Katrina Was Determined to Be a New Orleans Baby."

13. Wekker, *The Politics of Passion*, 67.

14. C. Johnson, ed., *The Neoliberal Deluge*; Klein, *The Shock Doctrine*.

15. Mbembe, "Necropolitics," 11–40.

16. Alexander, *Pedagogies of Crossing*; Gilroy, *The Black Atlantic*; Hartman, *Scenes of Subjection*.

17. Cohen, "Deviance as Resistance," 27–45; Ferguson, *Aberrations in Black*; Moynihan, *The Negro Family*.

18. Omolade, "Hearts of Darkness," 362–78; Gillman, *Difference and Pathology*; Collins, *Black Feminist Thought*.

19. Allen, "For 'the Children' Dancing the Beloved Community," 313; J. Brown, *Dropping Anchor, Setting Sail*; Wekker, *The Politics of Passion*.

20. Edelman, *No Future*.

21. Muñoz, *Cruising Utopia*, 94.

22. Allen, "For 'the Children' Dancing the Beloved Community," 313.

23. Kondo, *About Face*; Madison, *Critical Ethnography*; Conquergood, "Rethinking Ethnography."

24. Madison, *Critical Ethnography*, 186.

25. Collins, *Black Feminist Thought*; Abu-Lughod, "Writing against Culture."

26. A pseudonym has been used to protect this subject's identity.

27. Spillers, "Mama's Baby, Papa's Maybe," 65–81.

28. A pseudonym has been used to protect this subject's identity.

29. Delany, *Times Square Red, Times Square Blue*, 125.

30. Marable and Clarke, *Seeking Higher Ground*, x.

31. Agid, "Locked and Loaded," 55–75.

32. Delany, *Times Square Red, Times Square Blue*.

33. Livingston, *Paris Is Burning*.

PART 3

Engaging Politics

Southern Inhospitality

Latino Immigrant Attrition and Resistance in the South

GWENDOLYN FERRETI

On February 6, 2011, speaking to a Republican audience at a party breakfast, Alabama state senator Scott Beason said: "If you don't believe illegal immigration will destroy a community go and check out parts of Alabama around Arab and Albertville.... [Republicans need to] empty the clip, and do what has to be done."[1] Later in that legislative session, Senator Beason cosponsored a bill that was pushed into law: the "Beason-Hammon Alabama Taxpayer and Citizen Protection Act," hereafter referred to in this essay as HB56.

HB56 is a comprehensive, state-level immigration law that aimed for undocumented immigrants residing within the state to "self-deport" by increasing the number of circumstances where migrants' immigration status would be reviewed, denying them access to services, and criminalizing their actions so that they would be exposed to deportation. The "attrition via enforcement" approach to immigration control represents an effort by states to control the growth of undocumented immigration, particularly that of Latino migrants, by ratcheting up the enforcement of policies that exclude immigrants and policing them (and everyone else) on increasing fronts. It is best known for the fact that it created a requirement for law enforcement officers to inquire about a person's immigration status anytime a person is stopped, detained, or arrested, if the officer has "reasonable suspicion" that the individual may be an undocumented migrant, and mandated detention upon the lack of proof thereof. (This requirement is commonly known as the "papers, please" provision and was copied from Arizona's own state immigration law, SB1070.) The law also became infamous for including a provision that required K–12 public school officials to determine the immigration status of newly enrolled students and prohibited undocumented people from enrolling in public colleges and universities. The law aimed to criminalize mundane aspects of immigrants' everyday lives, such as driving, fishing, going to school, owning and living in a manufactured or mobile home, voting, not carrying state-issued identification or their legal permanent residency cards, entering into contracts, looking for work on the streets, and engaging in government transactions (including applying for a vehicle registration or trying to obtain public utilities, such as water). The legislators who supported HB56 aimed for undocumented immigrants' "attrition via enforcement" in the state, a goal popularly known as "self-deportation." Immigration restrictionists have promoted this as an alternative to mass detention and deportation, on the one hand, and to the legalization of the millions of undocumented immigrants living in the United States today, on the other. Restrictionists argue that undocumented immigrants can be pushed into leaving a state (and the country), in essence deporting themselves, if they face joblessness, increased criminalization, and stringent enforcement of already-existing immigration control measures such as the use of E-Verify and the Secure Communities program, discussed below. The policy of attrition via enforcement is viewed as an effective addition to the active hunt for undocumented immigrants, raids by the Immigration and Customs Enforcement Agency (ICE) or other law enforcement officials, and the stemming of unauthorized crossings at the border. The policy ignores undocumented immigrants' U.S. roots and communities and does not account for their strong motivations not to leave. The policy also shifts responsibility for immigration enforcement from institutions to individuals such as school staff and others untrained and unaccountable for misuse and abuse of these new powers.

HB56 targeted first- and second-generation immigrants by establishing a coding system that required K–12 public schools to record both a student's immigration status and the status of the student's parents. It also prohibited undocumented people from enrolling at state colleges and universities. The law also affected other Alabama residents who were not undocumented persons, making it a crime to harbor or transport anyone who was known to be undocumented or who it was reasonable to believe was undocumented, requiring all employers to verify new employees' immigration status by using the E-Verify federal database, making the solicitation of work on the streets (as done by day laborers) illegal, and establishing a photo identification requirement to vote. HB56 created an environment in which Latinos came under intense scrutiny and faced an increase in xenophobic and racist intimidation. In one instance in Tuscaloosa, a white neighbor knocked on the door of a Mexican family's trailer. When the head of the household opened the door, the neighbor took her picture and told her that she was going to report her to ICE.

HB56 was touted by both opponents and supporters as the harshest state law in the country aimed at curbing undocumented migration, and it was written with the intention of outdoing the infamous Arizona law. Provisions of both laws have been permanently blocked through litigation by civil rights organizations and in federal lawsuits, yet parts of them are in effect today.[2]

My research finds evidence that HB56 was intended to control, detain, and expel the growing Latino population in the state. A flurry of other southern states introduced similar bills into their legislatures, including Georgia, Mississippi, Tennessee, Florida, South Carolina, and North Carolina, which began to introduce attrition via enforcement laws in the 2011 legislative session. While bills in Mississippi, Tennessee, Florida, and North Carolina were defeated, "attrition via enforcement" laws were successfully passed in Alabama, Georgia, and South Carolina. For southern states, immigration has become a new issue with which to rehash arguments over states' rights, state autonomy, and regional boundaries. While immigration has traditionally been the purview of the federal government, states like Alabama have taken it upon themselves to police the growth of Latino populations through devolution of immigration enforcement.

My research also suggests that these laws have become the catalyst for an emergent immigrant justice movement in the South. In Alabama, HB56 prompted undocumented immigrants and their allies to engage in grassroots organizing to try to overturn the law. Undocumented immigrants in the state began to lobby at the state legislature and Congress. Some came out of the shadows and testified about their experiences, speaking at public rallies and federal hearings, such as a legislative field hearing organized by Illinois congressman Luis Gutierrez and a U.S. Civil Rights Commission hearing held in Birmingham. Working collaboratively with volunteers at the local level, and with statewide and regional immigrants' rights organizations, undocumented immigrants have gone so far as to engage in civil disobedience and risk arrest to challenge the state that tries to oust them.

In focusing on the effects of HB56, I aim to move the study of "new immigrant destination sites in the South," in the words of Jamie Winders, "away from describing and documenting Latino migration patterns and toward deconstructing the processes of exclusion worked upon Latinos in many southern communities."[3] I argue that although laws like HB56 are ostensibly race-neutral, referring to immigrants' legal status, they ultimately work to preserve white supremacy in the South by aiming to destroy the networks necessary for the social reproduction of people of color. I will further show how these laws have inadvertently prompted the emergence of a resistance movement. In doing this, I support contemporary efforts to incorporate Latino experiences within southern studies scholarship considering national demographic trends, the revival of states' rights and sovereignty discussions around immigration, and the current development of a southern immigrant rights movement. The work of Latino researchers in contributing to this scholarship should be highlighted. As a Latina/Chicana/Mexicana scholar and woman of color, my own positionality brings insight into the effects of essentially legislating xenophobia (as has been done with HB56) as it allows for a connection to my research subjects as fellow Latinos and because I have personally experienced some of the discriminatory practices that I describe. Lastly, I join fellow authors in this book in embracing the possibility that transdisciplinarity can deepen our understandings. I am an anthropologist who, through this work, has gained great insight from the fields of geography, legal studies, and history.

In this chapter, I begin with the backstory to HB56 in Alabama and then shift to my ethnographic research, conducted before and after the implementation of HB56, primarily employing the tools of participant observation and in-depth interview. As a brown-skinned woman and Latina scholar conducting ethnographic research, I was able to connect personally to my research subjects. I am a second-generation, mestiza Mexican immigrant born into a low-income family, a native Spanish and English bilingual speaker, and my parents were once undocumented immigrants themselves. As HB56 was implemented in Alabama, I became subject to the law as a brown woman and as someone who regularly interacted with undocumented persons.

Latino Attrition

Life in Alabama is not easy for low-income immigrants, regardless of documentation status. Many work one or two jobs six days a week and work shifts of more than ten hours without any labor protections such as sick pay, vacation, workers' compensation, or even an effective way to ensure the payment of wages. Many of my research contacts and family and friends in their extended networks have been victims of burglaries and armed home invasions. Latino immigrants across the state are more vulnerable because they are known to carry large amounts of cash either on their persons or in their homes, given that it is difficult for them to obtain bank accounts without a valid state driver's license or visa-stamped passport, and given immigrants' general lack of trust in banks.[4] The school systems are not friendly to immigrant parents and do a poor job of providing bilingual support so that they may effectively follow their children's progress. Many immigrants also do not have adequate access to regular, affordable health care, and undocumented immigrants (even those who have work authorization under programs such as Deferred Action for Childhood Arrivals [DACA]) are ineligible for the benefits of the Affordable Care Act.[5] The majority of my contacts in the Latino community in Tuscaloosa are Spanish monolingual, although there are also a significant number of Nahuatl indigenous peoples from Veracruz, Mexico, and Mayan Quiché and Kanjobal peoples from northern Guatemala.[6]

Despite the challenges, the Latino immigrant community has managed to survive and live in the state, calling Alabama home. Altha Cravey has described Latino communities in the South as living "microgeographies" of social reproduction. She sees these spaces as existing in a "parallel world" outside the scrutiny of native-born, non-Latino eyes. She points to how migrants adapt to the loss of traditional systems for social reproduction, ones they would normally have in their home countries, like household and family systems of support, by re-creating these spaces in their new social sphere.[7]

In Tuscaloosa, Latino community members can still identify pioneer migrants who first arrived in the city, but I was able to document second- and third-generation Latinos. They rely on extended social networks for financial security through things like house and car sharing, swapping of goods, private loans, and *tandas*—group savings pools that help to subsidize their low incomes. They also rely on these networks to maintain cultural traditions and sense of community. They frequent Latino family-run businesses such as grocery stores and barbershops. Families organize to engage in religious traditions such as *Las Posadas*, a Catholic tradition that reenacts Mary and Joseph's biblical search for lodging in Bethlehem, and hold regular house parties to celebrate boxing matches, birthdays, and homeland national holidays. These are conscious efforts to maintain their culture and provide their children with a sense of Latinidad that is otherwise invisible in the state.[8] Despite their hardships, many have been able to purchase their own trailer homes and live quiet lives. When I asked why people liked living in Alabama before HB56, I would often get the same response from many Latino immigrants: "[*Aquí en Tuscaloosa*] *es tranquilo y está bonito, hay muchos áboles*." (Here in Tuscaloosa, it's calm, and it's very pretty. There are a lot of trees.) Many compared Tuscaloosa to Atlanta and remarked that before HB56 police weren't as aggressive as in Georgia.

With HB56, the Latino community felt watched, plucked from the quiet anonymity of social marginalization. The law honed in on this community and catapulted them (and the rest of the state) into the middle of the national immigration debate. Latino undocumented migrants and their often mixed-status families were singled out despite being a relatively small population in the state, and this visibility was very jarring. Matilde, a Mexican single mother in her early thirties, recounted: "When I went back to work to clean the [university] stadium I felt like everyone was staring at me. It didn't help that lots of my coworkers didn't come back to work. I could tell people were thinking, what is she still doing here?" Imelda echoed this sentiment: "When I go to the Walmart I just feel the stares; it's not the same as before."

Having initiated my ethnographic research before HB56 was passed, I was able to observe firsthand the initial reactions of fear and panic that later transitioned into resistance and assertions of belonging and worth. The city was still recovering from an F4 tornado that had leveled much of Tuscaloosa only a few months before. Many Latino families had lost their homes to the tornado. Children were beginning the new school year. When the law went into effect, I observed that many families did not understand the scope of the law, did not know their rights, and did not have access to reliable sources of information beyond word of mouth.⁹ Many chose to keep their children home from school that week, and some opted to leave the state altogether. The law's implementation hit the news, and newspapers reported that Latinos were leaving the state in hoards on their own accord, just as the law's creators intended. Undocumented and mixed-status families prepared themselves in case of deportation, reducing their outings to essential trips such as going to work, school, and to buy food. Others began to sell or give away their things, looking to lessen their burden should they need to move. Jacinta, a Mexican woman in her late forties, told me, "I'm very sad. I went ahead and gave a lot of things to the secondhand store because, just imagine, what do [I do] with all of this stuff if I get deported?" Families turned inward, cutting off weekend activities like birthday parties and keeping one parent at home during outings, to make sure that if one parent was deported, then the other would remain to take care of the children.

In the face of inaction by Congress to pass laws that deal with inadequacies in our current immigration system, and desiring to solve the discursively convenient "immigration problem," some non-Latinos have sought to find more ways to control immigration locally. This follows a troublesome trend—the devolution of immigration enforcement to nonfederal agencies through programs such as Secure Communities, the deputization of law enforcement agents to enforce immigration law such as in 287(g) contracts, and interior checkpoints for snagging undocumented immigrants.¹⁰ Yet the difference between these programs and laws like HB56 is that immigration enforcement in the latter is handed in many cases to people who hold no official capacity and thus are not accountable.

HB56 was conceived of as part of a 2010 Alabama Republican Party campaign platform called "Handshake with Alabama." Alabama Republicans stated that one of their priorities that year would be to "create a new state criminal trespass statute that allows local law enforcement to arrest illegal immigrants for simply setting foot in Alabama. Another provision [would] make it a crime to provide an illegal immigrant transportation anywhere in Alabama, whether it is a trip across the state or simply to the corner store."¹¹ Proponents of the law, including its sponsors, have continuously made it explicit that they meant for HB56 to control the growing Latino population in Alabama and make local citizens responsible for enforcement. When Senator Beason claimed that immigration can destroy communities, he pointed to Arab, Alabama, and Albertville, Alabama, two cities with large Latino populations.

HB56 proponents often conflated "Hispanic" and "illegal alien" when discussing the law. An *Anniston (Ala.) Star* article reported that a state representative had responded to the paper's request for evidence to substantiate a claim that Alabama had the second highest rate of "illegal" immigrant growth by sending them a link to a Pew Research Center report that concluded that Alabama had the second highest rate of growth of its Hispanic population.[12] The terms "Hispanic" and "Latino" were frequently used in reference to the undocumented population during the passing of the law. In its decision to temporarily enjoin sections of the law, the U.S. District Court for the Middle District of Alabama noted, "While the record clearly establishes that concern about illegal immigration was a substantial factor behind the passage of HB56, there is substantial evidence that race and national origin also played a role."[13]

HB56 and other such laws demonstrate a backlash against changing regional and national demographics pointing to the United States becoming a "majority minority" nation—one in which former minorities, nonwhites, are no longer outnumbered. As evidenced by these laws, the South has become embroiled in a battle for the preservation of a white supremacist racial binary through the new lens of xenophobic hyper-nativism. Eduardo Bonilla-Silva describes the current racial order as the "new racism," saying that it "reproduces racial domination mostly through subtle and covert discriminatory practices which are often institutionalized, defended with coded language ... and bonded by the ideology of color-blind racism." He characterizes this as "killing me softly."[14] Attrition via enforcement effectively does this. This strategy of immigrant enforcement controls undocumented immigrants' lives and actions by hyper-regulating and criminalizing everyday transactions with the state and with other citizens (including "legal" aliens) to the point where the everyday lives of families and communities are stressed, broken, and for some, unbearable. The comprehensiveness of this law not only "structurally cut off [undocumented immigrants] in social reproduction terms from the society in which they nonetheless labor;"[15] it also cut them off from their own marginalized communities. Yet these actions are not race-neutral, as their application is explicitly racialized and aimed to excise Latinos from the state—to push them to "self-deport." HB56 and the general trend toward the devolution of immigration enforcement are a product of color-blind racism. They embrace the notion of color-blindness by using the language of immigrant "legality" (or lack thereof) to ultimately control, suppress, and annihilate communities of color, particularly Latinos and specifically people of Mexican descent. The election of the first black U.S. president in 2008, the release of 2010 census results that showed that Latinos had become the largest minority group, and projections that the United States will become a "majority minority" nation have fueled white supremacist fears. Leo Chavez describes a post-9/11 "Latino Threat Narrative," in which people of Latin American descent, especially those of Mexican descent, are not considered except as an internal threat to the nation at large.[16] This perceived threat has grown from marginalized, extremist sectors and become entrenched in mainstream thought, pushed forward by actors invested in gaining power through fear. Roxanne L. Doty describes how the white supremacist views of extremist vigilante groups like the Minuteman Project in Arizona and others who hunt down and chase border crossers have been adopted and rebranded by the anti-immigrant movement, camouflaged by research-oriented think thanks such as the Center for Immigration Studies.[17] She characterizes "attrition via enforcement" as a politics of exception, where segments of a population are segregated by the denial of rights and even denial of their humanity, and she credits the anti-immigrant movement with its conception.

The anti-immigrant movement relies on a manufactured discourse about brown "illegality," and it scapegoats undocumented immigrants, who are also a smokescreen to camouflage fear of the growth in Latinos' power. Unique to the South are attacks on people of color that transpire without much public comment, seemingly acceptable and even expected by many. There is a pervasive, pessimistic cynicism (even among local social justice community organizers) wherein the South is described as "the belly of the beast" in matters of structural racism. This is due, in part, to the South's history of black genocide through the institutions of slavery, the Confederacy, Jim Crow, and the continued exploitation of blacks, but this distinctiveness is worth further academic inquiry. This perception is not new, however, and these systems of oppression are not exclusive to the South. Malcolm X said, "Stop talking about the South.... Long as you south of the Canadian border, you're South."[18] Yet there is something to be said about the overt nature with which those who hold power in the South assert their power. Latinos today are pegged into this system through the legislation of xenophobic policies that institutionalize their second-class status—as people who are "illegal," without rights, and without a right to call the South home. Because the Latino population was relatively new and lacked strong institutional power, anti-immigrant laws were passed with limited preemptive resistance. I have since come to witness a shift, however, as described below.

Latino Immigrant Resistance

On a warm spring day in Tuscaloosa, a few dozen Latino families congregated on an open field by a local Catholic church. Many tried to fly handmade paper kites, but there was not enough wind for that. The kites had "No HB56" painted on them, and young children tried to get them aloft by screaming and towing them as fast as they could run. Even though the weather did not cooperate, the idea behind the event was beautiful. Held on *El Día del Niño* (the Day of the Child), a Mexican national holiday, it was intended as both a protest and a family affair. Invitation flyers read: "¡*Vamos a mandar volar* HB56!" (HB56 can go fly a kite!)

The light-hearted affair—organized by a volunteer grassroots group of immigrants who were members of the Alabama Coalition for Immigrant Justice—was a respite during otherwise tense times. Alabama's anti-immigrant law was in nearly full force, and the city was close to celebrating the first anniversary of surviving the tornado that had devastated the state in 2011. At the time when the protest happened in April 2012, only a few provisions had been blocked (mainly the K–12 school provision), and arrests and detention of immigrants were happening frequently. The would-be kite-flying protesters called on the state legislature to repeal the law that was tearing apart the community. They were working hard to achieve this and participating in activities many had never experienced before. For example, they had staffed a booth at an annual Latino health fair organized by regional social service providers. At that event, they urged attendees to join them in caravans to lobby directly at the state legislature in Montgomery, two hours away. They acted out skits in the tradition of popular theater, showing their audience a condensed, humorous explanation of what it meant to lobby lawmakers directly.[19] In one scene two friends shared their concerns about HB56, with a third friend inviting them to lobby directly. After a bit of convincing they agreed and jumped on an imaginary bus to travel to Montgomery. Once there, they acted out speaking to Senator Beason and Representative Mickey Hammon (the cosponsors of the bill), trying to convince them to drop the bill. The actors succeeded, and the Beason and Hammon stand-ins shook hands with their undocumented constituents. At the time, these new community organizers, and many others across the state, were visiting the statehouse every week or so, lobbying legislators to repeal HB56. Despite being undocumented immigrants, they were engaging the legislative process in ways that many citizens never do.

Their engagement in the civic process was a journey of learning how the process is supposed to work in the United States and a challenge to the taken-for-granted concept of constituency. They were working to save their families and community and stay in *their* "sweet home Alabama." In action, they were engaging in "cultural citizenship" practices, making claims of belonging that extended far beyond the traditional concept of political citizenship that excluded them.[20] But they would lose this battle.

HB56 was amended in 2012 to include more harsh provisions, including the creation of a public, online, searchable database that would reveal the names of some undocumented immigrants deemed "unlawfully present" by the state.[21] But this led to the development of an immigrant justice movement in Alabama that did not exist prior to the law. As the state sanctioned the attrition of this population, many members of the community resisted by digging in their heels and staying put.

In Alabama, immigrant families have worked collectively to counter the effects of HB56. New activists have emerged to maintain the social and relational networks that comprise the immigrant community. Here immigrants make the claim that they have deep ties to the state, claiming it as their home. "Este es *mi* dulce Alabama" (This is *my* sweet Alabama), says Anastasia, an undocumented Mexican immigrant involved in the movement. A mother of three children, including a DREAMer (an undocumented youth who would qualify for the proposed Development, Relief, and Education for Alien Minors Act), she is a domestic worker and the town baker who serves her famous *tres leches* cake at local quinceañera parties and weddings as well as at community meetings.[22] Ana says she fell into a depression after HB56 was passed—she feared for herself and her family. Yet involvement in the movement propelled her and others into the public sphere, and today she is a community leader who many turn to. She and other immigrant women in her church were the first to become involved in activism against HB56. They formed a grassroots volunteer organization, Somos Tuskaloosa (We are Tuscaloosa), to organize the kite-flying protest and other demonstrations against the law. The name of the group itself was a declaration. After the tornado, many signs boasted the phrase "We are Tuscaloosa" in red and white lettering with black-and-white houndstooth ribbons that highlighted the college town's famous football team: the Crimson Tide. The city had pushed the phrase in the earliest phases of recovery. Yet as families recovered from the storm, the state legislature passed HB56: making it explicit that immigrants were not wanted. Somos Tuskaloosa became a way for the group to assert their belonging and place within the city.

Latino immigrant families in Alabama are working to produce a new discourse where they are seen as a unit, with value and worth, regardless of each individual's immigration status. In her analyses of the U.S. immigrant justice movement, Amalia Palleres argues that the concept of family has become a political construct which activists claim as a political subjectivity and as collective identity in the contemporary immigrant rights movement.[23] As such, immigrant justice activists today conceive of the family unit as having the right to remain together and resist deportation. They use this argument to fight to repeal the current law. In their activism, the family itself as a discourse becomes a source of unity and distinction.[24] As they engage in acts of cultural citizenship, they work to redefine the parameters defining rights and what is legally available and to whom. In the South, these acts stand out. Immigrant activism in traditional immigrant-receiving states like Texas and California relies on larger, long-standing immigrant populations and the presence of physical, tangible symbols of oppression like border walls and fences to make their claims concrete. Immigrant communities in the South learn from discourses outside the regions, channeled through Spanish-language media, including social media. Yet they also produce new discourses specific to their local settings and targeting local people. In the South, the civil rights movement has become a major trope around which the emergent immigrant rights movement has been framed. This immigrant justice movement overlaps with the historic civil rights movement, as they both have addressed racially charged injustices and demanded equal rights; however, there are clear distinctions that fall outside the focus of this paper.

The growth of Latino political consciousness and activism in the South has led to solidarity and alliance work with southern black social justice movements.[25] At the state level, the Black Caucus of the Alabama legislature argued against HB56 before it passed and again when it was amended the following legislative year. Also, the Alabama Coalition for Immigrant Justice has worked with black civil rights organizations to make connections between the immigrant justice movement and the historic civil rights movement. The coalition launched its campaign against HB56 at the 16th Street Baptist Church in November 2011, the site where four black girls were killed in the 1963 attack by the Ku Klux Klan. In Tuscaloosa, HB56 also prompted new alliances with local black leaders. One example was how the local chapter of the Southern Christian Leadership Conference (SCLC) welcomed emergent Latino leaders as HB56 came to pass. The year after HB56 passed, the Tuscaloosa SCLC's annual Martin Luther King Jr. march hosted a Latino contingent for the first time, which has become a new tradition in the city. That year "Si se puede!" (Yes we can!) was chanted along with "Fed Up, Fired Up, Ain't Gonna Take it No More!" The fact that HB56 quietly embedded a voter identification requirement prompted black leaders across the state to engage the issue of immigration and find commonalities. The preservation of free access to voting continues to be important to African Americans in the South. The members of Somos Tuskaloosa reached out to the extended social networks they built at church and work, with friends and family, and got people to march as an act of solidarity with blacks, and as a way of bringing attention to their plight under HB56.

As HB56 has persisted despite protest, Latino activism has escalated to include acts of civil disobedience and other "crimes of dissent," as Jarrett S. Lovell calls them. Lovell describes these as protest strategies that, while varying in level of confrontation, risk, and playfulness, entail a level of criminality in their staging and execution. The intent is to appeal to the political imaginations of the greater populace and move them to resist a perceived oppression or injustice.[26] Because attrition via enforcement laws aim to inhibit undocumented immigrant life, I argue that refusing to leave and setting roots is itself an act of resistance. Fighting to defend their claims of belonging and choosing not to "self-deport," the undocumented Latino community in Alabama has found ways to survive, and these entail acts of dissidence, pushing the envelope, and challenging the state through nonviolent disobedience.

Moving Forward

Through the study of emergent social movements in the South and the development of laws aimed at population attrition, we see how the South is taking the lead on a national racial project to criminalize immigrant life, particularly that of Latino, mixed-status families. We gain an understanding of the ways that xenophobia and racism combine to advance white supremacy and how a community reacts to this pressure. As seen in my case study, the imposition of HB56 created an initial state of panic and fear in the Latino community and expanded the responsibility of immigration enforcement to the whole populace. Yet, as this community suffered and was pushed into the forefront of a national debate over immigration, the unexpected result was that it forged a grassroots resistance movement. Understanding these processes through ethnographic research brings them to life as we see how they are lived and experienced through participant observation. We can balance analyses of de jure institutionalized immigration with de facto experiences and come to understand how new communities make their homes in the heart of Dixie despite efforts by the state. As scholars, we must wait to see what implications this will have for the region and the rest of the country in the long term. Yet in this moment I honor the agency and resilience of the undocumented Alabama immigrant community.

Notes

1. Rolley, "Beason."

2. Various sections of HB56 have changed since it was originally passed in 2011. The U.S. Supreme Court upheld the "papers, please" provision of Arizona's SB1070, Section 2(B), stating that it was unclear whether requiring law enforcement to check the immigration status of detainees conflicts with federal law. See *Arizona et al. v. United States*. The requirement for public K–12 schools to review their enrolling students' immigration status was also blocked, but the provision that makes it illegal for undocumented people to attend public colleges and universities is still in effect. It continues to be a crime for undocumented people to attempt to register their vehicles; however, there is now an exemption for the registration of mobile and manufactured homes. The provision that made it illegal for undocumented people to engage in "government transactions" has also been amended to allow for the contracting of basic utilities such as water and waste collection. The provision of the law that criminalized renting to, housing, and driving undocumented people has also been removed. E-Verify continues to be mandatory for all new employees in both the private and public sector. The voter-ID provision that was embedded in HB56 is also still in effect. In 2012, the law was amended to include a provision that would have required the names of individuals the state deemed "unlawfully present" to be published on a public website (commonly known as the "scarlet letter" provision), but this provision has also been blocked.

3. Winders, "Changing Politics of Race and Region," 685.

4. Some undocumented immigrants who have been victims of violent crimes have gained legalization through U-visas. These are non-immigrant visas set aside for victims of certain crimes who have suffered mental or physical abuse. They require that victims help law enforcement in the investigation and/or prosecution of the criminal activities in which they were victims. For more information, see "Victims of Criminal Activity: U Nonimmigrant Status," U.S. Citizenship and Immigration Services, https://www.uscis.gov/humanitarian/victims-human-trafficking-other-crimes/victims-criminal-activity-u-nonimmigrant-status/victims-criminal-activity-u-nonimmigrant-status.

5. DACA is a U.S. immigration policy mandated through executive action by President Barack Obama that allows certain undocumented immigrants who arrived in the country as minors to receive a two-year, renewable work authorization permit without granting "legal" status or a pathway to citizenship. As such, these immigrants are ineligible for benefits under the Affordable Care Act. For more information, see "Executive Actions on Immigration," U.S. Citizenship and Immigration Services, http://www.uscis.gov/immigrationaction.

6. The factor of indigeneity within the Latino experience is complex but very important. My subject pool is marked by a higher concentration of Mestizo and indigenous Nahuatl Mexicans, but Tuscaloosa hosts a sizeable, albeit smaller, Guatemalan Mayan community, whose members speak Acateco, Kanjobal, and Mam. While I was able to work with some Guatemalan Mayans, I found this segment of the Latino community to be more insular and less fluent in Spanish, and thus harder to build rapport with. There were also issues of gender that arose as those who spoke more Spanish tended to be men, and my approach, as a then-unmarried woman, was a difficult social barrier given cultural norms. Working more with indigenous American peoples in the South would be a fruitful avenue of future research.

7. Cravey, "Transnationality, Social Spaces, and Parallel Worlds," 217–34.

8. Latinidad describes a place-specific understanding of pan-Latino ethnic identity, and belonging, that unifies those in Latino communities, based on shared experiences. For a specific use of this frame, in a particularly southern context, see Byrd, *The Sounds of Latinidad*.

9. HB56 went into effect on September 29, 2011, after a temporary injunction by the U.S. District Court Judge Sharon L. Blackburn. See *Hispanic Interest Coalition of Alabama et al. vs. Robert Bentley et al.*

10. See Varsanyi, ed., *Taking Local Control* (2010); Coleman, "The 'Local' Migration State"; Stuesse and Coleman, "Automobility, Immobility, Altermobility." The 287(g) program, "one of ICE's top partnership initiatives, allows a state and local law enforcement entity to enter into a partnership with ICE, under a joint Memorandum of Agreement (MOA). The state or local entity receives delegated authority for immigration enforcement within their jurisdictions." See "Delegation of Immigration Authority Section 287(g) Immigration and Nationality Act."

11. Hubbard, *Storming the State House*, 237.

12. "Hammon Doesn't Know Difference between 'Hispanic' and 'Illegal Immigrant.'"

13. Case 2:11-cv-00982-MHT-CSC, document 87, 68.

14. Bonilla-Silva, *Racism without Racists*, 213.
15. Coleman, "The 'Local' Migration State," 184.
16. Chavez, *The Latino Threat*.
17. Doty, *The Law into Their Own Hands*.
18. Malcolm X, "The Ballot or the Bullet."
19. Popular theater is a dramaturgic pedagogical style aimed at educating and bringing out critical consciousness, encapsulated by Paolo Freire's concept of "concientization" within an oppressed community to affect social change. See Freire, *Pedagogy of the Oppressed* (1972).
20. Rosaldo, "Cultural Citizenship, Inequality, and Multiculturalism," 253–64.
21. This provision was popularly called the "Scarlet Letter" provision by its opponents as it branded undocumented persons by making their names accessible on a public website if that person was arrested for any incident, including false arrests. It was prevented from being implemented as this information is considered confidential by the federal government. The state attorney general, Luther Strange, eventually reached a settlement to stop it from being enforced. "Civil Rights Coalition Victorious."
22. "DREAMers" are undocumented youths who would qualify for the Development, Relief, and Education for Alien Minors Act, a multiphase bill that would grant conditional residency with a pathway to citizenship to undocumented immigrants who entered the country while minors. This bill has failed to pass multiple times, but the name of the bill has led to a moniker for undocumented youths. While not all undocumented youths involved in the immigrant justice movement prefer this title, the young man to whom I refer in this chapter does.
23. Pallares, *Family Activism*.
24. Ibid.
25. Alvarado and Jaret, *Building Black-Brown Coalitions in the Southeast*.
26. Lovell, *Crimes of Dissent*.

Public History, Diversity, and Higher Education

Three Case Studies on the African American Past

JODI SKIPPER, KATHRYN GREEN,
AND RICO D. CHAPMAN

In 2014, Angela Thorpe, a recent graduate of the Museum Studies MA program at the University of North Carolina at Greensboro, began a series of blog posts on diversity in the field of public history for the National Council on Public History (NCPH). Thorpe, who is African American, wrote the posts after she witnessed the failure of the museum at which she interned to engage with the local African American community. African Americans did not seem to perceive the museum as a welcoming space, and "the museum was not confronting diversity [issues] head-on."[1] She also found a comparable inattention to diversity among the institutions that she considered for graduate school: "Each program director admitted their program 'struggled with diversity,'" while claiming that "they were 'working on it.'"[2] The four-part series included interviews with other public historians and attempted to understand what suggestions they had for better diversifying public history.

Thorpe was not the first to inquire into these questions. In 2009 an NCPH working group, "How Do We Get There? Racial and Ethnic Diversity in the Public History Profession," was co-organized by Modupe Labode and Calinda Lee "to discuss the profession's lack of diversity and share ideas about remedying the situation."[3] A recurring explanation for the lack of diversity in public history was described as the "'pipeline'—the process by which public historians are produced."[4] History majors tend to be perceived as the best candidates for public history graduate programs, and racial and ethnic minorities are underrepresented in the historical profession at large.[5] These concerns have been recognized by the Association for the Study of African American Life and History, the Association of Black Women Historians, and the American Historical Association's Committee on Minority Historians, but they have yet to be remedied. The recruitment of undergraduates from other disciplines is necessary, in addition to more conscious attempts to recruit and sustain minority history students, through an "encouraging environment" that counters "intellectual racism."[6] Minority students may "feel directly and personally connected to broader experiences of oppression and to struggles for empowerment," and white faculty "claims of objectivity are more apt to sound like self-serving maneuvers to preserve hierarchy and privilege," to them.[7] In turn, white cohort and faculty claims of subjectivity or subpar scholarship to students of color can create hostile environments. One participant specifically "urged the NCPH to engage in meaningful collaborations with minority-serving colleges and universities."[8] This means that their frameworks and "the idea of putting scholarship to the service of their own communities' empowerment" must be valued by potential collaborators.[9]

Even though "five years later, the implications of the session, and its impact on the field, [were] still being assessed and remain complex," its findings, and Thorpe's blog posts, offer a lens through which we, as three academics—two historians and one anthropologist—who work in public state universities on public history projects, can assess the practicality of doing public history work without formal public history program structures.[10] Chapman is a historian at Jackson State University, a historically black university in the Mississippi capital, Jackson; Green is a historian at Mississippi Valley State University, a historically black university in the Delta region; and Skipper is an anthropologist at the University of Mississippi, a historically white university in the North Mississippi Hill Country.

The NCPH's statement on best practices for undergraduate and graduate students recognizes that "history departments introduce public history to undergraduate students in a variety of ways," yet the NCPH does not adequately consider professionals working outside of history departments, in interdisciplinary programs like southern studies; those working in history departments, with limited means for doing public history projects; or instructors offering "a class or two on public history theories and/or practices."[11] Public history often requires efforts by individuals with limited departmental support or resources and explicit efforts to work across disciplines to introduce such methodologies. Our focus on the public history profession does not assume that it is the only way to do this kind of work but that this subdiscipline has offered the best methodologies thus far.

The goal of this chapter is to transdisciplinarily profile efforts to diversify public history at three universities in Mississippi. We believe that this comparative approach (across historical periods and state regions) allows us to adequately address a breadth of issues. Public history work (through historical consulting, museums, government work, archives, oral histories, cultural resource management, curation, film and media, historical interpretation, historic preservation, public policy advising, avocational history, and community activism) is pervasive in southern studies research. Most southern studies scholars will use public history methodologies, whether they name them such or not, at some point in their careers. As a result, we think that it is a model lens in which to consider diversity issues in southern studies. In addition, the interdisciplinary nature of public history work aligns with this edited collection's frame of transdisciplinary southern studies.

Our experiences show that many who claim to do public history work are unfamiliar with public history theory and methodologies. Some familiarity with public history scholarship is key. In addition, we recognize that public history methodologies alone are insufficient. Intersecting public history methodologies with fields outside of the discipline of history is crucial in instances where history departments do not prioritize public history projects or officially recognize them as beneficial to faculty tenure and promotion.[12] In the current economic and political environment, which might restrict some departments from supporting faculty and staff projects, people may be able to pool economic resources and human capital across disciplinary lines to complete projects.

The contributors to this chapter confront these issues in a variety of ways. We profile our personal findings on diversity through several concerns presented in Thorpe's work: 1) the lack of racial and ethnic diversity in the public history profession, 2) socio-economic inequality among African American undergraduate students who want to break the poverty cycle, and 3) the engagement in meaningful collaborations with minority-serving colleges and universities. The second issue is most pertinent in the U.S. South, where 55 percent of the black population in the United States lives, and even more evident in the state of Mississippi, which boasts the largest per capita black population (38 percent).[13] In addition, Mississippi is the state with the lowest median household income ($37,095 in 2012), disproportionately affecting student opportunities to break poverty cycles.[14]

The third issue is also most pertinent in the U.S. South, as 94 of the 113 current historically black colleges and universities (HBCUs) are located in historically southern states or border states such as Virginia and Kentucky.[15] In order to better assess what might make such collaborations meaningful, this chapter includes the perspectives of two faculty members with divergent experiences at different HBCUs. We contend that such an assessment of potential collaborations will not be productive without attempts to profile and better understand the positions and plights of those doing public history work at those colleges and universities.

Thorpe's assessment is one inspiration for this chapter, which evolved from conversations begun when the authors attended Roots/Heritage Tourism in Africa and the African Diaspora: Case Studies for a Comparative Approach, a conference at Florida International University in February 2015. We all work at universities in Mississippi, yet we had been unaware of each other's work. What we quickly observed is that our work intersected through the lenses of tourism and African American studies, yet our regional and chronological focuses diverged. This gave us a unique opportunity to compare and contrast notes on how the different focuses might affect public responses to and public support for our historic preservation work. We are still in the early stages of that assessment yet have chosen to present this chapter in the chronological order of our historical focuses, the antebellum, Jim Crow, and civil rights movement eras respectively.

Skipper Case Study: Antebellum North Mississippi

When Skipper arrived at the University of Mississippi in 2010, with joint appointments in anthropology and southern studies, she aspired to teach a course on southern heritage tourism. Increased student interest in blues tourism was evident.[16] Although students employed public history methodologies in their projects, their committees did not include a public historian. In fact, to date there is no public historian on the faculty.[17] Even with increasing student interests in public history–based projects, the University of Mississippi Department of History has no structured public history component.

The university's Center for the Study of Southern Culture (CSSC) has engaged in what can be considered public history work for years, recently through media and documentary projects and the Southern Foodways Alliance's oral history initiatives. But classroom discussions of public history as an applied approach or career are rare. Most public history projects are affiliated with the CSSC, others with the Department of History. Some faculty members use oral history methodologies and some assist local historic preservation organizations with interpretation projects. Still, the deficit in public history faculty is a huge oversight in a state university.

Skipper, a public archaeologist, connected her knowledge of public history methodologies and anthropological theories to design a southern heritage tourism course. She incorporated her graduate school training as a scholar-in-residence at the Women's Museum in Dallas and as a student of the Interpreting the Texas Past project, in which interdisciplinary teams of University of Texas at Austin graduate students worked at case study historic sites across the state. Rooted in that case study model, Skipper incorporated into her course Behind the Big House (BTBH), a grassroots tourism and education program in Holly Springs, Mississippi, that highlights the lives of the enslaved through extant slave dwellings.

Holly Springs is located in Marshall County, which by 1836 was a cultural and economic hub in northern Mississippi and which by 1850 had become the largest cotton producer in the state. In the twentieth century, tourism in the region grew considerably after the restoration of many old mansions built during this period of growth. For nearly eighty years now, the Holly Springs

Garden Club's annual "Pilgrimage" tour of historic homes and churches has historically interpreted this period through the furnishings in those houses.

The BTBH program began in 2012 when Jenifer Eggleston and Chelius Carter, two white homeowners, discovered that one of the structures on their property was a former slave dwelling. According to Carter, "The program was proposed to the Holly Springs Garden Club as an opportunity to do what other similar pilgrimages across the South had not done—to tell a more complete story of these antebellum homes. Holly Springs, Mississippi is well known [for] its antebellum architecture and this program offers the opportunity to give the visiting public a more accurate and inclusive historic narrative of our town by giving its enslaved population a rightful place in that narrative."[18]

Carter and Eggleston work through a local historic preservation organization, Preserve Marshall County and Holly Springs (PMCHS), Inc. In addition to attracting the average Pilgrimage visitor, whom Carter describes as "older and middle-aged Caucasian, largely retired and middle class," he and Eggleston made educational outreach a priority. With the help of Linda Turner, a local teacher, school visitation increased from just over 125 students in 2013 to 550 the next year.[19] There have also been successful efforts to increase African American visitation in a city in which they represent over 79 percent of the population. In 2014, Carter reported that the "prominence of the younger school-aged visitors and more from the local African-American community were encouraging. It will take time to develop more local support and interest, but we feel that [PMCHS] is steadily gaining credibility in the community at large and continued support . . . is critical towards our long-term goal to build a more unified community."[20]

As one remedy, part of that community engagement work is done through Gracing the Table (GTT), a local racial reconciliation group which recognizes that community healing and historic preservation are inextricably linked, especially when difficult heritages are being explored. Through GTT, Skipper met Alisea Williams McLeod, chair of the Division of Humanities at Rust College, a historically black college in Holly Springs. McLeod, a literature professor, works across the boundaries of her discipline to engage in several public history projects. Like Skipper, she struggles without a formal program but has been creative about involving students in public history work. She and her students helped to organize GTT, which aims to get local community members to invest in public history work around slavery. With a group motto of "Community Healing through Communication," its four basic tenets are uncovering history, making connections, working toward healing, and taking action. Related programs include a yearly libation ceremony in honor of enslaved and sharecropping communities who labored at the Davis Plantation in Holly Springs, film viewings and discussions on slavery, and family reunion tours of slave dwelling sites. Gracing the Table also helps to organize community member participation in the Behind the Big House program. Skipper's students worked directly with GTT members, including McLeod and her students. As a result, GTT has largely become a cooperative effort between private citizens, Rust College, and University of Mississippi faculty and students. This collaboration is significant, considering the call of the NCPH working group on racial and ethnic diversity for such alliances. More importantly, it has been mutually beneficial to McLeod and Skipper, who mainly work unaccompanied and without structured public history programs.[21]

Skipper was particularly attracted to the BTBH program's focus on community engagement and felt that such an emphasis was a key to student learning. Through graduate courses and mentorship, Skipper encourages students to think critically about the communities with whom they work. As a result, one course requirement was that students work as program docents, connecting them directly to program managers, site owners, and visitors. Skipper's conversations with members of the Holly Springs African American community revealed that they did not see the Pilgrimage as a welcoming space. They did not invest in its antebellum narratives, in which their ancestors were largely not represented. This began to slowly change with the BTBH program. Skipper's hope is that student engagements with local communities will lead them to stress to communities that public history projects are not just happening to them but that they are stakeholders with shared authority, one basic tenet of public history practice. This is especially significant to African American communities, who may feel historically ostracized from historic preservation work, and a necessary initial step in making this demographic more attractive to the field. Through BTBH community engagement efforts, several members of the local African American community now play significant roles as site interpretation volunteers.

These efforts, of course, do not bridge a gap to African American students who might not feel that public history work is relevant to them. Southern studies graduate students work with diverse communities, yet graduate program enrollees are largely white. As a result, the projects might embrace diverse southern communities but not racially diverse public history practitioners. The lack of public history professionals on the University of Mississippi campus, professionals who might be more conscious about the significance of attracting students of color, magnifies this problem. In addition, Skipper recognizes that it will likely be more difficult to get students attracted to public history work as a career, when other career options seem more economically attractive.

Thorpe covered this issue in an interview with Chris Taylor, director of inclusion and community engagement at the Minnesota Historical Society. She asked Taylor, "Why are there so few individuals from diverse backgrounds practicing public history?" He responded, "When you look at socio-economic inequality, a lot of the undergraduate students that I work with, they're chasing the money. They want to go into business or they want to be lawyers or doctors because they want to break that poverty cycle. We're not a real attractive source financially."[22] Skipper's experience is comparable. There is relatively little internship funding for undergraduate students. Many of them work in addition to attending the University of Mississippi and do not have the privilege of volunteer time. This is an issue that Skipper will better assess in her courses in the long run.

As evident in Skipper's work and that of Green and Chapman, described below, introducing underrepresented groups to public history work is essential. This seems basic, but if they aren't introduced and incorporated, then they will not know that such opportunities exist. If opportunities aren't readily available, then they should be created. Green uniquely introduces high school seniors to public history work and also to the possibilities of accessing higher education. Chapman's students work through a number of on-campus historic preservation institutions. Skipper's access to an African American student population presents unique circumstances. The African American student enrollment in her southern studies courses is low, with black students more likely to enroll in African American history courses. Skipper argues that this is possibly a reflection of whiteness equating to southerness, from the perspective of African American students.[23] In order to encourage African American students at the University of Mississippi to feel that public history work, in an institutional sense, belongs to them, Skipper incorporates the BTBH program in her African diaspora course, which generally has a black student enrollment of over 50 percent. Her southern studies introductory courses seem to average less than 10 percent black student enrollment. It is strongly encouraged that students in the African diaspora course assess local historic sites, volunteer with the BTBH program, or incorporate public history methodologies in their work. One student, an African American Holly Springs native, wrote after participating in the BTBH program:

> I felt a sense of pride in my town that I usually don't feel.... I was shocked because I had always seen the pilgrimage happening around Holly Springs, but I never really cared what it was, but I really enjoyed it. I think that this is something that needs to be a little more inclusive. I'm not sure how many people actually would take part in it, but I always found it weird that the pilgrimage seemed to be majority white, despite the fact that the town is majority black.... Part of me wonders why I've lived in Holly Springs for 21 years and have only now really learned what it was.

The student's response indicates both historical ostracizing from public history interpretations in the city and a desire to be more included. His experience in the course led him to anthropology as part of a double major.

Skipper's experience support's Thorpe's assertion that "at a baseline level, diverse audiences may not be comfortable going where they are not reflected—from the exhibits to the museum's professional staff."[24] Members of the Holly Spring African American community have not been reflected in the annual Pilgrimage. As a result, they have not largely attended. They are also fundamentally absent from historic preservation institutions, except as PMCHS board members. Of course, this does not mean that they are not doing historic preservation, through genealogical and benevolent societies, for example. What it does indicate is that much of their historic preservation work is being done outside of what Laurajane Smith calls an "authorized heritage discourse," which "naturalizes certain narratives and cultural and social experiences" based on "power relations and ideologies" reproduced through social practice.[25] Smith also frames this as "a professional discourse that privileges expert values and knowledge about the past," sometimes conflicting with popular conceptions of heritage or marginalizing those not considered heritage practitioners and policy makers.[26] Through these processes, many minority groups remain underrepresented.

This marginalization can shift to African American student populations who do not see themselves reflected in the public history profession. Thorpe asserts that "if our diverse communities feel that people like them 'don't work in museums,' the diversity issue immediately becomes more complex."[27] It is not only important that those doing public history work racially model possibilities as practitioners, but also that white public history professionals recognize those discrepancies, see the benefits in racial and ethnic diversity, and actively find ways of better incorporating African American students in such projects.

Unlike Skipper, Kathryn Green does not have difficulties choosing from a pool of African American students: she is on the faculty at a historically black university. This does not lessen the complicated nature of her public history work, with less than ideal institutional support, but her experiences offer an example of how one white public history professional perceives and responds to the lack of diversity in public history work.

Green Case Study: The Jim Crow Delta

Kathryn Green is a historian at Mississippi Valley State University (MVSU), which began in 1950 in the midst of the struggle against segregated education. The school, located in Itta Bena, was founded by the state as an industrial arts and teacher's college for African Americans in an attempt to avoid the desegregation of the public university system, especially nearby Delta State University. The students who were to attend the school were to be drawn from the African American population of the state—primarily the Mississippi Delta, as Alcorn State and Jackson State Universities were available for African American students outside of the Delta.

The state of Mississippi entered the Union in 1817, and the Mississippi Delta became a well-known center of cotton production after the expulsion of the Choctaw and Chickasaw peoples in the 1830s. In the Delta region, the Yazoo and Mississippi Rivers provided the means of transportation to export the cotton to market in New Orleans and made riverfront properties the most economically viable and valuable at the time. The rest of the Delta region was covered with dense forest and swampland, which required a great deal of labor to clear for cultivation. Much of this clearing of land away from the rivers took place after the end of the Civil War and was done by sharecroppers, the laborers of the agricultural system in the cash-poor society of the South that developed after the conflict ended. Prior to the Civil War, many of these same people and their ancestors had been the slave labor that worked the land to the enrichment of predominantly Euro-American landowners. Many of the descendants of these sharecroppers make up the current MVSU student population. The university itself was built on cotton land, and many of the early buildings and grounds were prepared by African American citizens who were proud to see an institution of higher learning developing across the highway from the little town of Itta Bena—at the time a majority-white town.[28]

In the summer of 2012, Green attended an organizing session for what would be called the Sweat Equity Investment in the Cotton Kingdom Symposium. Green, the coordinator of the history program in MVSU's multidisciplinary Social Sciences Department, was asked to attend the meeting by then–MVSU president Donna Oliver. At the end of the meeting Oliver asked Green to be the cochair of the symposium to be planned for that fall.

The meeting that summer was called at the request of Cassie Sade Turnipseed, the executive director of Khafre, Inc., a nonprofit organization in Indianola, Mississippi, about twenty miles from MVSU. Turnipseed is engaged in a long-term project to build the Cotton Pickers of America Monument and interpretive center to recognize the sweat equity of the cotton pickers of Mississippi, the Delta, and the South.[29] Negotiations for the site are ongoing outside of Mound Bayou, an all-black town founded by Isaiah Montgomery, a former slave from the Davis Bend plantation owned by Jefferson Davis's brother, Joseph Davis.[30]

Turnipseed proposed a partnership with MVSU to engage the university in the effort along with the Delta community in general. The symposium was envisioned as providing not only a platform to promote recognition and fundraising for the monument project but also to give high school seniors the experience of a university conference and to show them what MVSU has to offer them in the way of higher education. In addition, the symposium was seen as giving MVSU students (and interested faculty) a chance to present a prepared conference paper, an opportunity that is not often available given the school's relatively rural setting.

Both Skipper's and Green's projects work toward transforming perceptions of public history work, yet Green's work goes beyond Skipper's by facing diversity at the level of university enrollment. The BTBH program intentionally attracts a largely African American high school audience, who might not be introduced to the value of historic site representations otherwise. Green's work with Turnipseed is not only designed to introduce high school seniors to public history work but also to introduce them to the possibilities of accessing a higher education. At present, education requirements for public history practitioners tend to exclude—"traditionally marginalize," Thorpe says—underrepresented groups.[31] At a basic level, public history work requires an undergraduate degree but more often graduate studies. Few HBCUs offer graduate-level study in public history, museum studies, or library sciences. Green asserts that public history is a necessary field to begin offering, but state and university budget officers do not seem to see the necessity of history studies. A history undergraduate degree does not lead to well-paying jobs and therefore is not attractive to most students. Within the frame of Chris Taylor's discussion of socio-economic inequality, to Green this generation of college students are most interested in fully paid positions as soon as they graduate and look askance at the idea of additional debt (for graduate school) or unpaid internships.[32] This response may reflect the poverty of the region, the load of student debt they have accumulated to obtain bachelor's degrees, and the university's focus on celebrating the high salaries that STEM (science, technology, engineering, and mathematics) graduates receive on exiting with their bachelor's degrees. This administrative tactic has a negative impact on non-STEM fields, particularly on humanities and social sciences disciplines.

African Americans are less represented as public history practitioners and students, but this does not mean that they are not involved in public history work. According to Rhonda Jones, an assistant professor and director of the public history graduate program at North Carolina Central University in Durham, North Carolina, black people have been documenting their own histories for a long time but not publishing in academic journals.[33] According to Green, many citizens publish on historical topics in their local newspapers—something that was unheard of in the era of Jim Crow, outside of historically black newspapers. For example, debates on the Confederate battle flag and its symbolism, following the June 17, 2015, mass murder at the Emanuel African Methodist Episcopal Church in Charleston, South Carolina, brought out a kind of verbal tit-for-tat newspaper column war very instructive on the issue of "change over time" and the meaning of "heritage."

African American reluctance to engage topics that might be painful is a theme not covered by Thorpe yet evident in Skipper's and Green's work and also in public history work elsewhere in the U.S. South. As Katharine T. Corbett and Howard S. Miller write, "The stories public historians want to tell are sometimes not the stories the public wants to hear."[34] Scholarship in cultural representations at African American historic sites focuses on how some site managers choose to suppress discussions of slavery and other institutions of oppression and highlight the accomplishments of African Americans in spite of modes of oppression, sometimes at the request of African American community members.[35] Such strategies might be necessary to attract African American visitors who would otherwise be less likely to visit historic sites. In one instance, Skipper conversed with a black Holly Springs resident standing outside of the local library, just across the street from the historic Craft House, at the time headquarters for the BTBH program. Skipper described the goals of the program to the man, who seemed to be in his early forties, and asked that he check it out. He responded that he was not interested in hearing sad stories about black people. Even with some efforts to convince him that the BTBH narratives were more balanced than that, he conflated the experiences of enslaved people with sadness and oppression.

Green engaged comparable issues, as for many African Americans cotton in the Delta represents a topic to be avoided. "Cotton? Don't talk to me about that!" say many of the older citizens, remembering the hot sun, the poor pay, the torn-up hands and aching backs from planting, hoeing, and picking the crop. The message of the symposium was to inform the general public of the seminal role of cotton in the economic development of the United States and at the same time of the very real equity through their sweat that the laborers in those cotton fields are due. This is part of Green's and Turnipseed's efforts to help the local community recognize that public history work belongs to them, even if the history of that work is difficult to process and remember. The region in which MVSU is located remains racially polarized, as do understandings of African American oppression, so coaxing this recognition from descendants of the employers of the sharecroppers is a very difficult endeavor.

The Sweat Equity in the Cotton Kingdom Symposium, now an annual event, has come to be a significant aid in the teaching of public history at MVSU. Each fall the MVSU history program offers a research seminar course for senior history majors. In this course students engage in original historical research, learning historical research methods and oral history interviewing techniques. Since the introduction of the symposium project, Green has urged students to focus their research on local history on cotton. As students proceed with their projects, their interests are piqued. Part of their interest comes from Green's attempt to tangibly connect "a local story with events of national and global significance," as Libby Bischof put it in writing about witnessing the teaching of a course on the history of Maine.[36] Such teaching brings local history alive for students. Taking the story of cotton and its painful memories for the cotton workers of this region and bringing it full circle to the story of its role in the economic development of the entire country is a way to connect local stories to national ones.

Unfortunately, the Delta region's historic economic power, derived from cotton, led in our time to endemic poverty. Poverty in the Delta is pervasive and disproportionately a condition of African Americans. The MVSU focus is on STEM disciplines—where the grant money is.[37] This makes productivity difficult for Green.

The research seminar course for nine years has focused on Delta history, and, for those interested since 2012, specifically in telling the story of cotton in Mississippi. Before Green began teaching at MVSU there is no evidence that public history was ever considered. Upon her hiring, she met with local community groups to alert them to her interest in having MVSU students research and write on Delta history. This emphasis has been very useful for the students as they have discovered much about their familial or regional pasts while learning the process of research with locally available primary sources. Green has also attempted to interest the university in developing an alumni oral history project to be housed at the university archives, and she trained a group of students who were excited about the prospect of researching alumni and telling their stories. But as one instructor, operating on her own, Green could not get it off the ground. Public history programs are not sustainable when they are largely dependent on the efforts of one individual. The major problem for the MVSU history program is lack of faculty-supportive networks and personal time to do these projects. For example, the first professional university archivist was hired in 2012 but soon left for another job. Green, when an archivist is on staff, takes her research seminar classes to the archives to encourage a discussion of non-teaching careers for history majors, graduate school opportunities, and internship opportunities. A new professionally trained archivist was hired in August 2015, yet Green's class structure was compromised during the time the university was without an archivist. This required more effort and time from Green to supplement the archivist's role. These realities thrust public history practitioners, like Green and disproportionately scholars of color, into social justice work, with unpaid emotional labor and exhausting mental energy.

Green and Turnipseed had a recent meeting with a locally well-known cotton marketing board regarding sponsorship, attendance, and panel presentation at their annual symposium. The public relations person with whom they met stated her lack of knowledge that the sharecropping system of the Jim Crow era was unfair in any fashion to the sharecroppers. For Green, that was jaw-dropping and instructive. The frequent gap between the African American community's historical knowledge and the non–African American community's ignorance is discouraging, daunting, and frustrating. Green, who is white, was told by a middle-aged white lawyer in Greenwood that most of the slaves had signed up to be transported because they thought conditions would be better for them in America. She finds that a majority of white Deltans have no understanding of African American history, and academic prioritizing of STEM disciplines magnifies such historical disconnects. Green's work through the Sweat Equity Investment in the Cotton Kingdom Symposium attempts to make up for such lacks. In 2015 MVSU hosted its fourth symposium, which Green co-chaired.

In order for public history programs to benefit faculty members and educational institutions as a whole, departmental and university officials have to prioritize the qualitative value of history and leverage the human resources necessary to do this public history work. With no university public history program, Green is very involved in attempting to convince students, administrators, and colleagues to recognize the value of unearthing the history in the region. She has participated as a historical research consultant for the film *Booker's Place*, spoken in churches on Mississippi history, and held her weekly research seminar one semester in a regional museum (the Museum of the Mississippi Delta, located in Greenwood) to introduce the students to museum studies as a career option.[38] (The museum's executive director, Cheryl Taylor, provided museum studies instruction.) Another semester she held her research seminar in the university archives, for that same purpose. She has started an internship in public history for interested students who have worked in the university archives, the Museum of the Mississippi Delta, and the university library. She has also signed the university up to host the "Freedom Summer" exhibit prepared by the Mississippi Department of Archives and History (MDAH). All of this work comes at a sacrifice to her personal research goals and well-being.

For a few years, the program managed to access enough funds to take students to the state capital for a day to visit the state department of archives and history and the Old Capitol Museum—and to the Vicksburg National Military Park about forty miles to the west of Jackson. At each visit, faculty emphasized the role that African American students could play in telling the whole of Mississippi history. Green has an active, large bulletin board outside her department, and here she displays local newspaper articles and columns reflecting the importance of history as part of daily life. She is pleased to note the number of students, faculty, and staff who stop to read and comment on the articles. If she is present, she engages them on the role history plays in their daily lives. The most frequent response is rolled eyes. Recently, at the urging of a few of her students, she successfully passed through the university curriculum committee, which she chairs, a new minor field of study: Africana

Studies. The comments of the committee members were instructive. There was general astonishment that MVSU did not already have such a minor.

The awareness of public history work and associated fields of study is much more pervasive at Rico Chapman's institution, the historically black Jackson State University. Chapman has had better luck institutionalizing public history work than Green has. His strategic location in a larger city, the state capital, cannot be underestimated. Green is situated in the rural Delta, with disproportionately higher poverty levels and limited access to public transportation and local historic sites, a tangible barrier for some students.

Chapman's work features campus history as public history.[39] This places the NCPH working group's call for "meaningful collaborations with minority-serving colleges and universities" within the context of an HBCU as a model for supporting and featuring public history work.[40]

Chapman Case Study: Civil Rights Movement Era Jackson

Unlike the University of Mississippi and MVSU, Jackson State offers courses in public history, including ones titled Introduction to Museums, Historical Archaeology, Local History, and Introduction to Public Historical Studies, all offered by the Department of History and Philosophy (DHP). Of all the case studies, Jackson State best reflects the NCPH's best practice guidelines by offering a class on public history. It will better reflect those guidelines if efforts to develop a concentration in public history are successful. Unlike the University of Mississippi and MVSU, there are two associate professors at Jackson State DHP who direct centers that strongly support public history: Robert Luckett at the Margaret Walker Center (MWC), an archive and museum of the African American experience, and Rico Chapman at the Fannie Lou Hamer Institute @ Council of Federated Organizations (COFO), a human rights and civil rights education center. Chapman is an associate professor of Africana Studies and public history scholar.

According to Chapman, there is a growing interest in public history among Jackson State students taking courses in the history and philosophy department. Their interests are piqued through visits to museums and talks with museum professionals. For example, in the Introduction to Museums course, students visit several museums and are given behind-the-scenes tours of the facilities, where they learn about different positions in a museum. Chapman believes that this alternative to teaching as a career for undergraduate history majors is inspiring. Students gain volunteer experience at the MDAH, intern at the Saint Louis Art Museums, and work for the National Park Service. Recently a Jackson State graduate student was pursuing a PhD in art history, with a curatorial track at Virginia Commonwealth University.

Jackson State University was founded as the Natchez Seminary in 1877 by

Henry P. Jacobs and Dr. Charles Ayer in Natchez, Mississippi, about 150 miles southwest of its current location in Jackson. It became Jackson State College in 1899, and in 1927 it began conferring bachelor's degrees. In 1940, the Mississippi legislature changed the name to the Mississippi Negro Training School and four years later to Jackson College for Negro Teachers. In 1956 the school was again renamed, to Jackson State College, and its curriculum expanded to include general liberal arts. Jackson State College was designated Jackson State University in 1974.[41] The campus is centrally located in Jackson and in close proximity to the MDAH, the Old Capitol Museum, the Mississippi Museum of Art, and the Farish Street and John R. Lynch Street Historic Districts, where students have easy access to primary source documents, local history material culture, and oral histories.

Chapman emphasizes four historic sites in Jackson. The first is John R. Lynch Street, once a thriving black business district and major thoroughfare that ran through Jackson State College and Campbell College into downtown.[42] The second is the COFO building, which formerly housed an organization formed in 1961 to support jailed Freedom Riders and then developed to promote solidarity among civil rights organizations operating in Mississippi.[43] The third is Ayer Hall, one of the first buildings constructed on Jackson State's campus in 1903, with support from the American Baptist Home Missionary Society. The fourth is the Gibbs-Green Memorial, a stone monument dedicated to Phillip Lafayette Gibbs and James Green, gunned down by local police on the Jackson State campus on May 14, 1970.[44]

These sites reflect the capital city's status as a hotbed for civil rights movement activity. Jackson was the site of numerous civil rights demonstrations, such as the Tougaloo Nine read-in at the public library and a Woolworth's counter sit-in, and became the terminus for many of the 1961 Freedom Rides. Jackson was also home to one of the foremost civil rights leaders of the time, Medgar Evers. Jackson has several civil rights landmarks, and the state recently appropriated funds for a civil rights museum scheduled to open in 2017. The sites also display Jackson State University's storied past, sites that are opportunities for students to take campus tours, receive archival research training and experience interpretive learning via exhibitions and oral histories at the MWC and the Hamer Institute @ COFO.

The building once home to COFO was renovated and restored by Jackson State in 2011, after years of dilapidation, thanks to a grant from the U.S. Small Business Administration. This COFO Civil Rights Education Complex joined with the Fannie Lou Hamer Institute for Citizenship and Democracy to form the Hamer Institute @ COFO in 2013. It now serves as an interdisciplinary human and civil rights education center designed to inspire and support civic responsibility and activism through public programming, exhibitions, and community outreach.

Ayer Hall, named after Jackson State's cofounder and first president, has housed a chapel, president's office, library, classrooms, and dormitory. It was listed on the National Register of Historic Places in 1977 and designated a Mississippi landmark by the Historic Preservation Division of the MDAH in 1986. Ayer Hall now houses the Margaret Walker Center, dedicated to the preservation, interpretation, and dissemination of African American history and culture. The MWC is named after Margaret Walker, renowned writer and professor of English at Jackson State. She founded the Institute for the Study of History, Life and Culture of Black People in 1968. Its founding was unprecedented. At the time there were no other HBCUs with a black studies program other than Howard University. The Black Studies Institute, as it became known, appeared during an era when student unrest was rife on college campuses throughout the nation, following the height of the modern civil rights movement and the emergence of Black Power shortly thereafter.

The MWC now holds Alexander's papers, over two thousand oral histories, and a number of collections and artifacts that speak to the twentieth-century African American experience. Students and scholars can access the collection by visiting the campus or accessing documents online. Students serve the center as docents and receive training in archival processing while also working to help coordinate the center's public programs. In addition, campus tours are arranged by the Jackson State Welcome Center, MWC, and the Hamer Institute @ COFO to visit the historic John R. Lynch Street Corridor, the COFO Complex, Ayer Hall, and the Gibbs-Green Memorial.

Each year current and former students, faculty, and staff come together to commemorate the anniversary of the Gibbs and Green killings that played a crucial role in the university's history, at the memorial located at the site where the shootings took place. There are also panel discussions held to remember this tragic day. Students hear stories told by those who experienced this trying time and become aware of the importance of acknowledging the past while forging ahead into the future. Comparable to the function of Holly Springs's GTT, this memorial program serves as a healing opportunity for the community and students to reflect and consider the importance of racial reconciliation and ongoing current concerns about racial justice. This is one example of how Jackson State's public history projects serve the community as well as the campus in an effort to foster collaboration.

Chapman believes HBCUs should strongly consider program development in such areas, especially with the growing interest in African-American-focused museums and historic sites. A few do. Howard University has several public history courses as part of its graduate curriculum in history.[45] Morgan State University in Baltimore offers a master's in museum studies and historic preservation, and North Carolina Central University (NCCU) in Durham offers graduate-level study in public history, museum studies, and library science. It is likely no coincidence that NCCU's history department was recently awarded the American Historical Association's 2014 Equity Award, which "recognizes individuals or institutions for excellence in recruiting, retaining, and graduating members of underrepresented racial and ethnic groups in the history profession."[46] According to the university, it has "graduated more African American students who went on to earn a Ph.D. in history than any other undergraduate program in the country."[47] Jackson State's departmental attention to public history work likely influences its ability to recruit, retain, and produce minority history graduates.

Diversifying Public History: Our Findings

This chapter has profiled efforts to diversify public history at three Mississippi universities. Skipper does public history work through courses in anthropology and southern studies, and Green and Chapman through their history departments. Skipper's and Green's projects are more dependent on community networks, in the Hill Country and Delta respectively, while Chapman's university structure is innately tied to Jackson State's public history programs. At this point we hypothesize that Chapman's civil rights focus, although incorporating difficult histories, has a redeeming narrative of progress that local African American communities may find more attractive. As mentioned, the experiences of sharecropper and enslaved populations seem to be more difficult for local communities to support as valuable. In addition, Chapman's focus on civil rights in the state may make his projects more accessible to audiences more familiar with narratives of the state's civil right history than those represented by Green or Skipper. Even with unique circumstances and challenges, these projects generally reflect Thorpe's findings.

There is a lack of racial and ethnic diversity in the public history profession in the state, which likely stems from structural biases in the public history training of African American students. Socio-economic inequality among African American students magnifies this problem; to overcome it would require supportive university structures to fund training opportunities, as well as help students to make transitions from education to practice. Even with the economic opportunities available through STEM studies, public history work can positively affect African American student self-esteem and pride. In addition, there is much potential for "new jobs and cash flow from an underutilized industry like tourism," which is dependent upon the state's willingness to embrace black heritage tourism.[48] Of course, these potential benefits would have to be accepted statewide.

There are seven HBCUs in Mississippi. Even with some positive developments in public history training at Jackson State University, more meaningful collaborations between historic preservation institutions and minority-serving colleges and universities are necessary, as suggested through NCPH findings. Those like Green, attempting to do such work at HBCUs, do not have the economic or human support systems to make such work sustainable. It is our hope that our description of Green's experience offers an understanding of the barriers to some HBCU faculty and students.

Conscious attempts at public history collaborations between faculty members at historically white and historically black colleges and universities might help to minimize some of these barriers. Skipper has found these efforts somewhat productive, through her collaboration with Alisea Williams McLeod at Rust College, yet both scholars struggle with projects heavily dependent on the work of one or two individuals, with limited funding sources. Skipper is frustrated but not discouraged by this and hopes that continuing to think through these issues with HBCU colleagues will be helpful. One unpredictable benefit of this collaboration has been the opportunity for University of Mississippi students to learn from McLeod's students, who had more experience in public history methodologies. Some Rust College students also asked faculty collaborators at the University of Mississippi for assistance in thinking through graduate programs, even considering going on to graduate school there.

Connecting public history methodologies with other fields is necessary to those like Skipper, working outside of history departments. This is most important when students of color may be less likely to enroll in history programs, thus limiting opportunities for exposure. We recommend that public history practitioners look to programs and courses with higher enrollments of students of color. Skipper's African diaspora course began as an anthropology class, solely offered in the sociology and anthropology department. Her decision to make the title more inclusive and cross-list the course in African American studies increased her African American student enrollment. This created a more diverse pool of Behind the Big House program participants. Those without such course options should seek assistance from colleagues who do teach courses with more diverse classroom demographics, asking that they suggest public history–oriented courses to students or offer extra credit opportunities to students who participate. Skipper has broadened her BTBH volunteer base, through colleagues who have offered extra credit to students in both the University of Mississippi Department of History and its Department of Sociology and Anthropology.

We also found that it is most fruitful for those interested in diversifying public history work to look to African American historic preservation efforts outside of what Smith frames as "authorized heritage discourses." Green's collaboration with Turnipseed and Khafre, Inc., has been mutually beneficial. So has Skipper's work through Gracing the Table. Both of these organizations explicitly help local communities recognize that institutionalized public history work belongs to them. Such organizations can be invaluable not only as community partners but as community liaisons. The identification of true reciprocal partnerships is key. Community partners as dependents will likely lead to unsustainable projects, with disproportionately burdened public historians. This mode of operation can be especially difficult for academics, who fear relinquishing their authority, but true partnerships of equals are key to gaining underrepresented community interest. This means prioritizing the knowledge and interests of lay people.

Community members working outside of authorized heritage discourses will likely not be receptive to institutional projects without good evidence that the project managers have some experience in race relations and advocate tackling diversity concerns head-on, not covertly. Comparable concerns shift to academic institutions hoping to racially diversify undergraduate and graduate programs and "unblock the pipeline"—the route through which public historians are produced—for underrepresented students. Admitting that one is struggling with diversity and not creating strategic plans to help minimize those struggles is unacceptable, especially when working in regions with disproportionately high African American populations like the U.S. South.

It is our ultimate hope that those interested in how southern studies research is presently conducted will better consider the significance of racial and ethnic demographics to developments in the field. Racial and ethnic diversity is not an organic process, but it is a necessary one. This means that diversity initiatives must be intentional and perceived as rewarding to students of color. In addition, it is mandatory that white faculty and students engaged in public history work not only see the value in studying diverse topics but in diversifying public history practitioners. We hope to continue our collaborative work to better understand how the creation and consumption of Mississippi representations of African American historical experiences relates to the diversification of public history in the state and for the South at large.

Notes

1. Thorpe, "Rethinking Diversity."
2. Ibid.
3. Labode, "Diversity, Here to There," 7. As of September 2016, Modupe Labode is associate professor of history and museum studies at Indiana University–Purdue University Indianapolis, and Calinda Lee is historian at the Atlanta History Center.
4. Ibid. A 2008 survey of public history professionals revealed that out of nearly four thousand respondents, 88.5 percent identified as white, 7 percent identified as "of color" (multiracial, Native American/First Nation, Hispanic or Latino, Asian or Pacific Islander, or non-Hispanic black), and 4.5 percent chose not to answer. Labode, "Diversity, Here to There," 7.
5. In 2005 "the proportion of minorities among the cohort of new history PhDs" was

"13.3 percent of the U.S. citizens receiving the degree. This proportion is significantly lower than the average for all disciplines, which is 20 percent of the degree recipients. African Americans comprised 5.4 percent of the new history PhDs, while Hispanic/Latino Americans accounted for 4.2 percent and Asian Americans comprised 2.9 percent of those receiving the degree." See Townsend, "News: History PhD Numbers Lowest in Almost a Decade as Job Listings Continue to Rise." Townsend cited a "noticeable rise in the number of jobs in [history] fields" from 2005 to 2006. The number of history job openings is now decreasing. By 2016, the number of positions advertised with the American Historical Association "fell for the third year in a row," with no signs of improvement. See Townsend and Brookins, "The Troubled Academic Job Market for History."

6. See Carlton Wilson, "Viewpoints: Minority Students Pursuing History PhDs."
7. See Hale, Introduction to *Engaging Contradictions*, 3.
8. Labode, "Diversity, Here to There," 7.
9. Hale, Introduction to *Engaging Contradictions*, 3.
10. Thorpe, "Rethinking diversity."
11. NCPH Curriculum and Training Committee, "Best Practices in Public History."
12. An awareness of such issues among public history practitioners resulted in the Working Group on Evaluating Public History Scholarship, "Tenure, Promotion, and the Publicly Engaged Academic Historian," a 2010 report offering best practices for evaluating public history scholarship in history departments. Working Group on Evaluating Public History Scholarship, "Tenure, Promotion, and the Publicly Engaged Academic Historian."
13. Rastogi, Johnson, Hoeffel, and Drewery, "The Black Population: 2010 Census Brief."
14. Noss, "Household Income: 2012 American Community Survey Briefs."
15. Outside of the South, two of the institutions are in the District of Columbia (Howard University and the University of the District of Columbia). The other is the University of the Virgin Islands. See United States Department of Education, White House Initiative on Historically Black Colleges and Universities, "HBCUs and 2020 Goal."
16. At the time, Katharine Duvall Osteen was working on "The Blues Is Alright: Blues Music as a Root for Cultural Tourism and Public History" (master's thesis, University of Mississippi, 2011). That same year Cathryn S. Stout produced "A Place of Happy Retreat: Benefiting Locals and Visitors through Sustainable Tourism Practices at Beale Street, Graceland and the National Civil Rights Museum" (master's thesis, University of Mississippi, 2011). Two years later, under Skipper's direction, Kathryn Radishofski produced "Last (Un)Fair Deal Goin' Down: A Case Study on the Racial Ideologies and Projects Advanced by the Blues Tourism Industry in Clarksdale, Mississippi" (master's thesis, University of Mississippi, 2013). A subsequent analysis of that work is included in this volume.
17. The University of Southern Mississippi has a graduate program in public history, while Mississippi University for Women has an undergraduate program.
18. Chelius Carter, "Project Director's Report and Evaluation," written at the request of the Mississippi Humanities Council. In Skipper's possession.

19. Ibid.
20. Ibid.
21. As an exception, Skipper has had the support of her colleague Carolyn Freiwald, with whom she has co-managed an archaeology excavation at the Craft House slave dwelling, one of the BTBH tour sites.
22. Thorpe, "Rethinking Diversity."
23. For more on such racial perspectives, see Thompson and Sloan, "Race as Region, Region as Race."
24. Thorpe, "Rethinking Diversity."
25. L. Smith, *Uses of Heritage*, 4.
26. Ibid.
27. Thorpe, "Rethinking Diversity."
28. For historical contexts, see J. White, *Up from a Cotton Patch*; Hudspeth, "Mississippi Valley State University at the Millennium," 1–15.
29. The fund-raising project is described on the website of Khafre, Inc., http://www.khafreinc.org.
30. Hermann, *The Pursuit of a Dream*.
31. Thorpe, "Rethinking Diversity."
32. We do not mean to insinuate that this is the case for all or most students of color. We have not assessed that. In a conversation, one of Skipper's contacts, a historian at a historically white university, shared that most of the history majors in her department, who are overwhelmingly impoverished, want to go to graduate school but are not being adequately prepared for the admission requirements in their undergraduate program. This includes development of necessary writing skills. In 2009, historian W. Fitzhugh Brundage considered such issues in what he described as the University of North Carolina at Chapel Hill history department's model for increasing the "likelihood of successfully recruiting qualified [minority] applicants." Brundage wrote that the graduate program was "especially attentive to the files of minority applicants even before the closing date for applications because [they] have observed that many qualified applicants, for whatever reason, pay the application fee but fail to submit the remainder of their materials." Brundage is not clear on these reasons, but Skipper's contact seems to hint at some of these. See Brundage, "The Profession: Recruiting Minority Graduate Students."
33. Thorpe, "Rethinking Diversity."
34. Corbett and Miller, "A Shared Inquiry into Shared Inquiry," 22.
35. Eichstedt and Small, *Representations of Slavery*, 266.
36. Bischof, "The Lens of the Local," 531. For more on local history, see Kyvig and Marty, *Nearby History*; Bischof, "The Lens of the Local," 529–59.
37. See Rockoff, "Director's Message," in which he discusses how both declining enrollment and declining grant funding is leading to the elimination of humanities programs, including history, at institutions of higher education.
38. De Fellita, *Booker's Place*.
39. The NCPH recently organized a 2016 "Campus History as Public History" working group, from which we adopt this phrase.
40. Labode, "Diversity, Here to There," 7.

41. Rhodes, *Jackson State University*.

42. The first large student disturbance at Jackson State was precipitated by John R. Lynch Street traffic. The street became a troublesome bisector of the campus at a time when African Americans were asserting themselves all over the nation and black students had become the cutting edge of momentous change. Campbell College was a private historically black college located across the street from the Jackson State campus. Before being appropriated by the State of Mississippi in 1964, Campbell College hosted civil rights events and posted notices of boycotts on its campus. Campbell College also invited McComb (Miss.) High School students expelled due to a protest march to enroll at Campbell. Campbell College's activism and close proximity to Jackson State and downtown Jackson were likely the major reasons for its seizure by the state.

43. Sixties civil rights organizations in the state included the Student Nonviolent Coordinating Committee, the Congress of Racial Equality, the Southern Christian Leadership Council, and the National Association for the Advancement of Colored People. COFO was formalized in August 1962, at a meeting held in Clarksdale, Mississippi. In 1963 it relocated its headquarters to 1017 John R. Lynch Street. This location served as the state headquarters for the Mississippi civil rights movement and was considered to be the nerve center of the Mississippi freedom struggle. Making voter registration and education a top priority for the Mississippi movement, COFO was instrumental in organizing the 1963 Freedom Vote, the Mississippi Freedom Democratic Party, and the 1964 Mississippi Summer Project.

44. The Gibbs-Green shooting at Jackson State happened in the wake of the Kent State University shootings earlier in May 1970. The campus shootings prompted the White House to establish a commission to investigate campus unrest. The events are chronicled in *Campus Unrest*. Spofford's *Lynch Street* recounts the tragic night of May 14, 1970, in Jackson. Spofford interviewed students and eyewitnesses and examined newspaper accounts, public records, and court testimony.

45. Howard University College of Arts and Sciences, Department of History, Graduate Courses, http://www.coas.howard.edu/history/courses_graduate.html.

46. "North Carolina Central University Recognized for Promoting Diversity in the History Profession."

47. Ibid.

48. Enelow, "The Rise of Civil Rights Tourism in America's Deep South."

Where Do We Go from Here?

The Implications of Black Intellectual History in the Modern South

ROBERT GREENE II

When questions about race come to the forefront of American political, cultural, and intellectual discourse, arguments about the South are never far behind. John Egerton's *The Americanization of Dixie*, published in 1974, and Tracy Thompson's *The New Mind of the South*, published in 2013, both point to a tendency to hope that the South has changed and perhaps for the better. Yet when each of those books was written, scholars and intellectuals clearly had a role to play in reshaping what the South meant to southerners and the rest of American society. Violence, racism, and attachment to the past lie under the surface of all understandings of the American South. Intellectual history, a field dedicated to ideas and schools of thought among those willing to engage in public debate, can contribute to such understandings. The field will only matter, however, so long as southern studies scholars actively engage the wider community by adding to public debates.

The recent intellectual history of the American South—the intellectual and ideological contours within which southerners have debated ideas since 1965—is essential to understanding the roles of scholars, intellectuals, and academics in today's South. This leads to a question: what, precisely, should scholars give back to a region traditionally known for anti-intellectualism and quashing dissent?

This essay first gives a brief history of ideology and discourse in the South since the passage of the Voting Rights Act by Congress in 1965. This legislative achievement is acknowledged as the traditional end of the "heroic" phase of the civil rights movement, which began with the Supreme Court's *Brown v. Board of Education* decision.[1] This is the era of protest and activism remembered fondly by many Americans, coming before the rise of Black Power and white backlash. The post-1965 era in the South is one traditionally seen only through the lens of the "Southern Strategy" crafted by the Richard Nixon election team of 1968 and perfected by Ronald Reagan in 1980.[2] This was an attempt by Republican strategists to peel away white southern voters from their traditional home in the Democratic Party and to get them to become long-term supporters of the GOP. Despite recent works that have attempted to add nuance to discussions of this political shift, notably Matthew Lassiter's *The Silent Majority* (2006), the idea of white backlash in the Deep South tied to racism still maintains a powerful hold on historians. While this is an important part of the South's history after 1965, equally important are other political and intellectual changes: the ascension of African Americans back into the political realm as powerful actors; the rise of Latino immigration to the region, especially after the 1986 Immigration Reform and Control Act was passed by Congress; the increasing importance of women to southern politics through their political participation (not to mention the prevalence of "family values" issues); and the changing voting patterns of white Southerners on a local, state, and national level.

The intellectual history of this era takes into account all these changes, while arguing for the need to understand the complexity of intellectual and political discourse in the South during this era. I argue that changing questions about race—and racism—still shaped southern intellectual discourse from the late 1960s well into the 1990s. White-black relations still shaped most southern intellectual discourse after the civil rights movement ended, although augmented with questions about gender (especially after the battle over the Equal Rights Amendment of the 1970s) and immigration (beginning in the 1990s but intensifying in the early twenty-first century). My coverage of southern intellectual history argues that the 1970s set up an intellectual and political discourse that has lasted until the present.

This essay also aims to broaden the conversation about the role southern studies scholars can and should play in social justice debates. Events during the presidencies of George W. Bush and Barack Obama have opened new avenues for debating the lingering question of race in American society. Police violence against African Americans, fervent debate over immigration from Latin America, and fears among some conservative white Americans of losing their perceived place in society all allow for intervention by southern studies scholars in the public sphere.

The story of the United States cannot be told without understanding the story of the American South. The antebellum period of American history is filled with leaders from the South debating the future of the nation, from Thomas Jefferson and George Washington of Virginia to John C. Calhoun of South Carolina. The South's secession from the Union, and the postwar attempt at its reconstruction by the federal government, raised questions about the government's relationship to its residents of African descent that have still not been fully answered. Economic help from the federal government in the form of New Deal legislation was contingent upon support from southern Democrats, which meant that liberalism's greatest accomplishment in the twentieth century would be tainted by racism.[3] This is especially true of the last fifty years, as the South has become a political battleground between Republicans and Democrats, conservatives and liberals, and far too often between whites, African Americans, and other people of color.

Southern studies in recent years has undergone its own transformation. The *Journal of American Studies* edition of August 2014, for example, showcases a field that has published important scholarly texts but still has a rich future ahead.[4] There scholars such as historian Natalie J. Ring point out the many ways in which the South can be interpreted and reinterpreted by scholars to reflect how "the South" itself is a manufactured idea.[5] However, none of the scholars in that forum addresses the possibility or the need for southern studies to have an activist element. Many younger scholars (and quite a few seasoned veterans as well) wish to be involved in public debates as both scholars and activists. This essay expands the conversation about the future of southern studies and activism, and it considers the rich potential for working with scholars in other fields—in the humanities, social sciences, and STEM—in order to examine the South from a variety of angles.

This is not a call for all southern studies students, professors, and practitioners to become activist-scholars. Instead, this essay is meant as a challenge to historians, writers, sociologists, literary scholars, geographers, and others who have worked for years under the banner of southern studies. What can we contribute to the national conversation when, for instance, the Confederate flag remains a thorny topic of discussion? How can southern studies open up much-needed conversations about the legacy of Reconstruction as the sesquicentennial of that period in U.S. history begins? Finally, what can southern studies offer southerners faced with the rise of a growing Latino population?

Southern Intellectual History: Ideology and Discourse

The late 1960s in the South was an era of transition, peril, and promise for the region. References to the South being in the middle of a "Second Reconstruction" began to proliferate in both regional and national publications.[6] Yet, along with this idea was the issue of white backlash—not just in the South but also across the nation. Indeed, just as African American rights in the 1870s collided with white terrorism in the South and economic depression, so too nearly one hundred years later, in the late 1960s, whites began to turn away from the civil rights coalition, thanks partly to the Vietnam War, creeping economic malaise, and coast-to-coast urban riots.

As white and black southerners alike adjusted to a new normal, an increasingly politically and culturally assertive southern black population, southern politicians (especially in the Democratic Party) began to tailor their campaigns to this. The 1970 gubernatorial elections in Georgia, South Carolina, Florida, and Arkansas all proved important in showcasing a new politics of racial moderation that would prove important to southern politics for a generation. No longer would race-baiting carry the day in the region. A new politics of racial reconciliation, moving on from the bitter memories (for African Americans) of the Jim Crow era, would inform the New South.[7]

Intellectual discourse in the South followed a similar trajectory, albeit with a much larger space, within which an energized Left could operate. The creation of *Southern Exposure* magazine in 1973 by the Institute of Southern Studies, based in Durham, North Carolina, provided a new lens for southern history and culture. Cofounded by civil rights activist and Georgia politician Julian Bond, the magazine gave voice to young activists and intellectuals, most of whom came of age during the civil rights movement. The editors' goal, as they wrote in the first issue, was "to provide ideas, analyses, facts, and programs for groups and individuals building the South of the Seventies and beyond, to translate information into action for progressive change."[8] *Southern Exposure* has lasted for decades as a counterpoint to the traditional view of the South as a conservative, reactionary region.

Other magazines sprouted out of the rich soul of southern intellectual culture in the 1970s. Examples include *Southern Voices*, founded by the Southern Regional Council, and the *South Magazine*, devoted to business boosterism of the region, a time-honored tradition. Meanwhile, national publications also gave attention to the changing South, with publications from *Ebony* to *Time* expressing surprise at the region's many changes in such a short period of time.[9] It is not just important that the nation was paying attention to the South but that this attention followed the South's perceived transformation into a more racially harmonious place. During a period when urban rioting and a rise in crime were fresher in the minds of most Americans than images of innocent protesters being blasted by high-pressure fire hoses in Birmingham, the American South's evolution regarding race became a symbol to the entire nation.[10]

Not that the South had actually become paragon of virtue. Racial tensions still plagued the region. Jimmy Carter's 1970 candidacy for governor of Georgia was filled with race-baiting, which was noticed by some African American politicians in the region. Yet his 1971 inaugural address, which argued that racial discrimination no longer had a place in the state and in the South, propelled him to national prominence.[11] But racial violence would again tar the region, as seen in 1979 when the Ku Klux Klan experienced a national revival.

The Greensboro Massacre of 1979, in which Klansmen and neo-Nazis killed five pro-union African American demonstrators, chilled the national discussion on race.[12] The previous year's *Bakke* Supreme Court decision, which limited the reach and scope of affirmative action programs in higher education, gave many civil rights activists a sense of the tenuousness of the gains of the previous years.[13] For activists in the South, it appeared that racial progress in the region was grinding to a halt. Nonetheless, African Americans were becoming more assertive in politics, with African American mayors running Atlanta since 1973 and cementing the city's status as a leader of the New South of the 1970s.

African American intellectual culture was also on the rise in the South, even before the appearance of *Southern Exposure*. Harold Cruse's 1967 *Crisis of the Negro Intellectual*, while a hallmark publication in African American intellectual history, failed to mention the importance of the South to mid-twentieth-century African American intellectuals. Most notably, African American historian and activist Vincent Harding chided Cruse for his singular focus on Harlem-based intellectuals, writing, "Some of the southern group would surely have proved more profitable sources of analysis than a number of less important persons like Julian Mayfield, and even the editors of *Freedomways*."[14] Harding gave other African American intellectuals their due but wondered why the likes of southern civil rights leader James Bevel did not merit the same attention Cruse gave to Paul Robeson and Lorraine Hansberry.[15] The category of intellectual, argued Harding, included not just people in the academy or writers for elite publications but also activists like Martin Luther King Jr. and Robert Moses. After all, in order to craft and lead a movement, an activist had to put in the time to think deeply about what he or she was trying to change and to ponder and envision what kind of a world they wanted.

In the late 1960s, African American intellectuals in the South began to take on a more assertive role in the Black Power movement, as well as in the creation of black studies programs. The Atlanta-based Institute of the Black World (IBW), an African American think tank founded by Vincent Harding and others in 1969, would be the home for many black intellectuals in the South in the 1970s.[16]

In this way we need to continue the southern studies tradition of stretching the South beyond its geographic borders. Scholars such as C. Vann Woodward, in his essays in *The Burden of Southern History*, and Michael O'Brien and more recently Natalie Ring have examined Southern history in its relation to the international context more generally. Here Martin Luther King Jr. comes to mind (through his tying together of white supremacy and economic inequality at home with American militarism abroad), as do leaders of the IBW, who provided intellectual underpinnings of Black Power in the 1970s. The increasing importance of black studies departments on college campuses in the 1980s cannot be imagined without the contributions of the IBW.

These breakthroughs, as well as the racism they challenged, echo well into the twenty-first century, and concerns about southern racism dominate national discourse about the political and cultural trajectory of the region. Indeed, after the election of President Obama, it is impossible to avoid thinking about the legacy of racism in the South as part and parcel of a larger story of African American setback and triumph. *Oxford American*, a journal founded in 1992 and intended to both highlight and critique modern southern culture, gave evidence of this with an issue released shortly after Obama's first presidential election victory. Its 2009 roundtable discussion about race in the South included journalist Juan Williams, Southern Poverty Law Center founder Morris Dees, and Julian Bond, who said, "The region can never escape its history, but it can—with great effort—convince other Americans and those Southerners who worked for change and who hope for more that its public policies and political and economic leadership are committed to an integrated, bias-free region."[17] Bond, who died in 2015, captured an essential element of southern life: the lingering shadow of the past. That year, in 2015, as history made its presence felt in the South, it became clear that southern studies had a great deal to contribute to debates centered on race and public memory of the past.

Even before the mass killing of African Americans at the Emanuel African Methodist Episcopal AME Church in Charleston, South Carolina, on June 17, 2015, created a national moment of mourning and a regional moment of soul-searching, the nation was already being torn apart over questions of race and democracy. The death of Michael Brown in Ferguson, Missouri, in 2014, followed by the death of Eric Garner in Staten Island, both at the hands of police, created a national debate over both the use of force by police and, more broadly, racism and the continued concerns of African Americans and their place in society. Additional incidents between police and African Americans—most notably the shooting of twelve-year-old Tamir Rice in Cleveland and the mysterious death of Sandra Bland while in police custody in Texas—only added fuel to the fire.

Again, region and history both matter here. Ferguson's location in Missouri means that it sits at both the geographic and historic intersections of North and South. Likewise, after the April 2015 police shooting death of Freddie Gray in Baltimore and the riots that followed, Americans were reminded once more of Maryland's complicated relationship with the South. (The state included a strong pro-South current before and during the Civil War.) Scholars had much to contribute to national conversations about race during 2015—reminding people of the long history of police violence against African Americans, the countless policies—stretching back to the New Deal and before—that worked to concentrate impoverished African Americans in poorly served and nearly forgotten inner cities, and the inability of most white Americans to have substantial discussions about the continued racism.

Just as in the 1970s, intellectuals across the nation wrestled with questions of race. In the South, such questions intersected with concern about the future of the region. For forty years scholars and journalists asked, "Is the South still exceptional, still unique compared to the rest of the nation?" Such a question has never received a satisfactory answer. Yet the rise of new arenas for debate about the region's future, along with new questions about the region's past, have promised to put the lie to any idea of the end of an exceptional South. Magazines such as *Scalawag* and websites such as the Bitter Southerner present alternate versions of the South, clashing with perceptions of the region as being a solid red, conservative region. The South has never been a uniform place of white identity wrapped in a Confederate flag. Instead—as southern studies continues to showcase in many published works—the region is complicated and both haunted and inspired by its complicated past.

Southern Studies in Public Spaces

In the age of Black Lives Matter, economic malaise, and worry about immigration from Latin America, southern studies can act as an intellectual bedrock for scholars seeking a way to speak to the public about these and other issues.[18] Debates about race and identity in America today offer a wonderful opportunity to showcase the best of southern studies scholarship, writing, and discourse. My own experience in South Carolina during multiple protests against police brutality and the terrorist attack on the Emanuel AME Church in June 2015 is a testament to how southern studies analysis can make a difference publicly.

At this point, a brief biographical statement on my own public scholarship is necessary. As a writer and book review editor for the Society for U.S. Intellectual History blog since August 2013, I have used the online platform as a space to engage in scholarly debate.[19] The blog itself allows historians and scholars across the humanities the opportunity to write about the past and present, using intellectual history as a lens through which to examine identity, memory, and intellectual discourse in the United States. Since 2013 I have written a great deal about the American South and the African American experience.[20] In these and many other posts, I have tied together events and ideas from the past to present debates in American society. Eventually these online essays garnered the attention of editors at magazines such as *Dissent*, who offered me the opportunity to write about the South's experience with the Black Lives Matter movement. Having already done some work with the Columbia, South Carolina, chapter of Black Lives Matter, I was well positioned to tell the story of South Carolina's struggles with police violence.[21] This essay existed within a larger print and online context of discussion about the Black Lives Matter campaign, but writings on the movement have often included a reflection on the past and the use of that history to explain the present.[22]

Use of the history that follows in this essay was critical to my voice being part of the dialogue about race and U.S. society in 2014–15. Without that history, and without the ability to articulate clearly and concisely for a public audience, I would have had little new to add to an already robust conversation.

Dylan Roof's attack on Emanuel AME added additional fuel to the already heated conversation about race and memory in the South. I found myself thrust into this debate on the night of the attack. As an avid Twitter user, I found myself that evening desiring to get the word out about Emanuel AME's history as a center of African American freedom in South Carolina. Linking to the church's own history section, I sent out a tweet on the night of June 16, imploring curious users to learn more on their own.[23]

Soon this tweet was picked up by a reporter from the *Washington Post*, who was interviewing scholars about the church's history and asking why it might have been targeted by Dylan Roof. The ensuing article was the start of my public engagement on the issue of Emanuel AME, the South, and race relations.[24] I would later do interviews with BBC Radio and WNYC's "The Takeaway."[25] On both radio programs I attempted to explain why the Emanuel AME Church was such a powerful symbol for Roof, an avowed white supremacist, that he would attack with no remorse. Feeling the responsibility for explaining Emanuel's history to Americans (and, in the case of the BBC, to people around the world), I found myself called to a platform I never planned to be on.

Working across different media platforms is an important feature of being a publicly engaged scholar. Doing multiple radio interviews was something I did not expect to do in the aftermath of Charleston, but I adjusted to it as best I could. Thinking of it as being no different from taking questions during a seminar or a conference presentation, I offered as much information as I could to listeners who had not heard of Emanuel AME until after Roof's attack. Later, *Politico* requested a short essay about Emanuel's history, hoping that the attack would bring together South Carolinians instead of dividing them. The essay, "Racism Can't Destroy This Charleston Church," used another public forum to give context to the tragedy.[26] It was a difficult several days for South Carolinians. For me, as a historian, it was a welcome opportunity to use history to give context to current events. At the same time, however, it was hard for me—because it meant I had to be a scholar and postpone grieving until later.

Southern studies scholars like me also had a contribution to make to the Confederate flag debate, which began almost as soon as Dylan Roof was captured by South Carolina authorities. Columnists across the nation called for the flag to be brought down as a small but significant way to honor the nine Emanuel victims Roof killed. "Put it in a museum. Inscribe beneath it the years 1861–2015. Move forward. Abandon this charlatanism. Drive out this cult of death and chains. Save your lovely souls. Move forward. Do it now," wrote Ta-Nehisi Coates on the *Atlantic* website the day after the Roof shooting.[27] Coates's own career as a writer and public intellectual attests to the importance of public scholarship, as he reaches a far larger audience than most academics will ever know.

The creation of the #CharlestonSyllabus was the most important contribution by scholars in the aftermath of the Charleston shooting. Begun by Chad Williams, associate professor of African and Afro-American Studies at Brandeis University, #CharlestonSyllabus took advantage of the ease with which people can use Twitter.[28] First posted on the African American Intellectual History Society's blog, the syllabus immediately picked up steam thanks to the #CharlestonSyllabus tag on Twitter. Williams was inspired by the earlier #FergusonSyllabus (begun by Marcia Chatelain, professor at Georgetown University).[29] As Williams argued, "Social media and the blogosphere have emerged as vibrant spaces for both the production and dissemination of knowledge about African American history and its relation to our contemporary racial environment.[30] Discussion of the syllabus on Twitter and across other media sources helped the syllabus gain more entries.[31]

Debates about the Confederate flag included input from historians and other southern studies scholars. Already engaged in writing a piece for *Dissent* about South Carolina's forgotten progressive history, I was asked to also write about the fall of the flag for the *Dissent* website in July 2015.[32] Aware of my understanding of recent Southern history and my closeness to the situation, the editors of *Dissent* felt I had still more to add to the national conversation. The task I was given was to put the flag debate in additional context—in this case, to remind readers that only a year earlier Governor Nikki Haley of South Carolina had apparently cared little about taking down the flag, and to demonstrate how the Dylan Roof attack had profoundly changed the state's relationship to its history. The director for the Center for the Study of Southern Culture at the University of Mississippi, Ted Ownby, had also argued for changing Mississippi's state flag. As he said at that time, "In the past few days, it has been impressive to see so many historians and other scholars combining the immediacy of their reaction to the terrorism of Charleston with longstanding passions connected to their scholarship."[33] Ownby recognized, in the heat of public debate about Confederate flags and Civil War memory, why public scholarship mattered.

Social media operates as an easily navigable gateway between the academy and the curious public. Reflect, for a moment, on the explosion of articles, books, and entire magazine runs devoted to the changing South in the 1970s. As was the case in that decade, the first sixteen years of the twenty-first century have been cause for telling about the South in a variety of media forums.

Southern studies scholars such as Zandria F. Robinson and Karen Cox, among many others, have embraced Twitter and Facebook as places where they can communicate with non-academics and academics alike about the South.[34]

It is not easy to engage the public. In the case of Robinson, who had recently left the University of Memphis, pressure from conservatives was brought to bear on the administration's failure to clarify the details of her separation from the university. Through silence, university administrators allowed the public to assume that Robinson had been dismissed due to her public engagement of anti-white supremacist thought, rather than the reality: that she had voluntarily resigned from the university to take a position at another.[35] This is a warning of the price that public intellectuals engaging antiracist thought might have to pay.

Researching and reading history means confronting the brutality of the past. Studying the history of the South as an African American carries a particular burden: it means having to confront a past during which members of your immediate family suffered from oppression and the yoke of white supremacy. No one, least of all I, imagined having to deal with something like the Emanuel AME tragedy while in graduate school. That said, being a public intellectual, with the potential for immediate scrutiny by an ambiguous and anonymous audience, carries an additional burden: it means having to confront those who have yet to engage their own racism and who might highlight what they perceive as reverse discrimination on your part. While having a public electronic media persona requires lightning-quick responses and fierce arguments, online dialogue can alternate between being a source of mental and spiritual anguish and being a salve.

What Robinson endured online (as did Saida Grundy, a sociologist at Boston University who was also criticized by conservative bloggers and Twitter followers for comments made about white racists) is a reminder of the perils of being a publicly engaged scholar in the twenty-first century.[36] Regardless of the field you're in, taking on the mantle of public intellectual means having to speak to the public even when you're not ready to do so. Yet anyone driven by a passion to work with the public should do just that. Scholars in the humanities continue to argue about their place in a democracy. Southern studies scholars have a special role to play in giving back to the wider intellectual community, to say something about the South that helps others understand just how much the region has changed since the end of the civil rights movement. Debates about race and identity in twenty-first century America require that southern studies scholars take a seat at the intellectual table via monographs, scholarly journals, magazines, and the Internet. To engage fearlessly is not just a testament to our academic training but a tribute to southern-born intellectuals of yesteryear who tackled similar problems in a climate of even greater despair and mistrust across racial and ethnic lines.

Notes

1. Peniel Joseph and Jacquelyn Dowd Hall have both argued for the importance of understanding the black freedom struggle beyond the temporal parentheses of 1954 (*Brown v. Board of Education* decision) and 1965 (passage of the Voting Rights Act and the Watts Riots). Nonetheless, they have also argued that the traditional starting and end points for the civil rights movement hold considerable sway in American public memory of the era. See Joseph, "The Black Power Movement, Democracy, and America in the King Years," 1004; Hall, "The Long Civil Rights Movement and the Political Uses of the Past," 1233–34.

2. Crespino's *In Search of Another Country* and *Strom Thurmond's America* both bring to life the political upheaval of the South after the late 1960s. See also Link, *Righteous Warrior*; Perman, *Pursuit of Unity* (2009), especially 307–51.

3. Katznelson, *Fear Itself* (2013).

4. Ward, "Forum: What's New in Southern Studies—and Why Should We Care?," 691–733.

5. Natalie J. Ring, "An Irony of Ironies," in Ward, "Forum," 706–12.

6. C. Vann Woodward, most notably, began to promote the idea of a Second Reconstruction as being the best way to describe the civil rights movement and the federal government's passage of Civil Rights Acts in 1957, 1960, and 1964. See Woodward, "What Happened to the Civil Rights Movement."

7. The best monograph about this is Sanders, *Mighty Peculiar Elections*.

8. "Editor's Note." The first issue is also indicative of the ways in which these particular southerners viewed the region as locked into larger national and international problems—it was a review of the military-industrial complex's role in the building up of the South's economy since World War II.

9. *Ebony*'s August 1971 special issue, "The South Today," detailed how the region had changed for African Americans since the end of the civil rights movement.

10. Sokol, *All Eyes Are upon Us* (2014), especially 171–229, makes this argument from the point of view of the American Northeast. See also Cobb, *Away Down South*, 216–22.

11. T. Boyd, *Georgia Democrats*, 206–8.

12. Marable, *Race, Reform, and Rebellion*, 171. It is not a coincidence that the chapter in which Marable writes about this incident is titled "The Retreat of the Second Reconstruction, 1976–1982."

13. Ibid., 175.

14. Harding, "Beyond the Black Desert," 45–48, quote on 48.

15. This should also push both intellectual historians and other historians to think harder about whom we consider to be intellectuals, especially within oppressed communities.

16. Derrick White, *The Challenge of Blackness*.

17. Sabin, "A Great Debate."

18. The phrase "Black Lives Matter" rose in reference to the deaths of African Americans at the hands of police officers. From a hashtag on the social media site Twitter, "Black Lives Matter" became a phrase chanted at many anti-police brutality rallies in 2014 and 2015. The concern over immigration from Latin America began with the

failure of President George W. Bush to pass the Comprehensive Immigration Reform Act of 2007 due to a recalcitrant conservative wing of the Republican Party. This was followed up by the passage of bills by states such as Arizona (S.B. 1070), Alabama (H.B. 56), and South Carolina (S.B. 20) that were designed to, among other things, give law enforcement officers the right to stop anyone suspected of being an illegal immigrant and ask for documentation.

19. The Society for U.S. Intellectual History blog, s-usih.org, has been active since 2011.

20. See, for example, R. Greene, "The American South and American Minds"; R. Greene, "African American Activism and the Search for a Usable Past."

21. R. Greene, "The Southern Strategy," 67–72.

22. Other articles on Black Lives Matter and the South included Simonton's "We Have a Duty to Win."

23. Emanuel AME's website has been updated since then, but this is the current URL for the church history section: http://www.emanuelamechurch.org/church history.php.

24. Kaplan, "For Charleston's Emanuel AME Church, Shooting Is Another Painful Chapter in Rich History."

25. "The Charleston Shooting: A Crime of Hate amid Calls of Prayer."

26. R. Greene, "Racism Can't Destroy This Charleston Church."

27. Coates, "Take Down the Confederate Flag—Now."

28. Williams, "#CharlestonSyllabus and the Work of African American History."

29. It is also worth thinking about the earlier syllabi offered by Melissa Harris-Perry, an academic and public intellectual who hosts her own MSNBC show, *Melissa Harris-Perry*. Most notably, her "Black Feminism Syllabus," from the November 20, 2013, edition of her show, created in response to reporter Michelle Cottle referring to First Lady Michelle Obama as a "feminist nightmare," established a method by which scholars readily made available to the public reading lists about a wide variety of subjects. Harris-Perry, "The MHP Black Feminism Syllabus."

30. Williams, "#CharlestonSyllabus and the Work of African American History."

31. See Patton, "A Professor Crowdsources a Syllabus on the Charleston Shootings"; Williams, "Why I Founded #CharlestonSyllabus after the Charleston Shooting."

32. R. Greene, "The Southern Strategy," 67–71; Greene, "The Fall of the Confederate Flag."

33. Walton, "Center Director Ted Ownby on Current Efforts to Remove Confederate Symbols."

34. It is also important to note that both women have published important works of scholarship in monograph form (Robinson, *This Ain't Chicago*; Cox, *Dixie's Daughters*) and both have blogs: Robinson's *New South Negress*, http://newsouthnegress.com and Cox's *Pop South*, http://southinpopculture.com. In other words, they have established themselves as credible and important scholars through both traditional media and the Internet.

35. Robinson, "Zeezus Does the Firing 'Round Hurr," *New South Negress*, July 2, 2015.

36. Jaschik, "The Professor Who Wasn't Fired."

South Unbound

A Case Study in Ron Rash's Appalachian Fiction

DANIEL CROSS TURNER

In the green world of my early graduate school days, I'd begin my conference presentations—like so many of my fellow trainees in literary studies—with a rote disclaimer about how my paper would make only a tentative, provisional start on covering the topic at hand. The implication was that such inchoate ideas, given world enough and time, would gather and grow perforce into a fully formed, nigh irrefutable thesis that could explain all or nearly all. With sufficient intellectual labor clocked in, the promised day of closure would surely arrive. Back then, I didn't know what I didn't know. It has taken me six long, often dark years of graduate study and another ten longer, often darker years out on the tenure ladder to correct my vision. Such sought-for completion is false fire: beautiful, perhaps, but not so useful for warmth or protection. The bright and shining pride of a young firebrand scholar has met with a very real humility, some of my own making, some beyond my will. I've been humbled, humiliated at times, by thudding up against the rock ceiling of the theoretical monolith I'd so fool-heartedly—if full-heartedly—hoped to scale. And, like so many other young literary scholars, I've been simultaneously humbled, humiliated at times, by another strain of down- and black-heartedness: the vicissitudes, idiosyncrasies, and even the calculated, petty spite concomitant with the academic job market and with department, college, and university politics. I know now the Great Thesis lingers always just out of reach. I know now too, more acutely than ever before, that it's worth seeking, even if one never finds it completely. The day of closure never comes. May it never arrive, Lord, may it never arrive. Sufficient unto the day is the evil thereof. This means, fortunately, that our work as scholars is never done, even as we turn our critical gaze toward labor issues and institutional practices that impact academe, conditioning, if not controlling, our daily profession as professors.

What I imagined would be my version of the Great Thesis—my scholarly tome on contemporary southern poetics and cultural memory, eventually published as *Southern Crossings: Poetry, Memory, and the Transcultural South*

(2012)—begins with a passage from Appalachian poet and recent U.S. poet laureate Charles Wright's "The Southern Cross" (1981). My analysis played on various resonances of the controlling motif in his poem.

The title of Wright's poem most obviously cites the navigational constellation of the southern hemisphere as well as the Christian iconography of the Bible Belt, the poet's native territory. But it also suggests the famous and infamous battle flag of the Confederate States of America and the darker impulses of southern history in the use of the Southern Cross as a symbol for white supremacy and opposition to the civil rights movement. Thus, history returns obliquely to the evanescent surface of Wright's work, which gestures toward other forms of southern crossings, other indications of a time and region in flux, careful to note that absence, like the silences between musical notes, can be as revealing as the remembered presence of the past: "It's what we forget that defines us, and stays in the same place, / And waits to be rediscovered."[1]

My analysis was a mostly aesthetic appraisal of an image pattern in Wright's poetry, trimmed with broad strokes of historical, sociological, and political contexts. Although I was born in South Carolina and have lived most of my days here, the image of the so-called Confederate flag mostly served as a colorful backdrop for poetic analysis.

Things changed. On June 17, 2015, nine black citizens of Charleston, South Carolina, were shot to death during a Bible study and prayer session at Emanuel African Methodist Episcopal AME Church, one of the most historically significant African American churches in the South. The Emanuel Nine, several of whom, including state senator Clem Pinckney, were exemplary civic and religious leaders, were murdered by a twenty-one-year-old white supremacist under the sign of the Confederate battle flag on the anniversary of Denmark Vesey's failed slave rebellion in 1822 in the same city. (Vesey had been one of the founders of Emanuel AME.) As a number of historians duly reiterated to popular media in the aftermath of this terror attack, the Confederate flag had only been the battle flag of the Army of Northern Virginia and never served as a recognized political symbol for the Confederate States of America. Southern studies experts, such as historian Vernon Burton in a radio interview on NPR, further noted that the flag, long-adopted as a rallying symbol by the Ku Klux Klan, was placed atop the South Carolina Statehouse in 1961 by white-primacy legislators as a gesture of defiance against the burgeoning civil rights movement. Historically the flag had much more to do with race than nation.[2] In 2000, under pressure from the NAACP and other organizations, legislators agreed to a compromise: they would remove the flag from above the statehouse and put it instead in "a place of honor" next to a monument of a Confederate soldier directly in front of the statehouse, where the flag was even more prominent, inescapable. Even as the Emanuel Nine were mourned and laid to rest, the Confederate flag flew at full mast in front of the statehouse.

State senator Vincent Sheheen, a longtime proponent of removing the flag from the statehouse grounds, pointed out the bitter paradox: while the U.S. flag could be ordered down to half-mast by the governor to honor the dead, the Confederate flag was padlocked at full mast—as part of the 2000 compromise, only a legislative vote could lower the rebel flag. After mounting public pressure, national media scrutiny, majority votes in the South Carolina Senate (more than two-thirds) and in the House of Representatives (94–20), and Governor Nikki Haley's signature, a bill was enacted that led to the flag's removal from statehouse grounds on July 10, 2015.

Historical details merged with narrative, data blended with debate over "heritage" and "hate," and theory joined practice, and significant social, cultural, and political change was enacted, with subsequent ripples expanding out from local to state, regional, national, and transnational levels. The Emanuel Nine and the Confederate flag removal strongly affected the nation's image of the South, and the South clearly impacted the national imagination as well as how other nations viewed the United States. Thus was presented a powerful, if tragic, illustration of anthropologist James Peacock's concept of "grounded globalism," where the local and regional become primary sites influencing interregional and even transnational interconnections, where "globalism is grounded, even as it transforms that ground."[3] Indeed, the cover of Peacock's book is emblazoned with the Confederate flag, one that is inscribed "100% Cotton Made In China," therefore succinctly illustrating the global-southern economic implications of Peacock's thesis.[4] Southern studies crossed disciplines (history, sociology, politics), realms (from academe to "real world," classroom to statehouse), and media (from scholarly books to television, news websites, and social media), and knowledge directed action. Understanding the South, in no uncertain terms, mattered, and this form of transdisciplinary southern studies must matter still. The institutional stakes have never been higher in the United States, with conservative-leaning governors and state legislatures looking to severely cut funding and positions in higher education, especially in the red states and most especially in the red states in the South. The region remains in many respects arguably the nation's most intensive site of conflict and convergence, provoking ongoing ethnic and gendered conflict and conciliation as well as white political and cultural conservatism—a difference not in kind (read: regional exceptionalism) so much as in degree (read: the South as poster child for national ills). In approaching such a diverse, complex subject, our approaches should be equally diverse and complex. In terms of our disciplinary strategies, the way should be not one but many.

One of the important ways I've learned—or rather, I'm *learning*—to continue working, especially on the Big Idea of "the South," is simply (if not easily) to *listen*. There's a hollow, albeit popular practice that we're drawn to, particularly, I'm afraid, in the arena of literary criticism, where the competition—for entrance to highly rated graduate programs, for successful completion of said highly rated grad programs, for conferencing and publishing spots, for tenure-track positions, for earning tenure and promotion, et cetera—too often turns feral. Competition is further intensified as literati feel pressure to up the ante with specialized lingo and theoretical intricacy that mark us as intelligentsia, while at the same time alienating a broader popular audience, particularly one with more conservative cultural leanings. Consequently, there has been much spear-shaking and proclaiming in literary criticism that *whatever is theorized by us, is right.* We are caught in a bind in current southern studies. To lowball matters is to risk simplifying intellectual and political difficulties associated with regional definition and culture. This can be viewed by academic colleagues, who may peer-review our scholarship for publication or critique it afterward in reviews, as a form of dumbing down the field or even of selling out in hopes of more popular appeal. But to highball matters is to limit one's audience only to those who can speak the proper theoretical shibboleth. Too often we may find we are preaching to the choir, and a somewhat small, if fine-tuned, choir at that.[5] A more fully transdisciplinary brand of southern studies, one that I hope is signaled through the case study presented later in this essay, will enable us to productively balance these demands.

This competition within the literary studies discipline is exacerbated by competition between literary studies and other disciplines connected with southern studies, at a time when internal and external funding resources are scarce and becoming, it seems, ever scarcer. In addition to the widespread effort to increase participation in the science, technology, engineering, and mathematics (STEM) disciplines, the surrounding political climate, particularly in the solid-red southeastern states where most southern studies programs are anchored, is not very welcoming for what is perceived as "left-leaning" humanities research. These funding pressures tend to bring out the worst in interdisciplinary turf wars. As a result of these intra- and extra-institutional tensions, literary scholars who've fought long and hard for a glimmer of spotlight up on the academic stage often turn a deaf ear to other disciplines, merely lip-synching borrowed tropes without clear commitment to engaging with other disciplinary theories and practices that could inform current literary studies in crucial ways.

Several of these disciplines (e.g., history, sociology, politics, anthropology, ethnography, archaeology, linguistics, sociolinguistics, geography, and musicology) often show a heightened interest in merging theory with praxis, ideas with data, and abstractions with details. Literary critics tend to eschew number counting, much less statistical analysis, and what we cite as "history" or "context" often amounts to no more than generalized reference to categories of race, class, gender, and sexuality. Such tropes, if not fleshed out, can fade into pale ghosts, haunting the thin edges of transparent, oddly immaterial analysis, like when we write generally about deconstructing categories of racial identity when analyzing a particular literary work, but this remains disconnected from the newsfeed of our day-to-day lived experience. Don't get me wrong. With respect to current southern studies, negotiating the complexities of abstract thought is essential, and I do wish that some of our collaborating disciplines might join us more frequently up on the theoretical plane. But increasingly I've come to value efforts at deeper transdisciplinarity, which is slow work and hard, where numbers are indeed crunched, ideas and data matched, and the devil skulks behind all the details, details, details. These things matter.

So I offer here a case study of how interdisciplinary southern studies can deepen the value—aesthetic, yes, but also sociological and cultural—of depictions of methamphetamine use in short stories by one of the most compelling and highly touted contemporary Appalachian, southern, and U.S. writers. The main body of this essay will thereby sketch an overall framework of how literary studies might productively cross disciplines in order to illustrate significant ways that aesthetics can respond to and critique social life. I aim to propose in general terms how the fiction of Ron Rash, whose writing centers on life in the western North Carolina mountains, informs and is informed by a particular regional subculture, and at the same time I'd like to begin questioning the very defining lines of regional identity, claiming a level of site specificity for the Appalachian South as a microregion, while avoiding essentialist or exceptionalist clichés. I hope this contribution fulfills the etymological sense of "essay" ("to test" or "to experiment") in reflecting something of the importance of transdisciplinary southern studies as a vivid, forceful means to link world and page, to *make* things *matter*. The following account of representations of meth users in Ron Rash's short fiction makes—in truth, this time—a searching, tentative, provisional start on the topic at hand. However, I'd like to propose this essay as a general model for integrating other disciplines into literary analysis in order to foster a fuller, more trenchant understanding of this central conflict, not merely in Rash's work but also in the demographics of his home region of the western North Carolina mountains.

Meth Zombies in Ron Rash's Fiction

The American South, certainly in popular culture, has become a major repository for the undead over the past decade: from the arresting visual dynamics of the zombie-filled landscapes of *The Walking Dead*, both Robert Kirkman's comic book series (2003–present) and the AMC television show (2010–present), to the vampires and shape shifters of HBO's *True Blood* (2008–present), to the uncanny swamp-human revenants featured in David Sandlin's surreal pulp comic *Swamp Preacher* (2006), to the figurative walking dead who drag out their existence along the desiccated roadside terrain in Cormac McCarthy's *The Road* (2006) and John Hillcoat's cinematic adaptation (2009). In the wake of the terrorist attacks of September 11, 2001, one would think that cityscapes in the Northeast might make fitter spots for the recrudescence of the undead. Yet the contemporary South has become a powerful magnet for this popular explosion of zombified figures. The current rise of the undead in southern realms prompts the interrelated questions: Why zombies *now*? And why zombies *here*? The southern-bound undead speak truth—even (or especially) in their very inarticulateness, as is typically the case with the mumbling zombie brood—to underlying cultural anxieties that materialize within, across, and outside the geopolitical boundaries of the U.S. South: global economic transfers and tensions about the unsustainability of late capital; the instability of regional and national boundaries; the threat of ecological crisis; immigration and emigration pressures; the gutting of the urban-industrial environment; fears of pandemic; collapsing religious structures and values; and the dissolution of the neoliberal patriarchal family, among other things. Although beyond the scope of this essay, these social tensions merit further consideration as potential sources for the millennial uprising of the undead and almost necessitate multidisciplinary approaches. Indeed, the very issue of what constitutes "undeadness" deserves the collaborative attention of several disciplines.[6] The surging life of the undead down South unveils transformations in current regional economies and subcultures, disbanding old structures of identity while simultaneously engendering new possibilities for identification in an increasingly interregional world.

This essay gestures toward further geographic and cultural particularity in response to the above issues by focusing on a subsection of the U.S. South—the Appalachian or "mountain" South. In doing so, I outline potential convergences and conflicts between the *microregional* ("Appalachia"), the *macro-regional* ("the South"), the *transregional* ("the nation"), and even the *transnational* ("the Global South"). Appalachia has often been conceived as a bastion of cultural backwardness, a primitive subregion lost in its own time zone. Appalachian identity is stereotypically seen as being highly stable, even to an unhealthy, incestuous degree. Consequently, the southern Appalachians make a particularly interesting test case for navigating the cultural transformations washing through this subregion. Rodger Cunningham notes how the Appalachian South has conventionally been seen as a "timeless blank," a trope that engenders a "double alterity" for the area.[7] Cunningham argues for the redoubled oppositional status of the microregion in the regional and national imaginations: "Appalachia exists in a blank created by a double otherness—a *doubly* double otherness. For the region is not only an internal Other to the South as the South is the internal Other of America, but it is also the occupier of a simultaneous gap and overlap *between* North and South."[8] Similarly, Robert H. Brinkmeyer Jr. notes that Rash's primary fictive terrain is what Rash terms "the back of beyond" and is also "a good way to describe southern Appalachia's representation in the American cultural imagination," a space "somehow 'beyond' America": "Largely because the region remained isolated for so long, seemingly tucked away in a timeless zone where the march of history rarely intruded, the folk of the southern mountains often came to be seen by the rest of America (including Southerners) as somehow pure and undefiled." This sense of "purity" led to "other legends" that implied "mountain folk were degraded by their isolation, devolving through inbreeding and poor living conditions into deformed and monstrous creatures, not all that different from the zombies of the television series *The Walking Dead*." This "works as an allegory of what happens when hill people descend in large numbers upon Atlanta, *The Beverly Hillbillies* reimagined as apocalyptic nightmare."[9] Brinkmeyer's insightful interweaving of Appalachians and zombies is particularly apt, we'll see, in relation to Rash's meth-based short stories.

The stereotype of southern Appalachian culture as supposedly nontransformative, stuck within the amber of some other time, in part explains why Appalachia has spawned more than its fair share of undead figurations as of late. The microregion seems to open a wormhole to an antiquated, antimodern space-time, a place not quite dead despite modernity's incursions and attendant discourses of progress and nationhood. In *The Nation's Region* (2006), Leigh Anne Duck critiques the illusion of the South's backwardness as just that—an illusion, albeit a powerfully imprinted one, constructed and buttressed by literary and other media construing the belated South at odds with the progressive nation. In her essay on "hillbilly" horror films for *Undead Souths*, Duck hones her thesis on tropes used to represent residents of the mountain South, which

> exhibit a formidable consistency across literature, travel writing, cartoons, advertising, television, film, and other media: whether virtuously unspoiled, stalwart, and traditional or dangerously dysfunctional, lazy, and backward, purported "hillbillies" have been portrayed as inhabiting an amorphous space, in which differences between Appalachia and the Ozarks are typically effaced but isolation from the changing nation appears stark and definitive.[10]

Rash's fiction often shows mountain inhabitants as "virtuously unspoiled" and "dangerously dysfunctional," but he also reveals an awareness of the transparency of these types while unveiling ways that the microregion is linked to larger national transformations, thereby making us recalibrate received notions of Appalachianness as well as rurality more broadly.

The author of five novels, five short story collections, and four poetry collections, Rash has skyrocketed to national literary acclaim over the past few years. His novel *Serena* (2008) was a *New York Times* best seller and a 2009 PEN/Faulkner finalist, and it was adapted into a major motion picture, starring Jennifer Lawrence and Bradley Cooper, released in 2014. His short story collection *Burning Bright* (2010) won the Frank O'Connor International Short Story Award, with included stories garnering an O. Henry Prize as well as being selected for the Best American Short Stories and the Best New Stories from the South series. And his most recent collection of short fiction, *Nothing Gold Can Stay* (2013), has already inspired glowing critical response.

The primary locales of Rash's fiction are small-town settlements scattered among the Blue Ridge. Indeed, so tightly connected are his characters to their physical environments that Rash has described a kind of spatialized "blood memory" embedded in their native terrain, a binding causality between blood and land, as Rash told NPR's Scott Simon during an interview for "Weekend Edition": "One aspect that I'm fascinated by is how landscape is very often destiny, that the landscape a human being grows up in has an incredible impact on the way he or she perceives reality."[11] In a personal conversation in 2010, Rash told me he believes his ancestors who farmed these mountains (like my own Scots-Irish forebears in the southern Virginia mountains) felt an ominous presence when working these fields under the rock-cast shadows, the immensity of the hills summoning something of human fate and mortality, as if the rolling Appalachians were so many tombstones, an ever-expanding *mise en abîme* of memento mori.[12] However, as Elizabeth Rivlin has argued, Rash's stories often seem to tell a somewhat different story, mixing this almost deterministic notion of blood memory with awareness of the fraught contingencies of identity formation.[13]

In particular, tropes of undeadness in Rash's recent short stories call attention to contemporary Appalachian "zombies" produced by methamphetamine addiction. His work shifts the mountain South into a trans-southern, even global frame by illustrating the ways in which meth traffic influences and is affected by larger economic and sociocultural dynamics. "The Ascent" from *Burning Bright* and "Those Who Are Dead Are Only Now Forgiven" from *Nothing Gold Can Stay* present two of Rash's meth-based stories that intimate interweaving between literal and figurative undead. Specters and corpses commingle seamlessly with mind-numbed addicts, who appear equally possessed, aloof, and estranged from pressing realities of the present, entrapped in coreless redundancies of a mummified past. Their psyches rewired by bad chemicals, these meth zombies embody stereotypes of primitive Appalachians, subsisting almost fully on the brainstem's instinctual core; the pleasure principle overrides any abstract reality principle of the "modern" mind. Yet, despite their ostensible isolation, their situation reflects larger interregional schemata, unburying much of the dead landscape of U.S.-led late capitalism, from the financial non-sustainability of small farming to the operations of illicit narcotics markets and the quasi-legal trade in secondhand goods. The interconnected criminalization and securitization processes of local law enforcement also figure in Rash's meth tales.

"The Ascent" tells the story of a ten-year-old boy, Jared, who happens upon a small plane downed on Sawmill Ridge in Great Smoky Mountains National Park. Instead of reporting the find to the authorities, who are continuing helicopter searches in the snow-covered mountains to locate the missing plane, he conducts a kind of piecemeal grave-robbing of the two corpses, a man and a woman, left inside the wreckage. The scavenged wedding ring and Rolex watch are appropriated by the boy's parents, who immediately travel to Bryson City in order to pawn the goods to fuel their meth addiction. Not wishing to admit what he's done with the money from the pawned ring, the father tells his son the plausible lie that "the sheriff took it," invoking the network of legal surveillance that uses meth traffic as a nexus for the interrelated processes of criminalization and securitization: "When I showed it to the jeweler, he said the sheriff had been in there just yesterday. A woman had reported it missing."[14] The parents' efforts to perform the tradition of Christmas decorating become a grim parody of such family-centered nostalgic devotions, with chopped-up kindling serving as the tree and the mother substituting plastic fishing bobbers and aluminum foil for ornaments. In the end, the boy chooses a life with the dead over the death-in-life existence with his meth-addled parents. He returns to the plane as heavy snow accumulates, taking a seat behind the two corpses and entombing himself with them in the fuselage until hypothermia sets in.

"Those Who Are Dead Are Only Now Forgiven" connects the erasure of the small farm as a viable economic unit to the irruption of meth-undeadness in the area. An old farmhouse has gone to rot, a dead structure amid the influx of external capital and real estate development in the region: "The Shackleford house was haunted. In the skittering of leaves across its rotting porch, locals heard the whispered misery of ghosts. Footsteps creaked on stair boards and sobs filtered through walls. An Atlanta developer had planned to raze the house and turn the thirty acres into a retirement village. Then the economy flatlined."[15] In this haunted house we see intimations of a haunted housing market post-2008, one that has yet to adequately revive. The Atlanta developer's attempt to repurpose the decrepit farmhouse and surrounding acreage was forestalled by a deadened U.S. economy, and the story contains further evidence of the economic impacts of a transregional economy. Lauren cashiers at Walmart in Canton, while her boyfriend Jody works with his sister and mother at a poultry plant, where Lauren too eventually finds work to support her meth habit. Her brother handles nonlocal produce at the Winn-Dixie. Indeed, almost all of the food present in Rash's meth stories is processed, mass-produced for wide distribution, such as the "green leprechaun" sugary cereal that seems Jared's staple in "The Ascent," besides an occasional franchise "hamburger and a Co-Cola" his parents bring back from Bryson City along with their bags of powder.[16] Moreover, Lauren's father meets a bleak death via a work accident at the power plant, another symbol of impassive corporate production that disempowers the locals. What's left of the home place is rumored to be possessed by the Shacklefords, victims or culprits of some unspeakable, perhaps unforgivable trauma: "In a back bedroom were a bureau and mirror, a cardboard funeral-home fan, and a child's wooden rocking horse. Lauren had asked Jody if he knew why the house was supposedly haunted. He didn't, only that something had happened and it had been bad."[17] Lauren and two of her acquaintances from high school become contemporary doppelgängers shadowing this undead past, re-inhabiting the house as a trio of zombie-junkies. Lauren's brother tells Jody that there's no use in trying to "bring back" his girlfriend; she and her meth kin are beyond legal surveillance, too far gone for the local law enforcement to take any interest: "Sheriff Hunnicut told me he used to wonder why he never saw any rats inside a meth house. I mean, filth all over the place you'd expect them. Then he realized the rats were smart enough to stay clear."[18]

In terms of sociological context for Rash's portrayal of the meth-undead, one might look to Nick Reding's *Methland: The Death and Life of an American Small Town* (2009), which traces methamphetamine use in rural U.S. spaces, noting how media reports of crystal meth stigmatize those marked by race, class, and/or locale as hazards to a normative citizenry, an argument echoed in Travis Linnemann's "Governing through Meth" (2013). Linnemann traces how, through exaggerating risks, politicizing statistics, and "othering" meth users, government authorities link meth control to broader securitization projects, including the current wars on drugs and terror. According to Linnemann, government campaigning to regulate meth reflects an effusive disciplinary strategy, one of the "subtle yet pervasive ways social institutions 'know and act on their subjects'" that is "fundamental to fabricating, structuring and administering modern governance."[19] Duck's essay on "hillbilly" horror resets the meth controversy in a southern context. She contends that "because meth is deemed a 'white-trash drug,' stereotypes used to promote greater social control often stem from the savage-hillbilly tradition" associated with rural Appalachia.[20] Reding's account focuses on Iowa and Linnemann's on Kansas, emphasizing the interregional nature of meth traffic, yet their critiques are transferrable to southern arenas, such as Rash's North Carolina mountains or the meth-saturated Ozarks of Daniel Woodrell's *Winter's Bone* (2006), forming links between the Midwest and the South, heartland and Southland. In a fuller treatment, one might also consider Woodrell's meth-undead narrative as well as Debra Granik's 2010 film adaptation, in addition to the Albuquerque, New Mexico–based AMC series *Breaking Bad* (2008–13). These transregional connections unlink meth traffic and addiction from a specific locale (namely, the "white trash" mountain South) and reveal the national scope of meth production and distribution. Meth zombies are not cordoned off to the southern Appalachians, but they cross state and regional lines as a national concern.

Data released in 2013 by North Carolina attorney general Roy Cooper provides further sociological and demographic details to flesh out the cultural implications of Rash's meth tales. These numbers reflect the growing presence of meth production in western North Carolina but also suggest that this is not exceptional to this locality. Per the North Carolina Department of Justice, 177 meth labs were uncovered in 2003, while this number increased to an all-time high of 561 in 2013.[21] Lab busts in western North Carolina increased from 55 in 2012 to 62 in 2013, and these were mostly small-scale production labs.[22] Stronger legal surveillance techniques contributed to the spike in busts, including "new systems for tracking the sale of over-the-counter cold medicines containing pseudoephedrine," commonly used to create meth.[23] North Carolina takes part along with twenty-three other states in the National Precursor Log Exchange, a database that tracks frequent purchasers of pseudoephedrine. As a result of this increased capacity for local, state, and interstate authorities to log these numbers, they can focus surveillance efforts. In North Carolina, state law now "restricts anyone from buying more than two packages of pills containing pseudoephedrine at a time, or more than three packages a month."[24] Although rural western North Carolina contains hundreds of meth labs, the subregion is not exceptional: South Carolina recorded 617 meth lab busts in 2013 and Tennessee had more than 1,500 for the fourth consecutive year.[25] The fact that twenty-three other states are involved in the National Precursor Log Exchange database demonstrates that methamphetamine issues extend well beyond the isolated microregion depicted in Rash's fiction.

Like Reding, Linnemann, and Duck, Rash locates the proliferation of meth among working-class inhabitants of Appalachia vis-à-vis transregional economic shifts, from the emergence of large-scale agribusiness that swallowed up small farms, to corporate demands for greater productivity amid lower wages, to the federalization of land by the National Park Service, to the out-migration of locals from the area in search of better financial prospects. These tensions were exacerbated by the financial panic of 2008 and the continuing recession, which produced housing foreclosures as well as "zombie mortgages." Imbuing his Appalachia with a dark redundancy, the serial repetition of an undying past, Rash draws back to the history of hard times in the mountain South. He interlaces his tales of the meth-undead with echoes of the Great Depression as well as the Civil War among the folds of the Blue Ridge. No dramatic apocalypse, supernatural or secular, is to blame in Rash's world. What we find here is consumer capitalism extended to its illogical extreme, where zombie-junkies are walking allegories for the mindless repetition of cultural representations that have outlived their use. Futurity, it seems, is a thing of the past in Rash's Appalachia. His fiction urges us to reexamine the area's purported insularity, as strains of postinsularity well up between the plotlines of Rash's fictive contemporary Appalachia. Figures of undeadness in his stories enable us to uncover the striations of contemporaneous histories that irrupt in purportedly backwoods-equals-backwards Appalachia, to view the microregion not in isolation but in connection with other regions, even or especially when these cross-regional overlaps are grim or unsettling.

Regrouping/Regrounding

To return to the earlier image drawn from Charles Wright's poetry, Wright's oblique evocation of the Southern Cross as flag of the Confederate States of America connects with a scene from Rash's "Dead Confederates" (2010). The short story offers a warning against thoughtless, zombified devotion to the cult of the Lost Cause and the veiled danger of trading on the heritage of dead Confederates. In the opening pages, the narrator, a DOT road crew member, describes an unsavory coworker, Wesley Davidson:

> His uncle's the road crew boss, and he lets Wesley do about what he wants, including come in late, the rest of us all clocked in and ready to pull out while Wesley's Ford Ranger is pulling in, a big rebel flag decal covering the back window. Wesley's always been big into that Confederate stuff, wearing a CSA belt buckle, rebel flag tattoo on his arm. He wears a gray CSA cap too, wears it on the job. There's no black guys on our crew, only a handful in the whole county, but you're still not supposed to wear that kind of thing. But with his uncle running the show Wesley gets away with it.[26]

Rash's critique is subtle, understated, not unlike Wright's. But the quiet admonition that "you're still not supposed to wear that kind of thing" takes on astonishing, tragic resonances in the wake of the Emanuel Nine. The rebel flag version of the Southern Cross, with its star-blazoned St. Andrew's Cross, hails back to Scots and Scots-Irish settlement in the southern Appalachians during the mid-eighteenth century, post Culloden and the ensuing Highland clearances. There was a default whiteness, then, embodied in the Confederate battle flag design—reaching back across centuries and national boundaries—long before it resurfaced as an explicit symbol of white supremacy in the 1950s as part of the white southern countermovement against the civil rights movement. Just as "Dead Confederates" exposes marketable nostalgia for Confederate memorabilia as a careless—but not harmless—expression of white pride, the tale also self-reflexively notes that the southern Appalachians are typically conceived as an all-white space, for there were "no black guys on our crew, only a handful in the whole county."[27] From a certain vantage,

Ron Rash can be read (perhaps should be) as a premier writer of whiteness grounded in millennial Appalachia, in the same way that other contemporary writers are grouped as writers attuned to various other ethnicity-based perspectives: African American, Latino, Native, Asian American, Arab American, or mixed race. Likewise, Charles Wright can be recategorized as a trenchant poet of whiteness grounded in contemporary southern Appalachian suburbia.

Such regrouping and regrounding offer new alignments for re-envisioning what we find meaningful about the South, thereby renewing southern studies. Regrouping speaks more directly to the abstract patterning of theoretical discourse (i.e., the metacritical impulse of literary criticism). Regrounding offers the chance—more properly, the importance, if not necessity—for literary southern studies to avail itself of significant transdisciplinary modes of research. While regrouping invents new ideas about the thing, regrounding seeks something of the thing itself. That is, regrouping reconceives, recategorizes the larger meanings associated with southernness (and its subgroupings, including Appalachianness), where regrounding anchors this sensibility in an understanding of the American South as a material space, a plane (if "place" echoes too closely the old tropes of traditional southern studies) of activity and action that is measurable, definable. We can resee the South as a real ground(ing), even or especially on the level of its geographic elements as a structure—or a mass of structures, multiple, even contradictory—of environments, organic and built. A regrounded South encompasses a human-nonhuman, natural-cultural ecology, a geopolitical scape within which things happen and things matter. By combining regrouping and regrounding modes in a renewed southern studies, the natural or ecological plane merges with the ideological or virtual plane.

Keith Cartwright's recent work linking the U.S. South with the Caribbean and Gulf Coast lights a path for this kind of regrouping and regrounding in southern studies. His approach strives toward a South unbound from the traditional past, unloosing from the confines of what new southern studies critic Jon Smith has called out as the cliché obsession with "folklore, orality, the presence of the past, the sense of place, and the sense of community."[28] Though we shouldn't continue to mine the same old veins, Cartwright wishes to regroup and reground current and future southern studies in cognizance of "powerful southern countercultures of performance (and rememory, re-emplacement, restoration of community)." These, he says, "remain in need of proper respects" for "we may not need a New Southern Studies, just a deeper (more holistically conservative) one, hospitable to comings and goings beyond accustomed borders, beyond generational periodicities invented by professors and journalists, and beyond English."[29] Similarly, Taylor Hagood notes the way the South has assumed a reality on a virtual level, on the level of ideations and abstractions, yet nevertheless stresses the importance of continuing to see "ground" as efficacious. Intersecting material and virtual planes, "southern ground" provides "the kinds of liberating energies that can imagine new Souths" that reflect "not just the persistence but the refashioning of [the nation's] cherished other."[30] In such proliferating notions of southernness rubbing up against material formations of the region, the South rises again and again and again and again, never in the same form. The South is unbound.

And the same can be said for cross-domain studies that confront not just the persistence but the refashioning of the South's cherished internal other: Appalachia. This critical approach toward regrouping and regrounding is evident in current studies of southern Appalachian culture that add complexity and nuance to past understandings, challenging the traditional equation of "Appalachian" with "whiteness." For instance, in Emily Satterwhite's *Dear Appalachia* (2011), a reception studies account of the microregion, Satterwhite collects, counts, and analyzes detailed data on reading patterns, book reviews, and fan mail for Appalachian popular fiction across geographic areas from the 1870s to the present. Satterwhite grounds the perception and self-perception of Appalachians in empirical records while also regrouping the standard-issue linkage of "backwoods" and "backwards." Linguists Becky Childs and Christine Mallinson's collaborations, based in years of data collection and thoroughgoing statistical analysis, also help redefine Appalachia as a space of shared culture between whites and nonwhites, noting sociolinguistic forms in transit not merely across Appalachia but linking much of the Atlantic rim from Newfoundland to the Caribbean. Childs and Mallinson's scholarship is particularly invested in pointing out interchanges between white and African American English variants in the southern Appalachian microregion. Childs is also collaborating with J. Daniel Hasty to collect and interpret data about how language features that were marked as "country" or "uneducated" expressions for earlier generations of Appalachians (e.g., lexical features such as "y'all," "yonder," and "reckon" or morphosyntactic features such as double modals ["you *might could* say that"]) are in the process of being reintroduced in current speech within and beyond Appalachia. This self-conscious recycling of previous idioms by younger speakers projects a curvilinear pattern of linguistic change, suggesting that these throwback language variables are motivated primarily by intermediate groups in the sociolinguistic demographic—in this case, upper-working-class or lower-middle-class speakers of Appalachian English. Revivals of such traditional, even iconic Appalachian language practices are consonant with the emergence of the "New Appalachia," which balances the growing postinsularity of the microregion with a hip reclaiming of distinctive (if outmoded) figures of speech. These sociolinguistic features work alongside the popularity of other renovated tropes, including the rebranding of bluegrass music as well as mountain folk crafts for middlebrow consumption and the concurrent rise of "hicksterism" alongside the heavily bearded, plaid-shirt-wearing, overall-donning lumbersexual.[31]

As a final point, I should further note that the processes of regrouping and regrounding are already evident in much millennial literature representing the southern Appalachian microregion. If traditionally Appalachia has been synonymous with "mountain South," color-schemed as almost pure white, this stereotypical vision belies the mixed nature of Appalachia's often vexed histories. There are indeed *other* Appalachias, and these are reflected in recent literature about the area: for instance, the "Affrilachian" poetries engendered by Nikky Finney, bell hooks, Frank X Walker, and Ricardo Nazario y Colón, or the Native perspective on the microregion offered in poetry, fiction, and memoir by Allison Hedge Coke, a mix of Huron, Tsa la gi (Cherokee), French Canadian, and Portuguese heritage, who grew up working class in rural North Carolina. These writers point to transformations in our understanding of what counts as Appalachian as well as southern identities. Their diverse work offers effective means of resisting the typical racializing and primitivizing of the Appalachian South, calling attention to the dense strands of its multiethnic pasts that carry over into our present.

Notes

1. Wright, *The Southern Cross*, 54.

2. Schedler, *Racist Symbols and Reparations*; Bonner, *Colors and Blood*; K. Prince, *Rally 'Round the Flag, Boys!*; Coski, *The Confederate Battle Flag*.

3. Peacock, *Grounded Globalism*, 132.

4. Ibid., cover.

5. Scholarship on southern foodways may provide one recent illustration of these tensions between popular appeal and theoretical rigor. A call for papers for a proposed edited collection was circulated on various academic sites and listservs in June 2016 by two of the most prominent scholars in southern literary studies, Jon Smith (editor of the New Southern Studies Series for the University of Georgia Press) and Scott Romine (editor of the Southern Literary Studies Series for the Louisiana State University Press). The two criticize much southern foodways scholarship for being intellectually lightweight and therefore popular. Smith and Romine argue that their proposed collection will redress this by incorporating updated theoretical approaches to foodways while avoiding academic jargon (i.e., the essays will be written in a style accessible for the general public) and encouraging political activism. On July 8, 2016, Ted Ownby, a well-known southern historian and director of the Center for the Study of Southern Culture at the University of Mississippi, offered his balanced counterpoint to the call for papers on the website for the Southern Foodways Alliance, one of Smith and Romine's thinly veiled targets: Ownby, "The SFA TAKE."

6. The concept of undeadness in *Undead Souths* (2015), the collection of essays I co-edited with Eric Gary Anderson and Taylor Hagood, challenges traditional dividing lines between living and nonliving by drawing on developments in quantum physics,

biochemistry, and environmental studies, in connection with humanities fields such as post-humanist philosophy and aesthetic theory. How we recognize a "zombie" changes across various cultures, historical periods, and disciplinary contexts.

7. Cunningham, "Writing on the Cusp," 41, 44.
8. Ibid., 45.
9. Brinkmeyer, "Discovering Gold in the Back of Beyond," 219–20.
10. Duck, "Undead Genres/Living Locales," 175.
11. Simon, "'Nothing Gold' Stays Long in Appalachia."
12. Turner, "From Blue Ridge to Blue Sea," 18.
13. Rivlin, "The Ghost of Shakespeare in Ron Rash's *Serena*."
14. Rash, *Burning Bright*, 83.
15. Rash, *Nothing Gold Can Stay*, 127.
16. Rash, *Burning Bright*, 89.
17. Rash, *Nothing Gold Can Stay*, 139.
18. Ibid., 138.
19. Linnemann, "Governing through Meth," 40.
20. Duck, "Undead Genres/Living Locales," 184.
21. "Meth Lab Busts."
22. Elliston, "NC Sets record for Meth Lab Busts in 2013, with Slight Uptick in WNC."
23. Ibid.
24. Ibid.
25. Ibid.
26. Rash, *Burning Bright*, 46.
27. Ibid.
28. J. Smith, *Finding Purple America*, 30.
29. Cartwright, "Confederacies of Undead Imagination," 11.
30. Hagood, "Going to Ground," 259.
31. See, for instance, Childs and Mallinson, "African American English in Appalachia"; Childs and Mallinson, "The Significance of Lexical Items in the Construction of Ethnolinguistic Identity"; Childs, Mallinson, and Carpenter, "Vowel Phonology and Ethnicity in North Carolina"; Hasty and Childs, "The Old Is New Again."

PART 4

Southern Studies in Practice

Interlocality and Interdisciplinarity

Learning from Existing Models of the Global South

KIRSTEN DELLINGER, JEFFREY T. JACKSON,
KATIE B. MCKEE, AND ANNETTE TREFZER

The term "Global South" was coined in the 1970s by the United Nations when it established a special unit dedicated to "South-South cooperation"—development assistance shared between developing countries—and was originally used to describe those "less developed" countries of the world in terms of the UN Human Development indices or in terms of income per capita. Since the term has grown common, tending to replace the term "Third World," it has evolved to take on many meanings. One of the most interesting arenas in which we can observe these diverse and sometimes divergent meanings is post-1990s academic scholarship on the topic of globalization. While the Global South has become a well-recognized concept in both the humanities and the social sciences, we argue that usage of the term is anything but consistent and that this indicates uncertainty within the academy with regard to its meaning. This may create problems for academics who wish to have interdisciplinary conversations about the Global South, but, on a deeper level, the shifting meaning of the term indicates the complexity of defining power relations within the contemporary moment of intensely networked daily life. In order to more clearly understand this moment, and in an effort to move beyond disciplinary divides, this essay explores the concept of the Global South from the perspective of scholarship within both the humanities and the social sciences and draws on the direct experiences as scholars of an interdisciplinary working group at the University of Mississippi devoted to the topic of the Global South.

The goal of this essay is threefold. First, we offer an interpretation of some current models of the Global South and a response to them. This narrative is *not* a complete overview of all existing literature on the Global South, but rather a collective story of our own experiences interrogating this concept as an interdisciplinary working group. Central to this story is our own unique social location in Mississippi. Our attempt to conceptualize how Mississippi's place within the concept of Global South both afforded us insights into cross-disciplinary work and created certain terminological difficulties. Second, we outline how our own attempts to find common interdisciplinary ground on which to build collaborative research quickly revealed some of the limitations of individual scholarly approaches. Interrogating the various epistemological orientations of the scholars we studied became central to our discussions, and in this paper we will explore the implications of these different logics and frameworks, paying particular attention to where they overlap or contradict one another. Finally, we approach the Global South through the concept of "decentered interlocality," a term we used to integrate geographical and institutional locations by invoking a dynamic from one location while simultaneously raising an awareness of the power dynamics and inequalities inherent in other locations. Decentered interlocality allowed us to understand the complexities of our contemporary global culture and enabled us to work together across disciplinary lines.

The Global South Crosses the Disciplines

For three years, the interdisciplinary faculty working group on the Global South at the University of Mississippi welcomed social scientists and humanities scholars to discuss various definitions and applications of this concept with respect to our specific location here in Mississippi. As a working group, we immediately noticed that we were interested in borrowing from each other's disciplines. Literary scholars began incorporating sociology readings, and social scientists increasingly relied on literature and film in their classes. All of us were assigning the work of historians and geographers.

Nevertheless, as we read each other's canonical works and as we listened to invited speakers who were themselves transcending disciplinary boundaries in their research, the unique biases and norms of our epistemological orientations crept up. Sometimes these disciplinary fences were easily hurdled, and we moved forward. At other times differences between scholars in the sciences and the humanities surfaced that created tensions within the group and became opportunities to proselytize one another on the merits of our own academic perspectives.[1] In short, we became aware of the different priorities, agendas, perspectives, and biases of our fields. Alvin Gouldner called these the "domain assumptions" of theory, the basic epistemological orientations of scholars that involve key concepts used, key works cited, and the deeper fundamental (and often tacit) conceptualizations of human interaction present within a particular worldview or school of thought.[2] As we dug deeper into the foundations of scholarship on the Global South, we were looking for both the differences in the ways disciplines understand the term "Global South" and a common vocabulary.[3]

In our cross-disciplinary discussions, we observed that most social scientific scholarship uses the term "Global South" as a euphemism for "undeveloped" or "underdeveloped" regions or, most often, countries. The rubric is primarily economic and refers to global wealth disparities. "Global South" is used to mean the "poor" or "exploited" who suffer the worst depredations of global capitalism, while "Global North" stands for the wealthy beneficiaries of this contemporary political economic arrangement. Here the social scientists' primary goal is to be "power aware," and their concern is the people who occupy these various locations within the global social structure, what their conditions of life are like, and how these social structures themselves are maintained, resisted, or transformed. Particular attention is paid to the persistent structures of racism, sexism, and class inequality.

This is a different starting point from inquiry in literary scholarship, for instance, where most scholars use the term "Global South" as a way to think about space and as a euphemism for "subaltern." The rubric is primarily cultural and refers to the counter-hegemonic perspectives or "systems of meaning" that writers in different parts of the world create in order identify their social location (their "place") as well as to resist or survive their condition. Scholars in the humanities tend to be more "place aware" as literary canons are traditionally organized around nations, regions, and other locales. Their primary concerns are the textual and cultural expressions of people who occupy these various locations within the global social structure. Postcolonial scholars, for instance, attempt to describe how these expressions of meaning can be used to transform socially oppressive structures, and they pay particular attention to mind-sets, "discourses," texts, and cultural expressions of "(post)-coloniality." Working together, we realized that the Global South cannot be fully contemplated within either set of disciplinary domain assumptions. It is a concept best articulated as the interplay of power and place, and of textual representation and socio-economic conditions. Therefore, we sought a framework that allowed for a more collaborative discussion, one that emphasized matters of social structure, power, and wealth, as well as matters of cultural representation and the dynamics of "place" and meaning. On the way to this more comprehensive interdisciplinary view, we organized the key premises of our guest lectures and readings on the Global South into five predominant models of study, 1) the Global South as inflow/outflow model, 2) the comparative hemispheric model, 3) the geopolitical model, 4) the transnational feminist model, and 5) the decentered interlocality model.

The Global South as Inflow/Outflow Model

We approached the concept of the Global South first with the help of historian and anthropologist James Peacock, whose recent work gave us the impetus for thinking about a familiar U.S. South from the vantage point of globalization.⁴ With Peacock, we explored the question of whether what we mean by the Global South is the same as globalization in the South (it is not), what globalization has done to and for the South, and what the U.S. South can tell us about globalization in other places. We asked: what are the historical, cultural, and material *currents* of globalization that run through the U.S. South and link it with the world? This question led to a model of "inflow"—how foreign places reach into the U.S. South—and "outflow," how the U.S. South exports its ideas and institutions.

This idea of global import and export is central not only to the contemporary moment but also to an understanding of the U.S. southern past. Exploring such historical connections by following the traffic and trade of commodities, ideas, and people across the Atlantic and into the Indian Ocean, the scholarship of Gaurav Desai encouraged us to pay attention to the flows of people and goods. In his "Oceans Connect: The Indian Ocean and African Identities" he asked us to consider the ironies of the U.S. South's role in a system of oceanic trade between Salem, Massachusetts, Zanzibar, and South Africa: "Slave labor brought from Africa to the United States helped produce cotton that was manufactured into so-called *amerikani* cloth, which was shipped by Salem merchants to Zanzibar for trade."⁵ This Indian Ocean trading system that includes the U.S. South stretches the critical vantage point beyond the more familiar trans-Atlantic journeys.

Thinking in "flows" and paying attention to the global movements of people and goods is helpful. First, it makes visible cultural and demographic shifts caused by new immigration into the U.S. South, thereby transforming the former paradigm of a largely biracial landscape into a multi-ethnic mosaic. Second, foregrounding traffic and flows across regional and national borders detaches the region from a static, national North-South comparison. But, despite these promising advantages, this understanding of the Global South as flows keeps moving in and out of a relatively stable geography, as an ocean, a highway, or a rail line connect one stable location (say the cotton fields in Mississippi) to another (say South Africa). To what extent do these flows change the existing geographies into a relational concept? We began to conceive of the Global South, then, as not primarily or simply a flat geographical space traversed by people and goods, but instead as a space marked by relationships of global traffic that depend on deep historical structures, relationality, and contingency. Place as contingency—as opposed to a surface, continuous and given—appealed to us. Barney Warf argues that we are at a point today when the surface metaphor for space collapses and gives way to more convoluted geographies of the postmodern world. This shift is triggered largely by globalization technologies (fiber-optic networks, the Internet, satellites, etc.) that create an environment where software enables space to unfold in multiple ways, where the city gives way to the virtual city and "the notion of place as a discreet, bounded entity [becomes] increasingly problematic."[6] This model differs from the surface model of the globe produced by early modern capitalism when space was seen "as conducive to the circuits of capital accumulation stretching across the planet," in Warf's words, much like Gaurav Desai's example of the Indian Ocean trading system and its representation in literature.[7] Today geographies can be linked without transportation cost. New territorial configurations do not need the nation-state.[8] The surfaces of modernity—as structured by notions of systems, surfaces, levels, layers, or territories—give way to the "space of flows," not the flow between two points but flow itself as space, described by Manuel Castells as the "purposeful, repetitive, programmable sequences of exchange and interaction between physically disjointed positions held by social actors."[9]

The implications of this inflow/outflow model for the U.S. South fundamentally restructure traditional understandings of it. If the region is now and has always been crisscrossed by the footprints of other places—if the South is in the world and the world is in the South—then the South is not a unique enclave of identity. Under this model, the South is not exceptional; it is representative. These reflections take us beyond musings about a special "sense of place" that have become anathema to serious study. The immediacy and power of place—self-contained yet perpetually overlapping with other places—comes back through the sort of case study methodology the social sciences and thoughtful memoir and fiction employ. For those of us attempting to think of the U.S. South as part of the Global South, the "space of flows" emerges as crucial.

The Comparative Hemispheric Model

A second model that we encountered, the comparative hemispheric model, concentrates on the Western Hemisphere, orienting the U.S. South toward locations farther south, particularly Latin America, rather than defining it in relation to "the North," variously defined. In 1999, for instance, Deborah Cohn published *History and Memory in the Two Souths*, in which she explored at length connections between U.S. southern and Latin American literature by reading a series of texts and a range of authors, including William Faulkner, once famously claimed by Colombian author Gabriel Garcia Marquez "to be a writer from the Caribbean."[10] George Handley's study published the following year, *Postslavery Literatures in the Americas: Family Portraits in Black and White*, articulates the beginning of a paradigm shift lending momentum to U.S. southern literary study for the remainder of the twenty-first century's first decade. Here Handley posits the existence of "Plantation America," a construction unlimited by national boundaries that depends upon the site of the plantation as one of political, economic, and social power, "hardly a phenomenon that can be properly understood within a single nation's borders, especially since it was defined by large-scale, foreign capital investment, international trade and commerce, and external political control."[11] Ultimately Handley poses a provocative question: "How does the meaning of 'America' shift when we understand not simply the interdependency of black and white cultures in the United States, but also black and white cultures in the Americas?"[12] What's more, Handley outlines the long reach of the plantation, not only as an economic unit for organizing labor, but also as the political model that defines relations between the nation-states within his mapping project, concluding that the U.S. South acted as the training ground for the nation's subsequent imperial forays into Latin America, the Caribbean, and beyond.

The U.S. South as transitional space, rather than exceptional region, provides the foundation for Smith and Cohn's *Look Away! The U.S. South and New World Studies*. The editors of this collection "envision ... a liminal south, one that troubles essentialist narratives *both* of global southern decline *and* of unproblematic global-northern national or regional unity, of American or southern exceptionalism."[13] Smith and Cohn thus situate the U.S. South squarely within discourse about the hemispheric South but also within ongoing conversations about a Global South, locating it in relation to a Global North and Global South model that finds it oddly partaking of both halves. Pointing out that the "plantation—more than anything else—ties the South to both the rest of the United States and to the rest of the New World," they argue that the "very factors that allegedly make the South exceptional within the context of the United States thus make it acutely familiar within broader categories of Americanness and postcoloniality," particularly once we drive a wedge between "whiteness" and "southernness," thereby recognizing the region as "a space where the African diaspora's northern areas overlap the southern reaches of the English conquest of North America."[14] Smith and Cohn's driving question—how might we "conceptualize U.S. southern culture in a way that acknowledges its postcolonial status without ignoring the region's signal histories of oppression, its cultural specificity, *and* its cultural diversity?"—leads them to formulate the South "as a space of degrees of overlap *between*," "a space unique within modernity: a space simultaneously (or alternately) center and margin, victor and defeated, empire and colony, essentialist and hybrid, northern and southern (both in a global sense.)"[15] The U.S. South, then, is "compellingly ... both familiar and exotic, both Self and Other," something scholars of the region can recognize if "we redirect the central gaze of southern studies outward, away from nativist navel-gazing."[16]

The advantages of the hemispheric model are multiple. By paying attention to shared geographies and histories, especially those centered around the experiences and practices of colonialism and slavery, scholars can track connections between places and people that transcend fixed boundaries and reveal place to be "agentic," as Wanda Rushing employs that term. That is, events occur where they do not merely out of coincidence, but because of historical, material, and geographical circumstances converging there, regardless of the boundaries humans have used to fix space. By this token, for instance, nineteenth-century Haiti emerges not as an anomaly of revolution, but as a specter that haunts the power of the plantation by its potential to be representative. American exceptionalism, then, reveals itself to be a construction and regional exceptionalism within the national whole little more than the very point of contact that illuminates the hemisphere as an organizing principle.

Yet some of these very same characteristics underscore the limitations of this approach and its proclivity to reassert the very barriers it purports to dismantle. When they engage in comparative work, scholars can, for instance, reinscribe traditional borders and boundaries because the power of the similarities revealed often depends upon an initial difference linked to national characteristics. Even the frequently used moniker "New World studies," as Smith and Cohn acknowledge, is grounded in the perspective of a generalizing European colonialism, given that for the millions of indigenous people already here, the only thing "new" about their world was the startling appearance of strangers within it. By making these observations, we intend not to discount the obvious value of comparative study, but rather to deploy a variation of it that hinges upon the nuances of the local, suggesting that nations (and regions, towns, and square miles) are entities striated with difference so that elements of the Global South can be evident in one area of Mississippi but not another, despite the undeniable location of both firmly within the United States, just as those strains could be evident in Milwaukee or Tucson—if we disentangle the political ways in which place is demarcated from the ways in which power and place interact in specific locations. Hemisphere, then, is only one container for sorting shared experience. Our invocation of "Global South" seeks to unite highly specific locations across continents, not by discounting their national identities, but by examining the distributions of power within them.

The Geopolitical Model

In their introductory essay to a special issue of *Global South*, Caroline Levander and Walter Mignolo, as a follow-up to their participation as guest speakers in our University of Mississippi working group, outline a paradigm of similar but more painfully experienced geographic proximity, one in which "[a] Hemispheric South gestures to a South of the U.S. and a South of the Border—a Hemispheric South where the Third World grates against the First and bleeds."[17] This model shares with the inflow/outflow model an interest in the movement of people, goods, and ideas across borders, but it more centrally concerns itself with the nature of borders themselves and the marginal position of southern spaces in relation to centers of northern power and knowledge production. For Mignolo too, the creation of cartographic images of a region (like the U.S. South, the southern hemisphere, or Latin America) is related to and a consequence of "a geopolitics of knowledge."[18] In this model, the U.S. South as part of a Global South is situated in relation to colonialism and the long project of European modernity. As such, the U.S. South is subject to the fabrication of "northern" logics, and our challenge is to rethink the marginal position of southern spaces in relation to centers of northern power and knowledge production. The goal for Mignolo is not to trace an exchange or flow of goods and people across borders, but to interrogate the creation and function of those very borders. The questions Mignolo poses are particularly interesting for scholars working on historically disenfranchised populations or minority groups for whom this geopolitical concept of the Global South promises a re-centering on indigenous experience and knowledge.

Caroline Levander and Robert S. Levine take a "strategic comparativist approach" in their work to emphasize the "interconnections among nations, peoples, institutions, and intellectual and political movements in the larger context of the American hemisphere."[19] This approach to the Global South, while being anchored in a *geographical* landscape, goes much beyond it to sketch a geo*political* terrain that would include the U.S. South and many of its populations—Native American, African American, immigrant, working class—whose lives are marked by the effects of colonialism and whose existence is perceived to be outside of the aura of modernity because of their race, class, gender, or land of origin.[20]

Working with a Global South model based in the geopolitics of knowledge has its distinct advantages. Defining the Global South is not simply a question of how globalization may shape a particular "space of place" such as the U.S. South, but, more importantly, finding out how that place becomes constructed within social relations to begin with. Because these geographic constructions are created out of economic, political, and social power relations, we can direct our attention to historically disenfranchised or underrepresented groups and perhaps discover and develop counter-hegemonic logics, including the concept of "decoloniality," important to Mignolo's scholarship.

Nevertheless, we believe that too great an emphasis on counter-hegemonic logics as hopeful alternatives to existing power structures foregoes a direct discussion of the actual power dynamics at work. The academic fascination with Foucault, Said, and Gramsci sits upon a scholarly tradition that is in dialogue with Marx. But few scholars in the postcolonial tradition address the concept of capitalism in their writing. It comes up in spots but mostly framed as "power relations," as if the difference between people who have power and people who do not is based upon some other kind of logic than wealth. Capitalism fades into the background as a fundamental assumption of this school of thought, and it is not an explicit part of the analysis.

We must ask why racism, patriarchy, and capitalism are not foregrounded more often. We believe it is important to highlight these pervasive social inequalities. They are systemic forms of institutionalized oppression that persist due to concrete actions of powerful elites and ideological frames that support them. The language of the postcolonial critique is tentative when it comes to these systemic forms of oppression. "Subaltern" is preferred over "oppressed," "text" takes precedence over "the means of production," and "counter-hegemony" is all we have when revolution seems impossible. There are important historical and institutional reasons why this is the case, but our own interest in the Global South is fundamentally related to a desire to bring these social structures of inequality back into the discussion.

The Transnational Feminist Model

Exploring how gender as a system of power shapes (and is shaped by) the flow of people and goods into and out of the U.S. South seems essential to any globalized understanding of it. Existing work in feminist sociology and postcolonial feminism is useful for highlighting "the interconnectedness of the histories, experiences, and struggles of U.S. women of color, white women, and women from the Third World/South," as Chandra Mohanty puts it.[21] This work moves the focus to the "mutuality and coimplication" of the histories and power relationships within and between communities, between the local and the global, exploring what Mohanty refers to as "'common differences' as the basis for analysis and solidarity."[22] Working on the Global South de-emphasizes international relations, redirecting attention to uneven development and various forms of domination, including the intricate links between gender inequality, colonialism, and racism, emboldening scholars to use "Global South" as more than a fashionable substitute for "Third World."

We gleaned several lessons from transnational feminist scholarship. First, Global South analysis must remain attentive to material conditions. Feminist sociologists like Kim-Puri stress the ways that cultural and material conditions are tightly interwoven: "Materiality is thoroughly mediated and inflected by cultural meanings just as the cultural exists through material structures and relations. The point is that the material and cultural are conjoined and shaped through each other."[23] Second, while focusing on global networks, we must guard against the temptation of universalizing systems of power. Kim-Puri notes that "recognizing the plurality of imperialisms, as empires and subempires, eschews the notions of a universal or singular notion of imperialist domination."[24] Work on the Global South must be attentive to the importance of specific cultural, political, and economic contexts. Third, Kim-Puri writes that "the purpose of establishing linkages is to call attention to the complex, sometimes contradictory, and often unequal interconnections that exist across cultural settings, howsoever defined."[25] As an interdisciplinary model for social scientists and humanities scholars, the Global South can, then, highlight pockets of poverty, gender inequality, and racism everywhere around the globe, including in the so-called "First World," and deconstruct the old North-South or Western and non-Western fault lines of culture, poverty, and development. As Mohanty writes, "Affluent and marginal nations and communities obviously do not line up neatly within this [older] geographical frame." She urges us to develop a new place consciousness where "the challenge is to see how differences allow us to explain the connections and border crossings better and more accurately, how specifying difference allows us to theorize universal concerns more fully."[26]

The Decentered Interlocality Model

As a working group, we came to reframe our own situatedness in Mississippi via the concept of the Global South using an approach that we termed "decentered interlocality," that is, bringing to bear the experiences of other places as instructive in mapping the forces converging in a seemingly disparate location. This is not the same exercise as comparative study, which often seeks a point-by-point analysis. Rather, interlocality concentrates on an awareness of simultaneously parallel experiences and attempts to hold in mind the overlapping knowledge made possible by multiple approaches—the inflow/outflow model, the hemispheric model, the geopolitical model, and the transnational feminist model.

Reseeing Mississippi is not the same thing as saving the state from itself. Perennially ranked in the lowest tier of all drivers for success, from economic development to education, Mississippi as a place suffers from historically self-inflicted wounds and a persistent sense of embattlement that can make change slow to come. In pursuing our "re-envisioning project," we want to be clear that we are not trying to overlook dark moments or shameful events. We are trying to see Mississippi more clearly by confronting its intense locality at the same time that we heighten our awareness of its profound and persistent relationship to other places.

Drawing from the various models we studied, we suggest that interlocality widens our understanding of Mississippi by changing the backdrop from a strictly nation-based power struggle between North and South to one that plays out in a hemispheric and transnational context that intensifies our idea of the local by insisting on its instantiation at all times within the "global." This is not a new idea. People and products from around the world crisscrossed the U.S. South long before it took shape as a distinct region, and scholars, to varying degrees, have been aware of this phenomenon and written about it. What is noteworthy about our interdisciplinary approach to the Global South paradigm is its ability to reveal "the closed society" as anomalous within the state's history, a chapter in its development rather than its defining moment. Winding more tightly in upon itself as sectionalism intensified in the pre–Civil War years, the U.S. South drew harder lines of self-definition so that as the "peculiar institution" later reconstituted itself as Jim Crow segregation, the nation too could point to the region as an exotic holding bin for national sins sharpened with regional particularities. This model extends its reach into the present, in which a significant number of residents are apt to maintain that the area has grown beyond its racialized past but retained its exceptionalism. There's just something about the South that makes it distinctive and worthy of study, they might say, not for what it tells us about a national history or about global structures of power, but for what it tells us about itself as separate from those forces.

Following various scholars, most recently historians Matthew D. Lassiter and Joseph Crespino in *The Myth of Southern Exceptionalism*, we contend just the opposite, that in fact exceptionalist models of U.S. southern culture, some of which are rooted in the academy, are no longer representative of the region, if they ever were. Although it is certain that "southerners" have at crucial moments in national history distinguished themselves from their counterparts, and although it is clear that distinctive elements of geography, demography, and cultural preference continue to characterize the U.S. South, it has never been a place unto itself. If, as Matthew Guterl maintains, the central problem of the nineteenth century was the problem of labor—where to get it, how to get enough, how to make it produce at a maximum rate—then the challenges of agriculture in the U.S. South do not create an isolated scenario. They create a representative one that allows Guterl to track U.S. southern planters into the Caribbean as they pursue maintenance of their lifestyles, having already realized that they have a great deal more in common with large landowners in Brazil than with anyone in Boston.[27] They snap the thin bonds of nationhood in favor of a community built by capitalism. As a result, we can locate the nineteenth-century U.S. South on a continuum of power relationships across the globe that concentrate on labor and the threats to maintaining a compliant workforce class, for example. The Haitian Revolution and the specter of ascendant blackness that haunts white American culture from its beginnings straight into the present moment means that slavery is never simply about the white and black people living in U.S. South. It is also always about the oppressive reach of political, economic, and social power into the lives of the disenfranchised in various locations around the globe. Studying the way societies institutionalize racism, sexism, and classism in one location is instructive for unlocking the structures of power defining a seemingly unrelated location. Thus, confronted with the legacy of slavery and segregation in the U.S. South, the William Winter Institute for Racial Reconciliation at the University of Mississippi studies the Truth and Reconciliation Commissions in South Africa and travels to Northern Ireland for discussions with advocates for reconciliation there. We echo, then, Levander and Mignolo's assertion that the Global South is "a nested network of world dis/order in which reconfigurations of power become possible in places of struggle" by seeing Mississippi as a site on which such struggles have taken place and continue.[28]

Conclusion

Our interdisciplinary investigations revealed "Global South" as a conceptual framework for observing the contingent and interconnected pockets of poverty, gender inequality, and racism throughout the world, including the so-called "wealthy nations," a framework that attends to the importance of both local context and global interdependence and privileges the perspectives of the subordinate and subaltern in the production of knowledge. We privilege political economy and the meaning of place. We see the importance of attending to structure and culture. When we began our work we often debated whether we were looking for a new and improved definition of "Global South" and whether its discovery would help foster more productive work across disciplines. But efforts to move in that direction were often disappointing and ultimately proved futile. We have come to understand that it is the tensions between the various definitions of "Global South" that allow for productive discussion and debate and remind all involved that we are working with domain assumptions. Our awareness of these assumptions forces us to name them and helps us to seek ways to move beyond them. A power-aware and place-aware analysis of the Global South has required remaining conscious of the socially constructed boundaries, flows, and constructions of knowledge in a globalizing world, just as we are of the constructed boundaries within our own academic disciplines.

Notes

The authors are members of the University of Mississippi Working Group on the Global South and are listed alphabetically on the title page.

1. The social sciences and the humanities are based on different intellectual tradi-

tions, and these differences surfaced in our discussions. Immanuel Wallerstein discusses the transition from "the medieval university" to the "modern university" in the nineteenth century as follows: the "medieval philosophy faculty" was split into "at least two separate faculties: one covering the 'sciences'; and one covering ... the 'humanities' ... these two cultures were at war with each other, each insisting that it was the only, or at least the best, way to obtain knowledge. The sciences denied the humanities the ability to discern truth.... They bequeathed the search for the good and the beautiful to the ... [humanities who] ... agreed to this division of labor" (*World Systems Analysis*, 3). These disciplinary divisions are still with us, and they surfaced in our discussions.

2. Feagin, Orum, and Sjoberg, eds., *A Case for the Case Study*, 31–34.

3. The main distinctions that we faced were a product of our unique composition as a collaborative working group. Therefore, we cannot claim to have identified any universal truths with regard to interdisciplinary working group dynamics. We cannot even lay claim to an understanding of our own entire group due to the fact that many people have entered this conversation, but only the four of us are writing these words now. Nevertheless, we believe we came to understand the differences between us. As two literary scholars and two sociologists, we hope this understanding might be useful for scholars in other fields.

4. Peacock, *Grounded Globalism*; Peacock, Watson, and Matthews, eds., *The American South in a Global World*.

5. Desai, "Oceans Connect," 715.

6. Warf, "From Surfaces to Networks," 67.

7. Ibid., 59.

8. Sassen, *Territory, Authority, Rights*.

9. Castells, *The Rise of the Network Society*, 412.

10. Quoted in Cohn, *History and Memory in the Two Souths*, 43.

11. Handley, *Postslavery Literatures in the Americas*, 19.

12. Ibid., 31.

13. Smith and Cohn, *Look Away!*, 13.

14. Ibid., 3, 4, 6.

15. Ibid., 6, 9.

16. Ibid., 9, 13.

17. Levander and Mignolo, "Introduction," 8. In 2008 and 2009 our University of Mississippi faculty Global South Interdisciplinary Working Group hosted a Global South Speakers Series with lectures and workshops designed around the work of specific scholars and subthemes within Global South scholarship. Caroline Levander and Walter Mignolo were the co-presenters for our first lecture and workshop held on campus in September 2008, titled "The Global South: Literary, Cultural, and Theoretical Study."

18. Mignolo, *The Darker Side of Western Modernity*, xxi.

19. Levander and Levine, "Introduction," 2.

20. See, for example, Levander's discussion of "a borderlands South" in "Sutton Griggs and the Borderlands of Empire."

21. Mohanty, "'Under Western Eyes' Revisited," 522.

22. Ibid., 522, 523–24.
23. Kim-Puri, "Conceptualizing Gender-Sexuality-State-Nation," 143.
24. Ibid., 147.
25. Ibid., 148–49.
26. Mohanty, "'Under Western Eyes' Revisited," 505.
27. Guterl, *American Mediterranean*.
28. Levander and Mignolo, "Introduction," 7.

Finding Strength in Southern Studies Pedagogy

Cultivating Individual Resilience through a Representative Narrative

MICHELE GRIGSBY COFFEY

> The world is in a bad state, but everything will become still worse unless each of us does his best.
>
> Viktor E. Frankl, *Man's Search for Meaning*

When my co-editor and I began planning the structure of the symposium that ultimately led to this book, there was never any question that we would dedicate a session to the teaching of southern studies. We hoped that engaging the large cross section of scholars in attendance would shed light on the common struggles that southern studies instructors faced in the classroom. More importantly, we expected that these scholars, who taught the southern experience in institutions as varied as Simon Frasier University in Canada, the Carter G. Woodson Institute of African American and African Studies at the University of Virginia, the Gender and Sexualities Program at Tulane University, the University of Texas at Austin, and the University of South Carolina would have unique insights into how to approach these challenges. Sadly, it was instead the most dysfunctional roundtable of the symposium as it devolved almost immediately into a discussion of the ways in which these professors largely felt unable to break through to their classes filled primarily with white students who came to their courses invested in a pastoral vision of a white-dominated antebellum South or in fascination with African Americans as objects of expressive culture.

The two moderators who opened the dialogue and many of the audience members, including symposium participants and other University of Mississippi faculty and graduate students, shared stories of failures to teach complicated narratives of the South that opposed students' expectations. According to their accounts, acts of disrespect and resistance in the classroom were common, especially when issues of race were discussed.[1] And what was overwhelmingly clear at our symposium was that in southern studies, as is true throughout academia, professors of color are currently shouldering a far disproportionate share of the burden of doing most of the race work in our classrooms.[2] What was also apparent from the personal experiences shared was that faculty of color have no choice but to be perceived as hostile to the visions of those white students who are invested in pastoral, white narratives of the region. The very physical existence of these faculty, particularly when they are women of color, in a position of authority over these students challenges the white supremacy upon which those ideas are constructed.[3] As reported in the symposium, the backlash against faculty of color ranged from passive-aggressive behaviors in class to racial slurs yelled from passing vehicles and written in online forums. Those who, like me, are teaching southern studies while white, have a choice as to whether we will be perceived as hostile to that image of white supremacy. It can be more comfortable to choose not to actively confront the dominant narratives that so many of our white students bring to the classroom, but some of us are doing so anyway. And during the teaching roundtable at our symposium, some of us who are white also shared examples of public intimidation and threats used by students against instructors who challenged students' white supremacist worldviews, including being identified or threatened as "communists," "liberals," or "race traitors" in writing or verbally, sometimes in public spaces outside of campus.

Reflecting on this roundtable, as a southern white woman who specializes in the history of southern gender and racial politics, I realized that omitting discussion and dissection of white supremacy in class never seemed like an option to me, although I recognize that I had made the choice of specializations. And that choice, while it had been made years before I stepped into a southern studies classroom, was a privilege that many faculty members of color do not have. I could see why, in an environment in which some of us are currently facing negative consequences as a result of teaching more representative, multicultural narratives of southern experiences, others of us who can still choose are opting not to challenge the ideological demands that it appears a significant portion of our students bring to our classrooms. However, by choosing our own apparent comfort, those of us who are white professors of southern studies students are disproportionately burdening our colleagues of color, even when their own challenge to our students is their existence. And we are choosing to intellectually and developmentally stunt all of our students, regardless of race. This seems particularly tragic as our students do not know that they have already taken the necessary steps to make greater sense of the environment around them when they enrolled in our classes. The vague premise that Jon Smith put forward in that disheartening dialogue in Oxford was that teaching southern studies doesn't have to be this way. I am convinced that he is right, but more of us have to take ownership in believing that southern studies pedagogy can be different and in actively making it so in order for that to be true. As with many things, this apparently simple solution isn't really that simple at all. It involves understanding the psychology behind what is going on our classrooms and using that greater awareness to the benefit of our students and our colleagues who labor with us.

For me, the most promising related psychological research supporting this assertion came in the form of a series of studies conducted by Marshall P. Duke, Amber Lazarus, and Robyn Fivush of Emory University. Seeking to find useful indictors of likely psychological prognosis, these psychologists encountered a clinician who over the course of thirty years of practice had determined that she could, with an abnormally high degree of accuracy, predict the likelihood that her patients would positively respond to treatment or behavioral modifications based on how much a patient knew about his or her family history. In fact, she had come to view this factor as such a reliable indicator that she had "admittedly limited involvement with the formal clinical literature" by the time that Duke, Lazarus, and Fivush learned about her personal methodology.[4] Intrigued by this practitioner's contentions, the three researchers developed what they termed the "Do You Know" (DYK) scale of measurement to determine adolescents' knowledge of their familial histories. Using twenty yes-or-no questions, these psychologists analyzed the scores of forty adolescents between the ages of ten and fourteen who were not related to one another. All forty were also given the Family Functioning Scale, the Family Traditions Scale, the Rosenberg Self-Esteem Scale, the Children's Manifest Anxiety Scale, and the Child Behavior Checklist.[5] Using the data from all of these assessment tools, Duke, Lazarus, and Fivush determined that "the more children said they knew about their family histories the lower their anxiety, the higher their self-esteem, the more internally controlled they were, the better their family functioning, the fewer their behavior problems, and the more cohesive their families."[6] Basically, the more these children knew about their family stories, the more resilient they were likely to be moving forward in all aspects of their lives.

However, Duke, Lazarus, and Fivush caution against the idea that teaching an individual, simple, unrelated facts about their family would serve the same goal of increasing individual resilience. In their larger Family Narratives Project, Fivush, Duke, and their collaborators determined that those individuals who knew a broad range of information about their families had family members, generally mothers or grandmothers, who served as storytellers at family gatherings that happened with relative frequency.[7] These repeated family gatherings often fostered a high degree of family cohesion and the development in the children of what Duke and Fivush term an "intergenerational self" in a subsequent study with Jennifer Bohanek.[8] Those who possessed this intergenerational self not only knew facts about individual family members but also had clear senses of complex outcomes within their own families and realistic understandings of relative successes and failures. They understood themselves as being part of a complex system of people, each part of which had different experiences, attributes, challenges, and gifts.

Perhaps most importantly for those of us in education, according to Duke, Lazarus, and Fivush, it is this sense of an intergenerational self that indicates whether an individual has an internal locus of control.[9] An internal locus of control is an individual's fundamental belief that they have a great deal of control over what will and does happen in their lives. People with an internal locus of control view their own actions and choices as having logical consequences and as being the primary determinants of their life trajectories. A heightened internal locus of control has been positively correlated to academic achievement as well as decreased anxiety in academic environments in a number of studies.[10] Therefore, it is not surprising that Duke, Lazarus, and Fivush identified a positive correlation between knowledge of family history and fewer behavioral problems, including disruptive classroom and other social interactions.[11]

I contend that there is similarly a positive correlation between knowledge of one's multicultural regional identity and an individual's internal locus of control, behaviors, and even academic achievement. Just as Duke, Lazarus, and Fivush maintain that it is not adequate to teach individuals their family narrative as single-dimensional facts in order to stimulate positive personal outcomes, I also argue that it is not enough for us, as southern studies professors, to simply teach our students about the multicultural South as unrelated, segregated experiences in order to achieve the most potentially positive personal outcomes. Rather, like the family structures Duke, Lazarus, and Fivush observed in their Family Narratives Project, those of us who teach southern studies must actively engage our students in a multilayered, focused attempt to aid them in developing an intergenerational, intellectual self. Whether they are from this region or not, our students should be encouraged to see the connections between those living in the South (or who have lived in the South) as extending to them as part of complex and interrelated systems. Like the individuals in the studies by Duke, Lazarus, Fivush, and Bohanek, it is also imperative that our students gain complicated understandings of the region, fraught with successes, failures, ambiguities, conflicting outcomes, and continuing debates. Only then will we, as professors, be wisely using our "gathering" time to aid our students in developing and strengthening their internal loci of control.

I believe that many students are already taking action, without us, contextualizing themselves in our classrooms, often without our choosing to be aware of the ramifications of their doing so. To achieve more positive educational outcomes, we, as instructors, need to be more open to engaging our students productively and intellectually. One of the things that I found overwhelming when I first began teaching the freshman introduction to southern studies at the University of Mississippi was the frequency with which students came to my office and broke down crying. I have always made myself available, allotting office hours to meet with students, and, having taught for several years prior to coming to Mississippi, I was well aware that students cry for a host of reasons when they visit faculty offices.[12] However, what was happening at Mississippi was different. For one thing, the frequency of the tears was so intense that I had to stop stocking expensive tissues, being unable to afford to replace multiple boxes each month. The students were also crying for different reasons in Mississippi. There was the normal grade- and stress-related crying, but the bulk of the tears fell into what I began terming "southern identity crying." As we proceeded through southern studies lectures during my first semester, I believe that I was inadvertently stumbling into Duke, Lazarus, and Fivush's family narratives. Without my intentionally framing lectures and discussions as such, the students were placing themselves within the contexts of intergenerational, representative Souths. When discussing sharecropping and systemic poverty in the South, I would have a group of ostensibly upper-middle-class students, in this case primarily white, in my office, confessing to having income variances in their family or friendships. These students would often cry, and I would turn to pull books off of my shelves, recommending readings that placed whatever story they had to tell in much larger contexts, seeking to comfort them by letting them intellectually know that they weren't alone. The weeks we discussed mixed-race identities, multiracial families, and the legal implications of race in the region, the discussions in class were often tense and awkward, and then more students, of various races, ethnicities, and occasionally national origins, would come to my office asking questions about various personal situations in the present or past. More tears would flow, and more books came off of the shelves. Gendered lectures had the same effects. They brought confessions of rapes, miscarriages, and pregnancy scares, concerns about mothers, sisters, girlfriends, boyfriends, and transitions. More and more books came off of my shelves.

I maintain that many of the students in my office were crying in large part because they personally lacked the intergenerational self that Fivush, Bohanek, and Duke described. That deficit is representative in southern studies classrooms, which are disproportionately white, as white supremacy is based on the fallacy of a monolithic white experience within the structural politics of whiteness, particularly white womanhood, always being privileged.[13] That is why our white students so often come seeking the antebellum experience. They believe that it was a period in which whiteness was privileged above all else, and while that is true systemically, they do not recognize that many of their ancestors were also discriminated against within the white supremacist system for various reasons, including the fact that many of them were not considered white, were poor, or were female.[14] This conflicting reality of whiteness means that many white southerners, particularly those who are conditioned to prioritize Lost Cause explanations of "heritage," cannot reconcile an intergenerational self with the dominant narrative of white supremacy, which as Fivush, Bohanek, and Duke contend, compromises their resiliency, their very ability to thrive as individuals.

However, what southern studies can make possible for this specific kind of white student is a greater understanding of white supremacy while also personally reconciling the facts that they may know about the individuals in their experience, familial and otherwise, with a narrative that makes an intergenerational self more possible. It is based on an unconventional "family" in the sense that Duke, Lazarus, and Fivush present, but as Alix Chapman very effectively argues in his essay in this collection, at times the most functional kin networks for the individual are not familial. In this case, the intergenerational self would be formed based on an intellectual totality of one's personal and scholarly experience. The formation of this intellectual, intergenerational self can increase a southern studies student's resilience but only if the instructor is willing to take on the personal risk of becoming a target of backlash and do the heavy lifting of introducing the interconnected, diverse "family" narrative, one that includes individuals of varying races, ethnicities, religions, socio-economic backgrounds, sexual orientations, and gender identities, in fact, a representative South across time periods. As a historian, I am particularly drawn to the concept of the intergenerational self as a core educational principle as it results in classes that are more historically accurate. Catering to white supremacist, patriarchal, heteronormative illusions of history is far too limited and imprecise, which is why handing students books with more context helped to provide stability and eventually, as Duke, Lazarus, and Fivush argue, resiliency.

It would, however, be a mistake to view this pedagogical approach as a means to cure white supremacy as such. Taking this approach to teaching cannot be an attempt to somehow move students toward a singular political, social, or ideological position, even one as nearly universally defined as positive within southern studies as eliminating white supremacy. Rather, as Duke, Lazarus, and Fivush emphasize, the objective is to help students develop an internal locus of control, recognizing that they have the individual ability to control their educational experience and ultimately take from it what they, as individuals, most desire or need to accomplish their personal goals. As a result, the ultimate goal for students would be that they would internalize the information covered in a southern studies class in whatever ways they saw fit. As I have implemented this approach in my own classes, I have viewed my work with individual students as successful if they feel that they are in complete control of their worldview (as opposed to feeling that I am attempting to control them). Many of my white students who are invested in white supremacy remain confident in their convictions. If they are open to learning from the class, the difference that I see in them is that they are more secure in themselves. Even as their fundamental belief systems remain intact, they are, along with their classmates, more resilient and have more informed understandings of their region. Their decreased anxiety manifests in markedly less anger toward their classmates and usually toward me as well. And the point about their classmates is for me particularly important. More moderate whites, liberal whites, and students of color of various political bents, who have proven to be the vast majority of the students in all of my classes, are also more resilient and better informed, something that I would not have seen had I assumed that all of the white students were equally angry white supremacists.

Ultimately, over the course of my first year in Mississippi, I was able to stem the tide of tears in my office by moving more of this contextual work into the classroom. I did so in a number of ways. First, I introduced more theoretical work into my lectures. This did not mean that I devoted entire lectures to critical theory. Instead, I referenced specific works as they related to my subject matter, framing them in as simple terms as I could and expressing my excitement over having discovered these ideas myself. I tried to help my students see how the theory had helped me to make sense of what I was showing to them. My assumption was that if I demonstrated one application and made theory seem personally, intellectually liberating, as it had been for me, they would figure out other uses for themselves. I also began ending every class with a "suggested reading" list, explaining possible connections to class materials. Essentially, I was trying to make that step of self-revelation that often happened in my office less necessary for all of the students to have to take in order to get the books off of my shelves. The results of that process were mostly positive. Visits to my office hours continued, although tears became less frequent. Many students came prepared with questions related to the issues raised in class or via the reading lists themselves. During this transitional period in my pedagogical practices, I believe that I was witnessing the decreasing anxiety associated with the development of internal loci of control as my students' intellectual, intergenerational selves were maturing.

Negatives were nonetheless present and heartbreaking. One was a white frat boy from Louisiana who stayed after class many days to discuss his stereotypically white "southerness" with my white male colleague. He engaged in class and was doing marginally well, although he was quite wedded to a narrow, white conception of the region, and then I discussed Virginia Dominguez's research in Louisiana and the ways in which her findings had impacted my own understanding of race, including her conclusion that the vast majority of those who identify as white in the state are actually mixed race.[15] My co-editor, who is an African American woman from Louisiana, argues that such a revelation regarding race would not have been news to anyone from Louisiana. Based on my own experience and historical research in Louisiana, I come closer to agreeing with her when speaking about the African American population, which is much more open and informed about their complex racial pasts.[16] However, as Ruth Frankenberg writes, "whiteness, as a set of normative cultural practices, is visible most clearly to those it definitively excludes and those to whom it does violence. Those who are securely housed within its borders usually do not examine it."[17] I contend that even knowing that there is a sizable mixed-race population that is considered "black" by definitions constructed by a white supremacist system does not mean that white people would analyze whiteness in such a way that there would intellectually be an equivalent mixed-race "white" population. Here again, if a white person holds this belief that whiteness can somehow be "pure" while simultaneously knowing that their personal experience holds or might hold exceptions, this would also compromise their ability to form an intergenerational self as that information that conflicts with their ideology would have to be rationalized in illogical ways that would produce anxiety. I believe that when we teach about mixed-race identities, we can often see this anxiety at work in our classrooms.

During this discussion of Dominguez's work, several students engaged positively as we discussed the impossibility of using skin tone, even that as pale as my own, to identify race. All of them were initially either students of color or international students. Eventually a few white southern students joined into the discussion, although they were always careful to stress the Louisiana aspect of the study, as if to distance themselves from the implications.[18] Then I noticed this particular Louisiana student's "friends" laughing at him, elbowing him knowingly, clearly and visibly insinuating that he was not white. He never returned to class. For him, the anxiety was too high. If we are going to engage in the potentially psychologically traumatic work of challenging and expanding worldviews, which I believe that Duke, Lazarus, Fivush, and Bohanek's research makes clear that we should, I also believe that we must do so in a psychologically safe environment. That's why so many of my students chose to come to my office to do this work privately, and as I moved it into the classroom I had an obligation to them to be aware of that.

As Wharton Business School professor Adam Grant contends, psychological safety exists when those who are present "believe that [they] can take a risk without being penalized or punished."[19] And Amy Edmondson of Harvard Business School has proven in her research that an environment in which psychological safety is fostered promotes innovation, creativity, and learning.[20] In order to achieve the optimum educational experience in our classrooms, students, particularly undergraduate students, must not feel that they will be penalized or punished for the emotional and even at times the judgmental distance that they must traverse in order to process the new political, economic, demographic, historical, and sociological realities with which they are being confronted in southern studies courses designed to introduce them to a more complex understanding of the region.

It is imperative that as instructors we at times allow difficult conversations to take place. This becomes particularly complicated in the context of our subject matter, the admitted investment in white supremacy present in our subjects and our students, and the emotional toll that this can take on all of the students, regardless of race, as well as all of us as instructors, particularly those of color. It is important that some of the raw, insensitive questions be given vent in class, in an environment in which the professor has created the psychological safety for students to feel comfortable engaging and learning from one another and only marginally from the instructor.[21] However, as we are structuring our classes, we have to be aware that these sorts of issues are going to emerge and that the students are going to ineptly and sometimes painfully broach subjects and phrase comments and questions. Fundamentally, I have no good solution for this. There are times when I close my eyes and wish that a student had not said the horrible thing they let pass from their lips, but more often than not by the time I open my eyes to respond, another student is already dissecting the comment and providing supportive evidence. Other times, I wish I could take back my own words as I see the pain the past has inflicted on a student. And later I am grateful when that person comes to my office to discuss the beautiful and thought-provoking connection made in that moment. Ultimately, if we are going to make the development of an intellectual, intergenerational self a goal, then we must also pay close attention to how we structure our lectures and discussions so that those who need to personally process inner demons, pains, and conflicts have a better chance to do so outside the classroom—in office hours or on their own.[22] And then we must trust that, like all pedagogical decisions, it will not always work out as planned. Sometimes it will accidentally work out better.

Building on this bit of optimism, I contend that honestly believing in our white students' ability to embrace a representative multicultural southern narrative is an essential component in creating a psychologically safe environment in which personal growth and understanding is possible. While this may seem like a naïve statement of wishful thinking, I also base this contention on my research into educational psychology. In their work examining the connections between teachers' expectations of their students' giftedness and potentials as well as long-term intellectual development and performance, Robert Rosenthal and Lenore Jacobson discovered a direct correlation between teachers' beliefs and students' performance. In their study including eighteen different classrooms, 20 percent of the students were randomly selected and identified to their teachers as "bloomers," students who showed atypical and exceptional potential for growth during a school year. All of the students were given tests measuring their verbal and reasoning skills as well as their IQs at the beginning and end of the year, and those who their teachers believed were "bloomers" gained an average of twelve IQ points in that year as compared to the eight IQ points gained by the others.[23] Lee Jussim and Kent Harber argue that the reason why students like these "bloomers"—only exceptional in that their teachers believed them to be so—achieve disproportionately positive outcomes is because teachers' faith in their students leads them to create self-fulfilling prophecies for their students.[24] When we, as teachers, expect our students to perform in certain ways academically, we treat them in ways that are far more likely to yield positive results. We encourage them through our actions and our words. We create assignments that assume their success, and we frame our discussions anticipating that they will make positive contributions toward their own education. Fiseha Teklu and R. Sreevalsa Kumar have found this to be the case even when students have profound emotional and behavioral disorders. In their research into the impact of teachers' expectations, they found that teachers' beliefs in their students had potential positive impacts not only on educational outcomes but also on emotional and behavioral outcomes.[25] According to Teklu and Kumar, our students can feel better and act better if we believe that they can.

It might be tempting to argue that this research is all focused on children and therefore not applicable to the adults who we teach. Even Teklu and Kumar limited their work to studying secondary education and resisted what seems, at times, to be logical extensions of their sex education research into what they frame as something separate: adulthood. However, Don Eden has published two works analyzing the ways in which the Israeli Defense Forces have successfully applied the strategy of intentionally and randomly identifying recruits as gifted in an effort to positively impact training, and those who are serving in the Israeli military are roughly the same ages as those who sit in our southern studies classrooms.[26] I argue that we, as southern studies professors, should apply and extend this research to our teaching of southern studies. We should strive to believe that our students, all of them, even the white ones who come invested in the Lost Cause, can and will bloom in our classes, learning about representative, multicultural Souths and various theoretical approaches to understanding the region as a multiplicity of concepts that have evolved over time. If we believe that they, all of them, are capable of this intellectual growth, then they are more likely to excel at doing so.

Finally, I chose to open this piece with a Viktor Frankl quote for several reasons. Frankl, a Holocaust survivor, used his personal experience and training as a psychologist to found logotherapy, a psychiatric technique that encourages "therapists to look beyond patients' past or present problems to help them choose productive futures by making personal choices and taking responsibility for them."[27] Throughout his almost fifty-year career, Frankl also personally modeled and counseled others to maintain a commitment to inclusion and multicultural understanding, and in *Man's Search for Meaning* he combined autobiography and psychological theory to argue that the suffering of life could be used by individuals to find purpose for living and thus propel the sufferer to not only survive but thrive. Taking this approach to life meant that Frankl became popularly known as an advocate for what he termed "tragic optimism," being optimistic in the face of pain, guilt, and even death.[28] As we were gathered in Oxford, Mississippi, for the Transforming New South Identities Symposium, there was a great deal of focus on our collective pasts as southern studies professors. A number of us, myself included, have endured at times frightening and demoralizing treatment at the hands of the people in our workspace about whom we most care, our students.[29] As a result, when we had the opportunity to discuss solutions, we chose instead to become mired in the past, trying to process our personal pain. However, as is evident from our research, all of us who were at that symposium are, like Frankl, personally dedicated to inclusion and expanding a complex understanding of the region we study. Perhaps when assessing our personal experiences teaching southern studies, like Frankl, we should "choose productive futures," where there is, I think, also cause for "tragic optimism."[30]

Helping students to develop internal loci of control and confidence in their abilities to comprehend and address the pressing problems of the South can provide an invaluable service not only to the students themselves but also to the region. While we may prefer, as I do, to intellectually conceptualize the region as something other than geographic, most of us are doing so while living in states where our legislatures and governors justify political decisions using gendered and racialized Lost Cause rhetoric, and millennials dependably fail to vote. We would do well to think of Henry Giroux's arguments in *On Critical Pedagogy*: "Education is fundamental to democracy and ... no democratic society can survive without a formative culture shaped by pedagogical practices capable of creating the conditions for producing citizens who are critical, self-reflective, knowledgeable and willing to make moral judgments and act in a socially responsible way."[31] Fundamentally we would all benefit from a generation of students who possess an intellectual, intergenerational self and an understanding of the South as a complex multicultural space, even if achieving this requires all who teach southern studies to choose to experience the discomfort of having done so more effectively.

Notes

Acknowledgments: As I pondered the idea of the intergenerational self and the power that professors have in helping students to contextualize themselves, I was frequently reminded of those who were my mentors and role models when I was an undergraduate interested in the interdisciplinary study of the South. I am intensely grateful to have been the student of Paul Armitstead, John Boles, Tom Charlton, Jim SoRelle, and John Wood, who introduced me to a broad range of human experiences and interdisciplinary ideas. I am similarly thankful to my PhD advisor, Wanda Hendricks, who expanded my world personally, professionally, and intellectually.

1. This experience in the classroom is not limited to the teaching of the southern experience. For an excellent analysis of resistance among white students in American classrooms and the impact this has on white and black faculty, as well as strategies for addressing that resistance, see Elias and Jones, "Two Voices from the Front Lines."

2. There is an ever-increasing and sizable literature examining the disproportionately negative and often discriminatory experiences that faculty of color, particular women, experience in higher education. See Gutiérrez y Muhs, Flores Niemann, González, and Harris, eds., *Presumed Incompetent*; Niles and Gordon, eds., *Still Searching for Our Mothers' Gardens*; TuSmith and Reddy, eds., *Race in the College Classroom*; Deborah White, ed., *Telling Histories*. In "No Rest for the Weary," Babara Combs, who began teaching in southern studies at the University of Mississippi when I did, explores what she experienced as "racial battle fatigue" (1). Henry Giroux has specifically examined the negative impact that this hostile environment toward educators of color has on students of color as part of *Disposable Youth*. While this essay focuses on the overwhelmingly white student population of southern studies courses at majority institutions, the negative psychological and educational impact that these educational spaces have on students of color should not be ignored and must also be addressed in order for the discipline to attract and retain a more diverse student body.

3. Many scholars have shown the gendered dynamics of the white supremacist system that operates in the United States generally and the South more specifically. See especially Christina Greene, *Our Separate Ways*; Shaw, *What a Woman Ought to Be and to Do*; R. Williams, *The Politics of Public Housing*; Hunter, *To 'Joy My Freedom*; Deborah White, *Too Heavy a Load*; J. Jones, *Labor of Love, Labor of Sorrow*; DuRoucher, *Raising Racists*. Valuable insights specifically into the sexual exploitation of African American women by white men also were included in Deborah White, *Ar'n't I a Woman*; McGuire, *At the Dark End of the Street*; Coffey, "The State of Louisiana v. Charles Guerand." Constructive insights into gendered conceptions of race used as a justification for violence, particularly lynching, are contained in J. Hall, *Revolt against Chivalry*; Dorr, *White Women, Rape, and The Power of Race in Virginia*; Rise, *The Martinsville Seven*; C. Robinson, *Dangerous Liaisons*; Waldrep, *African Americans Confront Lynching*; Sommerville, *Rape and Race in the Nineteenth-Century South*; Feimster, *Southern Horrors*.

4. Duke, Lazarus, and Fivush, "Knowledge of Family History," 269.

5. McCubbin, Thompson, and McCubbin, *Family Assessment*; Rosenberg, *Soci-*

ety and the Adolescent Self-Image; Reynolds and Richmond, "What I Think and Feel"; Achenbach, *Manual for the Child Behavior Checklist*.

6. Duke, Lazarus, and Fivush, "Knowledge of Family History," 270.

7. Bohanek, Martin, Fivush, and Duke, "Family Narrative Interaction and Children's Sense of Self," 47–50; Bohanek, Fivush, Zaman, and Lepore, "Narrative Interaction in Family Dinnertime Conversations," 505–11.

8. Ibid.; Fivush, Bohanek, and Duke, "The Intergenerational Self."

9. Duke, Lazarus, and Fivush, "Knowledge of Family History," 270.

10. C. Jones, Slate, and Marini, "Locus of Control, Social Interdependence, Academic Preparation, Age, Study Time and the Study Skills of College Students"; Cone and Owens, "Academic and Locus of Control Enhancements in Freshman Study Skills and College Adjustment Course"; Hazard and Nadeau, *Foundations for Learning*, 95–99.

11. Duke, Lazarus, and Fivush, "Knowledge of Family History," 268.

12. As Myra Green argued in her piece for *Chronicle of Higher Education*, it is not uncommon for some professors, particularly female faculty, to become listening ears for students—and occasionally fellow faculty members—during times of stress, academic or personal (M. Green, "Thanks for Listening"). This function of academia is also excessively carried by faculty of color as they disproportionately serve as faculty advisors and as mentors to underrepresented students. June, "The Invisible Labor of Minority Professors."

13. I contend that the intensity of the anxiety suffered by those students at Mississippi was unique in large part because their personal experiences made them feel as if they were nonconformist at a university that so very publically celebrates a singular and undeniably white southern identity.

14. See especially Jacobson, *Whiteness of a Different Color*; Wray, *Not Quite White* (2006).

15. See Domínguez, *White by Definition*.

16. See ibid.; Kein, *Creole*; Brasseaux, Fontenot, and Oubre, eds., *Creoles of Color*; Hirsch and Logsdon, *Creole New Orleans*; Rohrer and Edmonson's *The Eighth Generation Grows Up*.

17. Frankenberg, *White Women, Race Matters*, 228–29.

18. While this is a description of the first time I introduced Domínguez's work specifically into one of my classes, this racialized pattern of discussion is completely representative of subsequent class interactions with my work both in Mississippi and now at Memphis. At Memphis, I actually have fewer white students who engage in discussions of mixed-race identity in class. I think because there are more students of color in the classroom to carry the burden of discussion, white students do not feel the same pressure to overcome their anxiety in discussing the topic publicly.

19. Grant, *Give and Take*, 85.

20. Edmonson, "Learning from Mistakes Is Easier Said Than Done"; Edmondson, "Psychological Safety and Learning Behavior in Work Teams."

21. I believe that those of us who are white should take a greater role in creating and sustaining this environment as faculty of color will likely experience a greater

degree of personal discomfort and psychological pain as well as much lower teaching evaluations doing this alone. See especially Lazos, "Are Student Teaching Evaluations Holding Back Women and Minorities?"; Chang, "Where's the Violence?"; TuSmith, "Out on a Limb."

22. For all of the controversy over trigger warnings in higher education at the moment, this simple reality of kindness and human decency is their fundamental purpose. (See Manne, "Why I Use Trigger Warnings.") *Teaching Tolerance*, a publication and program of the Southern Poverty Law Center, has excellent materials for helping teachers to think through teaching issues of difference and diversity in the classroom as well as materials that can be used in class. I use *Teaching Tolerance* both for my own classes and, more often, as reference material I provide to my students who are considering being teachers or who ask for recommendations for programs where they will be working with students of their own. See Teaching Tolerance, http://teachingtolerance.org. The program Facing History and Ourselves (http://facinghistory.org) is also beneficial for helping younger students contextualize their personal experiences.

23. Rosenthal and Jacobson, "Teachers' Expectancies"; Rosenthal and Jacobson, *Pygmalion in the Classroom*.

24. Jussim and Harber, "Teacher Expectations and Self-Fulfilling Prophecies."

25. Teklu and Kumar, "Teachers' Expectations on Academic Achievement and Social Skills and Behaviour."

26. Eden, "Pygmalion without Interpersonal Contrast Effects"; Eden, "Self-Fulfilling Prophecies in Organizations."

27. Frankl, *Man's Search for Meaning*, 164.

28. Frankl, "The Case for Tragic Optimism," in ibid., 137–54.

29. Since the symposium, the increase in high-profile shooting deaths on college campuses has generated much discussion and a general climate of fear in both *Chronicle of Higher Education* and *Inside Higher Ed*. In December 2015, in the aftermath of shootings at Umpqua Community College in Oregon and Delta State University in Mississippi, the *Chronicle* conducted an informal survey to get a sense of faculty fears related to the potential of mass shootings at their institutions. The resulting published piece is haunting, perhaps largely because it contains such familiar reflections. Thomason and O'Leary, "See How Worries about Shootings Affect Readers' Lives."

Most recently, Katherine Mangan, who teaches at the University of Texas, contributed a piece analyzing the atmosphere of apprehension among those teaching at her university, not only in an academic setting where a mass shooting is a historical reality as well as present fear but also as the State of Texas passed legislation allowing the open carrying of firearms on all state college campuses. This legislation specifically prohibited the banning of weapons in classrooms and was passed over the objections and protests of University of Texas faculty. Mangan's piece provides excellent context of both the legislative reality and the complex campus environment, including information on other state laws that allow open carry on college campuses. Mangan, "Under the Gun."

I recognize that these realities have added substantial weight to the concerns that many of my southern studies colleagues feel, especially as I take part in faculty meetings where we discuss responses to active shooters, as I teach political history in a large auditorium with multiple exits that cannot be locked or blocked, and as I work in a state that recently passed legislation making my campus open carry for full-time employees over the objections of many in education, including the universities' police chiefs. Izadi, "Faculty Can Carry Handguns on Public College Campuses Under Controversial New Tennessee Law."

Even in this environment, I, like John Warner in a recent piece in *Inside Higher Ed*, believe that the threats we face on campuses continue to disproportionately affect some of us more than others. And I still conclude as he does here: "As an instructor, there are limits to what I can do when I become afraid *for* my students.... At best, I can practice a pedagogy that takes student wellbeing into account.... I don't want to overreact to tragedies like the murder of [University of Southern California] Prof[essor] [William] Klug and the killer's spouse. But I can't ignore it either." Warner, "On Being Afraid of Students."

30. Frankl, *Man's Search for Meaning*, 137–54, 164.

31. Giroux, *On Critical Pedagogy*, 3. Giroux has written many works that are essential in conceptualizing the science of teaching critically in the context of modern politics. Of particular value to those who are not yet familiar with his work is *Teachers as Intellectuals*, which includes a forward by Peter McLaren that outlines Giroux's intellectual development up through the late 1980s. Giroux also wrote a recent piece exploring his analysis of the neoliberal politics surrounding Hurricane Katrina. This may be of particular interest to those in Southern studies. Giroux, "Drowning Democracy."

Southern Transformations

Three Documentary Films by Anne Lewis

ANNE LEWIS
LEIGH ANNE DUCK

Introduction
LEIGH ANNE DUCK

When I learned that Jodi Skipper and Michele Coffey had invited Anne Lewis to present a paper at their symposium Transforming New South Identities, I congratulated them on their brilliance: though better known in Appalachian than in southern studies, Lewis has been making vital documentaries about social and economic change in the region for decades. I came to know her work while looking for resources on globalization and the U.S. South, and *Morristown: In the Air and Sun* (2007) delivers. Combining the stories of Tennessean and Mexican workers seeking to navigate changing political regulations and economic circumstances, it provides insights into familial, union, and corporate cultures, into the efforts of workers to organize for better working conditions and to achieve better cross-cultural understanding, and even into macroeconomic forces. To me it has stood out as a model for engaged scholarship: it provides information people can use in a format they can appreciate.[1]

Accordingly, this chapter on transdisciplinarity combines Lewis's symposium essay, which discussed her motivations and methods in three of her films, with alternating sections in which I explore parallels between these documentaries and scholarly research. I consider *Anne Braden: Southern Patriot* (2012) in relation to debates over documentary representation and the question of how to render a film compelling as well as informative. *Morristown* and *Justice in the Coalfields* (1995) illuminate the dichotomy between efforts to represent cultural traditions and the challenges of depicting societies in the midst of transformation. By contextualizing Lewis's work in relation to documentary theory and history—especially concerning Appalshop, the film collective with which she has long been associated—I hope to demonstrate how these films speak to methodological questions in academic research as well, particularly how to conceptualize relationships between space, time, and identity, and how to present knowledge in ways invigorating for our students and publics.

Declaration
ANNE LEWIS

I start with an Austin, Texas (ATX), Declaration in the spirit of Werner Herzog's Minnesota Declaration, in which he attacks cinema verité as being "devoid of verité. It reaches a merely superficial truth, the truth of accountants."[2] My Austin, Texas (ATX), Declaration on Southern Documentary Film states:

1. No character who speaks English should be subtitled in English. (It's okay if you subtitle everyone.)
2. To ask a question when you know the answer is the truth of lawyers.
3. It is impossible to simply observe the truth. Cinema verité provokes the truth.
4. Never ask the subject to rephrase your question.
5. Members of the Republican Party must not be allowed near cameras.
6. No southern documentary film should cost more than a modest house.
7. The best documentary subjects are penguins. That creates a problem for southern filmmakers unless they live very far south indeed.
8. The best southern documentary filmmaker lived in Berkeley Hills.
9. Every southern documentary film is about race except for those set in Appalachia, which are about class and sometimes race too.
10. Any southern documentary film worth its salt has violence, sex, and lack of articulation. That's why we call each other's films stereotypical.
11. Southern documentary film budgets should rarely include air travel.
12. Don't hire vegans for southern shoots.

Although my content is almost opposite, I follow Herzog's form. I criticize the great maker of *Grizzly Man* because cinema verité is what inspired me to make films. So I figure that if Herzog could indulge himself so deeply, I should as well—in the spirit of freedom of speech and the silliness that comes from generalities.

Illuminating Truths, Engaging Viewers
LEIGH ANNE DUCK

However intensely Anne Lewis and Werner Herzog disagree about cinema verité, they share a taste for manifestos that combine distinctive wit with documentary wisdom.³ Herzog's version (which pauses to contemplate the efforts of Minnesota's governor at the time, ex-wrestler Jesse Ventura, to contend with a rash of snowmobiling accidents even Ventura regards as "stupid") posits a "poetic, ecstatic truth" against the "superficial[ity]" of mere "facts," which can seem as banal and uninformative as "stones" or, at their most revelatory, appear so "strange and bizarre" as to be "unbelievable." Though he attributes the obsession with facts to cinema verité—by which he actually appears to mean more narrowly "direct" or observational cinema—this tension between displaying information and, in Herzog's terms, "illuminati[ng]" truth is central to documentary filmmaking and arguably other forms of representing the world, including scholarship.⁴ In theorizing documentary, after all, Bill Nichols insists that it is at least "kin" to other "discourses of sobriety," including numerous social sciences.⁵ But while such modes of representation seek to provide information and analysis, documentary films, as Elizabeth Cowie argues, also stimulate desires for spectacle—the "fascinating pleasure" of seeing through another's gaze.⁶ Not simply a paradox, this duality suggests how documentary can move as well as inform: as Cowie claims, it "*engages us* with the actions and *feelings* of social actors" (emphasis added).⁷

For scholars, then, documentary offers not only a medium for conveying information but also a venue through which to contemplate problems and strategies in the representation of actuality. Researchers cannot go as far as "fabrication" in our quest for "deeper strata" of meaning—a practice Herzog advocates and which long diminished his reputation as a documentary filmmaker—but neither can we be satisfied with "the truth of accountants."⁸ Indeed, one volume in southern studies—Melanie Benson Taylor's *Disturbing Calculations*—argues that we must instead demystify the "fetish of number," the "principles of human quantification and commodification" that shaped both slavery and later capitalist practices.⁹ Such goals have always been central to Anne Lewis's films, which seek precisely to expose how southern and national wealth have derived from the abusive devaluing of entire swaths of the southern population—African Americans, Latinas and Latinos, and white poor and working classes.

But if a preoccupation with data threatens to obscure important questions about ethics and human relations, facts nonetheless remain necessary for understanding these issues—a need well demonstrated by Herzog's 2011 documentary set in Texas, *Into the Abyss: A Tale of Death, a Tale of Life*. This film's first shot positions Reverend Richard Lopez, described as a "Death House

Chaplain," in front of a field of grave-marking crosses with, as is revealed in later shots, only numbers to distinguish them. Herzog, in keeping with his quest for "mysterious and elusive" truths, asks the reverend to speak about his duties in the process of execution and also about chance encounters in his life, including one with a squirrel.[10] Their conversation reveals the wonder and sorrow of an individual seeking to behave compassionately in the midst of a lethal enterprise But those crosses suggest the need for an accountant's truth also, as they testify to a large but diegetically indeterminate number of lives taken by the state. Skillfully eliciting individual stories and affects, Herzog chooses not to situate them in relation to information concerning larger social dynamics and structures, but this context could have contributed to the film's revelatory power.[11]

This choice between spectacle or "stony" facts exists alongside another danger, as either strategy can marginalize persons being depicted, a danger abundantly apparent in documentaries concerning southern Appalachia. Lewis has focused on this area since 1973, when she began working with Barbara Kopple on *Harlan County USA* (1976) as associate director and assistant camerawoman.[12] During the 1960s, this region had been the subject of numerous televised exposés focusing on poverty, pieces that, however well intentioned, nonetheless represented the region as aberrational. One potent episode title from the CBS program *The Twentieth Century*, for example, was "Depressed Area, U.S.A.," and such representations left many in the region wary of "decontextualized images ... that only reinforced negative stereotypes and condescension."[13] In such a context, observational documentary, simply by departing from authoritative narration, could well seem a significantly more engaging and democratic form of representation. As visual anthropologist Jay Ruby argues, this representational mode offers viewers the opportunity "to hear people tell their stories and observe their lives instead of being told what they think and the meaning of their behavior."[14] This goal was vigorously embraced by the filmmakers at Appalshop, the collaborative workshop Lewis later joined, but she had already decided that, for her, documentary must involve a "point of human connection" with the subjects of the film—a way to "directly involve the community in the film."[15] Her work, then, exemplifies the interactive strain of the verité tradition.

Introducing her symposium paper, Lewis noted that it "in some ways contains the authenticity and subjectivity of documentary film since it quotes from film for source material," and these quotations reveal something of how she understands what documentary can convey, as well as to what purpose. Two linked themes emerge powerfully in her comments: an emphasis on the fullness and specificity of persons—who should be asked not to recite the expected but to provide their accounts of the truth—and an interest in social transformation. Noting, in a previous interview, the danger of making a film that turns out to be "obscure and unlikely to attract audiences," Lewis argues that, in documentaries focusing on musicians and artists, "you want as much of the actual person as you can get"—and that is clearly true of her "social justice pieces" as well, the films she calls her "most meaningful."[16]

Anne Braden: Southern Patriot (2012), though a biographical documentary, certainly fits in this category, as it uncovers a history of leftist organizing rarely discussed in the contemporary United States. While some of its images are familiar from popular and nationalist accounts of the U.S. mass civil rights movement, in which African Americans confronted southern white supremacy to win their constitutional rights to vote and access to public spaces and institutions, this film situates those images in a narrative concerning struggles that remain far more contentious, such as economic inequality and the right to challenge dominant national values.[17] As Braden argues in the film, "The powers that be in this country have just totally distorted what [Martin Luther King Jr.] was. . . . He wasn't a dreamer; he was a revolutionary!"[18]

Restoring this history through interviews and archival footage, *Anne Braden: Southern Patriot* demonstrates continuities between past organizing and contemporary movements against anti-black police violence, for LGBT rights, and over economic and environmental causes, but all of these are focalized in the film through one woman, her relationships, and the insights these provoke. As viewers see Braden develop from an adorably serious child to a still-determined elderly woman—images always embedded in retrospective commentary from her and from activist colleagues, as well as in documents and stories that provide social context—we are moved not simply to identify with Braden (the specificities of her life are too clearly defined) but rather to identify with her desire, which she names, in the film's last interview with her, as the "glimpse [of] a different world to live in . . . what you want to be a part of."[19] In this film, the seasoned activist Braden and the activist filmmakers Lewis and Mimi Pickering collaborate in illuminating and stimulating the desire for social transformation.

Inspiration
ANNE LEWIS

In 2004, Mimi Pickering and I convinced Anne Braden to be the subject of our documentary film, *Anne Braden: Southern Patriot*. That was not an easy task. Braden, hailed by Dr. Martin Luther King Jr. in his 1963 "Letter from Birmingham Jail" as eloquent and prophetic, was not enamored of the idea of a film about herself. She was much more interested in expressing ideas. A year before she died, Anne said, "I may not know a lot but I know something about white folks because I've been one for 80 years. And I know that us white folks, we will do anything in the world rather than face the truth about what racism—and I prefer to call it white supremacy which is what it is—has done to us and to the country."[20]

Anne spoke of the need for transformation—personal and social. And she railed against the notion of a New South, knowing full well that the race and class relationships that were the basis of the Old South remained intact. She said about her education during World War II at Randolph-Macon Woman's College, "All through history there's somebody coming along saying there's a new south. But we considered ourselves the new south and we rejected our parents' ideas of segregation. Sort of—kind of like we rejected their ideas about sex, which we did."[21] Her rejection of segregation was so complete that it landed both her and her husband in jail in a housing desegregation battle in Louisville, Kentucky, in 1954. Braden rejected any idea that made capitalism synonymous with progress and democracy and that failed to expose the system of white supremacy. Both ideas are the basis of formulations of a New South.

The term "New South" comes from Henry Grady of the *Atlanta Constitution* who sold the notion of societal change based on industrial development while stating that the supremacy of the white race in the South had to be maintained forever. In 1889 at the Bay State Club of Boston, he celebrated what he described as progressive transformation: "The old South rested everything on slavery and agriculture.... The new South presents a perfect democracy, the oligarchs leading ... a diversified industry that meets the complex needs of this complex age. The new South ... is thrilling with the consciousness of growing power and prosperity."[22] But Grady's vision called for continuing racial oppression. A year earlier, he stated: "The supremacy of the white race of the South must be maintained forever, and the domination of the negro race resisted at all points and at all hazards, because the white race is the superior race."[23] Where Grady suggested that the solution for poverty in the South was capital investment and industrialization, Anne Braden would say that we must challenge both race and class structures and their intersections. It's only then that we can achieve an understanding of the forces we must exert to achieve the transformation that is liberation. When Braden talks about transformation, she comes from a deeply personal and specific place, from her own heart. Unlike a Grady offering only what he thinks you want to hear, Braden always acknowledges her own identity as a white southerner and the hegemony of white supremacy. Here's a bone-chilling example from her life as a young newspaper reporter in Birmingham, Alabama:

> In the mornings before I came downtown I would call the courthouse, to see if anything big happened overnight, because if there had I'd have to skip breakfast usually and go on to the courthouse and get the details and get it into the first edition of the afternoon paper. When I would get downtown I often stopped

for breakfast and met a friend there. And the waitress was putting our food down on the table. And so he said anything doing? And I said no, just a colored murder. And I don't think I'd have ever thought anything about it if that black waitress hadn't been standing there. She was pouring coffee into our cups and her hand was sort of shaking, but there wasn't an expression on her face. It was like she had a mask. And my first impulse was that I wanted to get up and go put my arms around her and say, "Oh I'm sorry. I didn't mean that. It's not that I don't think the life of your people is important. It's my newspaper that says what news is." And then I just suddenly realized I had meant exactly what I'd said.[24]

The content, passion, and specificity of Anne's words give us real rather than abstract understanding. I try to picture myself using the same kind of words. Her honesty allows me to see myself, my upbringing, and my place for what they are—at least for that moment when I listen to her. My identity exposed, I am forced to move past what has been described by more arrogant people as white guilt to the personal and societal transformation that she demands. In my mind I hear and see Anne when I transcribe her words on transformation: "I was in a prison and life builds prisons around people and I had the prison that I was born white in a racist society. I was born privileged in a classist society. The hardest thing was class. I don't know that I could have ever broken out of what I call the race prison if I hadn't dealt with class. It's that assumption that is so embedded in you that you don't realize it's there, that your crowd is supposed to be running things."[25]

Anne does not see transformation as easy for white southerners. She describes transformation as gut-wrenching. "Our society—the one that had nurtured us and been pretty good to us—been pretty good to me. Our family, our friends, the people we loved and I never quit loving them, were just plain wrong. And that is painful. You really have to turn yourself inside out."[26] I remember she told us that progressive white southerners had an unusually easy time coming out against the Vietnam War because they'd already had to deal with race and after that all else was simple.

Anne saw identity as containing the possibilities of choice and change, perhaps even transformation, and in this way she created space for white southerners to join with blacks in struggle. She describes William Patterson, the black communist leader of Civil Rights Congress who wrote to her after she led a delegation of white women to protest their complicity in Willie McGee's execution in Mississippi under a false rape charge: "He said, you know you do have a choice. You don't have to be a part of the world of the lynchers. You can join the other America—the people who struggled against slavery, the people who railed against slavery, the white people who supported them, the people who all through Reconstruction struggled. He came on down through history of the people who have struggled against injustice—the Other America. And you know sometimes people will say just what you need to hear at that point. I was very young. And that's what I needed to hear. And that's what I felt like I joined."[27]

Changing Times, Changing Spaces
LEIGH ANNE DUCK

Documentary film has hardly been immune from the trend in social theory of which Doreen Massey has famously complained, in which space—associated with "stasis, ('simple') reproduction, nostalgia, emotion, aesthetics, the body"—is defined in opposition to time, which is aligned with "History, Progress, Civilization, Science, Politics and Reason."[28] On the contrary, particularly in its ethnographic variety, documentary has sometimes suggested—or at least staged the fantasy—that certain spaces, along with the people who live there, can be isolated in time as well, removed from the flow of history and the dynamism of politics. Fatima Tobing Rony dubs such films "salvage ethnography," as they purport to capture and reify ways of living far distanced from or threatened by the force of modernization.[29] Often generated by filmmakers fascinated with cultures they view as exotic or primitive, such trends can instead emerge as a form of resistance. For example, as a later academic consultant to Appalshop argued, the group's early films sought to represent "old-time, traditional forms of work," even though, taken as a whole, their oeuvre testifies to the anxieties, desires, and ambivalence created by socioeconomic change.[30]

Documentary style can exacerbate this tension or otherwise. As film scholar Jane Gaines argues, when verité (in its observational variant) determines to efface signs of the filmic apparatus and create the impression of direct transmission between a folk culture and a public characterized by its consumption of electronic media, it creates the impression of boundaries in time, "produc[ing] an image of the 'hold out' from modernization as a social isolate."[31] This danger helps to illuminate Anne Lewis's insistence that cinema verité must provoke—as opposed to simply observing—the truth. Rather than planning its representation of a scene (which reflects "the truth of lawyers," as well as an understanding that the space to be depicted is effectively frozen in time), it must learn from the setting it seeks to film and be open to contingency. Thus, for example, Gaines notes that even in situations where early Appalshop documentarists appeared to seek the illusion of pure and unmediated depiction of tradition, human interaction intervened. As documentary filmmakers and subjects conversed, the scene became recognizable as one of intergenerational dialogue, including a meeting of older and newer media.

This question of the relationship between space and time is important also for scholars in southern studies, for some of whom, like some specialists in Appalachian studies, the region constitutes, as Stephen L. Fisher and Barbara Ellen Smith note, a "beloved homeplace."[32] A resonant description of memories and feelings attached to a place, that phrase provides limited insight into social relations. Introducing an earlier set of brief essays in 2010, Smith asked an open question: "What are the pitfalls of place-based solidarity? What's wrong with nostalgia, insularity, or a homogenized view of Appalachia?"[33] In 2012 she and Fisher answered: such an approach "does not necessarily render [place] political for those in pursuit of social justice."[34] Analysis motivated by an interest in transformation must remain attuned to the dynamism within a space, as well as its relationships with other spaces. Massey argues that, even for the sake of accuracy, "it is necessary to insist on the irrefutable four-dimensionality (indeed, n-dimensionality) of things. Space is not static, nor time spaceless."[35] This seemingly abstract point was driven home to Appalshop filmmakers by changes in regional industry and the global economy. Elizabeth Barret, whose *Stranger with a Camera* (2000) focuses on how regional representations during the 1960s War on Poverty created acute and even dangerous feelings about "insiders and outsiders," later noted that structural economic change soon forced filmmakers to think about Appalachia—and their own audience—in relational terms: "What we know in this region because of coal mining is that national and international markets are affecting Letcher County, eastern Kentucky, and the mountains of Appalachia.... In the beginning, we probably saw Appalshop as a small, local, independent, filmmaking, sort of workshop. And then that changed pretty fast in terms of where the work was shown, how it got used, where the funding was coming from. There is no separation between the regional, local, national, and international."[36]

By the 1990s, when Anne Lewis began work on *Morristown: In the Air and Sun*, changing federal and international economic arrangements had led to a number of transformations. These included plant closings in Tennessee, an expansion of poorly paid jobs in Mexico along the northern border, and the flooding of the Mexican market with cheap agricultural products from the United States, all of which left laborers struggling and often moving to find jobs. In this context, Frances Ansley—a collaborator on *Morristown*—argued that effective organization for social justice campaigns "requires a serious engagement with issues of immigration and the global economy," including "cross-nation-solidarity."[37] But such a focus emphatically does not entail a lack of attention to local history. On the contrary, the film begins by remembering a previous instance of labor solidarity across differing social positions.

Morristown's first shot comprises a photograph of former slaves imprisoned under so-called Black Codes after Reconstruction as the narrator—Lewis herself—explains how late-nineteenth-century coal miners recognized that the oppression of convict laborers oppressed them too, depressing free workers' wages and making unionization nearly impossible. The Appalachians' response was to "storm the blockade" where the black workers were held. Linking this historical moment where racial divides had been profound and categorical to the contemporary one, in which "the global economy pits workers against each other," the narrator implies that now—as then—"solidarity" is the only answer.[38] Although the reference may be missed by some viewers, the film's title similarly embeds its values in Appalachian history: the phrase "in the air and sun" comes from a song written by Florence Reese during Harlan County's massive and violent 1931 mine strike, "Which Side Are You On?"

But *Morristown* also insists on the need to bridge differences. Focusing on developing relationships between Appalachian and Mexican workers, it subtitles every line in either Spanish or English, as needed. This anti-hierarchical practice—at a basic, affective level—establishes equivalence and challenge: there is no utterance that does not need to be translated, none without at least one simultaneous statement. Unlike films that—motivated by a fascination with the "exotic" or by resistance to modernization—might subtitle speakers of dialect in order to suggest their distance from social changes sweeping the globe, this film situates both Appalachian English and Mexican Spanish at the center of economic—and, as viewers soon see—sociopolitical transformation.

Transformation
ANNE LEWIS

Henry Grady's approach to New South development—capital investment and industrialization as the panacea for social ills—informed the recent crop of southern leaders who, unlike Grady, offered tolerance for a more integrated society. Coming more from the needs of industrial production and the service sector as well as self-interest, they promoted the South as a sunny place of complacent workers, low wages, lax regulations, and a hospitable culture.

In the 1990s, thousands of these New South workers were laid off as plants moved across international borders into the global South to find even cheaper wages. Barbara Knight, a Magnavox worker in East Tennessee, told us, "One day I came in and there was all this equipment that I worked on and it was in crates. And I said, well I'll just go over here and work on tuners. No, we're going to be boxing that up and sending it too. So all these big fixtures that I used to work on, these boards for big screen televisions—those were all in boxes and sent to Mexico."[39] A few years later she said, "There's not a VCR, there's not a radio, there's not a camcorder, there's none of that by any company built in this country. It's all gone."[40] Shirley Reinhart, a former General

Electric worker in Morristown, Tennessee, put it simply, "If they shut down the ports we'd be naked and barefooted."[41]

At the same time, a new group of disenfranchised and vulnerable workers, mainly from Mexico, were forced into the U.S. South by conditions in their own countries, in part caused by the expansion of neoliberalism. Agribusiness thrived, new temp agencies brokered workers and protected companies from questions of documentation, and processing plants were constructed with state and federal incentives in order to exploit the new workforce. The collective identity of small southern towns shifted with the changing demographics. Some saw this as broadening culture—a kind of cosmopolitan postracial identity—even though it was based on the exploitation of a new group of workers whose conditions at times resembled indentured servitude.

Filmed over an eight-year period in the mountains of East Tennessee, interior Mexico, and Ciudad Juarez, *Morristown: In the Air and Sun* is rooted in verité footage of factories, fields, union halls, Mexican stores, city parks, and employment agencies. The documentary travels to the U.S.-Mexican border with a group of black and white workers, to create deeper understanding of factory flight out of Morristown, and to interior Mexico to look at the forces that cause immigration. And then, abruptly, the story changes from workers jerked around and victimized by the neoliberal global economy to union solidarity, struggle, and victory. I remember an audience member with questionable exposure to documentaries asking me what I did to make *that* happen. I responded that it was inevitable. It's the age-old story of rebellion, organization, and victory. All we had to do was not finish the film and that wasn't so difficult given the major problems of funding an independent film.

Koch Foods had built a large chicken processing plant in the Morristown industrial park. Many of the Koch employees were undocumented, all were underpaid, and conditions inside the plant were horrendous—workers cut themselves and bled into the chicken, fluids from the chicken got in their eyes and infected them, and they (like Ford workers in the 1930s) didn't have bathroom breaks and worked dirty on the line. So, with the help of community members, they decided to organize into the United Food and Commercial Workers. On the election day, members of the organizing committee came out of the plant with hands held high. One woman from Oaxaca said, "I am also proud of my *compañeros* that finally broke through this barrier of fear in which the company held us. And we are so happy with their response because without being united we couldn't have done this. And now we won— 465 to 18!"[42]

Morristown, which had earlier gained recognition as one of the best places in the South for corporate incentives and a complacent nonunion workforce, emerged from the struggle of the workers as a place where it was possible to organize a labor union. This was a strange identity for a New South city that had sold itself time and time again to the highest corporate bidder on the backs of disorganized and exploited workers. As local activist Bill Troy put it: "It's going to be a good struggle. For the first time in this area, for a predominantly Hispanic workforce at a major corporation to elect to have an international union in the workplace is pretty remarkable. It's great. This won't be forgotten for sure. But if they would win, that would be amazing. Everywhere that these people come from in Mexico they will know that it's possible to come into the heart of the United States in the South and win an election and have a union and raise your wages and have dignity in the place and be able to stand up and talk for yourself. It will be terrific."[43]

Yet a few years after the organizing drive it would be hard to say that the city was transformed. Too many things remain the same. The undocumented Latina/o workers are still disenfranchised and vulnerable. The system of white supremacy forces black and brown workers into a downward spiral. Class oppression makes basic human need and dignity a matter of continuous struggle.

There's a contradiction between identity and transformation. Identity pushes the passive. We are what we are. It resists change, and in a good situation that's a good thing. But we don't live in a world where workers get a fair break.

"Transformation" is a polite way to say "revolution" in the social context. Transformation inevitably changes identity, which then resists change once more. And so the slow cycle of progress begins again.

The Place of Documentary
LEIGH ANNE DUCK

In describing the dialectic between identity and transformation, Lewis articulates a conceptual challenge familiar to scholars of the U.S. South but also to filmmakers—as well as researchers and activists—across much of the world. Contemplating documentary's role in helping viewers understand their position in a changing world, Michael Chanan argues that this medium informs "cognitive mapping: the construction of mental maps which encode the relative relationships between different locations in the spatial environment" and the "subject's Imaginary relationship to their Real conditions of existence."[44] "Cognitive mapping" became a keyword in aesthetic and social theory during the late twentieth century, after Fredric Jameson—borrowing the term from Kevin Lynch's *The Image of the City* (1960), in which he explored how individuals try to situate themselves in an "urban totality"—proclaimed such efforts, understood more broadly, the central challenge of the postmodern era, in which local cultures interact with (or, in apocalyptic accounts, get devoured by) global capitalism.[45] Chanan departs from Jameson's model, however, by insisting on the specific significance of locales in the global South, which are poorly represented (in terms of both quantity and quality) in global North media and from which vital documentaries rarely circulate in the global North.

The problem here is twofold: the "First World viewer, locked into the imaginary geography of the metropolis," typically lacks access to images and narratives that would assist in a more accurate understanding of global relations, and meanwhile, although media producers in the global South produce films attentive to local histories, epistemologies, and problems of economic development, they often struggle to find global distribution for their work.[46] Chanan focuses on how global South filmmakers—especially those of the radical Latin American documentary movement (*nuevo cine latinoamericano*)—sought to redress this balance, but we can also recognize Appalshop as participating in this moment when documentary worldwide sought to provide more abundant and critical accounts of relationships within and among spaces. Along with other community film workshops in the United States, Appalshop was established by the American Film Institute (AFI) and the U.S. Office of Economic Opportunity (OEO) in the late 1960s, with the twin goals of enabling marginalized communities—including African Americans, Native Americans, and Puerto Ricans—to produce media responsive to their concerns and cultures while also preparing participants for later employment in national media industries.[47] In comparison with other global film movements, these workshops had a very different structural relationship to their federal government and to a media industry already notorious for its pursuit of global hegemony: Stephen Michael Charbonneau describes the OEO/AFI developmental strategy as "managerial liberalism," in which marginalized groups are given tools that might enable them to join an economic system without fundamentally disrupting its values.[48] Nonetheless, this experience led many Appalshop filmmakers to understand their positions not only through the region of their birth, with its particular histories and cultures, but also through comparison with the experiences of other communities—particularly those of rural Vietnam and African Americans.[49]

Situating Appalshop amid global changes in media culture underscores Massey's understanding of the "four-dimensionality" of space: even as local filmmakers were given opportunities to depict, for themselves, a place they felt to be misrepresented in national media, they found it to be changing both internally and in its relationships with other areas—a change taking place in part, of course, in their own understandings. Appalshop films, particularly in an earlier period, were often noted for promoting, as one critic explains, "an identity, a sense of place and history that has otherwise been largely eroded by a dominant American culture."[50] At least one of its documentaries, *Strangers and Kin* (1984), focuses on the need to celebrate local culture as a way of resisting and confronting ascriptive stereotype. But Appalachia, as a space (like, presumably, most others) that involves local conflicts, also has a tradition of understanding "place" in terms of allegiance and solidarity. To return to Florence Reece's famous song, what matters is less where you're from than which side you're on.

Understood in this way—as Anne Lewis describes her work here and elsewhere—one's *position* is determined less by geographic origins than by allegiance. Filming a strike in Harlan County, for instance, Lewis "had to pick a side in order to function as a human being."[51] This approach to locale, a mental formulation based on transitory experiences in often shifting social networks (in other words, a process of cognitive mapping), facilitates not a static "identity" but rather a sense of commitment.[52] The political uses of such an approach are clear, but it provides analytic and narrative advantages also. Massey's recommendation of "4-D" analysis is compelling but abstract; methodologically, it serves more as a recommendation to generate new models than as a clear analytic path. In Lewis's work, however, we can see how recognition of problems and goals—and a desire to understand each more deeply—provides a vantage point from which to analyze changes in time and space, both locally and globally.

Confrontation
ANNE LEWIS

Appalachian identity is complex—both agrarian and industrialized. The part of the region that I know best, the southern Appalachian coalfields, has a wedge driven into its heart. The people who most care about its mountains are compelled by economic necessity toward their destruction. What's now become a movement against mountaintop removal, the modern form of strip mining, has brought new consciousness of the degraded environment to the nation. At the same time a kind of cultural strip mining based on class and regional stereotypes—especially of southern working-class men—flourishes.

The culture wars, an enormous time sump although a necessary part of the daily work of rooted filmmakers and academics alike, rage on. Fairly recently an atrocious commercial by DirecTV shows a kidnapped white businessman in a suit and tie in a shack inhabited by an attractive goat, a pregnant woman with rotten teeth, and a vaguely Hasidic looking man picking his few remaining ones. I love the comment from Harlan County resident Jeromey Smith in a story posted by a local TV station: "Goats and stuff running around? We don't have cats let alone dogs in the house." I rise to his defense as I write with a cat resting on my printer and a dog at my feet.

In spite of the fact that Appalachians are some of the last people that media can deride in politically correct America, Appalachian identity persists with common understanding of class; rootedness to land and culture, family, and community; and a fighting, resilient spirit. Even in a time of corporate control, widespread drug abuse, and economic decay, the history of a once proud, integrated, and militant labor union has the force of identity.

Justice in the Coalfields looks at resistance and civil disobedience during the Pittston strike.[53] Men and women, young and old, fight in a right-to-work state for their rights as workers, for their union, for care for the old and disabled, and for community justice. These coal miners and their families, during the time of the strike, transform themselves and their community. This transformation includes open defiance of the courts and police, the demand for inclusive health care, profound change in the relationships between men and women, solidarity between blacks and whites, four thousand civil disobedience arrests, and occupation of corporate property.

Married to a Pittston miner at the time, I decided to put the camera down and get arrested myself. I remember being dragged off by state troopers for blocking the entrance to the Moss 3 Coal Prep Plant, along with many others, including West Virginia writer Denise Giardina. They couldn't process us at the local jail because the jailer had refused to imprison supporters of the strike, so we were off on an hour-long bus ride to a 4H camp that had been converted for detention. I remember Denise reading the passage from her just published *Storming Heaven* about a black man thrown into a furnace for having a union card. As she read, the black state trooper driving the bus muttered, "oh, Lord."

We were processed, bailed out by pensioners, given a sandwich by the Daughters of Mother Jones, and driven back to our cars by a preacher–coal miner in a church bus.[54] I still think about the complexity of forging collective identity, class and regional solidarity, and that bold effort toward societal transformation.

Six months later, as the strike went on, ninety-nine miners and a Methodist minister occupied the plant where we had been arrested. We spoke with a black and a white miner who were sitting next to each other four stories up. One of them relayed, "Coming up the road you didn't really know what was going to be waiting on you. I was shaking in my boots. When we pulled up we saw all there was was the gate was open and there was two guards. So a hundred of us jump out and what are they going to do? You know, they either shoot us or they get out of the way. They got out of the way and we came on in.... I thought there'd be five or six of us shot before we got across that bridge."[55] Then the miner added: "When they talk about cutting retirees they ain't talking about strangers. They're talking about our uncles and our grandfathers. We've lived in the same area generation after generation. The man next door ain't no stranger. You went to school with him or his brother. They're not strangers, ain't talking about strangers. We're talking about family. They don't care what color their slaves are. They don't care if they're black, if they're white. A slave's a slave to them."[56] That collective identity was expressed late that night when Cecil Roberts, at that time vice president of the United Mine Workers of America, addressed a huge crowd outside the plant: "The thing that Pittston doesn't understand here is, we own the coal here in these hills. It belongs to us. It belongs to the people. And it's for the good of the people, not Paul Douglas and Joe Farrell. It's for the good of the people down here."[57]

Justice in the Coalfields ends with Gail Gentry, paralyzed after a roof fall in a Pittston mine, reading his letter to the local paper: "We the people who mine the coal are as much a part of these mountains as the seams of coal that lie in them. We have always been accommodating, independent people, but we, like all others, will not tolerate abuse whether corporate or government. We demand that we be treated with dignity and respect—certainly not an unreasonable request in the land of our heritage."[58] That truth coming from a southern white man is not the truth of privilege. Gail includes all the members of his union, black, white, and brown. All the New South rhetoric is meaningless in the face of that kind of collective identity that ties people together in mass action and principled belief and has, at its core, the seeds of transformation.

All of us in the South live in a place that has, in fact, been transformed. The unfinished revolution that began with the earliest slave revolts, and continued through Reconstruction and the mass civil rights movement, is the most important and active part of our collective identity—more important than the Civil War, more important than postbellum industrialization, more important than folk traditions and customs (no matter how beautiful), more important than neoliberal development. The possibility of passivity simply does not exist in the face of the murder of teenage Trayvon Martin and George Zimmerman's subsequent acquittal; Hurricanes Katrina and Rita; the Texas assaults on the rights of women, on civil liberties, and on the public sector; as well as the economic precariousness many of us experience.

Braden said it's a great time to organize for economic justice. She said that we need to know in our hearts that whatever gains one group makes benefit all. She believed that black liberation movements must lead the South. Braden said that it's only then that we can move toward the vision she describes eloquently in the film: a beloved community based on justice as well as love. Black lives matter! ¡Adelante!

Notes

1. This link between scholarship and documentary is explicit in the multimedia essay Lewis prepared with her collaborator Fran Ansley for the online open-access journal *Southern Spaces*. See Ansley and Lewis, "Going South, Coming North."

2. Herzog, "Minnesota Declaration."

3. They actually appear to be discussing somewhat different approaches. As Pat Aufderheide points out, "verité" has become a "popular umbrella term" for a variety of documentary approaches that shoot on location using synchronized sound, made possible by significant technological advances in the 1960s (*Documentary Film*, 44). One of these traditions, named "cinéma verité" by filmmaker and anthropologist Jean Rouch, insists that documentary must serve as a "catalyst" (or, in Lewis's words, "provoke the truth") and encourages filmmakers to reveal and even interrogate their presence in a scene (ibid., 86, 89). Bill Nichols distinguishes such approaches, which he terms "interactive," from the "observational" forms that "required a disciplined detachment from the events" being filmed and discouraged anyone involved—whether the subjects of the documentary or the crew—from acknowledging the recording apparatus (Nichols, *Representing Reality*, 33). Both Lewis and Herzog criticize the latter mode.

4. Ames, *Ferocious Reality*, 9.

5. Nichols, *Representing Reality*, 3, 9.

6. Cowie, *Recording Reality, Desiring the Real*, 2–3.

7. Ibid., 3.

8. Ames, *Ferocious Reality*, 3–4; Herzog, "Minnesota Declaration."

9. Taylor, *Disturbing Calculations*, 2.

10. Herzog, "Minnesota Declaration."

11. For instance, according to the Death Penalty Information Center, Texas leads other U.S. states in executions since 1976 (the year the Supreme Court ended the moratorium on uses of the death penalty) by a wide margin: 530, compared to Oklahoma's 112, Virginia's 111, and other states with smaller numbers. In 2011 Texas executed 13 inmates, one of whom, Michael Perry, is a subject of Herzog's film. As of April 1, 2015, 113 prisoners on death row in Texas were African American, 76 were white, 77 were Latino, and 5 were Asian. According to US census data from 2014, 12.5 percent of Texans are African American, 43.5 percent are white and non-Latino, 38.6 percent are Latina and Latino, and 4.5 percent are Asian American. While Lewis argues that "every southern documentary film is about race," that topic is only implicit in *Into the Abyss*, which focuses on white perpetrators, victims, familial and social connections, and investigators.

12. Beaver, Buckwalter, et al., "That Point of Human Connection," 60.

13. Aufderheide, "At Appalshop the 1960's Never Died." See also Harkins, *Hillbilly*, 185–86.

14. Ruby, "Speaking for, Speaking about, Speaking with, or Speaking Alongside," 48.

15. H. Lewis, "Appalshop," 81; Beaver, Buckwalter, et al., "That Point of Human Connection," 64, 65.

16. Ibid., 63, 72, 68.

17. I do not mean to suggest that the former rights have been fully achieved, as is sometimes influentially assumed. In 2013, for example, when the Supreme Court struck down the segment of the 1965 Voting Rights Act that required certain states to receive approval for any changes in voting procedures, the majority supported this change by arguing that "our nation has made great strides." Summarizing the dissent, Justice Ruth Bader Ginsburg contended that outright disfranchisement had been replaced by "second-generation barriers" that selectively pose obstacles to voting. See

Liptak, "Supreme Court Invalidates Key Part of Voting Rights Act." Meanwhile, the current organizing cry "Black lives matter!" is in many respects a demand for the opportunity to occupy public space without being harassed, arrested, or killed—a right too often denied over the suspicion of criminality. But while struggle continues over rights ostensibly guaranteed 150 years ago, other vital aspects of the movement for racial justice—the critiques of capitalism and colonialism—are still vigorously marginalized in public discourse. See Singh, *Black Is a Country*; Hall, "The Long Civil Rights Movement."

18. Lewis, *Anne Braden: Southern Patriot*.

19. Ibid. Noting that "identification" is a hoary term in film studies—once vigorously theorized and now not so fashionable—Cowie maintains that it is nonetheless central to both popular commentary about film and to psychoanalytic and ideological theory; her Lacanian approach focuses on the role of desire in documentary viewing. Cowie, *Recording Reality, Desiring the Real*, 88.

20. Lewis, *Transcript*, "Anne Braden: Southern Patriot."

21. Ibid.

22. *The South: Some Addresses*, 10.

23. Grady, "The South and Her Problems," 53.

24. Lewis, *Transcript*, "Anne Braden: Southern Patriot."

25. Ibid.

26. Ibid.

27. Ibid.

28. Massey, "Politics and Space/Time," 73.

29. Rony, *The Third Eye*, 14–15. Rony coins this term to describe Robert Flaherty's *Nanook of the North* (1922), but the director employed similar strategies—especially fictionalization and enactment of possible cultural "traditions" no longer employed by local people—in *Louisiana Story* (1948). See Suchy, Catano, et al., "Revisiting Flaherty's *Louisiana Story*."

30. H. Lewis, "Appalshop," 80.

31. Gaines, "Appalshop Documentaries."

32. B. Smith and Fisher, "Conclusion," 269.

33. B. Smith, "Introduction to Appalachian Identity," 56.

34. Smith and Fisher, "Conclusion," 268.

35. Massey, "Politics and Space/Time," 80.

36. H. Smith and Barret, "Appalshop Filmmakers Herb E. Smith and Elizabeth Barret Talk about Appalshop's Audiences," 30.

37. Ansley, "Doing Policy from Below," 104, 109.

38. *Morristown: In the Air and Sun*, transcript in possession of Anne Lewis.

39. Ibid.

40. Ibid.

41. Ibid.

42. Ibid.

43. Ibid.

44. Chanan, "Going South," 147–48.

45. Jameson, *Postmodernism*, 51. Jameson's early work on this subject elicited substantial critique; see, for example, Ahmad, "Jameson's Rhetoric of Otherness."

46. Chanan, "Going South," 150.
47. Charbonneau, "Branching Out," 138–39.
48. Ibid., 137–40, 145; Aufderheide, *Documentary Film*, 126–35.
49. Abbate-Winkel, "Voices, Mirrors, Names, and Dreams," 93–94.
50. Horton, "Film from Appalshop," 13.
51. Beaver, Buckwalter, et al., "That Point of Human Connection," 63.

52. Using Lewis's films as examples, I mean that her commitments to local movements enable her to recognize and even represent relevant spatial networks, but this sense of committed positionality is also embedded in Jameson's definition of "cognitive mapping," which he finally admits is "in reality nothing but a code word for 'class consciousness.'" See Jameson, *Postmodernism*, 418.

53. In 1987 the Pittston Company decided to cut health-care coverage at its coal mines, affecting United Mine Workers of America (UMWA) workers, some with work-related injuries. In 1989 over two thousand miners in Virginia, Kentucky, and West Virginia began striking. Along with non-union-affiliated protesters, they put pressure on the company to restore health coverage (see Brisbin, *A Strike like No Other Strike*). In addition to a 1990 settlement between Pittston and the UMWA to reinstate health and retirement benefits to miners, protests resulted in the Coal Industry Retiree Health Benefit Act of 1992, then Senator Jay Rockefeller's legislation to preserve "retirement benefits for miners and their families" (see Raby and Smith, "Jay Rockefeller Retiring").

54. For Daughters of Mother Jones involvement in the Pittston strike, see Birecree, "The Importance and Implications of Women's Participation in the 1989–1990 Pittston Coal Strike," 195–99.

55. *Justice in the Coalfields*, transcript in possession of Anne Lewis.
56. Ibid.
57. Ibid.
58. Ibid.

Surviving the Economic Apocalypse

Capitalism, Consumption, and the Indian Imaginary in Karen Russell's Swamplandia!

MELANIE BENSON TAYLOR

Karen Russell's *Swamplandia!* is like no book you've ever read before—and if you're like many adult readers, it may not sound like one you'd want to pick up in the first place. As a 2011 review in the *New York Times* put it, this is "a novel about alligator wrestlers, a balding brown bear named Judy Garland, a Bird Man specializing in buzzard removal, a pair of dueling Florida theme parks... a Ouija board and the dead but still flirtatious Louis Thanksgiving. Sound appealing? No, it does not."[1] The reviewer's point, however, was that this "noxiously fanciful" narrative nevertheless appeals on a visceral level. Indeed, the marvel of *Swamplandia!* is Karen Russell's ability to make the uncanny seem familiar and to render even the most implausible events shatteringly tangible. In a surprisingly affective way, this allegorical neo-southern family wrestles not just swamp demons and ghosts but the rapacious intrusion of advanced capitalism into their verdant idyll. It is a powerful rendering of the weird, pseudo-reality we inhabit in the twenty-first century and the fictions we marshal to make sense of it all.

Still, despite the positive reviews and the giddy buzz about the book in southern literature circles, I probably wouldn't have given it a chance but for one thing: it has Indians in it. At least, I thought it did. According to the dust jacket synopsis, "Thirteen-year-old Ava Bigtree has lived her entire life at *Swamplandia!*, her family's island home and gator-wrestling theme park in the Florida Everglades." The family surname instantly struck me as indigenous, albeit in the stereotypical way that any pairing of an animal or element of nature with a descriptive adjective immediately conjures a grim-faced Indian in a warbonnet. A few pages in, however, I discovered I'd been duped: while the Bigtree family considers itself a "tribe" and poses for advertisements and performances in makeshift headdresses and war paint, they are in fact the white descendants of a coal miner from Ohio. Ernest Shedrach, after losing his job at a pulp mill in 1932, had fled with his wife to the then-wild lands of South Florida, changing his name to "Sawtooth Bigtree" to evade his old boss (to whom he owed a sizable debt). The new identity is a cover, but Ernest clearly embraces the opportunity for a rebirth of sorts, an escape from the "pitiful wages," ringing ears, and "bleached vision caused by blinking into the chemicals" for so many years. He chooses the name "Sawtooth" in honor of the island's sedge, and "Bigtree" appealed to him with its "root-strong," indigenous sound.[2] In one swift act of self-reclamation, he and his descendants are reborn as Natives. On a tiny, swampy island in the Everglades reachable only by ferry, the Shedrachs-cum-Bigtrees effectively function as proxies for America's second-wave settlement of weary pioneers, looking to flee the hardscrabble industrialism of the early twentieth century in the wild, purchasing a "hundred-acre waste" marketed rhapsodically by northern realtors as an "American Eden."[3] There they spawn a dynasty of gator-wrestling—a vocation with an illustrious indigenous pedigree, particularly among local Seminoles. They "go Native" in an utterly pragmatic, shrewdly entrepreneurial, and uniquely American manner.

"Playing Indian" is, of course, a trope that dates back to the earliest moments of our national story: members of the Tea Party (then and now) have dressed up as Indians to express their indignation over taxation from external entities. For countless American authors, indigenous pasts and allies have frequently served to combat the incursions of colonial-capitalist development. The ideological Indian has shifted character and purpose along with the changing needs of the dominant national culture, absorbing its anxieties and desires like allegorical tofu. By far the most persistent and revealing flavor bestowed on the all-purpose, American Indian is the wise, romantic, ecological anticapitalist who protects the spirit and memory of our deepest national values particularly at the moments when we seem to be losing or forgetting them. As Iron Eyes Cody demonstrated enduringly in the popular television ad campaigns of the 1970s, weeping and paddling his way down a garbage-strewn river, Indians dislike littering and pollution, just as they dislike multisyllabic expression. Never mind that Cody was actually an Italian-American actor playing an Indian on screen (and equally fervently in his private life). Such pageantry simply underlines that the Native American trope has become a fungible celluloid fantasy, a mirror held up to a society anxious to gaze upon its own inherent well of alternative value. If the Indian somehow fails to surmount the crippling, corrosive forces of global capitalism, so too do those who depend on such fantasies of communal coherence, strength, superior values, and transcendence.

The allure of Indian alterity has proven especially seductive in the South, where it helps bolster narratives of nativist belonging, dispossession, and exploitation. Much of my published work so far has been invested in excavating the collisions between these Native and southern ideologies of exceptional loss and grace, looking for ways to force an admittedly uncomfortable dialogue between two groups that have far more in common than they'd generally like to admit.[4] For me, the conversation began abruptly when I found myself straddling these seemingly disparate worlds: I had recently moved from a position teaching American and southern literature in an English department to one housed solely in the historic Native American Studies program at Dartmouth College. That spring, while listening to the keynote address at the biannual Society for the Study of Southern Literature conference, it occurred to me that the rhetoric being used to signify "southern" preoccupations echoed uncannily those rampant in Indian country as well: these are fixations on land, tradition, community, sovereignty, dispossession, subjugation, purity, and violence—just to name a few. These groups at such cultural and ideological odds have in fact developed in suggestively analogous ways: both have been unsettled and dispossessed by alien regimes and colonized by federal forces issuing from northeastern headquarters of colonial-capitalism. Perhaps no two groups in the American context have been as persistently mythologized and made hyperreal as southerners and Indians. Indeed, neither "southerners" nor "Indians" would exist at all without the colonial processes and ideologies that introduced these categories of meaning into our cultural consciousness to begin with.[5] They occupy similar territory in the national imagination as monolithic others and foils, ways that America at large can know itself by contrast.[6]

While few would explicitly associate neo-secessionist ideologies with indigenous land claims and rights to self-government, the two groups tend to echo and borrow from one another's causes in their rhetorics of rebellion. Take, for instance, the numerous popular versions of the Confederate battle flag featuring American Indians in front of the stars and bars, presumably to authenticate the nativist pride fueling myths of the Old South.[7] The unquestioned assumption behind this phenomenon is that southerners and Indians share an anti-establishment ethos, that both have been cheated out of a birthright, and that their causes are compatible interests worthy of vigorous defense. Native Americans are just as likely to nurture myths of separatism and exceptionalism and grounds for rebellion, albeit for seemingly more justifiable reasons. Take, for instance, the arresting image of an Alabama Cherokee grass dancer stomping the powwow grounds in a vest emblazoned with thousands of tiny Confederate battle flags.[8] Despite the borrowed racist iconography, the rebel motif seems somehow less problematic because it appears to promote the rights of another historically oppressed group (and in this case, a relatively "new" tribe organized in 1997 and struggling for legitimacy).

But there are consequences for our lack of courage in interrogating the need of the oppressed to associate with such causes: we prop up new mascots for our own needs, ones no more authentic than those fashioned by outsiders. Most importantly, we shield ourselves from the knowledge that the sovereignty we crave rests not in tribe or community, not in any space of agency or power we might access, but in the economic structures that underlie both the destruction and the reformation of our identities. While both groups tend to position themselves warily against the industrial-capitalist character associated with the North and the federal government, both are patently and thoroughly enmeshed in fiscal enterprises that actively shape, sustain, and transform them.[9] The architecture of self-determination is mapped with money, and the very mechanisms of power and privilege that uprooted entire tribal nations and devastated regional plantation economies are now often the very same tools used to rebuild them. It is not this fact, however, but its denial that seems so deadly: the pretense for both groups that cultural distinctiveness and solidarity can save one from the predations of the market, despite the terrible knowledge that one's identity and autonomy are indistinct from—in fact, conditioned and colored by—primarily economic principles, priorities, and antagonisms.

For all its bizarre charm, then, *Swamplandia!* is not necessarily distinctive. In fact, Russell participates in a fairly conservative tradition of eliding southern distinctiveness with indigenous memory in order to service a mythology of anticapitalist, rabidly humanist exceptionalism. The question is whether or not Russell does so ironically, with the savvy tongue-in-cheek knowingness that marks her approach to the Bigtrees more generally and allows us to view their strange world with sympathy rather than pity or condescension. As Russell told an interviewer, "A lot of this book grew out of my sense that I had arrived a little late for the party, that a few generations ago... the Everglades was a wonderland. I grew up in a time when there was an increased consciousness of phosphor solution and development... [a] reckoning with the past twenty years of development and its consequences. So I think it must always be the case that you are in the shadow of an Eden that was more spectacular than your own."[10]

Hers is no Agrarian rhapsody on the lost splendor of porch-rocking days gone by, but rather a liberal lament for the new century, a clever screed against the poisons of industrial advances in Floridians' backwater paradise. Russell, like Americans in general—and southerners in particular—frequently view the present as a moment of waste, despair, of a just-past glory and nobility. What more stirring icon of such loss than the Indian who remains vaguely in our midst, just out of sight on the margins of society, a reminder of the depth of our roots and the terrible pain of social change? Shedding light on their victimization amounts to vicarious catharsis, but while this banding together of the dispossessed presumably heightens our ability to empathize, it also further occludes any recognition that we are all irrevocably entangled in the very mechanisms that undo us.

Swamplandia! is narrated by Ava, the thirteen-year-old daughter—and youngest—of the alligator-wrestling family, the Bigtrees. It seems plausible that she is a proxy for Russell's younger self, hovering in the liminal state between childhood fantasy and adolescent realism, between that "wonderland" of the past and the hardships of the present. For this reason, perhaps, she narrates the weird events of the novel with matter-of-fact acceptance, rarely indicating the obvious fissures in the family's alternative reality. Russell's empathy for Ava's wry innocence shines through plainly. Guilelessly enough, the contemporary Bigtrees merely consider themselves every bit as "indigenous" as *any* humans (Indian or otherwise) in the Ten Thousand Islands, where the Calusa Indians had long been extinguished, and where even the Seminoles, a reconstituted tribe of Creek migrants and refugees, were settlers. The Bigtrees fancy themselves just another "free and ancient swamp tribe" (Russell, 32) at the risk of being the next displaced by invasive species and programs. Ava's father—old Sawtooth's son Samuel—is the patriarch of the contemporary generation, and even the kids call him "Chief." The family don their plastic costumes, subdue the most formidable beasts of the swamp in spectacular fashion, and record their victories in their very own museum of Bigtree history—significantly, right next to the Swamplandia! gift shop, a clear indication of the weighted value of manufactured indigenous narratives. Apparently endowed with the agency of the resurrected oppressed, the Chief rewrites the family history at will. As Ava describes it: "Certain artifacts appeared or vanished, dates changed and old events appeared in fresh blue ink on new cards beneath the dusty exhibits.... You had to pretend like the Bigtree story had always read that way" (32).

This renegade authority over history, accompanied by an extravagant sense of subversive agency, seems doomed from the start of the book. The fragility of their makeshift tribe is immediately apparent. Sawtooth, who has become dangerously senile and combative, has been consigned to the "Out to Sea" rest home on the mainland. But the more poignant loss is that of Hilola Bigtree—the Chief's wife, and revered mother to the narrator and her siblings. The intrepid star of the "Swamplandia!" show, Hilola swims brazenly through the pit of alligators to the giddy fright of spectators, a petite package of almost inconceivable strength and nerve. But despite narrowly escaping every alligator in the pit, Hilola succumbs to ovarian cancer. The loss of this icon of impossible endurance leaves the Chief and their children off-balance and their gator show arrested. The fact that she dies of ovarian cancer in particular suggests an assault on the very mechanism of reproduction, a short-circuiting of a small and hardy troupe that, like their Indian inspirations, had long outlived their time and expectations. Tourists no longer wash ashore in boatloads for a show without a star, and the final few stragglers are poached by a fearsome new competitor on the mainland: the World of Darkness—a massive theme park of Disneyworld-like proportions. Swamplandia! is in catastrophic arrears, unlikely to survive, despite the Chief's blind belief in what he calls "Carnival Darwinism."

Kiwi, the oldest of the Bigtree children, harbors no such faith—he quickly defects to the mainland, ostensibly to earn money to help the family meet its ponderous debts. Really, though, he has long been seduced by the prospect of attending a mainland college. To finance his endeavor, he is forced to get a job at none other than the Bigtrees' competitor: the World of Darkness, aptly nicknamed "the World" in a parodic reminder that its uber-corporate, Disneyesque tyranny has supplanted the world as we know it. The education Kiwi craves is delivered instead in the dank basement dormitories of the World, where he lives and studies when he's not working. Rather than earning actual paychecks, his weekly stubs show him actually *owing* the company for board, uniform, and various incidentals, underscoring that his tutelage in the business of the World is a commodity he has purchased at considerable cost, and one he may never elude. Rather than save his family, he instead ends up reluctantly rescuing the granddaughter of the company's CEO from drowning in the theme park pool. This seems Russell's sardonic way of acknowledging how unwittingly, even unwillingly, we sustain the very economic structures that attempt to drown us. Yet it also conjures up memories of Swamplandia! and Hilola's death-defying swim through the pit of alligators, reminding us that Kiwi hails from an elect race that scrappily survives against formidable odds, although doing so often entails dragging capitalism's spawn to the surface too. It is no surprise that Kiwi and his damsel-in-distress have a brief and sloppy sexual encounter, executed with no more volition than her rescue: "How strange, Kiwi thought, that you could want so badly to insert a part of your anatomy into someone who you hated" (268).

Both the accidental rescue and the inadvertent fling dramatize the reluctance with which Kiwi succumbs to the allure of capitalism and its showy, false promises. But even back on the island he was always the only member of the family to resist the ballast of indigeneity, to feel embarrassed in the gaudy makeup and pasted-on feathers. While he declared staunchly at fourteen, "I'm a Not-Bigtree. A Not-Indian. A Not-Seminole. A Not-Miccosukee" (208), as the World's hero Kiwi in fact becomes the new poster child for "all that miraculous bullshit" (274). The press markets his rescue of the CEO's daughter as the work of a guardian angel, and the company welcomes the "free publicity and new clients from the 'crystals-are-my-medicine' crowd" (274). Despite himself, Kiwi uses the opportunities to promote Swamplandia! instead. He reverently hangs posters of his mother in his dorm room, and while the spectacle is sweet, it is also disturbingly sexual: all that she represents hovers in his view like a teenage fantasy, a masturbatory delight. Whereas the CEO's heir is flesh and blood, all drama and flash, Hilola is an absent presence, a dead promise, a glossy memory on paper that eventually gets torn by a careless friend. Both women are allegories for the competing seductions of Kiwi Bigtree's world, and he never fully gives himself over to either. Without the Indian guise, though, he acknowledges that identifying simply as white gives him "a whistling fear, a feeling not unlike agoraphobia" (208). It is human nature, Russell avers, to seek shelter in distinctiveness—not the vast expanse of anonymity, of not-belonging, that haunts white men like Sawtooth. It's practically our birthright to inhabit stories instead, ones that claim community and power while denying the dollars and cents that always underwrite such possessions.

The most delusional dreamer of the Bigtree family is the Chief himself, who is fond of claiming that "money appeared to be the one species that couldn't take root in the swamp—and this blight was a killer of dreams" (250). Yet Swamplandia! itself, its gift shop filled with campy postcards and sweatshirts with puffy logos, embodies both the "dream" and the "killer of dreams" all at once—knowledge that the Chief apparently knows but cannot know. He departs for the mainland as well, apparently to court investors who will save the family business. Kiwi, on a night out with his World of Darkness coworkers, accidentally discovers the truth: the Chief is moonlighting for cash at the southernmost Seminole casino. The casino itself expresses the collision between nature and its perversions, between the indigenous ideal and its ineluctable surrender. Built on the ruins of a Catholic church, the structure tacitly overwrites a costly colonial narrative with one of indigenous redemption and prosperity. But yet again this is a typically American palimpsest, a furious desire to believe in the power of new beginnings while the shadows of our past seep through, infuse, and infect all we think we have become. Much as we would like to believe otherwise, "indigenous capitalism" is no more virtuous because it is sanctified by colonial crimes. Neither is the "indigenous" Swamplandia! less prone to the fissures, evacuations, convections, and cancers of capitalism. Russell deepens the allegory by naming this fictional casino Pa-Hay-Okee, which is actually the Indian name for the Everglades. It doesn't matter, ultimately, whether the Chief is "free" on their island or in thrall at the mainland, the "chief" of Swamplandia! or a lowly casino worker named Sam, emceeing a second-rate beauty pageant while tripping over AV wires and being berated by his boss. Both are spaces of fantasy and desire that fail to pay out, that take root and "kill dreams."

With Kiwi and the Chief away on the mainland, Ava is left alone on the island with her fantasy-obsessed older sister, a teenager suggestively named Osceola after the legendary Seminole chief. "Ossie" begins telepathically communicating with—and dating—the ghosts of expired men. In particular, she falls for a Depression-era dredgeman named Louis Thanksgiving, whose ghost ship has run aground on their island. Ossie soon abandons Ava to elope with him in the underworld. In such ways, Russell creates a world where magic seems endemic but also the derivative of industry—a labored illusion crafted for economic survival. Indeed, part of the coming-of-age process in this novel seems to be reckoning with the terrible, mundane realities behind the fecund landscape of dreams that functions as Eden for Americans worn down by industrial development, debt, and depression. In this way, the novel invites history and fantasy together to blaze an illuminating path into the Bigtrees' befuddled present. Indeed, Louis Thanksgiving's apocryphal story uncannily echoes Sawtooth Bigtree's own arrival narrative. Like Sawtooth, Thanksgiving flees the Midwest, "bruised" and undone by hard labor, and remakes himself in the swampy frontier of South Florida. He falls in with a WPA dredge crew, working side by side with men of different races and backgrounds—a veritable fraternity of the American working class—until a horrible accident kills Louis and several of his mates (135, 138). Louis's European ancestry, like the Shedrach name, had already been cast aside by the miracle of his birth: he was "born dead" to an immigrant mother who died during childbirth, yet he revived miraculously and was thus christened "Thanksgiving." In his name is encoded the fictional harmony of the European settler and the indigenous host, the narrative of rebirth and the particularly American delusion of consecrated beginnings. Louis doesn't survive in the way that Sawtooth does, but this seems the point. His story functions as parable about the costs of such an existence, the illusion of a life sustained by fantasy and foolhardiness, and the haunting limits of America's multicultural fantasies. Osceola sets out to wed herself to an idea, an allegory, a promise.

The pivot point here, for both Thanksgiving (America) and Osceola (Swamplandia!), is the trap of the indigenous: the perception that "going Native" might deliver one from the noxious atmosphere of industry. When the "lone Indian" on Louis's crew, Euphon Tigertail, is beaten by the Everglades' severe environment and decides to leave, he urges Louis to escape with him. "You'll go in there and never come out," he warns. But Louis stays on, with no past or people to reclaim him, thinking, "How could you make a mistake when you had one option?" (138). Russell underscores here the poverty of choice that fuels the American Dream, leaving seemingly one path to survival. Louis's continued involvement with the Civilian Conservation Corps ends up executing the opposite of conservation—it is, for the human worker seeking to conquer a hostile environment, pure destruction. Their work is continued by the Army Corps of Engineers in the 1940s with their "Drainage Project," which involved sprinkling the area with the seeds of melaleuca plants that would grow kudzu-like for generations, strangling the Everglades' ecosystem into submission for agricultural development (96). The project failed, but the melaleucas remain, and the Bigtree girls routinely go on missions to "massacre" them: "We were tree *warriors*," Ava says (97, emphasis added). As an allegory, Louis's story suggests that Euphon Tigertail was right all along: the

Indian instinct for preservation is one's lifeline through the American wasteland of "progress"—a place where you go in and never come out. The catch, however, is that there is nowhere else to go.

Indeed, what depletes the Bigtree family most is not the demise of the island ecosystem but that of their tourist enterprise—which, to their grave folly, they see as one and the same. The crumbling of the Swamplandia! empire depletes the family that has over-identified with it: Ava watches Kiwi's body deteriorate, "robbed … of actual matter" (67), and sees herself "evaporating" (167). Kiwi defines the phenomenon as "convection": "the rapid cooling of a body in the absence of all tourists" (236). Significantly, Kiwi plumps up once on the mainland, eating fast food and accumulating "girlish hips" (275). Ossie's response too is to consume—in large quantities, senselessly, and irrepressibly—grains of rice, sticks of butter, heads of cauliflower, frozen steaks, and "Pick Up Club" meals—foods packaged, processed, and shipped from the mainland. It is presumably no accident either that her love interest bears the name of the American holiday associated with gorging oneself silly in a ceremony of patriotism and plenty. Together the Bigtree children demonstrate physically the fateful progress of consumer capitalism, and the literally haunting reminder of our American romance with the feast. Without the energy and profits of their business enterprise, they shift modes to pure and voracious consumerism, their bodies hungry for more and more "Burger Burger" and "Pick Up Club" satiation.

Russell's hope in all this seems to lie with Ava, who believes more romantically that the cure isn't money or tourists or food but "touch or speech with another human" (236)—a cure that becomes more and more elusive as she is slowly abandoned by the entire family. And again another suggestively indigenous supplement shows up just in time: a mysterious "gypsy Bird Man" (163) appears on the island, ostensibly to seek payment for his services of buzzard removal. Ava is drawn like gravity to this strange, unkempt man in a filthy coat of bird feathers, finding comfort in touching him and imagining that he might love her. The very etymology of her own name—"Ava," from the Latin "*avis*," for bird—parallels his and implies an unexpected kinship. Quickly she commissions him to help her rescue Ossie from the underworld, where she believes her sister has gone to elope with Louis Thanksgiving. The Bird Man whisks Ava off on their rescue mission in a skiff built on an "old Seminole blueprint" (196), spouting his swamp wisdom gleaned from gator hunters, moonshiners, and Indians alike: "Nobody can get to hell without assistance, kid" (183). It seems he's right: the fatal logic in this book seems to be that human companions can be our salvation, when in fact they routinely facilitate our ruin. Literally, Ava thinks the Bird Man is assisting her in getting to Hell—or to the fabled entrance to the underworld, which is really just a pair of ancient Calusa Indian mounds. (Who better than Indians to mark the gateway to the dead?) The Bird Man navigates this indigenous terrain with apparent ease. He is not an Indian per se, but he lives and dresses simply like one, and with his makeshift Seminole craft and navigational system, he leads her directly into the portals of fantasy.

Predictably their mission soon implodes: the "underworld" is emphatically alive, Ossie is nowhere to be found, and the Bird Man takes advantage of Ava's desire for intimacy by raping her. She manages to escape, and after muddling blindly through the swamps alone, covered with mud and stained by tannins, thinks, "The Chief would be proud—at last I'd turned the color of a real Indian" (342). It's a stunning admission, because she is literally stained now by her time in this very indigenous, very human "underworld"—the place where we are always born dead, like Louis Thanksgiving, and searching for the space, the community, the power to live. Her red skin here is a testament not to death or trauma or even to the blood of her unspeakable violation, but rather to the uncanny ability to survive, to blend in, to become intimate with a place rather than destroy it. The Bird Man's abuse reminds us that salvation frequently comes dressed misleadingly in the trappings of nature, of the wild, and of indigeneity. Such costumes are always a screen and a dangerous one. Ultimately, the Bird Man's coat of feathers is no more fraudulent and insidious than the Bigtrees' headdresses. Yet those fantasies guard us briefly from a World of Darkness that encroaches relentlessly and penetrates all the same.

Like so many American and southern authors, Russell makes her characters dance between such faith and despair. In the twenty-first century, this is no longer a racial or a regional compulsion but a human one, yet we still often reach for indigenous icons and parables as errant guides into both the lessons of history and the abuses of the present. Osceola's character in particular seems to underscore this phenomenon: the historical Osceola was of mixed Indian, Scottish, English, and African American descent, and he purportedly married a black woman and vehemently opposed chattel slavery. This genealogical hybridity did not dilute his tribal allegiance, though, as he fought fiercely on behalf of the Florida Seminoles in the Second Seminole War. His identity and commitments typify both the early mixture of peoples in the South and their suffering on behalf of the colonial forces that divided and enslaved them along violent lines of demarcation. Long after his death, Osceola's embalmed head circulated among numerous private hands and museums.[11] "Crudely put," says Florida Museum of Natural History curator Jerald T. Milanich, "parts of Osceola are everywhere."[12]

For the Alabama Creek poet Janet McAdams, Osceola's undead body speaks volumes about the cruel conflict between biological and communal affiliation, about the deadly demarcations that keep our imperial borders and fictions in place and literally tear our bodies asunder in the process. In a series of poems called "The Collectors," she describes the painful ways that history has become currency: when we dig into the past, we are searching for a usable history that feeds, fulfills, and enriches in some way. There, she says, you find "the broken skull of Osceola, stolen for a talisman, / teeth without their gold fillings, bits of skin.... / Oh, sweet adventure with pirates and map, a trunk / so stuffed with gold it will blind the one / who cracks it open."[13] The verse is distinctly reminiscent of Russell's characters probing for "adventure" and mystery in these layered sites of imperial histories, a trunk filled with the rewards of empire and the quiet extinction of its casualties. But McAdams knows, as Russell's characters soon discover, that the dazzling treasures will "blind" the bearer to the true cost of our escape from the violence and division that have marked our progress at every turn, in the same way that the chemicals of industry "blinded" Ernest Shedrach to the new life and industry he would set in motion. When Russell's Osceola attempts to marry the allegorical Thanksgiving, her failure is a commentary on the persistent fractures in our national consciousness, the desire for kinship that keeps us plundering the graves of those who might save us.

From their discrete subject positions, as both a southern Native woman and a fervent Everglades nativist, McAdams and Russell speak similarly about the seductions of indigeneity in this process, and particularly within a region that has long shared its histories and buried its secrets. As practitioners of discrete fields—Native, southern, and American studies, literary criticism, and history—we would do well to excavate this common terrain in the way that these authors and their subjects consistently do, even in ways that seem like incursions on others' sacred grounds and bodies. These are rude but necessary gestures of survival; they showcase a drive toward affiliation rather than isolation. When Ossie does return in the end of *Swamplandia!* Ava refuses ever to release her: "Until we are old ladies—a cypress age, a Sawtooth age—I will continue to link arms with her ... in a panic of love" (394). Ava clings to her now drugged and "paralytic" sister in the same way that she had attempted to hold fast to a strange red alligator born at Swamplandia! that she secreted away from the rest of the family; it eventually became another casualty of her disastrous trip to the underworld with the Bird Man. Ava never tells anyone about the "miraculous hatchling" (396), and after some time says she "can't seem to draw a stable picture of [her] in my mind's eye anymore—it feels like trying to light a candle on a rainy night, your hands cupped and the whole wet world conspiring to snatch the flame away from you. But in a dream I might get to see the part of the swamp where her body washed up, bloated and rippling, or where she escaped to, if the dream was beautiful" (396–97). In the end, Russell seems no less immune than her characters to the power of the "dream," the miracle, the antidote to being consumed whole by a world of darkness and hunger and rape, even if the fable leaves us "bloated and rippling" or "paralytic" in the end. Osceola and the red alligator are plainly ambassadors of indigeneity's promise, one from the past and one from the future, but the mystery and hope of both are snuffed out by the cures—institutional (Ossie's doctors) and criminal (the Bird Man)—of the wet, dark world.

This is the true loss of the Swamplandia! show: "It was your *weakness* that pinned the tourists to their seats," Ava knows. "They saw that you could *lose*" (19). What we purchase and perform, then, is the spectacle of triumph, the catharsis of power. All humans are, at bottom, fragile refractions of what society has made us and what fraternity now exacerbates—nobody can get to Hell without assistance. In their desperate attempt to "win"—on stage, seven days a week—the Bigtrees betray the debilitating human need to validate our pain, "under siege" by material forces and enemies, and to fight desperately to prevail. Although the Bigtree family abandons Swamplandia! for a new life on the mainland, Ava knows that the show, so to speak, will always go on. In the closing line of the book, she can't help but recall "this cardboard clock [we used to have on Swamplandia!] and you could move the tiny hands to whatever time you wanted, NEXT SHOW AT __:__ O'CLOCK!" (397). It is an apt, elliptical ending to a narrative both deeply suspicious and incurably sympathetic to the seductive power of fantasy, performance, and profit—and the stories we tell to survive it all.

Notes

1. Maslin, "In Florida Slough with the Gators and Family Ghosts."
2. Russell, *Swamplandia!*, 31.
3. Ibid.
4. See in particular Taylor, *Reconstructing the Native South*.
5. As Paul Chaat Smith avers in *Everything You Know about Indians Is Wrong*, "Indian" is "a word that exists only with the idea of the discovery that created the modern world" (54). Similarly in her recent monograph *Our South*, Jennifer Rae Greeson reminds us that "'The South' is a term that was originally constructed out of the discourse of modern empire.... 'The South' is first and foremost an ideological concept rather than a place" (10).
6. As Greeson explains, "A concept of the South is essential to national identity in the United States of America ... it is an *internal other* for the nation, an intrinsic part of the national body that nonetheless is differentiated and held apart from the whole" (*Our South*, 1). Similar arguments have been advanced by Leigh Anne Duck, Scott Romine, Jon Smith, and others, all of whom acknowledge the influential ways that the South became the scapegoat and repository for national anxieties about racial, cultural, and economic "backwardness." For a similar acknowledgement in American Indian studies, see, for example, Roy Harvey Pearce's now classic *Savagism and Civilization*.
7. The relationship between Native American groups and the Confederacy is actually quite complicated, given that numerous southeastern tribes had economic inter-

ests (e.g., slaveholding) that allied them with the Confederacy. In 2015, debate over the Confederate battle flag resurfaced in the wake of a racially inspired shooting at a black church in South Carolina. Many commentators and Native Americans themselves used the opportunity to make an analogy between the flag and Indian mascots as unacceptable racist symbols. See Houska, "The Racial Wallpaper of Slavery and Genocide."

8. Hitt, "The Newest Indians."

9. Elsewhere I have cited examples of indigenous tourism (such as that among the Eastern Band of Cherokee Indians in North Carolina) that explicitly blur the borders between traditional ideologies and capitalist mechanisms of survival and self-determination, which has the unavoidable effect of fundamentally refashioning the character of contemporary tribal identities. See Taylor, *Reconstructing the Native South*, especially 118–71.

10. Nicole Rudick, "Karen Russell on *Swamplandia!*"

11. See Wickman, *Osceola's Legacy*.

12. Milanich, "Osceola's Head," 48.

13. McAdams, "The Collectors," 6.

Last (Un)fair Deal Going Down
Blues Tourism and Racial Politics in Clarksdale, Mississippi

KATHRYN RADISHOFSKI

> Above all, cultural meanings are not only "in the head." They organize and regulate social practices, influence our conduct and consequently have real, practical effects... [including] mark[ing] out and maintain[ing] identity within and difference between groups.
>
> Stuart Hall, *Representation*

Since the 1970s, residents of the Mississippi Delta have developed events, monuments, and accommodations catering to travelers in search of regional blues experiences.[1] In Clarksdale, Mississippi, the Delta's crown jewel of blues history destinations, the past decade and a half welded tourism investments into a photogenic downtown infrastructure, where restaurants, hotels, nightclubs, and music and art retailers vie to service touristic cravings for the city's early twentieth-century musical heritage. Alan Lomax described Coahoma County, where Clarksdale lies, as "one of the capitals of the blues," and indeed, the city has been home to some of the genre's most venerated musicians.[2] W. C. Handy, Muddy Waters, John Lee Hooker, Charlie Patton, Son House, Bukka White, Robert Johnson, and Howlin' Wolf all either lived in Clarksdale at some point or played music in its juke joints regularly. The lives and music of these African American musicians—and the contemporary black Delta musicians believed to be carrying on their legacy—constitute the central attraction for the city's predominantly white blues tourism audience.[3]

As a critical component of meaning making in place-based identity, narratives developed for tourists can contribute to the defining of local residents through a commodification of their culture and history in consistent and highly visible forms. In Clarksdale, where African Americans constitute more than three-quarters of the population, blues tourism's burgeoning appeal as a monetary palliative for the depressed Delta economy has precipitated the intertwining of this demographic's musical heritage with the region's, and the city's, public face.[4] This has afforded Mississippi the opportunity to launch a public relations campaign that combats the state's popular image as a bastion of racial intolerance and conflict with claims that its participating communities are experiencing enhanced interracial harmony through an embrace of regional blues culture.[5] The Delta's blues tourism industry thus represents a high stakes cultural arena useful for divining responses to contemporary racial identities in the region, appropriation of these identities, and desires to shape them. With these considerations in mind, this case study deploys an interdisciplinary approach, bringing national and global discourses on race, heritage tourism, representation, and music to bear on the activities of the largely white cadre of civic leaders and entrepreneurs helming the blues tourism industry in Clarksdale. My aim here is to illuminate the processes through which these leaders shape racial representations and ideologies that both undermine and underwrite social, civic, and economic agendas in the region.

The primacy of race to this research environment has informed my interest in giving it precedence in the following analysis. Certainly race has always been, and remains, of crucial significance to the social experiences of African Americans in the Delta and beyond. In addition to the atrocities and inheritances associated with legal enslavement, as in many southern states, white Mississippians deployed Black Codes, Jim Crow laws, convict leasing, prison labor, tenant farming, and lynching in the postbellum era to secure the social and economic supremacy of whites.[6] The grim state of the Delta's contemporary economy reflects lingering racial inequity between whites and blacks in Mississippi. While Clarksdale has retained a sizable black majority since the 1930s, as of 2007, African Americans owned only a third of the city's businesses.[7] A 2010 study also revealed that, at 18 percent, the unemployment rate for blacks in Mississippi is well above the national average for African Americans, while white unemployment in Mississippi rated lower than the national average for that racial demographic and, at 6.4 percent, far lower than that of the state's African American population.[8] Moreover, in 2008, almost half of black Mississippians lived in poverty, while only 15.7 percent of their white counterparts suffered the same fate.[9]

In the Delta's blues tourism industry, these historical and contemporary contexts intersect with blues mythologies fortified by essentialized racial authenticity constructs, implicating it as a sociocultural domain with disparate parameters of involvement for whites and blacks.[10] Yet, while the racial politics of Delta blues tourism has gained traction as a research topic in recent years, many of these issues remain under-investigated. The following case study represents an effort to redress this by expanding the critical scope of Delta blues tourism research.

To that end, I have focused my analysis on superintendents in Clarksdale's blues tourism industry, those inhabiting a position of leadership via a managerial, proprietary, or organizational role. Though nearly all of the researchers working on Delta blues tourism have documented the fear among musicians and locals that the industry's racial dynamics may serve as yet another mechanism through which the region's white population safeguards its ascendency, no one has yet initiated a study that looks closely at trends among the racial ideologies of the industry's managerial class in order to gain a clearer idea of their role in this process.[11] In helping to fill this lacuna in blues tourism research, the following study serves as a form of oversight vis-à-vis the racial practices employed by the blues tourism industry's most influential strata. As Joe Feagin's research on U.S. racism demonstrates, "the majority of whites who do this more serious discriminating are those with significant power to bring harm, such as white employers ... [and] managers."[12] To be sure, where industry superintendents act as representational gatekeepers, and thus, "holders of symbolic power,"[13] they remain uniquely situated to wield a great degree of influence on Clarksdale's racial structure and semiotics.

In attending to this goal of invigilation, I have prized qualitative, ethnographic methods drawn from anthropology and critical race theory to manage the topical breadth of this interdisciplinary study. Such methods allow for the operationalizing of Stuart Hall's discursive approach, illuminating the commerce between the symbolic and the material in ways that quantitative studies cannot.[14] Indeed, in forging an analysis from data drawn from extended interviews with nine of Clarksdale's blues tourism superintendents, rather than surveys, this research is better equipped to reveal actual racial attitudes and the structural and institutional agendas they serve.[15]

I begin the subsequent analysis by discussing two contradictory racial ideologies used by white producers in Clarksdale's blues tourism industry: what Eduardo Bonilla-Silva has termed color-blind racism, which, in this context, serves as a rhetorical tool for circumventing explanations of racial phenomena that impugn white involvement in blues tourism, and blues authenticity, which invokes essentializing racial narratives for tourist consumption. Many of the white superintendents interviewed for this project consider the integration of public space to be blues tourism industry's greatest contribution to racial reconciliation in Clarksdale. I therefore also explore blues tourism's impact on the racial organizing of public space. Finally, I examine how white superintendents understand their work, and the work of their black counterparts, regarding questions of appropriate involvement, revealing the ways the industry's educational agendas inform understandings of who should participate in blues tourism, and in what manner. Ultimately, I show that while some of the perspectives of the industry's white producers seem to align with the reconciliation campaign promoted in Mississippi, the ideologies infusing much of their discourse make possible the instantiation of racial projects that are helping to produce a situation antithetical to it, in which blues tourism contributes to a widening of the racial divide in Clarksdale.[16]

Authenticity and Color-blind Racism

Claims of the "real" or "authentic" carry the potential to attach credibility to the ideological content advanced by cultural tourism attractions, which are forged "in terms of points of view [and] beliefs" and can entail "the projection of one's dreams, stereotyped images, and expectations onto toured objects" and "toured others."[17] As authenticity is likewise critical to music consumption in general, and blues in particular,[18] it remains a highly productive concept for understanding the interplay between racial fantasies, touristic endeavors centered on blues heritage, and local political economies.

White folklorists of the 1960s are largely responsible for contemporary blues authenticity tropes, as they revalorized the work of early southern bluesmen like Robert Johnson and Son House, eventually pushing perceived trends among the social and stylistic profiles of these musicians—including blackness, maleness, indigence, acoustic instrumentation, and rural provenance—to the center of conversations regarding blues authenticity.[19] In Clarksdale, white blues tourists and industry superintendents are especially wont to rhapsodize about, and revel in, notions of authenticity built with the more squalid details of the genre's history. Venue aesthetics offer the most palpable instantiation of this tendency to suture into the present a romanticized and seemingly timeless vision of rural black Delta poverty. Paragons of such aesthetics include the Shack-Up Inn, which, according to their website, offers guests the option of "pass[ing] out in one of . . . [the] authentic sharecropper shacks," or a room inside a former cotton gin; and Ground Zero Blues Club, an updated version of the classic juke joint featuring dilapidated couches on the porch, walls with missing bricks, peeling paint, and a thick coat of the graffitied signatures and sentiments of their patrons—the latter representing a practice the venue's owners explicitly encourage.[20]

The responses of several African American blues tourism superintendents reveal the ways actual experiences of "blackness" in the Delta can situate blues authenticity myths within historical-political contexts that impede accessing them as a source of pleasure or entertainment. One, a native Clarksdalian, explained that "a lot of African Americans [are] not going out [to the Shack-Up Inn] because . . . they know the story of [a] one-room shack with seven, eight children growing up in it and . . . sleeping in one room. . . . A lot of it is painful. . . . They don't want to relive that. . . . But the whites want to see the authenticity of it."[21] Similarly, having experienced this history firsthand, another brought an acute emotional tenor to our discussion of white blues tourists' interest in accessing "authentic" black Delta poverty and hardship. Informing me that he used to farm, that he has "done the till," he recalled working until it was too dark to see, a labor experience he began at the age of six or seven.[22] He also remembered going out with his mother to pick cotton when he was a very young child, sitting on her cotton sack as she worked. When I suggested that his white customers are after this kind of story, he angrily retorted, "You're right they want that kind of story. Because this is shit that they can't imagine. They can't imagine going through this stuff."[23]

The exigencies born of a tourism market capitalizing on African American cultural history require white blues tourism superintendents' romanticized displays of historical black indigence to take root adjacent to the contemporary poverty faced by many of Clarksdale's African Americans. However, as Mississippi's blues tourism campaign is also a public relations project designed to combat popular images of the state's history of racial conflict, the city's white superintendents often accessed color-blind racism to bury the implications aroused when their participation in the industry was viewed through the lens of the region's racial past and present. As the prevailing racial ideology in the contemporary U.S., this rhetorical strategy is deployed with the purpose of downplaying the role of racism in the experiences of contemporary people of color, while also constructing its users as racially progressive through a denial of their own racism.[24] Among other examples, white blues tourism producers accessed the frames of color-blind racism when denying the validity or existence of criticisms of the industry's racial structure. Some reduced African American complaints about racial discrimination and exploitation within blues tourism to cheap relativism, thereby constituting black testimony as a source of subjective perspectives but not hard data. Others embedded local racism in the past by associating any lingering discriminatory attitudes or behaviors with an older, white generation. Another common tactic of color-blind racism deployed by various white superintendents involved attempting to prove their irreproachability on racial issues by testifying to their friendships with African Americans, consumption of black culture, and disagreement with persons identified as racists.[25]

The superimposition of authenticity and color-blind racism in the city's blues tourism industry aids in the designing of experiences that pander both to white tourists' racial fantasies and their desires to maintain a sense of racial innocence. The conjunctive force of these ideologies also grossly delimits the constructions and applications of race that can circulate within the industry and in the city, supporting a white epistemology of disavowal.[26] This epistemology allows white superintendents to draw on *cultural* formations of blackness as they apply to the commodification of blues heritage, while suppressing or denying understandings of the way blues tourism intersects with or undergirds *social* experiences of race for Clarksdale's contemporary African Americans. This hampers the ability of local people of color to deal head-on with industry-produced, or other forms, of racial discrimination.[27]

Visions of Reconciliation, Fantasies of Public Space

As the majority of blues tourists are white, and the industry is catering to their symbolic appetites, blues tourism is expanding what anthropologists Helán E. Page and D. France Oliviera have called white public space, rather than creating integrated public space in Clarksdale as many white superintendents claimed it does. Such white space indirectly or directly imposes an "exclusionary sanction" on perspectives developed in opposition to white, mainstream interests and is an atmosphere we are discouraged from even acknowledging (and therefore questioning). It "is like the pink elephant that does not exist [because] ... we are expected to affirm that all public space is democratized and that its racial allocation is no longer an issue since the civil rights movement."[28]

Clarksdale's blues tourism superintendents implicitly testified to the industry's impact on the city's geo-social terrain in lamenting increasing instances of "white nights"—evenings in which white tourists make up the majority of the patrons at live blues events—and in sharing their concomitant frustration over the loss of local African American patronage at blues venues most frequently invoked as exemplars of industry-produced interracial space.[29] Paradoxically, several white superintendents shared their own, or others', plans to expand Clarksdale's and the Delta's blues tourism infrastructure into what are presently predominantly African American districts or venues, in some cases by refocusing the entertainment at such venues to encompass the "regular live blues" that would attract tourists.[30]

As the latter example demonstrates, the loss of black patronage and attendant expansion of white public space is tied to the local racial semiotics of music genres. According to King and several industry superintendents, much of the Delta's adult African American population prefers soul blues and R & B to country blues, the first two representing genres not included in blues authenticity constructs or supported by many of the industry's promoters, tourists, or venues.[31]

The types of services offered by the blues tourism industry similarly contribute to the likelihood that it is facilitating a racializing of public space on behalf of whites. A recent study on Clarksdale noted that two-thirds of the city's downtown businesses "have a close association with Blues music and Delta culture" and that most of them fail to "provide for the typical, day-to-day shopping needs of Clarksdale/County residents."[32] A similar outcome has been documented within the blues tourism industry in Helena, Arkansas, which lies some thirty miles northwest of Clarksdale and also hosts a largely African American population. Early on in the development of its blue tourism industry, the disappearance of spaces in Helena suitable for local interaction occurred in tandem with the growth of new construction designed to "meet the demands of increasing numbers of tourists," such that "recent photographs of the Cherry Street District show a great number of the juke joints that once made the district popular are now parking lots" that act as "open spaces for festival visitors."[33] As blues tourism continues to develop in Clarksdale, the city's considerable African American majority may encounter a comparable spatial marginalization through the encroachment of white public space into traditionally black domains. In misreading the expansion of white public space as the spreading of integrated public space, white superintendents fail to grasp their participation in the disappearance of places where contending African American perspectives can be voiced. Concomitantly, the production of domains wherein white racial epistemologies form the consensus on racial issues and conceptions of racial reconciliation assures the latter's failure and any real change in the racial status quo.

What's more, the spatial integration that *has* appeared in Clarksdale as a result of blues tourism may produce only negligible changes in local interracial relationships. Although African Americans make up a considerable portion of blues festival crowds in Mississippi, integration at such events is fleeting.[34] When asked if blues tourism was facilitating racial reconciliation in Clarksdale, one African American superintendent shared a story that corroborates scholar Stephen A. King's findings, stressing that the social proximity of local blacks and whites occurring during blues festivals is followed by the reappearance of segregated space. I was informed that if I were to stay in Clarksdale "till Sunday afternoon, around like six o'clock," following a blues festival, "the only thing you gonna see is the street sweeper.... Then Monday, it's almost like a ghost town. And some of the local people that you met through visitors—'Hey, Sally! Hey, Joe! You know, I own a place round here on Delta. You need to come by and holler at me.'—After the visitors are gone, you don't see them anymore until the next Juke Joint Festival, next Sunflower Blues.... It ain't the same on an everyday basis compared to special occasions."[35]

Only one superintendent, an African American, in Clarksdale's blues tourism industry expressed an interest in designing public space specifically with the city's African Americans in mind—including its blues musicians. While he does sponsor blues performances bimonthly and during festivals, he maintains a distance from the blues tourism industry itself, rejecting its black poverty authenticity aesthetic, limited musical purview, and lack of concern for the social comfort of African Americans.[36]

Participation and Racialized Labor Structures

When discussing who should participate in the industry, Clarksdale's white blues tourism superintendents focused on three main criteria: outsider, or nonlocal status, which they claimed would bring a much-needed, fresh perspective to blues tourism; passion for the blues; and, finally, business and scholarly credentials, a designation some claimed for themselves or their employees. As black Deltans are locals, and, as I will show, considered by some white producers to be dispassionate or unknowledgeable about the blues and lacking business acumen (or both), it comes as no surprise that a racialized distribution of labor exists within the industry.

This racialization of labor is naturalized and reproduced through the industry's educational projects, which build on assumptions regarding local black ignorance or indifference to the blues. One white superintendent observed that "private schools in Clarksdale . . . but not the public schools" patronize his establishment.[37] According to Stephen A. King and several superintendents, the Delta's private school system maintains almost entirely white student bodies, and the region's public schools generally service only African American children.[38] Thus, this superintendent's statement evinces a perspective that sees a lack of investment in blues heritage on the part of the Delta's African American community, a viewpoint he articulated overtly during our interview in arguing that "the black community takes [local blues heritage] for granted. It's just so everyday part of the history . . . it's not really appreciated." Similarly, when asked if the industry was trying to educate local African Americans about the blues, another white superintendent said yes, "exactly."[39] One white superintendent identified the region's African American youth and their parents as susceptible to incorrect notions about blues heritage, a "problem" he hopes to correct by bringing local schoolchildren to his establishment: "I want the locals, especially the people from this [community] here, the kids. I want to tell them that this is their heritage. And obviously when you go on this racial thing, most of them are black. So they should know that some people love this stuff . . . then they can form their own opinion. Not what their surrounding says . . . related to certain not-good environmental music too . . . So it's not only what you hear today that's in, because the kids at school think it's in. Or your parents don't like that. Make up your own mind."[40] Similarly, another white blues tourism superintendent shared that he believes public funding for blues tourism initiatives could help juke joint owners, a group he identified as African American, "to see, as they interact finally with tourists, . . . what are they coming here for"—instruction that this superintendent, specifically, believes himself to be uniquely capable of delivering.[41]

The general assumption among the white superintendents that local African Americans need to be educated about the blues and blues tourism sometimes invokes anthropologist Charles Valentine's myth of the "disorganized poor."[42] Culled from a culture of poverty stereotypes, this myth depicts the impoverished as "collectively weak and ineffective, incapable of organization, planning or sustained purposeful action, irresolute and lacking in will, dependent, helpless, and resigned."[43] Here Valentine's critique applies to the logic some white superintendents adduce to justify their right to manage the industry over the right of the region's African Americans, who, on account of the economic marginality associated with their geographical origins, are identified as possessing a sociocultural background that does not provide the same skill set their white middle- and upper-class counterparts access to produce managerial efficacy and consequently financial success. One participant in this study, for instance, distinguished between the relative prosperity of the white-managed Ground Zero Blues Club and Red's Lounge, a juke joint owned and managed by Red Paden, an African American.[44] This superintendent believes Paden isn't making money because "he's just not very efficient" and "is relying on others to promote it," while Ground Zero is successful because it "is promoting itself."[45] This superintendent eventually extended his use of the myth of the disorganized poor to suggest that a black and white division of the industry's various labors is necessary to its successful functioning. Discussing two African Americans currently participating in Clarksdale's blues tourism industry, the white superintendent claimed that he is not able to participate in blues tourism in the same way that these men do, but could only ever be a "fake" or "emulate" them because the capabilities these African Americans bring to the tourism industry are "just not in my background."[46] This superintendent further indicated that one of these African Americans, a superintendent himself, is less capable of dealing with various managerial responsibilities than his white counterparts. In subtracting the ability to successfully navigate the organizational aspects of running a club from the African American superintendent's professional qualifications, this white superintendent leaves little outside of the authenticity associated with black identity and geographical origins to support his contention that the African American superintendent, and not himself, can "run a juke joint and make it a juke joint."[47]

The central didactic project in Clarksdale's blues tourism industry that functions as an engine for a racialized labor schema is the Delta Blues Museum's Arts and Education program, which, according to its website, "keeps the history of the Delta blues alive" by teaching students "to play the blues on the instrument or instruments of their choice." A number of the industry's white superintendents showed support for the program, with one declaring that "the Blues Museum's doing a good job trying to teach blues music" to "young African Americans," saying that the program will help "put them to work ... playing music."[48] This superintendent's perception that the Blues Museum's program mainly targets local black youth and can train them for a career in the blues makes clear the program's role in fortifying the industry by refreshing its talent pool with young black Deltans, who satisfy the racial and regional conditionality required of "authentic" blues players. Indeed, as many of the older black blues musicians die out, some of the African American children tutored in the Arts and Education program have begun to take their place, playing blues music in Clarksdale's blues tourism venues.

The misguided paternalism apparent in this didactic project—ambitiously developed with the aim of offering "a way out" of the endemic poverty suffered by the region's African American population—can contribute to the premature entry of its younger members into scenarios that require adult sensibilities. At the same time, it may compromise access to other educational and career opportunities, while making appealing a labor domain that likely represents the blues tourism industry's least consistent or remunerative. Finally, it may push young black Deltans into inhabiting social roles that resemble minstrelsy through their reproduction of essentialized African American portrayals for white audiences. In discussing a recent performance by a local teen who trained in the Arts and Education program, one African American superintendent trenchantly critiqued the program in this vein, observing that some of the local African American blues players who started playing at a young age in the program began drinking, smoking, and looking prematurely haggard and old, and didn't finish school, or were homeschooled. This superintendent added, "You got a thirteen year-old kid ... you exposing him to this type of thing because you trying to keep blues alive.... Yeah, the tourism stuff, they love that. 'Cause he can play his ass off. But where he going from here?"[49]

Alternately, several of the industry's African American superintendents used different standards to determine who should participate in blues tourism. One placed the interests of the community at the center of his perspective, arguing that participants should be "people who are doing stuff for the community to keep it going. People who are trying to bring money into the town, to enhance the town, make the whole town better."[50] Another African American superintendent largely focused on racial considerations, as did white counterparts, but did so without using authenticity constructs and refrained from assigning specific forms of labor to particular racial groups. Instead, this superintendent argued for the participation of black Deltans in the industry on the premise that they are the rightful inheritors of blues heritage, wondering why the living relations of deceased or living Delta blues musicians being promoted in Clarksdale, many of whom live in the area, haven't been incorporated into local blues tourism. According to this superintendent, African Americans should participate in blues tourism because "when you talking about the blues, you talking about black folk."[51]

Conclusion

Such findings require us to consider the following question: can anything be done to effect a change that would allow for blues tourism to act as a more equitable racial institution? In answering this question, the differences between white and black assessments of blues tourism offered in this research are instructive. If the self-serving racial attitudes of white superintendents are currently dominating the industry, securing leaders whose intentions are informed by the interests of local African Americans would allow for a reworking of the industry's initiatives and historical narratives in ways remaining accountable to the diverse personal histories of black Deltans, the local and national asymmetries between contemporary racial groups, and the everyday needs of the local community. An inversion of the industry's educational agendas—wherein the critical investigation of white racial privileges and ideologies would inform didactic trajectories—could also aid in the redesigning of blues tourism as a less discriminatory phenomenon, as could a formal uniting of racial reconciliation and blues tourism, especially if overseen by an external body dedicated to and versed in the parameters and exigencies of rapprochement efforts in the Delta.

Considering the implications of this research more broadly, in inducting Clarksdale into national and global conversations about race and racialized music—such as the discourse orbiting color-blind racism, authenticity, white public space, and cultural tourism—the interdisciplinary framework employed here has the effect of discursively deprovincializing Mississippi and the South, which are often constituted as moral outposts and scapegoats in popular narratives about U.S. race relations. As such, this research is also useful for evincing how constructions of "place"—and the "South" in particular—shape the operations of racial ideologies. As this paper has shown, the region's racial reputation can affect how its contemporary inhabitants deal with its particular monuments to white supremacy, inspiring efforts that overcompensate for the inglorious position of Mississippi's racial legacies in the national racial imaginary by obscuring the ways African American music heritage has been co-opted to sustain white privilege in local settings.

Notes

1. King, *I'm Feeling the Blues Right Now*, 56.
2. Lomax, *The Land Where the Blues Began*, 24.
3. King, *I'm Feeling the Blues Right Now*, 16; Rotenstein, "The Helena Blues," 143.
4. United States Census Bureau, "State and County Quick Facts."
5. King, *I'm Feeling the Blues Right Now*, 9–11.
6. Ibid., 122–29. See chapter 1 of Lipsitz, *The Possessive Investment in Whiteness* for

a detailed discussion of the accumulated unjust inheritances racial minorities face as the victims of the West's racial hierarchy. For more information on the racial experiences of African Americans in the Mississippi Delta during the antebellum and postbellum eras, see Berrey, *The Jim Crow Routine*; Cobb, *The Most Southern Place on Earth*.

7. United States Census Bureau, "State and County Quick Facts."
8. D. Hall and Austin, "Distressed Mississippi."
9. King, *I'm Feeling the Blues Right Now*, 10.
10. Ibid.
11. Dempsey, "Refuse to Fold," 6; King, *I'm Feeling the Blues Right Now*, 177–92; Rotenstein, "The Helena Blues."
12. Feagin, *Racist America*, 141.
13. Lidchi, "The Poetics and Politics of Exhibiting Other Cultures," 179.
14. S. Hall, *Representation*, 6.
15. Bonilla-Silva, *Racism without Racists*, 11.
16. Omi and Winant's notion of the racial project identifies collective movements that are "simultaneously an interpretation, representation or explanation of racial dynamics and an effort to reorganize and redistribute resources along particular racial lines" (*Racial Formation in the United States*, 56).
17. Wang, "Rethinking Authenticity in Tourism Experience," 351; King, *I'm Feeling the Blues Right Now*, 104.
18. Gibson and Connell, *Music and Tourism*; Grazian, *Blue Chicago*; King, *I'm Feeling the Blues Right Now*.
19. Grazian, *Blue Chicago*, 36; King, *I'm Feeling the Blues Right Now*, 45–46; Wald, *Escaping the Delta*, 2004.
20. Shack Up Inn.
21. Anonymous, interview with the author, February 2013.
22. Ibid.
23. Ibid.
24. Bonilla-Silva, *Racism without Racists*, 1, 131.
25. See Radishofski, "Last (Un)Fair Deal Goin' Down," chapter 1 ("Authenticity and Color-blind Racism") for an extended analysis of framings of these ideologies in superintendents' discussions on the industry and Clarksdale's racial past and present.
26. Milazzo, "White Supremacy, White Knowledge, and Anti-West Indian Discourse in Panama."
27. Tatum, "Breaking the Silence," 117–19.
28. Page and Oliviera, "Visual Images of the Postcolonial Blues on the Corner of Toulouse and Royal," 86.
29. Anonymous, interview with the author, February 2013.
30. Anonymous, interview with the author, January 2013.
31. Anonymous, interview with the author, February 2013; King, *I'm Feeling the Blues Right Now*, 101; anonymous, interview with the author, January 2013.
32. Henshall, "Downtown Clarksdale," 33.
33. Rotenstein, "The Helena Blues," 140–43.
34. King, *I'm Feeling the Blues Right Now*, 101, 182.
35. Anonymous, interview with the author, February 2013.

36. Ibid.

37. Anonymous, interview with the author, February 2013.

38. King, *I'm Feeling the Blues Right Now*, 182; anonymous, interview with the author, February 2013; anonymous, interview with the author, January 2013.

39. Anonymous, interview with the author, February 2013.

40. Ibid.

41. Anonymous, interview with the author, January 2013.

42. Valentine, *Culture and Poverty*.

43. Valentine quoted in Gregory, *Black Corona*, 10.

44. Anonymous, interview with the author, January 2013. Although Ground Zero Blues Club is co-owned by a multiracial group of investors, including actor Morgan Freeman, the club is managed solely by one of its white co-owners Bill Luckett. As the study participant is here making distinctions between management styles, the racial identity of the managers of the establishments, and not the owners, takes precedence here.

45. Anonymous, interview with the author, January 2013.

46. Ibid.

47. Ibid.

48. Ibid.

49. Anonymous, interview with the author, February 2013.

50. Ibid.

51. Ibid.

The Politics of Hillbilly Horror

EMILY SATTERWHITE

Hillbilly horror films have been an important locus of interdisciplinary research.[1] Scholarship about rural-set horror films employs a wide array of disciplinary frameworks to examine the ways in which the films map space, stereotype place, and criticize uneven geographic development. Lead theorists of the hillbilly horror subgenre have emerged especially from literary studies but also from geography, anthropology, and Appalachian studies.[2] Such work on the subgenre is made possible in part by scholars of the horror genre more broadly who trained in communication, media and film studies, sociology, anthropology, and philosophy.[3] Many of the most influential horror film scholars, including those working on hillbilly horror, approach films through the lenses of feminist or queer theories. The form of interdisciplinarity practiced by scholars of hillbilly horror traverses social sciences and humanities disciplines, incorporating qualitative and quantitative analyses. Hillbilly horror scholarship, then, constitutes a form of collaboration that is both inherent in southern studies and a model for future work.

Nonetheless, to date these collaborations have been unable to bridge an impasse in our understanding of the political valences of hillbilly horror films. Some scholars and most lay observers find the politics of hillbilly horror films anathema to efforts for social justice in the films' sexism, racism, and classism, yet hillbilly horror scholars frequently claim the films to be transgressive in their progressive critiques of U.S. norms. Both sets of claims—hillbilly horror as promoting or challenging hegemony—generally rely on close readings of the films themselves, without much or any evidence beyond close readings to support their interpretations.[4]

Skepticism about the progressive politics of hillbilly horror films is patently warranted. Laden with vulgar stereotypes, rural-set films often appear to emphasize the depravity, danger, and monstrosity of white rural people and places. As one blogger noted about the film *Staunton Hill* (2009), "If this [movie's] goal was to give white small town Americans a worse cinematic rep than they already have, well then it certainly succeeded."[5] Yet sophisticated close readings of particular films within the hillbilly horror subgenre have argued persuasively that horror films can marshal the figure of the mutinous redneck antihero for the purpose of critique of U.S. nationalism, capitalism, class hegemony, or uneven geographic development and hierarchies of geography.[6] While scholars' close readings are compelling, actual viewers' interpretations of, and investments in, hillbilly horror films remain under-documented and under-analyzed. Methods and insights from the field of reception studies can contribute a valuable additional dimension for assessing films' consequences—for the construction of overlapping imagined geographies of Appalachia, the South, and rural U.S. locales more broadly, and for the sociopolitical consequences of these geographic imaginaries for rural-identified Americans.

Beyond hillbilly horror, audience studies have often been undertaken as a social science endeavor, relying on surveys, focus groups, or ethnography, commonly with the assumption that a text's "preferred reading" is a hegemonic one.[7] "Fan studies" scholarship, on the other hand, has tended toward ethnographies that underscore the potential for human agency and resistance to the dominant ideologies presumed to be embedded in mass media texts. Since the year 2000, reception studies in the United States have promoted a third set of methodologies that emphasize the qualitative study of evidence produced by readers and viewers. Reception studies may employ ethnography, but frequently they rely especially on textual evidence such as fan mail, letters to the editor, online customer reviews, or film adaptations.[8]

For this essay, I work in this more recent tradition of reception studies to examine reactions to two recent low-budget "nightmare visions of the rural," *Wrong Turn 2: Dead End* (2007) and *Staunton Hill* (2009), both selected because they so deliberately follow in the tradition of the now-canonical *The Texas Chain Saw Massacre* (1974) in their representation of decimated rural economies and because of my particular interest in Appalachian settings. I thematized reviews posted to websites for Amazon, IMDb, and Netflix, as well as a selection of online horror blogs, to assess whether viewers registered the films' commentaries on American capitalism, urban exploitation of the rural, and the social injustice that results from deliberate and unequal processes of capitalist development (see table 1). As David Church notes, "texts cannot fully dictate their reception," but "they still provide interpretive cues to which viewers may respond in varied ways for more or less ideological reasons."[9]

My findings support both readings of hillbilly horror—as contributing to a normative condemnation of white Americans marginalized by class and region and as opening up a public space for discussion of the consequences of industrial capitalism. In the case of *Wrong Turn 2*, at least, customer reviews suggest some viewers indeed recognize in the film a critique of the consequences of irresponsible industrial capitalism and its attendant environmental injustices.

Analysis of customer reviews points to a third set of responses, heretofore unanticipated by close readings of the films themselves, in which a sort of sympathy for rural villains serves not progressive but reactionary ends. In other words, while cheering for monstrous hillbillies certainly might translate into a challenge to hegemonic geographic and class norms—a kind of talking back from margin to center—the tenor and content of *Staunton Hill* reviews suggest the film at times promotes a reactionary populist politics in defense of rural white landowners trespassed upon by leftist urban-identified outsiders. In this context, rooting for hillbilly monsters that prey on trespassing outsiders may translate into an affirmation of xenophobia and a conservative "states' rights" white supremacist stance on race and immigration. In my conclusion, I will explore whether such politics might appeal in particular to white males who see themselves as entitled to power via the "wages of whiteness" but resentfully feel themselves to be marginalized by class and geography instead.

The Cultural Work of Rural Dystopia in *Wrong Turn 2* and *Staunton Hill*

The depravity of the countryside is, of course, a much older trope than the inventions of Appalachia and the South that solidified in the late 1800s. Just to give two examples of works in the U.S. context, Richard Slotkin's foundational American studies text *Regeneration through Violence* (1973) charts American stories about the white male hero in the wilderness who gains the power of the primitive by acts of violence in the service of saving civilization (dramatized as the rescue of a white woman), while Bernice Murphy's *The Rural Gothic in American Popular Culture* (2013) makes abundantly clear the persistence into the twenty-first century of cultural productions that appear to "return to the scene of the crime" in their worrying over the perils and brutalities of European settlement of North America and the founding of the United States. Repeatedly in the white European narrative of American civilization, "the city on the hill" stands as a beacon of progress, wherein city equals good and country equals bad. Whether in the guise of wilderness savagery, rural barbarism, or provincial small towns, the countryside has been understood as a static relic of a past that deigns to linger on out of obstinacy toward the clear-the-frontier push for violent expansion.[10]

Visions of rural dystopia like those found in hillbilly horror have functioned in service of this narrative of progress and in resistance to it. In service of this narrative, horror films cast the countryside as deserving of misery because of its monstrosity, its refusal to conform, and its opposition to urban progress. In resistance to this civilizing narrative, blame for the miseries of the countryside—and the obfuscation of those miseries in idyllic versions of the countryside—are laid at the feet of the city. Films that highlight the realities of uneven economic development and environmental injustice—if in fantastical ways, in the case of the hillbilly horror subgenre—"bring squarely into view the realities that notions of progress seek to obscure" and "talk back to a cannibalizing urban core that gobbles up land and everything else in its way."[11] Like Walter Benjamin's reflection on history as catastrophe rather than progress, and the future as an irresistible storm, the hillbilly horror film sees "piles of rubble" where we would like to see a neat "chain of events."[12]

Assessing the cultural work performed by the hillbilly horror subgenre has become more urgent since a surge in its production after the release of *The Blair Witch Project* in 1999 (a rush of production paralleled in the horror genre as a whole).[13] Comments posted in Internet customer reviews indicate that the subgenre is readily recognized by viewers, who tend to refer to rural villains with some combination of at least two of the following terms: "mutant," "inbred," "cannibal," "hillbilly," and "redneck." (These terms are interchangeable as adjective or as noun, as in "Hideously deformed inbred hillbilly cannibals," "the usual bunch of Southern inbreds," or "superhuman inbred religious hillbillies.")[14] Films scholars identify as "hillbilly horror" or "urbanoia" are in fans' terminology usually identified as "backwoods horror" or "backwoods slashers."[15]

Wrong Turn 2 and *Staunton Hill*, both of which were released straight to video without a theatrical release, feature Appalachian settings and explicitly implicate a capitalist market economy in the creation of the "monstrous-rural."[16] In *Wrong Turn 2*, the hillbilly cannibals are figured as the victims of environmental injustice and deindustrialization, poisoned by tainted water supply and toxins from an abandoned factory. In *Staunton Hill*, an Appalachian farm family has turned from a struggling livelihood based in slaughtering pigs to a more profitable black market trade providing human body parts to wealthy accident victims. As the table below illustrates, neither film won high praise from viewers. Nonetheless, the longevity of the *Wrong Turn* franchise (2015 witnessed its sixth installment and *Wrong Turn 7* is slated for release in 2017) and the marketing of *Staunton Hill* as the work of horror maestro George Romero's son have ensured familiarity of the films among horror aficionados.[17]

Customer reviews of slasher films are highly conventionalized. Reviews sometimes give a thumbnail sketch of the plot and pass judgment on its realism or predictability. They frequently exhibit great familiarity with conventions of the subgenre and describe the film in relation to its obvious predecessors, such as *The Texas Chain Saw Massacre*. Typically, slasher reviews

TABLE 1 *Wrong Turn 2* and *Staunton Hill* Online Customer Reviews and Ratings as of October 15, 2013

	Wrong Turn 2		Staunton Hill	
Review Source	Rating	Number of Reviews	Rating	Number of Reviews
Amazon	3.5 (out of 5)	100	2.9 (out of 5)	20
Netflix	3.1 (out of 5)	324*	2.7 (out of 5)	98
IMDb	5.4 (out of 10)	148†	3.7 (out of 10)	25
TOTAL		572		143

*Of 324 Netflix reviews of *WT2*, I analyzed 166 (approximately the first half dating from the time of the film's release), making my analysis based on a total of 413 of 572 *WT2* reviews. Mediocre ratings and relatively low numbers of reviews suggest the films were not popular with audiences.
†Two reviews are duplicates, leaving 146 distinct reviews.

address the quantity of the gore as well as its quality (e.g., in terms of creativity, makeup, and special effects). Horror fans also routinely pass judgment on scariness, female hotness and nudity (or both), and the quality of the actors, director, and screenplay. Representative comments include these: "Lots of awesome killings and you can feel the suffering in the characters eyes" (*Staunton Hill*).[18] "Gore, Ugly freaks, and some hot chicks, what more do you want??" (*Wrong Turn 2*).[19] "This movie is 1000 times better, scarier and gorier than the first. It is a must see for all horror fans and gorehounds. The gore is just nonstop" (*Wrong Turn 2*).[20] A reviewer who gave *Wrong Turn 2* four out of five stars was impressed: "The gore. OH MY GOD the gore . . . I nearly spit beer across my living room when I saw the first kill."[21]

The conventions of customer reviews make it admittedly difficult to use them to discern viewers' interpretation and construction of nuanced ideological messages, although, as these quotes illustrate, the vast majority of customer reviews unreflectively express support for crass hegemonic norms regarding the importance of women's appearance (and nudity), the savagery of the poor, disgust for physical variation, and—given that the physical abnormalities of the mutant hillbillies are codes for class and race—endorsement of classism and racism. Effusiveness about filmic violence and its appeal for "gorehounds," while not conforming in some ways to broader cultural norms, is seldom linked to recognition of structural or symbolic violence. It is rare to find meta-commentary on a slasher film's cultural politics or ideological content with regard to the setting or villains, although disparaging comments about the cultural politics of violence and to a lesser extent gender are slightly more common. Nonetheless, reviews provide evidence that at least some viewers are able to use the occasion of backwoods horror films to articulate sympathy with country people, lament the conditions of rural economies, or critique the U.S. economic system.

Wrong Turn 2: "These Inbred Cannibals Were People Once"

The six-film *Wrong Turn* franchise, set in southern West Virginia, features cannibals with a variety of physical deformities. In *Wrong Turn 2: Dead End*, a straight-to-video release distributed by 20th Century Fox Home Entertainment, "a clan of mutant hayseed cannibals" prey on producers and contestants filming a *Survivor*-like reality TV show who mistake "the flesh eaters' woodland turf" for uninhabited forest.[22] *Wrong Turn 2* is the only film in the franchise that posits the hillbillies' deformities and cannibalism as the result of rural industrial capitalism.

As of September 2013, *Wrong Turn 2* had garnered 572 reviews on Netflix .com, Amazon.com, and IMDb.com combined.[23] Reviewers regularly commented upon the differences between the original and *Wrong Turn 2*, with many characterizing the first film as more "atmospheric" versus the shockingly gory sequel. According to reviewers, *Wrong Turn 2* was less atmospheric in part because the villains were less elusive than in the original. Rather than seen only in fleeting glimpses, the hillbillies get a great deal more screen time, in part because viewers are introduced to what many called the cannibals' backstory.

In *Wrong Turn 2*, we learn that the cannibals are products of environmental injustice. They are figured less as products of inbreeding due to isolation in the wilderness (as implied in the first *Wrong Turn*) and more as victims of a toxic post-industrial landscape (see photo 1). As one reviewer explains, *Wrong Turn 2* informs us that "an abandoned pulp mill released chemical wastes on the creek, killing the animals and transforming the descendants of a local family in[to] deformed mutants. Without animals to hunt or fish to catch, the next generation chases travelers to feed themselves."[24] Reviews on horror film blogs were even more likely to articulate the film's argument. A reviewer for *DVD Verdict* noted that the "hill-country family" was "mutated by pulp mill pollution" and their "diet of man-flesh and toxic waste."[25] This backstory shifts the blame for the cannibals' deviance away from the cannibals themselves to the system that produced them, and it casts their cannibalism as necessary for survival following the devastation of their ecosystem and economy.

Though just eighteen of the 413 reviews that I examined explicitly mention that the hillbilly cannibals are the products of toxic pollution, it is clear that the film's statement regarding the consequences of industrial pollution was legible for average viewers (see photos 2 and 3).[26] Indeed, almost a third of reviewers give at least some hint of what Carter Soles would call "sympathy for the devil."[27] (An additional eleven mention that the film gives the cannibals' "backstory," though it is not clear what the viewers understand that story to be.)

In the words of one reviewer, *Wrong Turn 2* tries "to 'develop' the hicks

PHOTO 1. One of the mutant cannibal family in the abandoned pulp mill (*Wrong Turn 2*, 20th Century Fox Home Entertainment, 2007)

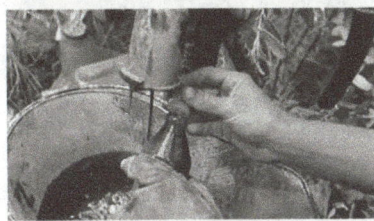

PHOTO 2. Polluted water supply (*Wrong Turn 2*, 20th Century Fox Home Entertainment, 2007)

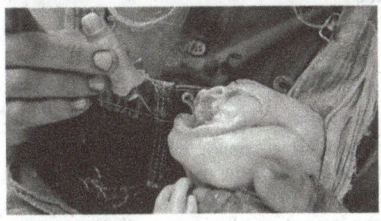

PHOTO 3. Effects of toxic waste on the local population (*Wrong Turn 2*, 20th Century Fox Home Entertainment, 2007)

by fleshing out their story and showing them as a family."[28] A number of reviewers commented upon the dinner table scene, when the cannibal family "join hands and say grace before devouring a potful of human stew."[29] A few reviewers mentioned the "very touching moment . . . , when the father, [lets] his boy shoot the bow and arrow, and like the two just look at each other in a cool, father and son moment."[30] While some reviewers saw such scenes as "cheeky touches" or "macabre humour," others felt that such scenes humanized the inbred mutants.[31] In one reviewer's words, "The mutants have much more screen time and human appeal than the original. They watch television, eat, and pray together. All the things that normal families do."[32] Almost all of those who commented upon this aspect of the film were disappointed by the way in which it reduced the fear factor, although in one instance a reviewer found it *more* frightening to think that the family behavior was portrayed as "normal."[33] Tellingly, some reviewers referred to the cannibals not as "bloodthirsty" but as "hungry," evoking images of suffering and poverty rather than wickedness or soullessness (see table 2).

In one singular, striking, and highly visible instance, reviewer Michael J. Tresca of Fairfield, Connecticut, combined into social commentary the observations that *Wrong Turn 2* explained the genesis of the hillbillies' cannibalism and humanized the cannibals. Although he acknowledges that the film is "so

TABLE 2 Topics Mentioned by Reviewers Sympathetic to *Wrong Turn 2*'s Rural Villains

Topics Mentioned	Number of Reviewers
Cannibals	51
—as products of toxic pollution	18
—as victims of toxics from pulp mill or factor	11
—backstory of	17
—pity for	3
—poverty of	2
Hillbillies	103
—as normal	20
—as hungry	12
—and food	40
—and hunting	26
—as too human or not scary enough	5
Positive appreciation for or defense of the rural	13
Understanding of cannibals as agents of just vengeance	8
Appreciation of landscape	3
Backtalk	2
(TOTAL SYMPATHETIC REVIEWERS)	(167)

This table identifies topics or themes common to reviews that express some sympathy for the rural villains in *Wrong Turn 2* or some attempt to contextualize or humanize the violence they commit. It is based on 413 reviews examined (out of 572 reviews available as of October 15, 2013), including all Amazon and IMDb reviews and one half of Netflix reviews (see note 26). Reviews mentioning more than one topic are counted in multiple categories.

violent, so vile, that you can't see the social commentary because you're wiping blood out of your eyes," Tresca asserts that the film "is probably as good as the mutant-slaughter genre gets." According to Tresca, *Wrong Turn 2* is "always reminding us that these inbred cannibals were people once."[34]

Tresca admires what he sees as the film's critique of consumer capitalism in the media industry, calling *Wrong Turn 2* "rife [with] commentary on our cannibalistic tendencies to feast on celebrities in the media." He makes an explicit link between reality shows and slasher flicks when he says their plots are facile and not "deep." For Tresca, when the character of the TV show director "tries to force Jake (Texas Battle) into an onscreen liaison with Elena" for the sake of sensational reality TV, he finds it little less morally repugnant than the "incestuous relationship between 'Brother' and 'Sister' mutants." Tresca links the critique of reality television to social commentary on class disparity: "While upper class folks are stumbling around for cash on television, the people we can't see have to survive every day." The cannibals "are the underclass, the underprivileged, the people who don't need a reality show to get their thrills and can't afford cable."

Of course, the number of viewers who recognized the presence of an explanatory backstory does not necessarily indicate that the viewers share the film's implied critique. One reviewer simply combined the inbreeding origins narrative with the explanation in the sequel, calling the cannibal family "the product of generations of inbreeding, combined with exposure to chemicals and poisons from an abandoned pulp mill."[35] Another liked that the film "explained a lot things that I didn't understand in part 1" such as the "aftermath of pollution and [its] effect on the people who refused to leave the polluted area," somehow managing to blame the victim after all.[36] And one reviewer, who recognized the film's claim that "the superhuman freaks are victims of environmental pollution," called it "a rather silly premise."[37]

Staunton Hill: That's What You Get for "Invading the Houses of Country Folks"

While there is some evidence of the potential for critique of the effects of industrial capitalism in response to *Wrong Turn 2*, reviews of *Staunton Hill* point to the potential for nurturing reactionary politics in the service of capitalism. *Staunton Hill* is another straight-to-video release (distributed by Anchor Bay Entertainment, which has a distribution agreement with 20th Century Fox Home Entertainment) that gained the attention of horror buffs thanks to the cult fame of director Cameron Romero's father, George Romero, director and co-writer of *Night of the Living Dead* (1968).[38] Despite its pedigree, *Staunton Hill* failed to attract much of a following, and as of October 2013 it had garnered just 143 reviews on Netflix.com, Amazon.com, and IMDb.com combined—fewer than any of the films in the popular *Wrong Turn* franchise. A majority of critics complained that the film is derivative, with most of those identifying it as a "'Texas Chainsaw Massacre' knock off."[39] As one blogger commented, "'Staunton Hill' may be a big hit with the small niche of horror fans who love southern-fried-slashers but for the more broader-based genre fan, it's just another 90 minute clich[é]."[40]

Staunton Hill is set in 1969, when a group of young friends are hitchhiking "up to D.C. for the [political] rallies." Forced by ruse to spend the night in a barn "on a remote family farm in the hills of Virginia," the activists "fall victim" to what the IMDb plot summary contributor calls a "clan's brutal harvest."[41] As is hinted at in the choice of the word "harvest," the film proposes that collecting human body parts and selling them to wealthy accident victims on the black market is simply the natural evolution of an Appalachian farm family's search for a livelihood once small-scale raising and slaughtering of pigs is no longer a viable line of work. *Staunton Hill* therefore features a kind of metaphorical cannibalism, rather than the actual cannibalism in *Wrong Turn 2*, as in the way one might cannibalize a discarded piece of equipment to keep more desirable equipment running.

A film that sees the logical end of market capitalism as the commodifica-

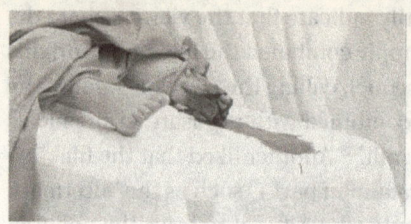

PHOTO 4. A wealthy accident victim awaits a foot transplant (*Staunton Hill*, Anchor Bay Entertainment, 2009)

tion of body parts for those who can afford them offers a tremendous potential for progressive critique, but in the case of *Staunton Hill* this potential appears to have gone largely unrealized. Not quite half of twenty-three horror bloggers mentioned the role of the organ trade in the film, and no bloggers pursued its implications.[42] Of all 143 customer reviews of *Staunton Hill*, only five indicate that the viewer recognized that "a mad doctor pays for body parts provided by the deranged family" and correctly identified the motivation of the rural villains as financial profit.[43] Another twelve viewers almost grasp the plot but throw up their hands in befuddlement: "Buddy, Momma and Grandma ... make their living on body parts.... There is also a backstory about a lab, a doctor and surgery being performed on a young girl but that really has no explanation."[44] One reason so few reviewers identify the villains' profit motive is that the film's cuts between the farm and the operating room make the plot confusingly difficult to follow—as evidenced by numerous frustrated complaints. In at least one instance, a reviewer identified the organ trade as linked not to the family's desire for profit but to their religiosity: they "slaughter innocent people for their 'parts'" because they are "convinced that they are doing a good deed for God" (see table 3).[45]

There is a historical precedent for capitalist hicks in *Texas Chain Saw Massacre* and especially its 1986 sequel (in which the hicks sell their human victims as barbecue). Like *Texas Chain Saw Massacre*, *Staunton Hill* implies that the young people pitted against the hicks are cosmopolitan—middle-class hippies. The hitchhikers' class is suggested by their nice jackets and blue jeans and especially by their attitude toward the junkyard they approach for help finding a ride. One of the young men says with sarcasm, "It's a nice place," to which a young woman replies with a knowing giggle, "Gorgeous." The youth include as one of their number Boone, an African American male, whose girlfriend, Raina, is white. Given the 1969 setting and the fact that Washington, D.C., is their destination, the hitchhikers may be civil rights activists, but, while they accuse the Staunton family of racism, the only other directly political talk they engage in is Boone's criticism of butchering animals for meat. The Stauntons, by contrast, are depicted as working-class, highly religious, and racist. Cooper Huckabee plays the owner of the junkyard (Burgh, whom

TABLE 3 Reviewers' Comments about What Motivates the Family's Violence in *Staunton Hill*

Category	Comments	Number of Reviewers
Reviewers accurately identifying the family's motive for violence as market economics	—reviewers mentioning organ harvesting, black market, blood-soaked trade, etc.	5
Reviewers giving some indication that they see the family's motive for violence as more complex than "bloodthirst"	—reviewers recognizing that the violence stems from something more than "bloodthirst"	8
	—reviewers correctly identifying black market subplot but express confusion anyway	4
Reviewers failing to identify family's motive as market economics	—reviewers mentioning flashbacks but saying they are confusing or nonsensical	14
	—reviewers saying that story is confusing or nonsensical	11
	—reviewers incorrectly identifying motive as cannibalism	5*
Reviewers not commenting on plot		96
TOTAL		143†

*One reviewer noted that the motive was both cannibalism and market economics, and this review was counted twice. No others were counted twice.
†The total includes 20 reviews from Amazon, 98 reviews from Netflix, and 25 reviews from IMDb posted prior to October 15, 2013.

we later learn is the Staunton patriarch), who tells the travelers that he will not serve them "long as you got that nigger fella with you." Quintin, another traveler, whom we later learn is a Staunton son and a failed medical student, comes to their aid. At this point in the film, audience sympathies are directed to Boone, who expresses pity that Burgh is "holding on to all that hate," and his antiracist companions.

Sympathies shift on the part of some reviewers, however, after the young travelers find themselves stranded by the side of the highway and are encouraged by Quintin to seek shelter for the night in a barn. While a horror scholar might read into *Staunton Hill* a critique of large-scale industrial capitalist slaughterhouses that pushed the farm family to seek an alternative livelihood, members of this subset of reviewers were more likely to complain about the young interlopers. All rural horror films feature some sense of trespass by outsiders, but usually the places featured are implicitly public—town squares, national forests, roadways, gas stations. *Staunton Hill* is a departure in that,

PHOTO 5. The villainous Staunton family prays before dinner (*Staunton Hill*, Anchor Bay Entertainment, 2009)

PHOTO 6. The Staunton family farm (*Staunton Hill*, Anchor Bay Entertainment, 2009)

instead of wilderness cannibals who hunt for meat, it features "a family of god-fearing southern farm folk" who are property owners.[46] This distinctive feature of the plot seems to have translated into some viewers' reactionary reading in defense of property rights.

A few reviews in particular blame the youthful *Staunton Hill* hitchhiking victims for their fate because they are trespassers. One reviewer put it this way: the young travelers "take it upon themselves to camp out in the barn for the night."[47] Another complained, "Don't they know that if you trespass on someone's property you can get a lot worse than that, no matter where you are or how deranged or not-deranged the homeowners are? . . . Seems to me if you're going to go around invading the houses of country folks (or any folks) uninvited, you kinda just get what you get."[48] Such viewers sided with the farm family over the integrated group of countercultural friends.

Just as southern white readers in the 1970s, ones who resented what they characterized as an intrusion by 1960s civil rights activists, may have "identified with hillbillies' attempts to discipline interlopers" in *Deliverance* as much as with James Dickey's novel's victimized outsiders,[49] some white viewers of *Staunton Hill* adopted a masculinist "get off my land" sentiment that aligned them with the religious white farm family. Reception studies of customer reviews suggest that even when there is textual potential for progressive subversion in films featuring a hillbilly antihero, certain viewers may marshal such texts for decidedly reactionary purposes. In the case of *Staunton Hill*, the usual sympathy for the middle-class victims is absent for some viewers, for whom the film instead animates white racial identities more closely aligned with a "stand-your-ground" sentiment that rationalizes violence against people of color.

The Political Uses of Hillbilly Horror

Customer reviews suggest that the political uses of backwoods slasher films vary widely across the subgenre and across viewers. Certainly crazed hillbillies contribute to a normative condemnation of white Americans marginalized by class and geography when reviewers appear to sincerely believe in "crazy inhabitants of the woods, whose total isolation from the civilization promotes the violence and the cannibalism."[50] At the same time, customer reviews indicate that some viewers are indeed able to register and articulate what hillbilly horror film scholars have identified as progressive critiques of capitalism and class oppression.

But then again, customer reviews also show us something that close readings have not: hillbilly horror films may be put to reactionary purposes that likely appeal in particular to white males who feel themselves entitled to power but marginalized by class and geography. The "'backwoods family preys on unsuspecting folks' sub-genre of horror film,"[51] with its clear geographical lines between urban middle-class outsiders and desperately poor rural whites, may allow some viewers to retrench the political dichotomy between "red states" and "blue states." Affronted by urban claims to superiority, such viewers may desire to recoup the figure of "the yeoman," the lower-class good-ole-boy white "who was both henchman and victim in the expansion of white elite capitalism and patriarchy."[52]

Viewers who align themselves with hillbilly villains against "outsiders" may see the empowerment of people of color, people of non-normative sexualities, and women as threatening what little sense of power they gain via the "wages of whiteness."[53] An outlier review, although just one of 413 *Wrong Turn 2* reviews I examined, illustrates the alienation and outrage that a racist hillbilly-identified viewer may feel when interpreting a film as siding with urban outsiders. The reviewer, who identified himself as "Leonard Smalls [the name of the bounty hunter in *Raising Arizona*], the Lone Biker of the Apocalypse from Arizona," complained that *Wrong Turn 2* blames hillbillies—"(white people, of course)"—for "nonsensical killings." Leonard complains that the victims are "politically correct caricatures," including "a hispanic lesbo," a "sex-crazed white surfer/loser guy," and a "heroic, doctoral, all-knowing wise black guy." "Leonard" objects that "it ain't the white guy" who is the last man standing. He finds it sheer "lunacy" that "the WHITE guy is the sex-crazed moron" in the film. For the reviewer, the "sex-crazed moron" character type belongs in a "BLACK" body; only the filmmakers' desire to avoid charges of racism would cast this character with a white actor.

Even as "Leonard" correctly notes the tendency of horror films to villainize "hillbillies," still his defensive response is not to see the ways in which the hillbillies are racialized as unworthy whites ("not quite white") in the service of white elite power.[54] Instead, he insists on the whiteness (and therefore goodness) of hillbillies and the depravity of blacks. His unabashedly racist proposal for retribution is to have the next film in the franchise "take place in Compton or West Baltimore. They could title it: 'Wrong Turn 3: Dis Time Dey Ghetto.'" To "be fair," the sex-crazed moron will be "hispanic or black." Villainous "drug-dealing, crack addict mutant killers" can stalk a "group of kids" (presumably white) who are saved by a "lone punk rocker or biker," "played by a white guy for sure ... who ends up killing the deformed hood rats!"[55] Leonard pretends that such a narrative would break from convention.[56]

The geographic affiliations of "Leonard Smalls" are not clearly southern. He presents himself as punk rocker and biker more so than hillbilly, although his IMDb "recommended" lists indicate his appreciation for "Redneck Mayhem Horror Films" and "White Trash Films." His review of *Wrong Turn 2* and his recommendations, including his "Top 10 Neo Nazi Movies" list, nonetheless provide an explicit link between hillbilly horror fandom and white supremacist sentiment. He may represent one end of a spectrum of white viewers, those who look to hillbilly horror as a comeuppance against threats to white power from overprivileged white elites and underprivileged people of color alike. Like defenders of the Confederate battle flag, who may believe that detractors seek only to further defame white working-class southerners and exacerbate unevenly geographically distributed class inequities, these viewers perhaps look to hillbilly horror to "affirm and avenge their white-masculinity-made-monstrosity."[57] "Leonard" may represent a set of white viewers who choose to demand the wages of whiteness rather than form alliances with people of color in rural communities who, despite being entirely invisible in hillbilly horror, are even more egregiously disadvantaged by class, health, education, and other measures of attainment than are rural and working-class whites.[58]

At a time when anti-immigration hysteria is palpable, and stand-your-ground laws seem to encourage whites to brazenly attack African Americans, some viewers may find in hillbilly horror affirmation of their sense that white rural people deserve recognition as the truest of Americans rightfully defending their status against all comers. For some viewers, the hillbilly slasher seems to reject values of inclusion, tolerance, and change. Its "xenophobia" may target not predatory urban white elites but those newcomers and immigrants seeking a place in an American landscape imagined as peopled with white farmers.[59] It is only through interdisciplinary inquiry, historically contextualized and augmented by studies of audience reception, that we discern the full range of cultural work performed by hillbilly horror.

Notes

Acknowledgments: Special thanks to Michele Grigsby Coffey and Jodi Skipper, whose Transforming New South Identities Symposium put Zandria F. Robinson, Robert H. Brinkmeyer, Leigh Ann Duck, Anne Lewis, and Daniel Cross Turner in conversation with my work at a critically formative stage. I am particularly indebted to Zandria, who saw straight through to the heart of the matter and helped me perceive the larger stakes. Leigh Ann Duck and Barbara Ellen Smith provided valuable feedback, and Virginia Tech students Meghan Oakes and Brittany Ferris provided welcome research assistance.

1. The term "hillbilly horror" is from Bell, "Anti-Idyll," 97. Like Bell, I use the term to refer to horror films in which the monster is a rural local and the victims are urban visitors.

2. Hillbilly horror scholars from the discipline of English include Carol Clover, Linnie Blake, Bernice Murphy, Carter Soles, and English teacher and professional film critic Robin Wood. Hillbilly horror scholars in other disciplines include David Bell (geography) and Justin M. Nolan and Gery W. Ryan (anthropology). In Appalachian studies, Douglas Reichert Powell's "Panoramas of Gore and other Social Inventions: Region on Film," provides a wonderful analysis of the rural-as-monster (Reichert Powell, *Critical Regionalism*, 100–46).

3. From the field of communication: Janet Staiger, Stephen Prince, and Mary Beth Oliver and Meghan Sanders; media and film studies: Matthew Hills and Barbara Creed; sociology: Andrew Tudor and Isabel Cristina Pinedo; philosophy: Noël Carroll.

4. While here I suggest that horror scholarship's focus on close readings of texts themselves ought to be augmented by analyses of films' reception, other scholars have compellingly argued that close readings must also be augmented by analyses of production. See the fascinating work of Bernard, *Selling the Splat Pack*.

5. Mr. HoRrOr, Horrormoviesandstuff Database, http://ottofries.proboards.com/thread/20731/staunton-hill-review.

6. Cf. Sharrett, "The Horror Film as Social Allegory." Also: Robin Wood (capitalism), David Bell (narratives of civilization), Carter Soles (class inequality), Linnie Blake (nationalism), and Bernice Murphy (ecological damage). Clover, *Men, Women and Chainsaws*, demonstrates the horror film's recognition of class-based and place-based environmental injustice, although in her reading the films ultimately redeem the city.

7. For Stuart Hall, a "dominant" and "preferred" reading is "encoded" into most texts. The intended reading is dominant but not "'determined,' because it is always possible to order, classify, assign and decode" a text in multiple ways. Nonetheless, "there exists a pattern of 'preferred readings'; and these both have the institutional/political/ideological order imprinted in them and have themselves become institutionalized." S. Hall, "Encoding/Decoding," 128–38.

8. Machor and Goldstein, eds., *Reception Studies*. See also Goldstein and Machor, eds., *New Directions in American Reception Study*. For ethnography, compare Radway, *Reading the Romance*; Long, *Book Clubs*; Chabot Davis, *Beyond the White Negro*.

9. Church, *Grindhouse Nostalgia*, 177.

10. I am grateful to Zandria F. Robinson for this formulation. Robinson, Review of Emily Satterwhite's "Hillbilly Horror."

11. Ibid., 1. For a savvy and insightful overview of the rural and urban in black popular culture, see Z. Robinson, "Finding the Black South," in *This Ain't Chicago*, 30–59. Robinson notes that rural spaces were actual dystopias in many ways for African Americans from slavery to World War II. Escape narratives like Richard Wright's *Black Boy* situated the South, and by proxy its rural communities, as the "scene of the crime." Yet, by the 1960s, African American authors like Maya Angelou were writing of a black southern idyllic community, one in which racism existed but was contained in a way, warded off by the strength of isolated black communities. By the 1990s, African American films were situating urban space as an alienating and ruinous force for black folks—and the rural South as a site of redemption—in order to critique the failure of the Great Migration project and racial conditions in northern cities.

12. Benjamin, "On the Concept of History."

13. "Horror films are currently enjoying a resurgence in production, popularity, and inventiveness unparalleled since the rise of the indie horror movement in the 1970s." Museum of the Moving Image, quoted in Bernard, *Selling the Splat Pack*, 1–2.

14. "Family" and "psycho" are commonly included as well, as in "oddball inbred family," JB Beverley (United States), "Let's Be Fair about This," review of *Staunton Hill* [hereafter *SH*], November 23, 2009, IMDb. "Hideously deformed inbred hillbilly cannibals" is from IAmNo4 (California), "Probably the Most Entertaining Horror Sequel I've Ever Seen," review of *Wrong Turn 2: Left for Dead* [hereafter *WT2*], October 14, 2007, IMDb. "The usual bunch of Southern inbreds" is from bigdarvick (United States), "Staunton Hill Went Downhill Fast!," *SH*, November 2, 2009, IMDb. "Superhuman inbred religious hillbillies" is from JuRK (Our Vast, Cultural Desert), "How Much Garbage Are We Supposed To Take?," *SH*, December 29, 2011, Amazon.

15. "Urbanoia" is from Clover, *Men, Women and Chainsaws*, 124. "Backwoods horror" is used in, for example, Trebe, "Outwit, Outlast, Outplay, or Die," February 8, 2011, *WT2*, Amazon; BA Harrison (Hampshire, England), "Reality Show Contestants vs. Hillbilly Cannibals. Cool!," *WT2*, September 8, 2007, IMDb; kosmasp (Germany), "Rollin(s)," *WT2*, November 24, 2009, IMDb; Woodyanders from The Last New Jersey Drive-In on the Left, "Worthy Sequel," *WT2*, May 20, 2010, IMDb. "Backwoods slasher" is found, for example, in lost-in-limbo from the Mad Hatter's tea party, "Blood Soaked Soap Opera," *WT2*, February 13, 2008, IMDb; Paul Andrews (UK), "Outrageously Gory Sequel, Probably the Best Straight-to-Video/DVD Sequel Ever in Fact," *WT2*, December 5, 2007, IMDb; LoneWolfAndCub (Australia), "An Awful Sequel to an Average Movie, but Not without its Charms," *WT2*, October 29, 2009, IMDb.

16. Bell, "Anti-Idyll: Rural Horror," 105.

17. As of July 2015, *Wrong Turn 2* is available as a DVD via Netflix, and can be rented streaming on Amazon; *Staunton Hill* is available as a DVD via Netflix. Earnings data is not available for *Wrong Turn 2* (which had a $4 million budget) or *Staunton Hill* (budget not available). In its opening year alone, the original *Wrong Turn*'s gross earnings were double its $12 million budget (IMDb, last accessed July 13, 2015).

18. D. Kerr, "Horror Junkie" (Birmingham, Alabama) (REAL NAME), "Awesome Horror Thriller," *SH*, September 18, 2009, Amazon.

19. BIG T (Louisville, Kentucky), "Gore, Ugly Freaks, and Some Hot Chicks, What More Do You Want??," *WT2*, October 12, 2010, Amazon.

20. Recent Reviews #7, *WT2*, Netflix.

21. Silvio "The Heathen" Dante "I ate your mom's brains," "This was STV? Could Have Fooled Me," *WT2*, October 30, 2007, Amazon.

22. Synopsis from "*Wrong Turn 2: Dead End*," Netflix, last accessed July 17, 2015.

23. Of these, I examined all 99 Amazon reviews, all 148 IMDb reviews, and 166 of 324 Netflix reviews, for a total of 413 of the 572 reviews. The structure of the reviews on the three websites delivers different benefits and limitations in terms of information useful for assessing audiences. IMDb has the advantage of offering fairly long reviews (often 175–600 words) and of including date and usually geographic location of reviewer—at least the country of origin if not the city or town. IMDb is less useful for characterizing numerous reviews by U.S. viewers as, of all its *Wrong Turn 2* reviews, just 35 percent are identified as posted from the United States. Amazon and Netflix likely have a larger percentage of American reviewers given that Amazon has separate websites for other countries and that Netflix's subscriber base initially was composed of U.S. postal customers. Netflix usually provides a greater quantity of reviews than the other two sites, but its reviews are frequently quite short (under 125 words) and therefore lean toward brief evaluation over descriptions that allow for more nuanced assessments of individual interpretation. The greatest disadvantage in relying on Netflix is that it does not include any information regarding the reviewer (name or location) or the date of the review. Amazon reviews typically run 125–75 words, and the site provides the most metadata of the sites, including a title, a reviewer's online nickname or name plus sometimes "Real Name" verification, the date of the review, and sometimes a geographic location.

24. Claudio Carvalho (Rio de Janeiro, Brazil), "A Replay of Many Other Movies—but with More Gore and Originality in the Deaths," *WT2*, November 30, 2007, IMDb. I use this as illustration even though it is not from a U.S. viewer because it mentions the mill and because it may have been influential given that it was rated highly useful.

25. Judge Ian Visser, *DVD Verdict*, September 18, 2007, http://www.dvdverdict.com/reviews/wrongturn2bluray.php, accessed July 16, 2015. See also Rick L. Blalock, review of *WT2*, September 11, 2007, *Terror Hook*, http://www.terrorhook.com/reviews/w/wrongturn2.html: "Within the woods lives a cannibalistic family, when chemical spills drove everyone away from the area and killed off all the wildlife, they chose to stay, hunting any human life that passes through for survival—all the while still reproducing to keep their bloodline alive."

26. Of 572 available customer reviews as of October 15, 2013, I examined all those on Amazon and IMDb plus one-half of the Netflix reviews for a total of 413. On Netflix, I looked at the first three reviews to appear, which are those rated by other customers as "Reviews voted most helpful," plus the next 163 reviews listed as "Recent Reviews." The "most helpful" reviews were designated as such by 75 to 134 "members"; by contrast, the remainder of the reviews were endorsed by fifteen members at most.

27. Soles, "Sympathy for the Devil," 233–50.

28. Recent Reviews #5, *WT2*, Netflix.

29. Reviewers praised or jeered the film's mimicry of the dinner table scene in *The Texas Chain Saw Massacre*.

30. kairingler (United States), "Inbreeding 2," *WT2*, August 21, 2009, IMDb.

31. Recent Reviews #11, *WT2*, Netflix.

32. sabenge (United States), "Sue Me," *WT2*, February 15, 2008, IMDb.

33. happyendingrocks (United States), "If Peter Jackson Was Still Making Horror Movies, They Might Look a Lot like *Wrong Turn 2*," *WT2*, April 24, 2011, IMDb.

34. Michael J. Tresca "Talien" (Fairfield, Connecticut), "Sweet Meat," *WT2*, November 3, 2010, Amazon. Tresca argues that the film itself makes a connection between the two unscrupulous couplings when Sister gets excited by Brother's wearing the scalp of Elena. As of September 2013, all three raters weighing in on Tresca's review deemed it helpful, making it the first review listed and so highly visible and possibly relatively influential. In March 2014 and July 2015, four out of four rated it helpful, and Tresca's review continued to appear on the first page of reviews.

35. Trebe, "Outwit, Outlast, Outplay, or Die," *WT2*, February 8, 2011, Amazon. A Canadian reviewer also dismissed the distinction as frivolous, saying the "hillbilly cannibals" were "disfigured likely due to their notions of whetting their sexual appetites with kin (or was it toxic waste—I can't remember)"; Greg (Oakville, Ontario), "Gorefest!", *WT2*, October 10, 2007, IMDb.

36. ororomonroe "blknstl" (St. Charles, Missouri), "Gory, Gory, Gory . . . and I Loved It!!!!!!!!," *WT2*, February 21, 2008, Amazon. Similarly the Blalock review of *WT2* in *Terror Hook* says the hill people "chose to stay."

37. Recent Reviews #11, *WT2*, Netflix. A disgruntled reviewer in the United Kingdom noted, "There may also have been a bit of subtext about not judging others by their appearance," but "with people this ugly that's really not a good idea" since "the villains were so utterly repulsive, any message about not judging others on their looks is sort of lost as you reach in desperation for the sick bucket." ian_bell (United Kingdom), "This Whole Film Is a Complete Dead End," *WT2*, August 23, 2010, IMDb.

38. Anchor Bay is "dedicated to film makers just getting started and is usually a good place to go if you are in the mood for something different." Douglas MacLean, "Staunton Hill," *Home Theater Info*, January 12, 2010, http://www.hometheaterinfo.com/staunton_hill.htm.

39. James Mudge, "Staunton Hill (2009) Movie Review," *Beyond Hollywood*, October 24, 2009, http://www.beyondhollywood.com/staunton-hill-2009-movie-review. *Staunton Hill*'s debt to *Blood Salvage* (1990), about organ harvesting, is also mentioned by critics.

40. Mr. HoRrOr, Horrormoviesandstuff Database.

41. Irishlass240 (smmorr240@aol.com), *Staunton Hill* Plot Summary, IMDb, http://www.imdb.com/title/tt1118693/plotsummary?ref_=tt_ov_pl.

42. English-language horror blog reviews that mention or discuss the organ trade as a feature of *Staunton Hill* include Tom Leins, *D&C Film*, http://www.devon-cornwall-film.co.uk/2009/10/22/halloween-horror-special-tom-leins-peeps-over-his-sofa-at-the-latest-scary-dvd-releases/#staunton-hill; TheHrunting, *From Black to Red*, http://fromblacktoredfilmreviews.blogspot.com/2011/11/staunton-hill-2009.html; Porfle, *HK and Cult Film News*, http://hkfilmnews.blogspot.com/2009/10/staunton-hill-dvd-review-by-porfle.htm; Mr. HoRrOr, Horrormoviesandstuff Database, http://www3.webng.com/horrormoviesandstuff/StauntonHillReview.html; Mark R. Hasan, KQEK,

http://www.kqek.com/dvd_reviews/s/3504_StauntonHill.htm; Jared Roberts, *Lair of the Boyg*, http://www.lairoftheboyg.com/2009/11/staunton-hill-2009.html; Rick L. Blalock, *Terror Hook*, http://www.terrorhook.com/reviews/s/stauntonhill.html; Horror Bob, *The Horror Review*, http://www.horrorreview.com/2009/stauntonhill2009.html; PiddeAndersson on *Xomba*; and perhaps also *Horror Movie a Day* and Douglas MacLean at *Home Theater Info*, http://www.hometheaterinfo.com/staunton_hill.htm.

43. qormi (United States), "Hostel Meets 'The Texas Chainsaw Massacre,'" *SH*, December 4, 2011, IMDb.

44. Recent Reviews #97, *SH*, Netflix.

45. Rick L. Blalock, "*Staunton Hill*," *Terror Hook*, October 12, 2009, http://www.terrorhook.com/reviews/s/stauntonhill.html.

46. Mr. HoRrOr, Horrormoviesandstuff Database. http://www3.webng.com/horrormoviesandstuff/StauntonHillReview.html

47. FrightMeter from FrightMeter.Com, "*Texas Chainsaw Massacre* Part 156," *SH*, March 31, 2010, IMDb.

48. Recent Reviews #8, *SH*, Netflix. See also Recent Reviews #4, *SH*, Netflix: "this is stupid. i would bet most people will shoot trespassers not a thing wrong with them. no psycho is needed to shoot a trespasser you think might be a thief, or vandal."

49. Satterwhite, *Dear Appalachia*, 135.

50. Argemaluco (Argentina), "It's Not Great but It's Totally Entertaining," *WT2*, February 18, 2008, IMDb.

51. Recent Reviews #87, *SH*, Netflix.

52. Z. Robinson, review of Emily Satterwhite's "Hillbilly Horror," 2.

53. Ibid.; Roediger, *The Wages of Whiteness*.

54. On the concept of almost or not quite white, see D. Wilson, "The Felicitous Convergence of Mythmaking and Capital Accumulation"; Wray, *Not Quite White*.

55. Leonard Smalls, the Lone Biker of the Apocalypse from Arizona, "Aging Alternative Icons Even Suck Now," *WT2*, October 3, 2009, IMDb. An IMDb "top reviewer," this reviewer's current screen name is coldwaterpdh, http://www.imdb.com/user/ur17816817.

56. For analysis of anti-black violence as real-life convention at odds with horror film conventions in which the girl is saved rather than being beaten by a police officer, see Z. Robinson, "Nightmare on Main Street."

57. Z. Robinson, review of Emily Satterwhite's "Hillbilly Horror," 3.

58. Ibid.

59. "Xenophobia": Bell, "Anti-Idyll," 98.

PART 5

Drive and Desires

For They Know Not What They Do

Southern Studies Centers, Normativity, and Fantasies of White Redemption

JON SMITH

When describing how she and Jodi Skipper decided whom to invite to the groundbreaking Transforming New South Identities symposium that led to this book, Michele Coffey has joked that one of the things it involved was going to a bunch of mainstream "southern studies" conferences and looking around to see who in the room looked angry. As the symposium amply demonstrated, they found a lot of us, in fields ranging from literary studies to anthropology. Yet there seems to be a presumption among more mainstream southern studies scholars—a presumption that may echo or simply drag out the kerfuffle fifteen years ago in southern literary studies over Patricia Yaeger's "angry" tone in *Dirt and Desire*—that this anger, coming chiefly from the left, is mysterious, unjustified. "Some of the criticisms by figures in [the new southern studies] are pretty harsh," the director of the Center for the Study of Southern Culture at the University of Mississippi, Ted Ownby, has recently opined, "and plenty of the students and working scholars have read some of the critiques, apparently intended to be glib and pithy, as being something closer to smug and unwelcoming."[1] I cannot speak for everyone, but the "harshness" of my own critiques has derived largely from frustration with what I will call an *unearned normativity* at the core of too much of what mainstream southern studies still does. Even now, old southern studies can too often offer a subject—"southerners" or, worse, "we southerners"—followed by a predicate that does not reflect what "we" do at all. Much of the time it reflects a particularly narrow, upper-class white notion of "southern," or, perhaps paradoxically, an upper-class white notion of "inclusiveness." We southerners love barbecue. We southerners are great storytellers. We southerners have a sense of place.

It has been decades since American studies felt the need to do anything like this. American studies centers do not, as a rule, celebrate the putative distinctiveness of American foodways or host vaguely old-timey "American music" sessions on the front porch of whatever building houses their offices. And the more people at southern studies centers and in the corresponding lifestyle magazines and websites—*Garden and Gun*, the *Oxford American*, *Bitter Southerner*, and even at times *Southern Cultures*—celebrate "southern identity," the more it can look, to those trained in American studies, not like a celebration but a narcissistic overcompensation. It can look like an overreaction to the general perception that the South is inferior to the rest of the nation (so "we" have to claim it's the best, most beautiful, most authentic, foodiest, whatever), but more fundamentally (for those of us who get Lacan), it overcompensates for the gnawing anxiety that no such identity exists. I have written about how most new southern studies scholars grew up in the southeastern United States after the most obvious mark of southern distinctiveness—de jure apartheid—had been struck down.[2] In arguing against southern exceptionalism, we have been largely measuring exceptionalist claims against our really rather unexceptional upbringings—"not to absolve the south," as historians Matthew Lassiter and Joseph Crespino have put it, "but to implicate the nation."[3] Mainstream southern studies, on the other hand, just can't seem to let go. Its practitioners can still seem desperate to forge an alternate, more benign version of "southern identity," one grounded in foodways and music and attempting, at least, to be "inclusive"—unless, of course, you're one of the millions of vegetarian southerners, or southerners who find "southern storytelling" to be wildly predictable, or who find a sense of place in lots of places, from Manhattan to the Canadian Rockies, but not so much in southern small towns, with their tedious strips of identical Walmarts, their Applebee's and Advance Auto Parts and Hardee's, or who come from border states like Virginia and appreciate far more similarities with, say, Marylanders than Mississippians. The need for group identity seems wildly to override the available evidence, and that's bad enough for any putatively scholarly enterprise, but what can seem worse is the emotional neediness that seems to motivate the whole thing. It's tempting to take the position—perhaps from the Olympian distance preferred by Scott Romine in *The Real South*—that even in their neediness such folks aren't hurting anyone, that this is just how culture works. What I want to suggest, however, is that this fantasy does real harm.

One revealing but unfortunate mark of a number of southern studies centers at present is the mixed messages they can send about all this. Ownby—whose 1999 call for scholars to stop contemplating whether various putative southern essences have been "lost" has had a big impact on my own work—now argues that such clichés as southerners distinctively loving barbecue, telling stories, and having a unique sense of whatever are largely behind us, dead horses no longer to be beaten. "We study the body and physical senses more," he writes, "but it's not a time to offer central themes or to come up with new Senses. Also gone is the search for essences—a few facts, habits, beliefs that one can say are essential to the American South."[4] Yet open the pages of the *Palmetto Bluff* announcing "John T. Edge to host culinary festival," and the horse seems very much alive. "Potlikker is the distilled essence of the South," proclaims an insert provided "Courtesy of the Southern Foodways Alliance," the most visible outreach branch of the center Ownby directs. "When the greens have finished cooking, Southerners know that the pork-infused liquid in that pot is precious. They don't waste it. . . . Potlikker is more than just a cooking liquid, and Potlikker Film Festivals are more than just movie screenings."[5] Of graduate students coming to southern studies, Ownby writes, "Some hope to pursue greater understanding through the listening and watching essential to documentary film, still photography, audio recording, and oral history," which certainly seems reasonable and scholarly enough.[6] Yet while the website of the Center for the Study of Southern Culture mentions that "documentary studies at the Center include photography, film, and oral history," those words are preceded, in all caps and a more elegant sans serif font, by the tagline, "TELLING THE STORIES OF THE MOST STORIED PLACE," subordinating that scholarly mission to just the essentialist mythologies of storytelling and place (notably not even *region*) that Ownby would disavow. In his conclusion to the collection of foodways scholarship essays *The Larder*, Ownby pointedly notes that "one thing that unifies most, and perhaps all, of the articles is the lack of nostalgia—or in most cases, even affection—for the food itself."[7] He claims that "most of the authors in this book, I suspect, would accept [Andrew] Warnes' suggestion to study foodways without having a fixed point for judging authenticity."[8] Yet the *Southern Foodways Alliance Community Cookbook*, copyrighted just three years earlier, nostalgically models both its physical form and its content after mid-twentieth-century spiral-bound church and community cookbooks. In his foreword, Alton Brown cheerily judges the resultant work "authentic," based on four fixed points ranging from "such books must be spiral-bound or they are not to be trusted" to "all the recipes must be directly attributed to a member of the community" to "community cookbooks must be truly democratic" to "community cookbooks convey a strong sense of place."[9] (As I write in the late summer of 2015, *The Larder* has sold 1,115 copies in all formats; the *Southern Foodways Alliance Community Cookbook* has sold 11,588. If one counts only hardbacks, the cookbook has, unsurprisingly enough, outsold the scholarly collection 10,835 to 89, a ratio of 121 to 1.) These are, of course, very different kinds of books, but that's my point: especially when it comes to foodways, southern studies books and essays written as "outreach" to the general public have too often tended to advocate precisely the comforting, essentialist, even agrarian positions on "authenticity" and "sense of place" that academics have, with good reason, moved well past. Yet the sugarcoating of the cookbook or "creative nonfiction" form, particularly in the absence of rigorous scholarly oversight, ensures a much larger audience for now-reactionary models of the South and southern identity.

Perhaps, then, it should come as no surprise that at the Transforming New South Identities symposium, what seemed to be two exasperated University of Mississippi social scientists presented the group with this activity: "Imagine one of your students wants to make a documentary about a Memphis barbecue joint. How do you help the student make it more than just a celebration of foodways?" (It *did* come as a surprise to the presenters that many in the audience, especially the literary critics, took offense that anyone would think they had any investment in celebrating foodways either.) But such frustration is hardly limited to the University of Mississippi or to the symposium's participants. At a recent St. George Tucker symposium, historian Fitzhugh Brundage ended a well-received talk on changes to southern studies at the University of North Carolina as follows: "I am not advocating a return to [sociologist Howard] Odum's regional studies, but I do regret that outside of History classes, most students who take courses that focus on the South will learn almost exclusively about foodways, music, and identity politics. Of course, I have the same concerns about the current field of 'Southern Studies' beyond my own institution."[10]

Thus, while Ownby's take on the present situation of southern studies is characteristically earnest and thoughtful, it also appears necessarily partial—reflective, perhaps, of its author's closeness to the subject matter. (In *Finding Purple America*, I predicted that "the first part of this book is likely to anger people in direct proportion to how personally and professionally invested they are in enjoying their dominant disciplinary fantasy.")[11] Even in the situation Ownby describes, one's desire to enter a problem-solving profession, and more particularly which problems one seeks to solve, are necessarily shaped, by virtue of our being human, by unconscious desires and drives. This is the fundamental—and pretty uncontroversial—tenet of psychoanalysis, and it is only bolstered by recent work in empirical psychology.[12] When we pretend we are other than deeply flawed, fallen human beings—to put things in a Christian register perhaps more legible to traditional southernists—we run into problems.

Historians, however, have seemed particularly resistant to such lines of argument, at least when applied to them. Part of the reason may be that, as historian Brian Ward has asserted in a recent state-of-the-field essay assessing "where among southernists and Americanists the influence of [new southern studies] has been most keenly felt, and where it has so far failed to make much impression," "historians are less comfortable or adept" in "areas of cultural representation and consumption, performance practices, affect, and emotion."[13] But part of the reason too may be the not-unrelated fact that too many historians still see themselves—in terms that recall how not long ago white males described themselves vis-à-vis white women and people of color—as the last bastion of rigor and objectivity in the humanities. "Insofar as these are postmodern literary scholars," historian Michael O'Brien recently sniffed of the new southern studies, "they seem to assert the right to seek out unexpected juxtapositions, which may or may not be demonstrable to the dogged historicist.... It would be inconsistent to demand consistent patterns and tight logics from the New Southern Studies, which believes in the constitutive power of the imagination."[14]

Of course, this apparent lack of self-awareness is hardly limited to southern historians. When the editors of a 2014 collection of literature-meets-foodways scholarship, both literary scholars trained in Chapel Hill's traditional program, declare on the first page of their introduction, "We are both native southerners, raised on grits and greens,"[15] their claim reveals the insufficiently examined conservative identity politics, the unconscious identitarian needs and anxieties, underlying much traditional southern studies (especially foodways scholarship) and critiqued by new southern studies. Thanks to the native turn in southern studies, for example, phrases like "native southerner" and "native South" mean something different nowadays, and when the descendants of settler colonialists call themselves "natives," they can be accused of erasing, even perpetrating, violence against the Natives they displace.[16] Equally fundamentally, as scholars such as Scott Romine have most thoroughly argued, most contemporary southerners, including those "born here," are not, in fact, "raised on grits and greens."[17] Whether we use Romine's more recent Weberian theoretical terminology of enchantment and disenchantment, or my own Lacanian references to fantasy and the *objet petit a*, we all have as much of a moral obligation to understand how our desires and drives shape—and distort—our scholarship as we do to understand ourselves.

So it is unfortunate that Ownby, in his treatment of new southern studies, constructs what to me constitutes a false binarism similar to O'Brien's: hardheaded pragmatism versus useless theory. Few graduate and undergraduate southern studies students, Ownby reports, "to use a religious metaphor, seem to convert to [new southern studies], and many seem to think, as I do, that it offers a set of tools that go along with lots of other tools. I suspect my biggest concern," he continues, "is that the New Southern Studies does not seem to offer anything particularly useful to the large number of students who come to the field for two pretty conventional reasons. Some hope to understand the American South better so they can fix problems. Some hope to pursue greater understanding through the listening and watching essential to documentary film, still photography, audio recording, and oral history."[18]

Ownby's description of his students' motivations may actually offer the most generous explanation I have yet seen for the complaint I have heard from English professors that southern studies students "don't work as hard" as English majors: perhaps, as hard-headed pragmatists, those students just don't see the relevance of southern literature, or of literary-critical methods, to their activist concerns. (I say this not to be snarky but to resist the temptation to treat students, especially southern studies students, as more virtuous or insightful than they are.) Yet I also cannot help thinking what is really at stake here is that most southern studies students are nowhere nearly as impatient with "southern identity" as, to his credit, Ownby is. Ownby approves of a hemispheric, global approach, he says, in part because "taking a global perspective means studying people for whom the concept of southern identity may or may not be important."[19] In my admittedly anecdotal experience (but also that of many at the symposium), people who go into southern studies tend to be much more likely not only to identify as "southern" than most folks who live in the South, but also to cherish that identity. The "southern identity" they most often perform, moreover, tends to consist of just the "symbolic southernness" that sociologists Larry J. Griffin and Ashley B. Thompson described nearly fifteen years ago: "Largely ancestral, honorific, and selectively enacted rather than rooted in the routines of daily life or the attributions of nonsoutherners, 'symbolic southernness' need not rest on an actually existing distinctive South. Indeed, symbolic southerners are able to proclaim their heritage and differentiate themselves from the mass of Americans by grounding their sense of who they are in a mythic place existing mainly in cultural memory—the South as an imagined community—rather than in a 'real' space."[20] In short, such students are much more likely than the average citizen of the southeastern United States to end up, whether they stay in academia or not, proclaiming themselves "native southerners, raised on grits and greens."

In fact, we may have entered an era in which the chief fault line in southern studies no longer lies between literary scholars and historians (a line Barbara Ladd accurately noted a decade ago), but between progressive social scientists, historians, and literary scholars, on the one hand, who insist on the need for critical distance from such symbolic southernness, and, on the other, more traditional scholars and students—not always older, and not always white—who seem unable or unwilling to think outside that rather tight box, the unearned normativity of "raised on grits and greens."[21] Historian Natalie Ring has recently written that "it seems unlikely that the newest field of southern studies will reveal a true interdisciplinarity if historians and literary scholars cannot agree that there is something known or understood as 'the South.' Just because we realize that the South is not now, or never was, distinctive, doesn't mean that the discourse about its distinctiveness didn't shape national policies and people's lives inside and outside the South."[22] Of course, no one in literary studies would argue with the premise that "there is something known or understood as 'the South'"; Ring too may be attacking a straw opponent here, echoing O'Brien's weird equation of new southern studies with philosophical idealism. Sounding more like Ownby, however, she continues, "I am not advocating that southern historians . . . reinvigorate what I would call old southern history—that is, identify material southern distinctiveness, tracing the assault of southern identity over time, explaining the consumption of southernness, and recycling the never-ending debate over change versus continuity."[23] If I am reading her correctly, by rejecting southern distinctiveness, Ring is suggesting that those who study the South should eschew embracing "symbolic southernness." If southern studies centers tend to attract students who embrace just that, however, we all have a problem. Such students' refusal to "convert" to new southern studies may, in such cases, derive less from pragmatism than from simple affect, from identitarian resistance to that movement's critique of so much they hold dear about their own specialness.[24]

To tease out the implications of Ownby's own religious metaphor (or Griffin and Thompson's "mythic" model), we might say that a certain kind of fervent young southerner seeks out a southern studies master's program for not a few of the same reasons that a certain kind of fervent young Baptist or Methodist applies to divinity school: to make the world a better place, yes, but also to consolidate, as an identity-seeking adolescence comes to a close, a group identity.[25] In both cases, the professors may gamely assign a few works by atheists (the term Michael O'Brien, deploying the same metaphor, has used to describe new southern studies scholars vis-à-vis the old), but nobody would expect the students—or, for that matter, many of the faculty—to convert.[26] In fact, *convert* is not quite the right word, because while old southern studies (especially foodways scholarship) resembles a faith (as Romine has most trenchantly argued) and offers many of the benefits of church (identity, belonging, fellowship), new southern studies is just a skepticism. Pushing students to make their work "more than just a celebration of foodways" simply asks students to take an appropriate, scholarly critical distance from the rituals of identity, belonging, and fellowship more traditional work uncritically celebrates and performs. It asks southern studies centers to function less like divinity schools and more like every other department of a research university. It asks them to *de*convert.

Dogged historicists demanding empirical support for the above argument about the affects still shaping many southern studies centers might look to the website of the Mercer University Southern Studies Center, which contains an illustrative page entitled "What Is Southern Studies?" Aimed at prospective undergraduate majors, the page does not directly answer the question. Instead, it simply lists the sorts of courses one takes in the major ("in southern history, literature, religion, politics, and African American studies"), major events (the Lamar Lectures, "the most prestigious lecture series on southern history and culture"), and the sorts of careers and graduate schools majors have entered. And it offers testimonials: one student says the classes "rocked my understandings of race relations, religious experience, and southern history" and praises "professors whose affirmation and guidance ultimately directed me to my future career." Another describes at some length why he entered the major: "I've always felt a deep desire to understand and come to terms with the place where I grew up, and southern studies is one way to satiate that longing. On one hand, I want to be able to be proud to call the South home, and I've been conditioned for most of my life to glorify the mythical southern ideals of hospitality, kinship, and magnolia-scented charm. On the other hand, however, I can't help but recognize the many problems with the place I call home, and I've often sought to downplay it as part of my identity out of fear of appearing responsible for its flaws."[27] This is not primarily the language of a problem-solver seeking a tool kit. From "deep desire" and "longing" and "proud" straight through "want" and "charm" and "fear" and on to "place," "home," and "identity," the passage is suffused with affect.

On one level, of course, such permeation simply constitutes very smart branding in an era of declining humanities enrollments. The website attempts to offer what marketing professor David A. Aaker calls a "value proposition" about the "emotional benefits" of establishing a relationship with a brand: southern studies, apparently, will help you both satiate your longing and overcome your fear—and even, by implication, your white guilt ("appearing responsible").[28] But it is not just about branding: the passage suggests the unusual degree to which not only the student but also southern studies itself, as a field, really does remain shot through with affect. (Mercer's English and history departmental web pages, in contrast, generally limit their discussions to the specific skills—the tool kit—with which students will emerge.) The student describing his reasons for entering the major seems remarkably unaware that he is performing the very old emotional script of the melancholy, "longing" white southerner who loves his native "place" yet is ashamed of its "flaws" (so ashamed, apparently, that unlike the "ideals" they are not to be enumerated here). Yet the web page seems to assert that southern studies works because—rather than interrogating this old script—his professors enjoy performing it as well: self-identified white "southerners" of the traditional type, they have felt these very things—they too, we may safely conclude, love barbecue and hate racism—and hence their "affirmation."

Undergraduate testimonials, then, do offer a few provisional clues as to what southern studies is, at least as an institution: 1) a set of courses in discrete disciplines (which are presumed to converge on a single topic, just as Henry Nash Smith decades ago thought American studies should do); 2) an attempt to unteach, especially at the introductory level, the sort of bad, racist, religiously bigoted versions of southern history white students pick up from family and, not infrequently, their high school teachers and textbooks; 3) a brand of pastoral counseling for guilty or otherwise tortured white southerners in the Quentin Compson vein (in a recent blog post, Ownby seems to confirm this view, optimistically suggesting that reading in southern studies might have helped Elvis Presley "have a healthier, more focused life, maybe a longer life"); and 4) an exercise in "identity" construction.[29]

Rhetoric about inclusiveness notwithstanding, the target demographic of southern studies sketched by such testimonials remains very much a certain sort of upper-class white southerner. After all, southern studies centers, overwhelmingly, are not found at HBCUs or even at land-grant schools. They occupy the old-money public universities of their respective southern states and a few private southern universities: most visibly, the University of Mississippi, the University of South Carolina, the University of North Carolina at Chapel Hill, and Mercer University.[30] Not coincidentally, as the Southern Focus Polls wrapped up in the early twenty-first century, the only group not experiencing a decline in percentages identifying as "southern" over the previous decade were conservative, affluent, Republican whites. It is perhaps also no surprise, then, that so much of the "outreach" programming offered by the majority of southern studies centers happens to constitute stuff such white people like: bluegrass concerts on the porch, a Lee Bains III private concert and discussion, a visit from the founders of the *Bitter Southerner*, celebrations of foodways said to mark southern distinctiveness (rather than less statistically questionable but decidedly unpleasant marks of regional distinctiveness in public health or education or income inequality), readings by writers who produce a certain strainingly "southern" variety of fiction set in small towns and hunting camps, and nonthreatening blues rather than angry-sounding hip-hop.

To their credit, some of the upper-class white people who run the Southern Foodways Alliance know they have a problem. In a recent blog post, its director, John T. Edge, optimistically describes a "visioning" retreat to assess where the SFA will be in 2020: "Interacting with members, observers, influencers, and press, SFA actively and persuasively dispels beliefs that our work preserves some past. Instead, we document the present, which we believe instructive for our future. SFA has convinced its audience that us versus them, north versus south, old versus new, native versus immigrant, are not frames for our work. We are broad because our region is broad. We recognize that we only succeed in documenting the cultural landscapes of the changing South through rigorous adherence to breadth and inclusion."[31] Other foodways scholars also seem convinced that "breadth and inclusion" are the wave of the future, the cutting edge. In *The Edible South*, Marcie Cohen Ferris even claims that "the 'new southern studies' considers landmarks of southern identity other than the Civil War, Reconstruction, and barbecue [and] recognizes the diverse cultures and ethnicities of the South, whose global influences shape the region and its foodways."[32]

Ownby acknowledges that "inclusiveness [has] been a recurring, if challenging, goal for decades."[33] What so many fail to realize, however, is that for new southern studies scholars, the problem is not that "southern identity" is not inclusive enough in its "landmarks," it's that "southern identity" itself is a chimera. In the era of the #solidarityisforwhitewomen hashtag and the new southern studies' firm rejection of "landmarks of southern identity," the concern for "breadth and inclusion" looks not just quaint but also chiefly symptomatic of the emotional needs of upper-middle-class, self-identified white southerners. And what they need, it seems, isn't just solidarity. It isn't just "reconciliation." It's the redemption—for themselves—that such solidarity and reconciliation would bring.

That may sound harsh, but my thinking is guided here by recent progressive and indigenous critiques of Canada's Truth and Reconciliation Commission. As my Simon Frasier University colleague Sophie McCall notes, "The term 'reconciliation' suggests a return of order between two equals, thereby downplaying power asymmetries, and naturalizing an imagined past of unity, cooperation, and friendliness. It also produces an illusory sense of resolution that conveniently brackets ongoing colonial injustices."[34] Elsewhere McCall writes, "For many writers and thinkers who have considered deeply the challenges of decolonization, reconciliation is a top-down initiative that, far from addressing the root causes of the fractured relationship between Indigenous people and the state, fixates upon resolution and absolution. In the memorable words of Kanien'kehaka scholar Taiaiake Alfred, reconciliation often works as a 'pacifying discourse,' demanding that Indigenous people become 'reconciled with imperialism.'"[35]

Consider an essay of Edge's in the Spring 2015 issue of *Oxford American*, "Going Deeper with Red Dog." The piece celebrates Goren "Red Dog" Avery, the recipient of the 2014 SFA "Ruth Fertel Keeper of the Flame Award," "given annually to an unsung hero or heroine of the food world, a tradition-bearer whose work and life bear witness to the better impulses of the Southern experience."[36] Avery, as it happens, is a black waiter at white chef Frank Stitt's flagship restaurant Highlands Bar and Grill in Birmingham, Alabama. Because the former is not a "garrulous jester" or "faithful retainer," as black waiters once used to be figured, Edge paradoxically sees great progress even as he celebrates Avery's tradition-bearing. Sitting down to lunch with Avery—whom he has known "for nearly twenty years" but with whom he has had just two "substantive discussions," both in the wake of the Ruth Fertel Keeper of the Flame Award—is also a mark of progress for Edge, who is old enough to remember when such public luncheons would have been difficult in Birmingham. "What I see" in Avery's career, Edge writes, "is a kind of redemption, an earned equity that Avery broadcasts to those he serves. That's the true gift of his career." And there is this: "With a surety that matches the mien of owners Pardis and Frank Stitt, Avery shepherds the flocks who seek purchase nightly in this reliquary of a restaurant, the most vaunted in the South. This place, and, by extension, this city, are his domain."[37]

In southern studies even more than most fields, overwriting can generally be read profitably as overcompensation. Most of the time, it reflects an attempt to create, through sheer linguistic effort, the southern identity it purports to describe. (This is what I take Romine to mean in arguing that "the *discourse* of the foodway makes it possible to eat the South.")[38] Sometimes, however, it goes beyond overcompensation. Edge notes that Avery's tips from the previous night average 34 percent. At a restaurant where the tabs generally start in three figures, that's good money. Over time it will pay off the mortgage on a very nice house in Eastlake or Norwood or Bush Boulevard or any other of the rather precariously middle-class black neighborhoods in Birmingham. But it will not get you so much as a townhouse in an over-the-mountain white suburb like Mountain Brook (whence hail most of Highlands' customers) or even Homewood. As countless scholars and even journalists have noted, that reality, the racialized geography of metropolitan Birmingham and virtually all other U.S. cities, reflects a continuing national history of massive, un-redressed structural inequity. By focusing on affect—Avery's "surety," the way he "physically and emotionally ... commands the social moment" and "exerts control like a munificent dictator"—Edge elides the real power relations, the structural racism, that such affect exists to hide. He insists on progress: "Progress has been made. Change has come. . . . [Avery's] strength of character and force of personality subvert prevailing expectations about race and how it's lived in the South. . . . Goren Avery has helped curate a more welcoming and inclusive South."[39]

It would be easy to treat the oversight as simply an innocent mistake. Unfortunately, there seems to be an element of bad faith here that goes to the heart of what southern studies centers do. Edge, after all, has not just read such writers on the challenges still facing black men as journalist Ta-Nehisi Coates, novelist and essayist Kiese Laymon, and entrepreneur/writer/chef Tunde Wey. Moved by Coates's essay "The Case for Reparations," he invited Coates to speak at the SFA's 2014 Fall Symposium.[40] Laymon spoke the next year, and most recently Edge gave part of his *Oxford American* column to Wey, who rather brilliantly used the opportunity to offer critiques not unrelated to those advanced here.[41] In the "Red Dog" essay, Edge points out that "faithful retainer" narratives are bad, even though anyone familiar with the genre (and such nostalgic phrases as "remained in service") will realize that is precisely what his own essay is. "He's a loyalist," Edge writes approvingly of Avery, "who walked through the door in November of 1982 and has remained in service at Highlands, despite insistent offers from other employers."[42] In Christian terms, it seems, he "knows not what he does," but as Slavoj Žižek notes, "psychoanalysis is much more severe than Christianity: ignorance is not a sufficient reason for forgiveness since it conveys a hidden dimension of enjoyment. Where one doesn't (want to) know, in the blanks of one's symbolic universe, one enjoys, and there is no Father to forgive."[43]

At the conceptual center (and literal conclusion) of "Going Deeper with Red Dog" lies the familiar notion of the reconciling, redemptive "welcome table": "Goren Avery has helped curate a more welcoming and inclusive South.... Now is our time to take a seat at the welcome table he sets."[44] As Edge himself notes, the whole essay takes place against the backdrop of what he euphemistically calls "recent racially enflamed events in Ferguson, Missouri, and elsewhere."[45] For Edge, however, those events merely "make clear why Avery's life and work shine brightest when projected opposite the lives of black waiters of previous generations." Avery's "strength of character and force of personality subvert prevailing expectations about race and how it's lived in the South."[46] Except, of course, that they don't. In the South as in the nation, black men are still waiters in white men's fancy restaurants vastly more often than the reverse. What has changed is that over the past forty or fifty years, white people have moved from anxiously wanting to be reminded of their privilege to anxiously not wanting to be reminded of it. In Lacanian terms, Black Lives Matter disrupts white Americans' enjoyment, their symbolic order, by calling attention to the Real of continuing inequality enforced by violence against black bodies, while Avery's story, like the upbeat fantasy of the inclusive welcome table, conversely documents yet another fantastic white attempt not to face the Real, not to be reminded of their privilege and the violence that sustains it.

Of course, as the quote from Taiaiake Alfred above suggests, it hardly takes a Lacanian to recognize how "reconciliation" and "inclusion" and "welcome table" can mean "redemption for white people on the cheap." Shortly after the 2015 Charleston church shooting, Kiese Laymon wrote a piece for the *Guardian* in which he recalled his upbringing at Concord Baptist Church in Forest, Mississippi: "We members of Concord were supposed to love white folks because they knew not what they did. We were supposed to heal them because they knew not who they were. We were supposed to forgive them because salvation awaited she or he who could withstand the wrath of the worst of white folks. We were supposed to pray for them, often at the expense of our own healthy reckoning. Grandma and her church taught me that loving white folks in spite of their investment in our terror was our only chance of not becoming them morally." But after the shooting, his grandmother rethinks things. "God says you must forgive them for they know not what they do. Shit. Maybe God says something else." Laymon responds, "Loving white supremacists in the face of white supremacy is a hallmark of American evil, and a really a fundamental part of the black American experience in this country." Then the essay turns even darker: "Tomorrow, President Obama will smile and sit down with white people, white power, and white supremacy. I know that, like most of us, he will let them in again and again because he was elected to have faith in tomorrow. He was elected to have faith in tomorrow. And even after he is no longer president, he will still want to be chosen as someone who represents a better tomorrow for people who hate him. I wonder sometimes what he does with his pain and his shame."[47] It is safe to say Laymon knows exactly what is up when he is chosen to sit at the southern studies welcome table, and it is fairly safe to say we know exactly how he feels about it.

When I began this essay, I thought I was going to address the question of how one does progressive work at a southern studies center whose student, alumni, and donor bases consist of relatively conservative white people. I thought the point at issue was one of creatively resisting external pressure. Over time, I came to see the question as a rhetorical one: how do you tell the truth to rich white people who tend to need to be flattered? Minus the flattery part, this is Edge's own concern: "Through the years, when I tried to tackle those matters [of race and class, gender and justice] head-on, I often lost an audience."[48] The more I read, however, the more I came to see the problem as one of disavowal within southern studies centers themselves. And that's a harder problem to solve. It may be an impossible one. In looking at the possibility of change in southern literary studies, I have always been comforted by the advice a dean gave me at a difficult time early in my career: "People don't change, demographics do." He was thinking generationally, and when I wrote *Finding Purple America*, it seemed to me that so many senior people in southern literary studies and American studies were so invested in their own fantasies that the best I could do would be try to reach younger scholars who weren't yet in such a rut. I have spent much of the past fifteen years arguing with older people, fairly confident that their ideas would depart the field when they did. But while the demographics of southern studies faculty are somewhat more diverse than they were a quarter century ago, the leadership and the student, alumni, and donor bases seem almost freakishly the same. To see disavowal going on in leaders of southern studies centers not much older than I am, and in master's students much, much younger, is disheartening.

But of course we try anyway. It's tremendously easy, if you work in a place like Mississippi or North Carolina or Georgia, to consider yourself progressive if you're somewhere to the left of Confederate flag-wavers. (It's also tremendously easy, if you work in a place like British Columbia, to point fingers from a distance, to be the sort of scholar whose sole "activism" now lies in publishing scholarly articles like this one.) Younger scholars such as Coffey and Skipper and many other contributors to this volume somehow have to go to work with people still so busy comparing themselves to the white southerners of their childhoods that they don't see how they might, themselves, know not what they do. Such younger scholars have to work within a kind of church for white people, knowing that white people's emotional needs are not, in fact, the greatest needs out there, and they also have to support students and other faculty of color in deeply, deeply white spaces. ("Step onto the campus of one of the country's great sites of learning," writes Robert Reid-Pharr in *Southern Spaces*, shifting the metaphor, "and you are quite likely stepping onto a plantation.")[49] Little of what I have written here will come as news to them or to people of color working or studying at southern studies centers. My hope, however, is that if a balding, middle-aged cis-het white guy can write it, it might help make it a little harder for my people to know not what they do.

Notes

1. Ownby, "The New Southern Studies and Rethinking the Question," 873.
2. J. Smith, "Toward a Post-postpolitical Southern Studies," 82–3.
3. Lassiter and Crespino, introduction to *Myth of Southern Exceptionalism*, 7.
4. Ownby, "The New Southern Studies and Rethinking the Question," 872.
5. "John T. Edge to Host Culinary Festival."
6. Ownby, "The New Southern Studies and Rethinking the Question," 875.
7. Ownby, "Conclusion. 370.
8. Ibid.
9. A. Brown, foreword to *The Southern Foodways Alliance Community Cookbook*, xi.
10. Brundage, "Southern Studies at University of North Carolina."
11. J. Smith, *Finding Purple America*, 6.
12. For a popular treatment of the latter developments, see, for example, moral psychologist Jonathan Haidt's metaphor of the rider and the elephant in his books *The Happiness Hypothesis* and *The Righteous Mind*.
13. Ward, "Forum," 723, 728–29. In his thoughtful and balanced treatment of disciplinary methods, strengths, shortfalls, and biases in recent scholarship on the South, Ward notes that "while there may be something to the charge that literary and cultural scholars occasionally claim too much on the grounds of too little evidence, historians, economists and political scientists are hardly immune to that interpretive vice. More importantly, this kind of accusation can quickly degenerate into caricature, with historians smugly contrasting their supposed analytical rigour, deep immersion in archival sources, and concern for context with the whimsical, overdetermined readings of randomly selected, highly idiosyncratic texts undertaken by literary and cultural studies

scholars. This mythology certainly does a grave disservice to sophisticated scholars who do demonstrate a firm grasp of the empirical detail; respect for the nature and limits of sources; and a feel for the social, political, and economic contexts that historians like to privilege" (728).

14. M. O'Brien, "Place as Everywhere," 274. For a full counterargument, see J. Smith, "Toward a Post-postpolitical Southern Studies," 79–85.

15. D. Davis and Powell, "Reading Southern Food," 3.

16. See, for example, M. Taylor, *Reconstructing the Native South*, 21, 26–71; Caison, "Red States."

17. Romine, *The Real South*, 108–15; Romine, "God and the Moon Pie," 49–71.

18. Ownby, "The New Southern Studies and Rethinking the Question," 874–75.

19. Ibid., 874.

20. Griffin and Thompson, "Enough about the Disappearing South," 52–53.

21. Ladd, "Literary Studies," 1634. The editors of this volume point out that many social scientists have moved well past this debate into actual activism. Still, as I hope to show, that activist agenda will be necessarily hobbled until the majority of southern studies scholars in history and English departments also get past the question—a major goal, of course, of their symposium.

22. Ring, "An Irony of Ironies," 710.

23. Ibid., 710–11.

24. See Haidt's *The Happiness Hypothesis* and *The Righteous Mind*.

25. Haidt, *The Righteous Mind*, 285–318.

26. M. O'Brien, "Place as Everywhere," 275.

27. "What Is Southern Studies."

28. Aaker, *Building Strong Brands*, 95–102.

29. Ownby, "Ted Ownby on Elvis Presley as a Southern Studies Student."

30. In this essay, I do not further discuss the University of South Carolina's Institute for Southern Studies, because it offers an undergraduate minor only and its programming rather scrupulously avoids the most important problems, the rituals of identity, I seek to counter here.

31. Edge, "SFA Visioning with Ari."

32. Ferris, *The Edible South*, 3.

33. Ownby, "The New Southern Studies and Rethinking the Question," 873.

34. McCall, *First Person Plural*, 111.

35. McCall, Reder, and Anderson, "First Nations and Native Souths on Both Sides of the 49th Parallel," 43. McCall cites Alfred, "Restitution Is the Real Pathway to Justice for Indigenous Peoples," 182–83.

36. Edge, "Going Deeper with Red Dog," 102.

37. Ibid.

38. Romine, "God and the Moon Pie," 50.

39. Edge, "Going Deeper with Red Dog," 103.

40. Dixler, "Why Southern Food Authority John T. Edge Is 'Not Giving Up on the South.'"

41. Edge and Wey, "Who Owns Southern Food?"

42. Edge, "Going Deeper with Red Dog," 102.

43. Žižek, *For They Know Not What They Do*, 2.
44. Edge, "Going Deeper with Red Dog," 103.
45. Ibid.
46. Ibid.
47. Laymon, "Black Churches Taught Us to Forgive White People."
48. Edge, "Why Southern Food Matters," 5.
49. Reid-Pharr, "Writing at the Plantation's Edge."

BIBLIOGRAPHY

Aaker, David A. *Building Strong Brands*. New York: Free Press, 1996.

Abbate-Winkel, Dee. "Voices, Mirrors, Names, and Dreams: A Case History of Participatory Management at Appalshop." PhD diss., Northern Illinois University, 1995.

Abu-Lughod, Lila. "Writing against Culture." In *Recapturing Anthropology: Working in the Present*, edited by Richard G. Fox, 466–79. Santa Fe, N.Mex.: School of American Research Press, 1991.

Achenbach, Thomas. *Manual for the Child Behavior Checklist/4-18 and 1991 Profile*. Burlington, Vt.: Department of Psychiatry, University of Vermont, 1991.

Adams, Jessica, Michael P. Bibler, and Cécile Accilien, eds. *Just Below South: Intercultural Performance in the Caribbean and the U.S. South*. Charlottesville: University of Virginia Press, 2007.

Agid, S. "Locked and Loaded: The Prison Industrial Complex and the Response to Hurricane Katrina." In *Through the Eye of Katrina: Social Justice in the United States*, edited by K. A. Bates and R. S. Swan, 55–75. Durham, N.C.: Carolina Academic Press, 2007.

Ahmad, Aijaz. "Jameson's Rhetoric of Otherness and the 'National Allegory.'" *Social Text* 17 (1987): 3–25.

Aja, Alexandre, and Grégory Levasseur. *The Hills Have Eyes*. DVD. Los Angeles: 20th Century Fox Studios, 2006.

Alexander, M. Jacqui. *Pedagogies of Crossing: Mediations on Feminism, Sexual Politics, Memory, and the Sacred*. Durham, N.C.: Duke University Press, 2005.

Alfred, Taiaiake. "Restitution Is the Real Pathway to Justice for Indigenous Peoples." In *Response, Responsibility, and Renewal: Canada's Truth and Reconciliation Journey*, edited by Greg Younging, Jonathan Dewar, and Mike DeGagné, 179–87. Ottawa: Aboriginal Healing Foundation, 2009.

Allen, Jafari Sinclaire. "For 'the Children' Dancing the Beloved Community." *Souls* 11, no. 3 (2009): 311–26.

Alvarado, Joel, and Charles Jaret. *Building Black-Brown Coalitions in the Southeast*. Atlanta: Southern Regional Council, 2009.

Ames, Eric. *Ferocious Reality: Documentary according to Werner Herzog*. Minneapolis: University of Minnesota Press, 2012.

Anderson, Eric Gary, Taylor Hagood, and Daniel Cross Turner, eds. *Undead Souths: The Gothic and Beyond in Southern Literature and Culture*. Baton Rouge: Louisiana State University Press, 2015.

Anderson, Joe, and Sean McEwen. *Albino Farm*. DVD. Miami: MTI Home Video, 2009.

Ansley, Frances. "Doing Policy from Below: Worker Solidarity and the Prospects for Immigration Reform." *Cornell International Law Journal* 41 (2008): 101–14.

———. "Tennessee Industrial Renewal Network (TIRN) Scrapbook." *Southern Spaces*,

May 19, 2011. http://southernspaces.org/content/tennessee-industrial-renewal-network-tirn-scrapbook.

Ansley, Frances, and Anne Lewis. "Going South, Coming North: Migration and Union Organizing in Morristown, Tennessee." *Southern Spaces*, May 19, 2011. http://southernspaces.org/2011/going-south-coming-north-migration-and-union-organizing-morristown-tennessee.

Arizona et al. v. United States. Slip Opinion. Supreme Court of the United States. October Term, 2011. http://www.supremecourt.gov/opinions/11pdf/11-182b5e1.pdf.

Aufderheide, Patricia P. "At Appalshop the 1960's Never Died. They Just Grew Up." In *Appalshop: Celebrating Thirty-Five Years*, edited by Mia Frederick and Laura Sohn, 3–7. Whitesburg, Ky.: Appalshop, 2004.

———. *Documentary Film: A Very Short Introduction*. New York: Oxford University Press, 2007.

Aulette, Judy. "North-South." In *The Wiley-Blackwell Encyclopedia of Globalization*, edited by George Ritzer. West Sussex, UK: Blackwell Publishing, 2012: 1547–48.

Ayers, Edward L. "The Inevitable Future of the South." In *South to the Future: An American Region in the Twenty-First Century*, edited by Fred C. Hobson, 87–106. Athens: University of Georgia Press, 2002.

———. *The Promise of the New South: Life after Reconstruction*. New York: Oxford University Press, 1992.

———. "What We Talk about When We Talk about the South." In *All over the Map: Rethinking American Regions*, edited by Edward L. Ayers, Patricia Nelson Limerick, Stephen Nissenbaum, and Peter S. Onuf, 62–82. Baltimore, Md.: Johns Hopkins University Press, 1996.

Ayers, Edward L., and Christy Coleman. "Three Recommendations to the University of Mississippi." In *Action Plan on Consultant Reports and Update on the Work of the Sensitivity and Respect Committee*. August 1, 2014. http://web.archive.org/web/20150907094432/http://chancellor.olemiss.edu/wp-content/uploads/sites/17/2013/08/2014-ActionPlanonConsultantReportsandUpdateontheWorkoftheSensitivityandRespectCommittee.pdf.

Baker, Houston, Jr., and Dana D. Nelson, eds. "Preface: Violence, the Body, and 'the South.'" *American Literature* 73, no. 2 (June 2001): 231–44.

Barker, Deborah E., and Kathryn McKee, eds. *American Cinema and the Southern Imaginary*. Athens: University of Georgia Press, 2010.

Bates, Denise, ed. *We Will Always Be Here: Native Peoples on Living and Thriving in the South*. Gainesville: University of Florida Press, 2016.

Beaver, Patricia, Jesse Buckwalter, et al. "'That Point of Human Connection': An Interview with Filmmaker Anne Lewis." *Appalachian Journal* 40, nos. 1–2 (2012–13): 58–76.

Bell, David. "Anti-Idyll: Rural Horror." In *Contested Countryside Cultures: Otherness, Marginalisation, and Rurality*, edited by Paul Cloke and Jo Little, 94–108. London: Routledge, 1997.

Benjamin, Walter. "On the Concept of History." Translated by Dennis Redmond (2005) from Benjamin, *Gesammelten Schriften*, 1:2. Frankfurt am Main: Suhrkamp Verlag, 1974. http://members.efn.org/~dredmond/ThesesonHistory.html.

Benson, Melanie R. *Disturbing Calculations: The Economics of Identity in Postcolonial Southern Literature, 1912–2002*. Athens: University of Georgia Press, 2008.

Bernard, Mark. *Selling the Splat Pack: The DVD Revolution and the American Horror Film*. Edinburgh, UK: Edinburgh University Press, 2014.

Berrey, Stephen A. *The Jim Crow Routine: Everyday Performances of Race, Civil Rights, and Segregation in Mississippi*. Chapel Hill: University of North Carolina Press, 2015.

Berry, Wendell. "The Regional Motive." In *A Continuous Harmony: Essays Cultural and Agricultural*, 61–68. New York: Harcourt Brace Jovanovich, 1972.

Birecree, Adrienne M. "The Importance and Implications of Women's Participation in the 1989–1990 Pittston Coal Strike." *Journal of Economic Issues* 30, no. 1 (1996): 187–210.

Bischof, Libby. "The Lens of the Local: Teaching an Appreciation of the Past through the Exploration of Local Sites, Landmarks, and Hidden Histories." *History Teacher* 48, no. 3 (May 2015): 529–59.

Blake, Linnie. *The Wounds of Nations: Horror Cinema, National Identity and Historical Trauma*. Manchester: Manchester University Press, 2008.

Blood, Peter, and Annie Patterson, eds. *Rise Up Singing: The Group Singing Songbook*. Bethlehem, Pa.: Sing Out! Publications, 2004.

Bohanek, Jennifer G., Kelly A. Martin, Robyn Fivush, and Marshall P. Duke. "Family Narrative Interaction and Children's Sense of Self." *Family Process* 45, no. 1 (2006): 39–54.

Bohanek, Jennifer G., Robyn Fivush, Widaad Zaman, and Catlin E. Lepore. "Narrative Interaction in Family Dinnertime Conversations." *Merrill-Palmer Quarterly* 55, no. 4 (October 2009): 488–515.

Boles, John B., ed. *A Companion to the American South*. Malden, Mass.: Blackwell, 2004.

Bone, Martyn. *The Postsouthern Sense of Place in Contemporary Fiction*. Baton Rouge: Louisiana State University Press, 2005.

Bone, Martyn, Brian Ward, and William A. Link, eds. *Creating and Consuming the American South*. Gainesville: University of Florida Press, 2015.

Bonilla-Silva, Eduardo. *Racism without Racists: Color-Blind Racism and Racial Inequality in Contemporary America*. 3rd ed. Lanham, Md.: Rowman and Littlefield, 2010.

Bonner, Robert. *Colors and Blood: Flag Passions of the Confederate South*. Princeton, N.J.: Princeton University Press, 2002.

Boorman, John. *Deliverance*, deluxe ed. DVD. Burbank, Calif.: Warner Home Video, 1972.

Boyce Davies, Carole. *Left of Karl Marx: The Political Life of Black Communist Claudia Jones*. Durham, N.C.: Duke University Press, 2008.

Boyd, Julian P., ed. *Papers of Thomas Jefferson*, vol. 8, *1785*. Princeton, N.J.: Princeton University Press, 1950.

Boyd, Tim S. R. *Georgia Democrats, the Civil Rights Movement, and the Shaping of the New South*. Gainesville: University Press of Florida, 2012.

Brasseaux, Carl A., Keith P. Fontenot, and Claude F. Oubre, eds. *Creoles of Color in the Bayou Country*. Jackson: University Press of Mississippi, 1994.

Brinkmeyer, Robert H., Jr. "Discovering Gold in the Back of Beyond: The Fiction of Ron Rash." *Virginia Quarterly Review* 89, no. 3 (Summer 2013): 173–77.

———. *The Fourth Ghost: White Southern Writers and European Fascism, 1930–1950.* Baton Rouge: Louisiana State University Press, 2009.

Brisbin, Richard A. *A Strike like No Other Strike: Law and Resistance during the Pittston Coal Strike of 1989–1990.* Baltimore, Md.: Johns Hopkins University Press, 2002.

Brown, Alton. Foreword to *The Southern Foodways Alliance Community Cookbook*, edited by Sarah Roahen and John T. Edge, xi. Athens: University of Georgia Press, 2010.

Brown, Jacqueline Nassy. *Dropping Anchor, Setting Sail: Geographies of Race in Black Liverpool.* Princeton, N.J.: Princeton University Press, 2006.

Brundage, W. Fitzhugh. "The Profession: Recruiting Minority Graduate Students: The UNC Model." *Perspectives on History: The News Magazine of the American Historical Association*, December 2009. http://www.historians.org/publications-and-directories/perspectives-on-history/december-2009/recruiting-minority-graduate-students-the-unc-model.

———. *The Southern Past: A Clash of Race and Memory.* Cambridge, Mass.: Belknap Press of Harvard University Press, 2005.

———. "Southern Studies at UNC-CH." Paper presented at the St. George Tucker Society annual meeting, Atlanta, 2014.

Burton, Vernon. "The Confederate Flag's History in South Carolina." *Here & Now*, June 22, 2015. http://www.wbur.org/hereandnow/2015/06/22/history-confederate-flag-sc.

Butler, Judith. *Gender Trouble.* New York: Routledge, 2002.

Caison, Gina. "Red States: Literature, Indigenous America, and the U.S. South." Unpublished book manuscript.

Campus Unrest: The Report of the President's Commission on Campus Unrest. Washington, D.C.: Government Printing Office, 1970.

Carlton, David, and Peter Coclanis, eds. *Confronting Southern Poverty in the Great Depression.* Boston: Bedford St Martin's, 1996.

Cartwright, Keith. "Confederacies of Undead Imagination." In Anderson, Hagood, and Turner, eds., *Undead Souths*, 10–22.

Cash, W. J. *The Mind of the South.* New York: Vintage, 1941.

Castells, Manuel. *The Rise of the Network Society.* Boston: Blackwell, 1996.

Central Alabama Fair Housing Center, et al. v. Julie Magee, et al. Decision Granting Preliminary Injunction. US District Court for the Middle District of Alabama Northern Division. Case 2:11-cv-00982-MHT-CSC, document 87, filed December 12, 2011: 68.

Chabot Davis, Kimberly. *Beyond the White Negro: Empathy and Anti-Racist Reading.* Champaign: University of Illinois Press, 2014.

Chanan, Michael. "Going South: On Documentary as a Form of Cognitive Geography." *Cinema Journal* 50, no. 1 (2010): 147–54.

Chang, Grace. "Where's the Violence? The Promise and Perils of Teaching Women of Color Studies." In Gutiérrez y Muhs, Flores Niemann, González, and Harris, eds., *Presumed Incompetent*, 198–220.

Chapman, Alix. "The Punk Show: Queering Heritage in the Black Diaspora." *Cultural Dynamics* 26, no. 3 (November 2014): 327–45.

Charbonneau, Stephen Michael. "Branching Out: Young Appalachian Selves, Autoethnographic Aesthetics, and the Founding of Appalshop." *Journal of Popular Film and Television* 37, no. 3 (2009): 137–45.

"The Charleston Shooting: A Crime of Hate amid Calls of Prayer." *Takeaway*, June 18, 2015. http://www.thetakeaway.org/story/gunman-inflicts-terror-hate-crime-attack-historic-black-church.

Chavez, Leo R. *The Latino Threat: Constructing Immigrants, Citizens, and the Nation*. Stanford, Calif.: Stanford University Press, 2008.

Childs, Becky, and Christine Mallinson. "African American English in Appalachia: Dialect Accommodation and Substrate Influence." *English World-Wide* 25, no. 2 (2004): 7–50.

———. "The Significance of Lexical Items in the Construction of Ethnolinguistic Identity: A Case Study of Adolescent Spoken and Online Language." *American Speech* 81 (2006): 3–30.

Childs, Becky, Christine Mallinson, and Jeannine Carpenter. "Vowel Phonology and Ethnicity in North Carolina." In *African American English Speakers and Their Participation in Local Sound Changes: A Comparative Study*, edited by Malcah Yaeger-Dror and Erik R. Thomas, 23–47. Durham, N.C.: Duke University Press, 2010.

Ching, Barbara. *Wrong's What I Do Best: Hard Country Music and Contemporary Culture*. New York: Oxford University Press, 2001.

Church, David. *Grindhouse Nostalgia*. Edinburgh, UK: Edinburgh University Press, 2015.

"Civil Rights Coalition Victorious in Challenge to Alabama's Anti-Immigrant 'Scarlet Letter' Law." Press release. National Immigration Law Center, October 10, 2014. http://www.nilc.org/2014/10/10/nr101014.

Clover, Carol. *Men, Women, and Chainsaws: Gender in the Modern Horror Film*. Princeton, N.J.: Princeton University Press, 1992.

Coates, Ta-Nehisi. "Take Down the Confederate Flag—Now," *Atlantic*, June 18, 2015. http://www.theatlantic.com/politics/archive/2015/06/take-down-the-confederate-flag-now/396290.

Cobb, James C. *Away Down South: A History of the Southern Identity*. New York: Oxford University Press, 2005.

———. *The Most Southern Place on Earth: The Mississippi Delta and the Roots of Regional Identity*. New York: Oxford University Press, 1992.

———. *Redefining Southern Culture: Mind and Identity in the Modern South*. Athens: University of Georgia Press, 1999.

Cobb, James C., and William Stueck, eds. *Globalization and the American South*. Athens: University of Georgia Press, 2005.

Coffey, Michele Grigsby. "*The State of Louisiana v. Charles Guerand*: Interracial Sexual Mores, Rape Rhetoric, and Respectability in 1930s New Orleans." *Louisiana History* 54, no. 1 (Winter 2013): 47–93.

Cohen, Cathy J. "Deviance as Resistance: A New Research Agenda for the Study of Black Politics." *Du Bois Review* 1, no. 1 (2004): 27–45.

Cohn, Deborah N. *History and Memory in the Two Souths: Recent Southern and Spanish American Fiction*. Nashville, Tenn.: Vanderbilt University Press, 1999.

Coleman, Mathew. "The "Local" Migration State: The Site-Specific Devolution of Immigration Enforcement in the U.S. South." *Law and Policy* 34, no. 2 (2012): 159–90.

Collins, Patricia Hill. *Black Feminist Thought: Knowledge, Consciousness, and the Politics of Empowerment*. New York: Routledge, 2002.

"The Combahee River Collective Statement." In *Home Girls: A Black Feminist Anthology*, edited by Barbara Smith, 264–74. New Brunswick, N.J.: Rutgers University Press, 2000.

Combs, Barbara Harris. "No Rest for the Weary: The Weight of Race, Gender, and Place inside and outside a Southern Classroom." *Sociology of Race and Ethnicity* (December 2016): 1–15.

Cone, A. L., and S. K. Owens. "Academic and Locus of Control Enhancements in Freshman Study Skills and College Adjustment Course." *Psychological Reports* 68 (1991): 1211–17.

Conquergood, Dwight. "Rethinking Ethnography: Towards a Critical Cultural Politics." *Communication Monographs* 58 (June 1991): 179–94.

Corbett, Katharine T., and Howard S. (Dick) Miller. "A Shared Inquiry into Shared Inquiry." *Public Historian* 28, no. 1 (Winter 2006): 15–38.

Coscarelli, Don. *Incident on and off a Mountain Road*. DVD. Masters of Horror. Troy, Mich.: Anchor Bay Entertainment, 2005.

Coski, John. *The Confederate Battle Flag: America's Most Embattled Emblem*. Cambridge, Mass.: Belknap Press of Harvard University Press, 2005.

Cowie, Elizabeth. *Recording Reality, Desiring the Real*. Minneapolis: University of Minnesota Press, 2011.

Cox, Karen. *Dixie's Daughters: The United Daughters of the Confederacy and the Preservation of Confederate Culture*. Gainesville: University Press of Florida, 2003.

———. *Pop South: Reflections on the South in Popular Culture*. http://southinpopculture.com/.

Craven, Wes. *The Hills Have Eyes*. DVD. Chatsworth, Calif.: Image Entertainment, 1977.

Cravey, Altha J. "Transnationality, Social Spaces, and Parallel Worlds." In *Latinos in the New South: Transformations of Place*, edited by H. A. Smith and O. J. Furuseth, 217–34. Burlington, Vt.: Ashgate, 2006.

Creed, Barbara. *The Monstrous-Feminine: Film, Feminism, Psychoanalysis*. New York: Routledge, 1993.

Crenshaw, Kimberlé. "Demarginalizing the Intersection of Race and Sex: A Black Feminist Critique of Antidiscrimination Doctrine, Feminist Theory, and Antiracist Politics." *University of Chicago Legal Forum*, 1989, 139–67.

Crespino, Joseph. *In Search of Another Country: Mississippi and the Conservative Counterrevolution*. Princeton, N.J.: Princeton University Press, 2007.

———. *Strom Thurmond's America*. New York: Hill and Wang, 2012.

Cunningham, Rodger. "Writing on the Cusp: Double Alterity and Minority Discourse in Appalachia." In *The Future of Southern Letters*, edited by Jefferson Humphries and John Lowe, 41–53. New York: Oxford University Press, 1996.

Dailey, Jane, Glenda Gilmore, and Bryant Simon, eds. *Jumpin' Jim Crow: Southern*

Politics from the Civil War to Civil Rights. Princeton, N.J.: Princeton University Press, 2000.

"Databases of Megachurches in the U.S." Hartford Institute for Religion Research. hirr.hartsem.edu/megachurch/database.html.

Davis, Angela Y. *Women, Race and Class*. New York: Vintage Books, 1983.

Davis, David A., and Tara Powell. "Reading Southern Food." In *Writing in the Kitchen: Essays on Southern Literature and Foodways*, 3–12. Jackson: University Press of Mississippi, 2014.

Davis, Thadious M. *Southscapes: Geographies of Race, Region, and Literature*. Chapel Hill: University of North Carolina Press, 2011.

Death Penalty Information Center. "Number of Executions by State and Region since 1976." http://www.deathpenaltyinfo.org/number-executions-state-and-region-1976 (accessed December 28, 2015.).

———. "Current Death Row Populations by Race as of July 1, 2015." In "Race of Death Row Inmates Executed since 1976." http://www.deathpenaltyinfo.org/race-death-row-inmates-executed-1976?scid=5&did=184#deathrowpop (December 28, 2015).

De Felitta, Raymond. *Booker's Place: A Mississippi Story*. DVD. New York: Tribeca Films, 2012.

Delany, Samuel. *Times Square Red, Times Square Blue*. New York: New York University Press, 1999.

"Delegation of Immigration Authority Section 287(g) Immigration and Nationality Act." US Immigration and Customs Enforcement. https://www.ice.gov/287g.

Dempsey, Brain David. "Refuse to Fold: Blues Heritage Tourism and the Mississippi Delta." PhD diss., Middle Tennessee State University, 2009.

Desai, Gaurav. "Oceans Connect: The Indian Ocean and African Identities." *PMLA* 125, no. 3 (May 2010): 713–20.

Dixler, Hillary. "Why Southern Food Authority John T. Edge Is 'Not Giving Up on the South.'" *Eater*, August 7, 2014. http://www.eater.com/2014/8/7/6175389/why-southern-food-authority-john-t-edge-is-not-giving-up-on-the-south.

Domínguez, Virginia. *White by Definition: Social Classification in Creole Louisiana*. New Brunswick, N.J.: Rutgers University Press, 1986.

Dorr, Lisa L. *White Women, Rape, and the Power of Race in Virginia, 1900–1960*. Chapel Hill: University of North Carolina Press, 2004.

Doty, Roxanne Lynn. *The Law into Their Own Hands*. Tucson: University of Arizona Press, 2009.

Douglass, Frederick. *Narrative of the Life of Frederick Douglass, an American Slave, Written by Himself*. New Haven, Conn.: Yale University Press, 2001.

Doyle, Don H. *Nations Divided: America, Italy, and the Southern Question*. Athens: University of Georgia Press, 2002.

Duck, Leigh Anne. *The Nation's Region: Southern Modernism, Segregation, and U.S. Nationalism*. Athens: University of Georgia Press, 2006.

———. Review of *The Real South*, by Scott Romine. *Journal of Southern History* 76, no. 3 (2010): 801–2.

———. "Undead Genres/Living Locales in *The True Meaning of Pictures* and *Winter's Bone*." In Anderson, Hagood, and Turners, eds., *Undead Souths*, 173–86.

Duke, Marshall P., Amber Lazarus, and Robyn Fivush. "Knowledge of Family History as a Clinically Useful Index of Psychological Well-Being and Prognosis: A Brief Report." *Psychotherapy Theory, Research, Practice, Training* 45, no. 2 (2008): 268–72.

Duke, Marshall P., Robyn Fivush, Amber Lazarus, and Jennifer Bohanek. "Of Ketchup and Kin: Dinnertime Conversations as a Major Source of Family Knowledge, Family Adjustment and Family Resilience." Emory Center for Myth and Ritual in American Life, Working Paper no. 26, May 2003.

DuRoucher, Kristina. *Raising Racists: The Socialization of Children in the Jim Crow South*. Lexington: University of Kentucky Press, 2011.

Edelman, Lee. *No Future: Queer Theory and the Death Drive*. Durham, N.C.: Duke University Press, 2004.

Eden, Don. "Pygmalion without Interpersonal Contrast Effects: Whole Groups Gain from Raising Manager Expectations." *Journal of Applied Psychology* 75 (1990): 394–98.

———. "Self-Fulfilling Prophecies in Organizations." In *Organizational Behavior: State of the Science*, edited by Jerald Greenberg, 91–122. Mahwah, N.J.: Erlbaum, 2003.

Edge, John T. "Going Deeper with Red Dog." *Oxford American* 88 (Spring 2015): 102–3.

———. "SFA Visioning with Ari." Southern Foodways Alliance, August 21, 2015. https://www.southernfoodways.org/sfa-visioning-with-ari.

———. "Why Southern Food Matters." In *The Southerner's Handbook: A Guide to Living the Good Life*, edited by David DiBenedetto, 3–7. New York: Harper Wave, 2013.

Edge, John T., Elizabeth S. D. Englehardt, and Ted Ownby, eds. *The Larder: Food Studies Methods from the American South*. Athens: University of Georgia Press, 2013.

Edge, John T., and Tunde Wey. "Who Owns Southern Food?" *Oxford American* 93 (Summer 2016). http://www.oxfordamerican.org/magazine/item/870-who-owns-southern-food.

"Editor's Note." *Southern Exposure* 1, no. 1 (Spring 1973).

Edmondson, Amy. "Learning from Mistakes Is Easier Said than Done: Group and Organization Influences on the Detection and Correction of Human Error." *Journal of Applied Behavioral Science* 32 (1996): 5–28.

———. "Psychological Safety and Learning Behavior in Work Teams." *Administrative Science Quarterly* 44 (1999): 350–83.

Eichstedt, Jennifer L., and Stephen Small. *Representations of Slavery: Race and Ideology in Southern Plantation Museums*. Washington, D.C.: Smithsonian Institution Press, 2002.

Elias, Karen, and Judith C. Jones. "Two Voices from the Front Lines: A Conversation about Race in the Classroom." In Tusmith and Reddy, eds., *Race in the College Classroom*, 7–18.

Ellison, Curtis W. *Country Music Culture: From Hard Times to Heaven*. Jackson: University Press of Mississippi, 1995.

Elliston, Jon. "NC Sets Record for Meth Lab Busts in 2013, with Slight Uptick in WNC." *Carolina Public Press*, January 10, 2014. http://www.carolinapublicpress.org/.

Enelow, Sarah. "The Rise of Civil Rights Tourism in America's Deep South." *Skift*, August 25, 2016. https://skift.com/2016/08/25/the-rise-of-civil-rights-tourism-in-americas-deep-south.

England, Eric. *Madison County*, DVD. Chatsworth, Calif.: Image Entertainment, 2011.

Englehardt, Elizabeth S. D. *A Mess of Greens: Southern Gender and Southern Food.* Athens: University of Georgia Press, 2011.

Engelhardt, Elizabeth S. D., et al. "Letter: Activists Correctly Call Silent Sam Racist." *Daily Tar Heel*, October 29, 2015. http://www.dailytarheel.com/article/2015/10/letter-activists-correctly-call-silent-sam-racist.

Escobar, Arturo. "'Post-development' as a Concept and Social Practice." In *Exploring Post-development: Theory and Practice, Problems and Perspectives*, edited by Aram Ziai, 18–30. New York: Routledge, 2007.

Eskew, Glenn T. *Johnny Mercer: Southern Songwriter for the World.* Athens: University of Georgia Press, 2014.

Ethridge, Robbie Franklyn. *From Chicaza to Chickasaw: The European Invasion and the Transformation of the Mississippian World, 1540–1715.* Athens: University of Georgia Press, 2010.

"Executive Actions on Immigration." U.S. Citizenship and Immigration Services. http://www.uscis.gov/immigrationaction.

Feagin, Joe. *Racist America: Roots, Current Realities, and Future Reparations.* New York: Routledge, 2001.

Feagin, Joe R., Anthony M. Orum, and Gideon Sjoberg, eds. *A Case for the Case Study.* Chapel Hill: University of North Carolina Press, 1991.

Feiler, Bruce. "The Stories That Bind Us." *New York Times*, March 15, 2013.

Feimster, Crystal. *Southern Horrors: Women and the Politics of Rape and Lynching.* Cambridge, Mass.: Harvard University Press, 2010.

Ferguson, Roderick. *Aberrations in Black: Towards a Queer of Color Critique.* Minneapolis: University of Minnesota Press, 2004.

Ferris, Marcie Cohen. *The Edible South: The Power of Food and the Making of an American Region.* Chapel Hill: University of North Carolina Press, 2014.

Fireman, Gary D., Ted E. McVay and Owen J. Flanagan. *Narratives and Consciousness: Literature, Psychology and the Brain.* New York: Oxford University Press, 2003.

Fivush, Robyn, Jennifer G. Bohanek, and Marshall Duke. "The Intergenerational Self: Subjective Perspective and Family History." In *Self Continuity: Individual and Collective Perspectives*, edited by Fabio Sani, 131–43. New York: Psychology Press, 2008.

Fivush, Robyn, and Catherine A. Haden. *Autobiographical Memory and Construction of a Narrative Self: Development and Cultural Perspectives.* Mahwah, N.J.: Erlbaum, 2003.

Flancranstin, Archibald. *Header.* DVD. Synapse Films, 2006.

Foucault, Michel. *The History of Sexuality.* London: Allen Lane, 1979.

Frankenberg, Ruth. *White Women, Race Matters: The Social Construction of Whiteness.* Minneapolis: University of Minnesota Press, 1993.

Frankl, Viktor E. *Man's Search for Meaning.* Boston: Beacon Press, 2006. First published 1946.

Frederickson, Mary. *Looking South: Race, Gender, and the Transformation of Labor from Reconstruction to Globalization.* Gainesville: University Press of Florida, 2011.

Freeman, Elizabeth. "Queer Belongings: Kinship Theory and Queer Theory." In *A Companion to Lesbian, Gay, Bisexual, Transgender, and Queer Studies*, edited by George E. Haggerty and Molly McGarry, 295–314. Oxford, UK: Blackwell, 2007.

Freire, Paulo. *Pedagogy of the Oppressed.* New York: Herder and Herder, 1972.
Gabriel, Kathleen F. *Teaching Unprepared Students: Strategies for Promoting Success and Retention in Higher Education.* Sterling, Va.: Stylus, 2008.
Gaines, Jane M. "Appalshop Documentaries: Inventing and Preserving Appalachia." *Jump Cut*, no. 34 (1989), 53–63.
Gibson, Chris, and John Connell. *Music and Tourism: On the Road Again.* Clevedon, UK: Channel View, 2005.
Giggie, John. *After Redemption: Jim Crow and the Transformation of African American Religion in the Delta, 1875–1915.* New York: Oxford University Press, 2007.
Giglio, Tony. *Timber Falls.* DVD. Los Angeles: Slowhand Cinema Releasing, 2007.
Gillman, Sander L. *Difference and Pathology: Stereotypes of Sexuality, Race and Madness.* Ithaca, N.Y.: Cornell University Press, 1985.
Gilroy, Paul. *The Black Atlantic: Modernity and Double Consciousness.* Cambridge, Mass.: Harvard University Press, 1993.
Giola, Ted. *Delta Blues: The Life and Times of the Mississippi Masters Who Revolutionized American Music.* New York: W. W. Norton, 2008.
Giroux, Henry A. *Disposable Youth: Racialized Memories and the Culture of Cruelty.* New York: Routledge, 2012.
———. "Drowning Democracy." In *Critical Studies of Southern Place: A Reader*, edited by William M. Reynolds. New York: Peter Lang, 2014.
———. *On Critical Pedagogy.* New York: Continuum, 2011.
———. *Teachers as Intellectuals: Toward a Critical Pedagogy of Learning.* Westport, Conn.: Bergin and Garvey, 1988.
Goldstein, Philip, and James L. Machor, eds. *New Directions in American Reception Study.* New York: Oxford University Press, 2008.
Grady, Henry W. "The South and Her Problems." In *The New South and Other Addresses*, edited by Edna Henry Lee Turpin, 43–91. New York: Haskell House, 1969. First published 1904.
Grant, Adam. *Give and Take: A Revolutionary Approach to Success.* New York: Viking, 2013.
Gray, Richard. "Inventing Communities, Imagining Places: Some Thoughts on Southern Self-Fashioning." In *South to a New Place*, edited by Suzanne W. Jones and Sharon Monteith. Baton Rouge: Louisiana State University Press, 2002.
Grazian, David. *Blue Chicago: The Search for Authenticity in Urban Blues Clubs.* Chicago: University of Chicago Press, 2003.
Green, Myra. "Thanks for Listening." *Chronicle of Higher Education*, October 19, 2015.
Greene, Christina. *Our Separate Ways: Women and the Black Freedom Movement in Durham, North Carolina.* Chapel Hill: University of North Carolina Press, 2005.
Greene, Robert. "African American Activism and the Search for a Usable Past." *U.S. Intellectual History*, August 30, 2015. http://s-usih.org/2015/08/african-american-activism-and-the-search-for-a-usable-past.html.
———. "The American South and American Minds," *U.S. Intellectual History*, May 11, 2014. http://s-usih.org/2014/05/the-american-south-and-american-minds.html.
———. "The Fall of the Confederate Flag." *Dissent*, July 15, 2015. https://www.dissentmagazine.org/blog/the-fall-of-the-confederate-flag-south-carolina-charleston.

———. "Racism Can't Destroy This Charleston Church." *Politico*, June 19, 2015. http://www.politico.com/magazine/story/2015/06/charleston-shooting-emanuel-african-methodist-episcopal-church-119205.

———. "The Southern Strategy." *Dissent* 62, no. 3 (2015): 67–72.

Greeson, Jennifer Rae. *Our South: Geographic Fantasy and the Rise of National Literature*. Cambridge, Mass.: Harvard University Press, 2010.

Gregory, Steven. *Black Corona: Race and the Politics of Place in an Urban Community*. Princeton, N.J.: Princeton University Press, 1998.

Grewal, Inderpal, and Caren Kaplan, eds. *Scattered Hegemonies: Postmodernity and Transnational Feminist Practices*. Minneapolis: University of Minnesota Press, 1994.

Griffin, Larry J., and Ashley B. Thompson. "Enough about the Disappearing South: What about the Disappearing Southerner?" *Southern Cultures* 9, no. 3 (Fall 2003): 51–65.

Guerrero, Franklin, Jr. *Carver*. DVD. Fort Mill, S.C.: Allumination Filmworks, 2007.

Gussow, Adam. *Seems Like Murder Here: Southern Violence and the Blues Tradition*. Chicago: University of Chicago Press, 2002.

Guterl, Matthew Pratt. *American Mediterranean: Southern Slaveholders in the Age of Emancipation*. Cambridge, Mass.: Harvard University Press, 2008.

———. "South." In *Keywords for American Cultural Studies*, edited by Bruce Burgett and Glenn Hendler, 230–33. New York: New York University Press, 2007.

Gutiérrez y Muhs, Gabriella, Yolanda Flores Niemann, Carmen G. González, and Angela P. Harris, eds. *Presumed Incompetent: The Intersections of Race and Class for Women in Academia*. Boulder: University Press of Colorado, 2012.

Hagood, Taylor. "Going to Ground: The Undead in Contemporary Popular Southern Culture Media and Writing." In Anderson, Hagood, and Turner, eds., *Undead Souths*, 248–60.

Haidt, Jonathan. *The Happiness Hypothesis: Finding Modern Truth in Ancient Wisdom*. New York: Basic Books, 2005.

———. *The Righteous Mind: Why Good People Are Divided by Politics and Religion*. New York: Vintage, 2013.

Hale, Charles R. Introduction to *Engaging Contradictions: Theory, Politics, and Methods of Activist Scholarship*, 1–28. Berkeley: University of California Press, 2008.

Hall, Douglas, and Algernon Austin. "Distressed Mississippi: Unemployment Rate for African American Workers Is Significantly Higher than for Whites." *Economic Policy Institute Issue Brief*, no. 303, 2011. http://www.epi.org/page/-/old/issuebriefs/IB303_Mississippi_FINAL.pdf.

Hall, Jacquelyn Dowd. "The Long Civil Rights Movement and the Political Uses of the Past." *Journal of American History* 91, no. 4 (March 2005), 1233–63.

———. *Revolt against Chivalry: Jessie Daniel Ames and the Women's Campaign against Lynching*. New York: Columbia University Press, 1979.

Hall, Stewart. "Encoding/Decoding." In *Culture, Media, Language: Working Papers in Cultural Studies, 1972–79*, 128–38. London: Hutchinson, 1980.

———, ed. *Representation: Cultural Representations and Signifying Practices*. London: Sage, 1997.

"Hammon Doesn't Know Difference between 'Hispanic' and 'Illegal Immigrant.'" *Anniston Star*, June 23, 2011.

Handley, George B. *Postslavery Literatures in the Americas: Family Portraits in Black and White*. New Brunswick, N. J.: Rutgers University Press, 2000.

Harding, Vincent. "Beyond the Black Desert." *Motive* 28, no. 6 (1968): 45–48.

Hardy, Sarah Madsen, and Marisa Milanese. "Teaching Students to Be Public Intellectuals." *Chronicle of Higher Education*, June 29, 2016.

Harkins, Anthony. *Hillbilly: A Cultural History of an American Icon*. New York: Oxford University Press, 2004.

Harris-Perry, Melissa. "The 'MHP' Black Feminism Syllabus." MSNBC, November 13, 2013. http://www.msnbc.com/melissa-harris-perry/the-mhp-black-feminism-syllabus.

Hartman, Saidiya. *Scenes of Subjection: Terror, Slavery, and Self-Making in Nineteenth-Century America*. New York: Oxford University Press, 1997.

Harvey, David. *The Condition of Postmodernity: An Enquiry into the Origins of Cultural Change*. Cambridge, Mass.: Blackwell, 1989.

Harvey, Paul. *Freedom's Coming: Religious Culture and the Shaping of the South from the Civil War through the Civil Rights Era*. Chapel Hill: University of North Carolina Press, 2005.

———. *Moses, Jesus, and the Trickster in the Evangelical South*. Athens: University of Georgia Press, 2012.

———. *Redeeming the South: Religious Cultures and Racial Identities among Southern Baptists*. Chapel Hill: University of North Carolina Press, 1997.

———. *Through the Storm, through the Night: A History of African American Christianity*. Lanham, Md.: Rowman and Littlefield, 2011.

Hasty, J. Daniel, and Becky Childs. "The Old Is New Again: Curvilinear Patterns of Linguistic Change in Appalachia." Presentation at NWAV 42 (New Ways of Analyzing Variation conference), Carnegie Mellon University, Pittsburgh, Penn., October 2013.

Haygood, Atticus. *The New South: Gratitude, Hope, Amendment*. Oxford, Ga., 1880.

Hazard, Laurie L., and Jean-Paul Nadeau. *Foundations for Learning: Claiming Your Education*. 3rd ed. New York: Pearson, 2012.

Hemphill, Essex. "American Wedding." In *Ceremonies: Prose and Poetry*, 170–71. New York: Plume Books, 1992.

Henninger, Katherine. *Ordering the Facade: Photography and Contemporary Southern Women's Writing*. Chapel Hill: University of North Carolina Press, 2007.

Henshall, John. *Downtown Clarksdale: An Action Plan for Economic Revitalization*. Carlton, Australia: Essential Economics, 2008.

Herberg, Will. *Protestant, Catholic, Jew*. Garden City, N.Y.: Doubleday, 1955.

Hermann, Janet Sharp. *The Pursuit of a Dream*. Jackson: University Press of Mississippi, 1999.

Herzog, Werner. *Into the Abyss: A Tale of Death, a Tale of Life*. New York: IFC Films, 2012.

———. "Minnesota Declaration: Truth and Fact in Documentary Cinema." *Walker Magazine*, April 30, 1999. http://www.walkerart.org/magazine/1999/minnesota-declaration-truth-and-fact-in-docum.

Heyrman, Christine. *Southern Cross: The Beginnings of the Bible Belt*. Chapel Hill: University of North Carolina, 1997.

Hill, Samuel. *Southern Churches in Crisis*. Boston: Beacon Press, 1966.

Hills, Matt. *The Pleasures of Horror*. New York: Bloomsbury Academic, 2005.

Himley, Margaret. "Response to Phillip P. Marzluf, 'Diversity Writing: Natural Languages, Authentic Voices.'" *College Composition and Communication* 58, no. 3 (February 2007): 449–63.

Hirsch, Arnold R., and Joseph Logsdon. *Creole New Orleans: Race and Americanization*. Baton Rouge: Louisiana State University, 1992.

Hispanic Interest Coalition of Alabama et al. vs. Robert Bentley et al.; Rt. Rev. Henry N. Parsley, Jr. et al. vs. Robert Bentley; United States of America vs. State of Alabama; Governor Robert J. Bentley. Order. United States District Court Northern District of Alabama Northeastern Division. September 29, 2011. http://www.babc.com/files/upload/Blackburn%20Order.pdf.

Hitchcock, Alfred. *Psycho*. DVD. Los Angeles: Paramount Pictures, 1960.

Hitt, Jack. "The Newest Indians." *New York Times Magazine*, August 21, 2005. http://www.nytimes.com/.

Hobson, Fred. *Serpent in Eden: H. L. Mencken and the South*. Chapel Hill: University of North Carolina Press, 1974.

———. *The Southern Writer in the Postmodern World*. Athens: University of Georgia Press, 1991.

Hooper, Tobe. *The Texas Chainsaw Massacre*. DVD. Bryanston Distributing, 1974.

Horton, Andrew. "Film from Appalshop: Documentary Film-Makers in the Appalachians." *Film Quarterly* 33, no. 4 (1980): 11–14.

Houska, Tara. "The Racial Wallpaper of Slavery and Genocide." *Indian Country Today*. June 24, 2015. http://indiancountrytodaymedianetwork.com/2015/06/24/houska-racial-wallpaper-slavery-and-genocide-160840.

Howard, John. *Men Like That: A Southern Queer History*. Chicago: University of Chicago Press, 1999.

Howe, Julia Ward. "Battle Hymn of the Republic." *Atlantic Monthly* 9, no. 52 (February 1862): 145–46.

Hubbard, Mike, with David Azbell. *Storming the State House: The Campaign that Liberated Alabama from 136 Years of Democracy*. Montgomery, Ala.: NewSouth Books, 2012.

Hudspeth, Harvey Gresham. "Mississippi Valley State University at the Millennium: A Sixty-Year History, 1943–2003." *Griot* 23, no. 2 (2004): 1–15.

Hull, Gloria T., Patricia Bell-Scott, and Barbara Smith, eds. *All the Women Are White, All the Blacks Are Men, but Some of Us Are Brave: Black Women's Studies*. Old Westbury, N.Y.: Feminist Press at CUNY, 1982.

Hunter, Tera W. *To 'Joy My Freedom: Southern Black Women's Lives and Labors after the Civil War*. Cambridge, Mass.: Harvard University Press, 1997.

Indian Country Diaries. Lincoln, Neb.: Native American Public Telecommunications and Advando Vision, 2006.

"It Feels Like a Dagger to the Soul." BBC World Service, June 18, 2015. http://www.bbc.co.uk/programmes/p02vogtr.

Izadi, Elahe. "Faculty Can Carry Handguns on Public College Campuses under Controversial New Tennessee Law." *Washington Post*, May 2, 2016.

Jackson, Jeffrey T., Kirsten Dellinger, Kathryn McKee, and Annette Trefzer. "Interdisciplinary Perspectives on the Global South and Global North." In *The Sociology of Development Handbook*, edited by Gregory Hooks. Oakland: University of California Press, 2015.

Jacobson, Matthew Frye. *Whiteness of a Different Color: European Immigrants and the Alchemy of Race*. Boston: Harvard University Press, 1999.

Jameson, Fredric. *Postmodernism, or, The Cultural Logic of Late Capitalism*. Durham, N.C.: Duke University Press, 1991.

Jaschik, Scott. "The Professor Who Wasn't Fired." *Inside Higher Ed*, July 1, 2015. https://www.insidehighered.com/news/2015/07/01/twitter-explodes-false-reports-u-memphis-fired-professor-why.

Johnson, Cedric, ed. *The Neoliberal Deluge: Hurricane Katrina, Late Capitalism, and the Remaking of New Orleans*. Minneapolis: University of Minnesota Press, 2011.

Johnson, E. Patrick. "Mother Knows Best: Black Gay Vernacular and Transgressive Domestic Space." In *Speaking in Queer Tongues: Globalization and Gay Language*, edited by William L. Leap and Tom Boellstorff, 251–78. Urbana-Champaign: University of Illinois Press, 2004.

"John T. Edge to Host Culinary Festival." *Palmetto Bluff*, Fall 2012, 36, http://issuu.com/palmettobluff/docs/pb_thebluff_fall2012/38.

Jones, Anne Goodwyn, and Susan V. Donaldson, eds. *Haunted Bodies: Gender and Southern Texts*. Charlottesville: University Press of Virginia, 1997.

Jones, C. H., J. R. Slate, and I. Marini. "Locus of Control, Social Interdependence, Academic Preparation, Age, Study Time and the Study Skills of College Students." *Research in the Schools* 2, no. 1 (1993): 55–62.

Jones, Jacqueline. *Labor of Love, Labor of Sorrow: Black Women, Work, and the Family, from Slavery to the Present*. New York: Basic Books, 1985.

Jones, Suzanne W., and Sharon Monteith, eds. *South to a New Place: Region, Literature, Culture*. Baton Rouge: Louisiana State University Press, 2002.

Joseph, Peniel. "The Black Power Movement, Democracy, and America in the King Years." *American Historical Review* 114, no. 4 (October 2009): 1001–16.

Joshi, Khyati Y., and Jigna Desai, eds. *Asian Americans in Dixie: Race and Migration in the South*. Urbana-Champaign: University of Illinois Press, 2013.

Joyner, Brian. "Whither Diversity?" *History@Work*, April 22, 2016. http://ncph.org/history-at-work/whither-diversity.

June, Audrey Williams. "The Invisible Labor of Minority Professors." *Chronicle of Higher Education*, November 8, 2015.

Jussim, Lee, and Kent Harber, "Teacher Expectations and Self-Fulfilling Prophecies: Knowns and Unknowns, Resolved and Unresolved Controversies." *Personality and Social Psychology Review* 9 (2005): 131–55.

Kaplan, Sarah. "For Charleston's Emanuel AME Church, Shooting Is Another Painful Chapter in Rich History." *Washington Post*, June 18, 2015.

"Katrina Brides and Babies." CBS News, August 25, 2006. http://www.cbsnews.com/videos/katrina-brides-and-babies.

Katznelson, Ira. *Fear Itself: The New Deal and the Origins of Our Time.* New York: W. W. Norton, 2013.

Kein, Sybil. *Creole: The History and Legacy of Louisiana's Free People of Color.* Baton Rouge: Louisiana State University, 2000.

Kim-Puri, H. J. "Conceptionalizing Gender-Sexuality-State-Nation: An Introduction." *Gender and Society* 19, no. 2 (April 2005): 137–59.

King, Stephen A. *I'm Feeling the Blues Right Now: Blues Tourism and the Mississippi Delta.* Jackson: University Press of Mississippi, 2011.

Kirby, Jack Temple. *Mockingbird Song: Ecological Landscapes of the South.* Chapel Hill: University of North Carolina Press, 2000.

Klein, Naomi. *The Shock Doctrine: The Rise of Disaster Capitalism.* New York: Macmillan, 2007.

Kondo, Dorinne. *About Face: Performing Race in Fashion and Theater.* New York: Routledge, 1997.

Kreyling, Michael. *Inventing Southern Literature.* Jackson: University Press of Mississippi, 1998.

———. "Toward 'A New Southern Studies.'" *South Central Review* 22, no. 1 (Spring 2005): 4–18.

Kyvig, David E., and Myron A. Marty. *Nearby History: Exploring the Past around You.* Lanham, Md.: AltaMira Press, 2010.

Labode, Modupe. "Diversity, Here to There." *Public History News* 29, no. 4 (2009): 7.

Lacan, Jacques. *The Ethics of Psychoanalysis 1959–1960.* Translated by Dennis Potter. Seminar of Jacques Lacan, book 7. Edited by Jacques-Alain Miller. New York: Norton, 1992.

Ladd, Barbara. "Dismantling the Monolith: Southern Places—Past, Present, and Future." *Critical Survey* 12, no. 1 (2000): 28–42.

———. "Literary Studies: The Southern United States, 2005." *PMLA* 120, no. 5 (October 2005): 1628–39.

Lando, Jeffery Scott. *Savage Island.* DVD. Santa Monica: Ardustry Home Entertainment, 2004.

Lassiter, Matthew. *The Silent Majority: Suburban Politics in the Sunbelt South.* Princeton, N.J.: Princeton University Press, 2006.

Lassiter, Matthew D., and Joseph L. Crespino, eds. *Myth of Southern Exceptionalism.* New York: Oxford University Press, 2010.

Laymon, Kiese. "Black Churches Taught Us to Forgive White People. We Learned to Shame Ourselves." *Guardian*, June 23, 2015.

Lazos, Sylvia R. "Are Student Teaching Evaluations Holding Back Women and Minorities? The Perils of "Doing" Gender and Race in the Classroom." In Gutiérrez y Muhs, Flores Niemann, González, and Harris, eds., *Presumed Incompetent*, 164–85.

Lein, Laura, Ronald Angel, Julie Beausoleil, and Holly Bell. "The Basement of Extreme Poverty: Katrina Survivors and Poverty Programs." In *Displaced: Life in the Katrina Diaspora*, edited by Lynn Weber and Lori Peek, 47–61. Austin: University of Texas Press, 2012.

Levander, Caroline. "Sutton Griggs and the Borderlands of Empire." *American Literary History* 22 (2009): 57–84.

Levander, Caroline F., and Robert S. Levine. "Introduction: Essays beyond the Nation." In *Hemispheric American Studies*, edited by Caroline F. Levander and Robert S. Levine, 1–17. New Brunswick, N.J.: Rutgers University Press, 2008.

Levander, Caroline, and Walter Mignolo. "Introduction: The Global South and World Dis/Order." *Global South* 5, no. 1 (2011): 1–11.

Lewis, Anne. *Anne Braden: Southern Patriot*. DVD. Whitesburg, Ky.: Appalshop, 2012.

———. *Justice in the Coalfields*. DVD. Whitesburg, Ky.: Appalshop, 1995.

———. *Morristown: In the Air and Sun*. DVD. Whitesburg, Ky.: Appalshop, 2007.

———. *Transcript, "Anne Braden: Southern Patriot."* California Newsreel. http://www.newsreel.org/transcripts/Anne-Braden-Southern-Patriot-transcript.pdf.

Lewis, Helen M. "Appalshop: Preserving, Participating in, and Creating Southern Mountain Culture." In *Cultural Heritage Conservation in the American South*, edited by Benita J. Howell, 79–86. Athens: University of Georgia Press, 1990.

Lewis, John, and Michael D'Orso. *Walking with the Wind: A Memoir of the Movement*. New York: Mariner Books, 1999.

Lewnes, Pericles. *Redneck Zombies*. DVD. Long Island: Troma Entertainment, 1989.

Lidchi, Henrietta. "The Poetics and the Politics of Exhibiting Other Cultures." In *Representation: Cultural Representations and Signifying Practices*, edited by Stuart Hall, 151–222. London: Sage, 1997.

Link, William. *Righteous Warrior: Jesse Helms and the Rise of Modern Conservatism*. New York: St. Martin's Press, 2008.

Linnemann, Travis. "Governing through Meth: Local Politics, Drug Control and the Drift toward Securitization." *Crime Media Culture* 9 (2012): 39–61.

Lipsitz, George. *The Possessive Investment in Whiteness*. Philadelphia: Temple University Press, 1998.

Liptak, Adam. "Supreme Court Invalidates Key Part of Voting Rights Act." *New York Times*, June 25, 2013.

Livingston, Jennie. *Paris Is Burning*. DVD. Los Angeles: Off White Productions, 1991.

Lomax, Allen. *The Land Where the Blues Began*. New York: New Press, 1993.

Long, Elizabeth. *Book Clubs: Women and the Uses of Reading in Everyday Life*. Chicago: University of Chicago Press, 2003.

Lovell, Jarrett S. *Crimes of Dissent: Civil Disobedience, Criminal Justice, and the Politics of Conscience*. New York: New York University Press, 2009.

Lowe, John, ed. *Bridging Southern Cultures: An Interdisciplinary Approach*. Baton Rouge: Louisiana State University Press, 2005.

Lynch, Joe. *Wrong Turn 2: Dead End*. DVD. Los Angeles: 20th Century Fox Home Entertainment, 2007.

Machor, James L., and Philip Goldstein, eds. *Reception Study: From Literary Theory to Cultural Studies*. New York: Routledge, 2001.

Madison, D. Soyini. *Critical Ethnography: Method, Ethics, and Performance*. Thousand Oaks: Sage Press, 2005.

Malcolm X. "The Ballot or the Bullet." *Digital History*. http://www.digitalhistory.uh.edu/disp_textbook.cfm?smtid=3&psid=3624.

Mangan, Katherine. "Under the Gun: Faculty Members in Some States Prepare for 'Campus Carry' to Become Reality." *Chronicle of Higher Education*, July 18, 2016.

Manne, Kate. "Why I Use Trigger Warnings." *New York Times*. September 19, 2015.

Marable, Manning. *Race, Reform, and Rebellion: The Second Reconstruction and Beyond in Black America, 1945–2006*. Jackson: University Press of Mississippi, 2007.

Marable, Manning, and Kristen Clarke. *Seeking Higher Ground: The Hurricane Katrina Crisis, Race, and Public Policy Reader*. New York: Palgrave Macmillan, 2008.

Marty, Martin. "The Revival of Evangelicalism and Southern Religion." In *Varieties of Southern Evangelicalism*, edited by David Harrell, 7–21. Macon, Ga.: Mercer University Press, 1981.

Marzluf, Phillip P. "Response to 'Diversity Writing': Natural Languages, Authentic Voices." *College Composition and Communication* 58, no. 3 (February 2007): 463–65.

Maslin, Janet. "In Florida Slough with the Gators and Family Ghosts." *New York Times*, February 16, 2011.

Massey, Doreen. "Politics and Space/Time." *New Left Review* 196 (November/December 1992): 65–84.

Mathews, Donald G. "The Southern Rite of Human Sacrifice." *Journal of Southern Religion*, August 22, 2000. http://jsr.fsu.edu/mathews.htm.

———. "We Have Left Undone Those Things Which We Ought to Have Done: Southern Religious History in Retrospect and Prospect." *Church History* 67, no. 2 (June 1998): 305–25.

Mathews, Donald, Samuel Hill, Beth Barton Schweiger, and John Boles. "Forum: Southern Religion." *Religion and American Culture* 8, no. 2 (Summer 1998): 147–77.

Mbembe, Achille. "Necropolitics." Translated by Libby Meintjes. *Public Culture* 15, no. 1 (2003): 11–40.

McAdams, Janet. "The Collectors." In *Feral*, 1–7. Cambridge, UK: Salt Publishing, 2007.

McCall, Sophie. *First Person Plural: Aboriginal Storytelling and the Ethics of Collaborative Authorship*. Vancouver: University of British Columbia Press, 2011.

McCall, Sophie, Deanna Reder, and Eric Gary Anderson. "First Nations and Native Souths on Both Sides of the 49th Parallel." *Global South* 9, no. 1 (2015): 39–61.

McCubbin, H., A. Thompson, and M. McCubbin. *Family Assessment: Resiliency, Coping and Adaption: Inventories for Research and Practice*. Madison: University of Wisconsin Press, 1996.

McDannell, Colleen. *Picturing Faith: Photography and the Great Depression*. New Haven, Conn.: Yale University Press, 2004.

McGuire, Danielle. *At the Dark End of the Street: Black Women, Rape and Resistance: A New History of the Civil Rights Movement from Rosa Parks to the Rise of Black Power*. New York: Vintage Books, 2011.

McKee, Kathryn, and Annette Trefzer. "Preface: Global Contexts, Local Literatures: The New Southern Studies." *American Literature* 78 (December 2006): 672–90.

McKinney, Louise. *New Orleans: A Cultural History*. New York: Oxford University Press, 2006.

McLean, Kate C., and Monisha Pasupathi. *Narrative Development in Adolescence: Creating the Storied Self*. New York: Springer, 2012.

McPherson, Tara. *Reconstructing Dixie: Race, Gender, and Nostalgia in the Imagined South*. Durham, N.C.: Duke University Press, 2003.

Mencken, H. L. "Americana." *American Mercury*, October 1924, 170–74.

———. "Editorial." *American Mercury*, November 1924, 290–92.

———. *Prejudices: Second Series*. New York: Alfred Knopf, 1920.

"Meth Lab Busts." North Carolina Department of Justice. July 24, 2015. http://www.ncdoj.gov/getdoc/b1f6f30e-df89-4679-9889-53a3f185c849/2-0-1-1-3-3-Meth-Lab-Busts.aspx.

Mignolo, Walter. *The Darker Side of Western Modernity: Global Futures, Decolonial Options (Latin America Otherwise)*. Durham, N.C.: Duke University Press, 2011.

———. "Delinking: The Rhetoric of Modernity, the Logic of Coloniality and the Grammar of De-Coloniality." *Cultural Studies* 21, nos. 2–3 (2007): 449–514.

———. "Epistemic Disobedience, Independent Thought and De-colonial Freedom." *Theory, Culture, and Society* 26 (December 2009): 159–81.

Milanich, Jerald T. "Osceola's Head." *Archeology* 57, no. 1 (January/February 2004), 48.

Milazzo, Marzia. "White Supremacy, White Knowledge, and Anti-West Indian Discourse in Panama: Olmedo Alfaro's *El peligro antillano en la América Central*." *Global South* 6, no. 2 (2012): 65–86.

Miller, Karl Hagstrom. *Segregating Sound: Inventing Folk and Popular Music in the Age of Jim Crow*. Durham, N.C.: Duke University Press, 2010.

Mohanty, Chandra Talpade. "'Under Western Eyes' Revisited: Feminist Solidarity through Anti-Capitalist Struggles." *Signs* 28, no. 2 (Winter 2003): 499–535.

"'Mother Emanuel' A.M.E. Church History." http://www.emanuelamechurch.org/churchhistory.php.

Moynihan, Daniel Patrick. *The Negro Family: A Case for National Action*. Washington, D.C.: Government Printing Office. 1965.

Muñoz, José Esteban. *Cruising Utopia: The Then and There of Queer Futurity*. New York: New York University Press, 2009.

NCPH Curriculum and Training Committee. "Best Practices in Public History: Public History for Undergraduate Students." October 2009. http://ncph.org/wp-content/uploads/2010/08/Undergrad-Best-Practice.pdf.

Nelson, Katherine. "The Psychological and Social Origins of Autobiographical Memory." *Psychological Science* 4, no. 1 (January 1993): 7–14.

Nichols, Bill. *Representing Reality: Issues and Concepts in Documentary*. Bloomington: Indiana University Press, 1991.

Niles, Marnel N., and Nickesia S. Gordon, eds. *Still Searching for Our Mothers' Gardens: Experiences of New Tenure-Track Women of Color at "Majority" Institutions*. New York: University Press of America, 2011.

Nolan, Justin M., and Gery W. Ryan, "Fear and Loathing at the Cineplex: Gender Differences in Descriptions and Perceptions of Slasher Films." *Sex Roles* 42, nos. 1, 2 (2000): 39–56.

"North Carolina Central University Recognized for Promoting Diversity in the History Profession." *Journal of Blacks in Higher Education*. November 21, 2014. https://www.jbhe.com/2014/11/north-carolina-central-university-recognized-for-promoting-diversity-in-the-history-profession.

Noss, Amanda. "Household Income: 2012." American Community Survey Briefs,

U.S. Census Bureau, September 2013, 1. http://www.census.gov/prod/2013pubs/acsbr12-02.pdf.

Nystrom, Derek. *Hard Hats, Rednecks, and Macho Men: Class in 1970s American Cinema*. New York: Oxford University Press, 2009.

O'Brien, Declan. *Wrong Turn 3: Left for Dead*. DVD. Los Angeles: 20th Century Fox Home Entertainment, 2009.

———. *Wrong Turn 4: Bloody Beginnings*. DVD. Los Angeles: 20th Century Fox Home Entertainment, 2011.

———. *Wrong Turn 5: Bloodlines*. DVD. Los Angeles: 20th Century Fox Home Entertainment, 2012.

O'Brien, Michael. "Place as Everywhere: On Globalizing the American South." In *Creating Citizenship in the Nineteenth-Century South*, edited by William A. Link, David Brown, Brian Ward, and Martyn Bone, 271–89. Gainesville: University of Florida Press, 2013.

O'Connor, Flannery. *Mystery and Manners*. New York: Farrar, Straus and Giroux, 1969.

Odum, Howard. *Southern Regions of the United States*. Chapel Hill: University of North Carolina Press, 1936.

Oliver, Mary Beth, and Meghan Sanders. "The Appeal of Horror and Suspense." In *The Horror Film*, edited by Stephen Prince, 242–59. New Brunswick, N.J.: Rutgers University Press, 2004.

Omi, Michael, and Howard Winant. *Racial Formation in the United States from the 1960s to 1990s*. 2nd ed. New York: Routledge, 1994.

Omolade, Barbara. "Hearts of Darkness." In *Words of Fire: An Anthology of African-American Feminist Thought*, edited by Beverly Guy-Sheftall, 362–78. New York: New Press, 1995.

Ownby, Ted. "Conclusion: Go Forth with Method." Edge, Englehardt, and Ownby, *The Larder: Food Studies Methods from the American South*, 345–62.

———. "Director's Column." *Southern Register*, Winter 2010, 2–3.

———. "The New Southern Studies and Rethinking the Question, 'Is There Still a South?'" *Journal of American Studies* 49, no. 4 (November 2015): 871–78.

———. "The SFA Take: A Call to Listen." Southern Foodways Alliance, July 8, 2016. https://www.southernfoodways.org/the-sfa-take-a-call-to-listen.

———. "Ted Ownby on Elvis Presley as a Southern Studies Student." Center for the Study of Southern Culture blog, November 11, 2014. http://southernstudies.olemiss.edu/ted-ownby-elvis-presley-southern-studies-student.

Page, Helán E., and D. France Oliviera. "Visual Images of the Postcolonial Blues on the Corner of Toulouse and Royal: Discord and Identity in *Songs of my People*." In *Cultural Portrayals of African Americans: Creating an Ethnic/Racial Identity*, edited by Janis Faye Hutchinson, 75–111. Westport, Conn.: Bergin and Garvey, 1997.

Pallares, Amalia. *Family Activism: Immigrant Struggles and the Politics of Non-Citizenship*. New Brunswick, N.J.: Rutgers University Press, 2015.

Parker, Ryan. "Snoop Dogg Asks Fans to Boycott 'Roots': "Let's Create Our Own Shit Based on Today." *Hollywood Reporter*, May 30, 2016. http://www.hollywoodreporter.com/news/snoop-dogg-asks-fans-boycott-898225.

Patton, Stacey. "A Professor Crowdsources a Syllabus on the Charleston Shootings." *Chronicle of Higher Education*, June 23, 2015.

Peacock, James L. *Grounded Globalism: How the U.S. South Embraces the World*. Athens: University of Georgia Press, 2007.

Peacock, James L., and Carrie R. Matthews. "Globalization." In *The New Encyclopedia of Southern Culture*, vol. 3, *History*, edited by Charles Reagan Wilson. Chapel Hill: University of North Carolina Press, 2006.

Peacock, James L., Harry L. Watson, and Carrie R. Matthews, eds. *The American South in a Global World*. Chapel Hill: University of North Carolina Press, 2004.

Pearce, Roy Harvey. *Savagism and Civilization: A Study of the Indian and the American Mind*. Berkeley: University of California Press, 1988.

Percy, Walker. *The Second Coming*. New York: Ivy, 1980.

Perman, Michael. *Pursuit of Unity: A Political History of the American South*. Chapel Hill: University of North Carolina Press, 2009.

Pinedo, Isabel Cristina. *Recreational Terror: Women and the Pleasures of Horror Film Viewing*. Albany: State University of New York Press, 1997.

Prince, K. Michael. *Rally 'Round the Flag, Boys! South Carolina and the Confederate Flag*. Columbia: South Carolina University Press, 2004.

Prince, Stephen, ed. *The Horror Film*. New Brunswick, N.J.: Rutgers University Press, 2004.

Raby, John, and Vicki Smith. "Jay Rockefeller Retiring: West Virginia Senator Won't Run Again when Term Ends in 2014." *HuffingtonPost.com*, March 13, 2013. http://www.huffingtonpost.com/2013/01/11/jay-rockefeller-resigns_n_2455812.html.

Radishofski, Kathryn. "Last (Un)Fair Deal Goin' Down: A Case Study on the Racial Ideologies and Projects Advanced by the Blues Tourism Industry in Clarksdale, Mississippi." Master's thesis, University of Mississippi, 2013.

Radway, Janice. *Reading the Romance: Women, Patriarchy, and Popular Literature*. Chapel Hill: University of North Carolina Press, 1984.

Raimi, Sam. *Evil Dead II*. DVD. Santa Monica, Calif.: Lionsgate Entertainment, 1987.

Rash, Ron. *Burning Bright*. New York: Ecco, 2010.

———. *Nothing Gold Can Stay*. New York: Ecco, 2013.

Rastogi, Sonya, Tallese D. Johnson, Elizabeth M. Hoeffel, and Malcolm P. Drewery Jr. "The Black Population: 2010." 2010 Census Briefs, U.S. Census Bureau, September 9, 2011. http://www.census.gov/prod/cen2010/briefs/c2010br-06.pdf.

Ray, Celeste. *Southern Heritage on Display: Public Ritual and Ethnic Diversity within Southern Regionalism*. Tuscaloosa: University of Alabama Press, 2003.

Rechdahl, Katy. "Boy Born a Day before Hurricane Katrina 'Was Determined to Be a New Orleans Baby.'" *Times Picayune*, August 27, 2010.

Reding, Nick. *Methland: The Death and Life of an American Small Town*. New York: Bloomsbury, 2009.

Reichert Powell, Douglas. *Critical Regionalism: Connecting Politics and Culture in the American Landscape*. Chapel Hill: University of North Carolina Press, 2007.

———. "Panoramas of Gore and Other Social Inventions: Region on Film." In *Critical Regionalism: Connecting Politics and Culture in the Regional Landscape*, 100–146. Chapel Hill: University of North Carolina Press, 2007.

Reid-Pharr, Robert F. "Writing at the Plantation's Edge." In "Authorship in Africana Studies," *Southern Spaces*, October 28, 2015. http://southernspaces.org/2015/authorship-africana-studies.

Religious Landscape Study. Pew Research Center: Religion and Public Life. http://www.pewforum.org/religious-landscape-study.

Reynolds, C., and B. Richmond. "What I Think and Feel: A Revised Measure of Children's Manifest Anxiety." *Journal of Abnormal Psychology* 6 (1978): 271–80.

Reynolds, William M., ed. *Critical Studies of Southern Place: A Reader*. New York: Peter Lang, 2014.

Rhodes, Lelia Gaston. *Jackson State University: The First Hundred Years, 1877–1977*. Jackson: University Press of Mississippi, 1979.

Richards, Gary. *Lovers and Beloveds: Sexual Otherness in Southern Fiction, 1936–1961*. Baton Rouge: Louisiana State University Press, 2005.

Richardson, Bonham. "The South and the Caribbean: A Regional Perspective." In *The South and the Caribbean*, edited by Douglas Sullivan-Gonzalez and Charles Reagan Wilson, 3–20. Jackson: University Press of Mississippi, 2001.

Ring, Natalie. "An Irony of Ironies: The Discipline of History in the New Southern Studies." *Journal of American Studies* 48, no. 3 (2014): 706–12.

Rise, Eric W. *The Martinsville Seven: Race, Rape, and Capital Punishment*. Charlottesville: University of Virginia Press, 1995.

Ritchie, Don. "Good News for Scholars Doing Oral History! The Federal Government Is Preparing to Grant Them the Right to Be Excluded from IRBs." *History News Network*, October 13, 2015. http://historynewsnetwork.org/article/160885.

Rivlin, Elizabeth. "The Ghost of Shakespeare in Ron Rash's *Serena*." Conference presentation, Southern American Studies Association, January 31, 2013, Charleston, South Carolina.

Rizzo, Mary. "NCPH so white?" *History@Work*, March 11, 2016. http://ncph.org/history-at-work/ncph-so-white.

Robinson, Charles F. *Dangerous Liaisons: Sex and Love in the Segregated South*. Fayetteville: University of Arkansas Press, 2003.

Robinson, William I. *A Theory of Global Capitalism: Production, Class, and the State in a Transnational World*. Baltimore, Md.: Johns Hopkins University Press, 2004.

Robinson, Zandria F. "Nightmare on Main Street: On Racial Violence and the Problem of Convention." *Gawker*, November 7, 2015. http://gawker.com/nightmare-on-main-street-on-racial-violence-and-the-pr-1741195462.

———. Review of Emily Satterwhite's "Hillbilly Horror" at Transforming New South Identities Symposium, 1–3, in possession of Emily Satterwhite.

———. *This Ain't Chicago: Race, Class, and Regional Identity in the Post-Soul South*. Chapel Hill: University of North Carolina Press, 2014.

———. "Zeezus Does the Firing 'Round Hurr." *New South Negress*. http://newsouthnegress.com/zeezusyear.

Rockoff, Stuart. "Director's Message: The Chronic Illness of the Humanities." *Forum on the Humanities* (Mississippi Humanities Council Newsletter), October 20, 2015.

Roediger, David. *The Wages of Whiteness: Race and the Making of the American Working Class*. New York: Verso, 2007.

Rohrer, John H., and Munro S. Edmonson. *The Eighth Generation Grows Up: Cultures and Personalities of New Orleans Negroes.* New York: Harper and Row, 1960.

Rolley, Sam. "Beason: Dems Don't Want to Solve Illegal Immigration Problem." *Cullman (Ala.) Times,* February 6, 2011.

Romero, George. *Staunton Hill.* DVD. Troy, Mich.: Anchor Bay Entertainment, 2009.

Romine, Scott. "God and the MoonPie: Consumption, Disenchantment, and the Reliably Lost Cause." In *Creating and Consuming the American South,* edited by Martyn Bone, Brian Ward, and William A. Link, 49–71. Gainesville: University of Florida Press, 2015.

———. *The Real South: Southern Narrative in the Age of Cultural Reproduction.* Baton Rouge: Louisiana State University Press, 2008.

Romine, Scott, and Jennifer Rae Greeson, eds. *Keywords for Southern Studies.* Athens: University of Georgia Press, 2016.

Rony, Fatimah Tobing. *The Third Eye: Race, Cinema, and Ethnographic Spectacle.* Durham, N.C.: Duke University Press, 1996.

Rosaldo, Renato. "Cultural Citizenship, Inequality, and Multiculturalism." In *Race, Identity, and Citizenship: A Reader,* edited by R. D. Torres, L. F. Mirón, and J. X. Inda, 253–64. Malden, Mass.: Blackwell, 1999.

Rosenberg, Morris. *Society and the Adolescent Self-Image.* Princeton, N.J.: Princeton University Press, 1965.

Rosenthal, Robert, and Lenore Jacobson. *Pygmalion in the Classroom: Teacher Expectation and Pupils' Intellectual Development.* New York: Crown, 2003.

———. "Teachers' Expectancies: Determinants of Pupils' IQ Gains." *Psychological Reports* 19 (1966): 115–18.

Rotenstein, David S. "The Helena Blues: Cultural Tourism and African-American Folk Music." *Southern Folklore* 49, no. 2 (1992): 133–46.

Rubin, Louis D., Jr., and Robert D. Jacobs, eds. *Southern Renascence: The Literature of the Modern South.* Baltimore, Md.: Johns Hopkins Press, 1953.

Ruby, Jay. "Speaking for, Speaking about, Speaking with, or Speaking Alongside: An Anthropological and Documentary Dilemma." *Journal of Film and Video* 44, nos. 1–2 (Spring and Summer 1992): 42–66.

Rudick, Nicole. "Karen Russell on *Swamplandia!*" *Paris Review: The Daily* (blog). February 3, 2011. http://www.theparisreview.org/blog/2011/02/03/karen-russell-on-swamplandia.

Rushdie, Salmon. "In the South." *New Yorker,* May 18, 2009. http://www.newyorker.com/magazine/2009/05/18/in-the-south.

Rushing, Wanda. *Memphis and the Paradox of Place: Globalization in the American South.* Chapel Hill: University of North Carolina Press, 2009.

Russell, Karen. *Swamplandia!* New York: Vintage, 2011.

Sabin, Warwick. "A Great Debate." *Oxford American* 64 (2009): 21.

Sanders, Randy. *Mighty Peculiar Elections: The New South Gubernatorial Campaigns of 1970 and the Changing Politics of Race.* Gainesville: University Press of Florida, 2002.

Sani, Fabio. *Self Continuity: Individual and Collective Perspectives.* New York: Psychology Press, 2008.

Santora, Tommy. "Generation K: Post-Katrina Baby Boom Populates New Orleans Hospitals." *New Orleans City Business*, December 11, 2006.

Sassen, Saskia. *Territory, Authority, Rights: From Medieval to Global Assemblages*. Princeton, N.J.: Princeton University Press, 2006.

Satterwhite, Emily. *Dear Appalachia: Readers, Identity, and Popular Fiction since 1878*. Lexington: University Press of Kentucky, 2011.

Schedler, George. *Racist Symbols and Reparations: Philosophical Reflections on Vestiges of the American Civil War*. Lanham, Md.: Rowman and Littlefield, 1998.

Schmidt, Rob. *Wrong Turn*. DVD. Los Angeles: 20th Century Fox Home Entertainment, 2003.

Sedgwick, Eve Kosofsky, and Adam Frank. *Touching Feeling: Affect, Pedagogy, Performativity*. Durham, N.C.: Duke University Press, 2003.

Shack Up Inn. http://www.theshackupinn.com/.

Shafer, Byron E., and Richard Johnston. *End of Southern Exceptionalism: Class, Race, and Partisan Change in the Postwar South*. Cambridge, Mass.: Harvard University Press, 2006.

Sharrett, Christopher. "The Horror Film as Social Allegory (and How It Comes Undone)." In *A Companion to the Horror Film*, edited by Harry M. Benshoff, 56–72. Chichester, UK: Wiley-Blackwell, 2014.

———. "The Idea of Apocalypse in *The Texas Chainsaw Massacre*." In *Planks of Reason: Essays on the Horror Film*, edited by Barry Keith Grant and Christopher Sharrett, 255–76. Scarecrow Press, 1990.

Shaw, Stephanie. *What a Woman Ought to Be and to Do: Black Professional Women Workers during the Jim Crow Era*. Chicago: University of Chicago Press, 1996.

Simmons, Ann M. "Baby Boom Adds Life to Rebirth of New Orleans." *Los Angeles Times*, August 14, 2006.

Simon, Scott. "'Nothing Gold' Stays Long in Appalachia." Interview with Ron Rash. *Weekend Edition Saturday*, NPR radio broadcast, February 16, 2013. http://www.npr.org/2013/02/16/172175237/nothing-gold-stays-long-in-appalachia.

Simonton, Anna. "We Have a Duty to Win: Vignettes trom Atlanta," *Scalawag* 1, no. 1 (2015): 31–36.

Singh, Nikhil Pal. *Black Is a Country: Race and the Unfinished Struggle for Democracy*. Cambridge, Mass.: Harvard University Press, 2004.

Smith, Barbara, ed. *Home Girls: A Black Feminist Anthology*. New Brunswick, N.J.: Rutgers University Press, 2000.

Smith, Barbara Ellen. "Introduction to Appalachian Identity: A Roundtable Discussion." *Appalachian Journal* 38, no. 1 (2010): 56–57.

———. "Place and the Past in the Global South." *American Literature*, 78, no. 4 (December 2006): 693–95.

Smith, Barbara Ellen, and Stephen L. Fisher. "Conclusion: Transformations in Place." In *Transforming Places: Lessons from Appalachia*, edited by Barbara Ellen Smith and Stephen L. Fisher, 267–92. Urbana-Champaign: University of Illinois Press, 2012.

Smith, Herb E., and Elizabeth Barret. "Appalshop Filmmakers Herb E. Smith and Elizabeth Barret Talk about Appalshop's Audiences." In *Appalshop: Celebrating*

Thirty-Five Years, edited by Mia Frederick and Laura Sohn, 30–31. Whitesburg, Ky.: Appalshop, 2004.

Smith, Jon. *Finding Purple America: The South and the Future of American Cultural Studies*. Athens: University of Georgia Press, 2013.

———. "Toward a Post-Postpolitical Southern Studies: On the Limits of the 'Creating and Consuming' Paradigm." In *Creating and Consuming the American South*, edited by Martyn Bone, Brian Ward, and William A. Link, 72–94. Gainesville: University of Florida Press, 2015.

Smith, Jon, and Deborah Cohn, eds. *Look Away! The U.S. South in New World Studies*. Durham, N.C.: Duke University Press, 2004.

Smith, Laurajane. "Editorial." *International Journal of Heritage Studies* 18, no. 6 (2012): 533–40.

———. *Uses of Heritage*. London: Routledge, 2006.

Smith, Mark M. *How Race Is Made: Slavery, Segregation, and the Senses*. Chapel Hill: University of North Carolina Press, 2006.

Smith, Paul Chaat. *Everything You Know about Indians Is Wrong*. Minneapolis: University of Minnesota Press, 2009.

Soja, Edward W. *Postmodern Geographies: The Reassertion of Space in Critical Social Theory*. London: Verso, 1989.

Sokol, Jason. *All Eyes Are upon Us: Race and Politics from Boston to Brooklyn*. New York: Basic Books, 2014.

Soles, Carter. "Sympathy for the Devil: The Cannibalistic Hillbilly in 1970s Rural Slasher Films." In *Ecocinema Theory and Practice*, edited by Stephen Rust, Salma Monani, and Sean Cubitt, 233–50. New York: Routledge, 2013.

Sommerville, Diane M. *Rape and Race in the Nineteenth-Century South*. Chapel Hill: University of North Carolina Press, 2004.

The South: Some Addresses. Charlotte, N.C.: Observer Printing House, 1910.

Sparks, Randy. *Religion in Mississippi*. Jackson: University Press of Mississippi, 2001.

"Spelman College Establishes a Curatorial Studies Program." *Journal of Blacks in Higher Education*, April 29, 2016. https://www.jbhe.com/2016/04/spelman-college-establishes-a-curatorial-studies-program.

Spillers, Hortense J. "Mama's Baby, Papa's Maybe: An American Grammar Book." *diacritics* 17, no. 2 (1987): 65–81.

Spofford, Tim. *Lynch Street: The May 1970 Slayings at Jackson State College*. Kent, Ohio: Kent State University Press, 1988.

Staiger, Janet. *Perverse Spectators: The Practices of Film Reception*. New York: New York University Press, 2000.

Stuesse, Angela. *Scratching out a Living: Latinos, Race, and Work in the Deep South*. Oakland: University of California Press, 2016.

Stuesse, Angela, and Mathew Coleman. "Automobility, Immobility, Altermobility: Surviving and Resisting the Intensification of Immigrant Policing." *City and Society* 26, no. 1 (2014): 51–72.

Suchy, Patricia, James V. Catano, et al. "Revisiting Flaherty's *Louisiana Story*." *Southern Spaces*, April 27, 2010. http://southernspaces.org/2010/revisiting-flahertys-louisiana-story.

Szabo, Liz. "New Orleans Births Soar." *USA Today*, August 29, 2006.

Tatum, Beverly. "Breaking the Silence." In *White Privilege: Essential Readings on the Other Side of Racism*, edited by Paula S. Rothenberg, 115–20. New York: Worth, 2002.

Taylor, Helen. *Circling Dixie: Contemporary Southern Culture through a Transatlantic Lens*. New Brunswick, N.J.: Rutgers University Press, 2001.

Taylor, Melanie Benson. *Reconstructing the Native South: American Indian Literature and the Lost Cause*. Athens: University of Georgia Press, 2011.

Teklu, Fiseha, and R. Sreevalsa Kumar. "Teachers' Expectations on Academic Achievement and Social Skills and Behaviour of Students with Emotional and Behavioural Disorders." *Eastern Africa Social Science Research Review* 29, no. 2 (June 2013): 79–95.

Thomas, Lynnell L. *Desire and Disaster in New Orleans: Tourism, Race and Historical Memory*. Durham, N.C.: Duke University Press, 2014.

Thomason, Andy, and Brian O'Leary. "See How Worries about Shootings Affect Readers' Lives." *Chronicle of Higher Education*, December 2015. http://chronicle.com.ezproxy.memphis.edu/interactives/shooting-worries.

Thompson, Ashley, and Melissa Sloan. "Race as Region, Region as Race: How Black and White Southerners Understand Their Regional Identities." *Southern Cultures* 10, no. 4 (2012): 72–95.

Thorpe, Angela. "Rethinking Diversity: Introduction." *History@Work*, November 13, 2014. http://ncph.org/history-at-work/rethinking-diversity-introduction.

Tichi, Cecelia. *High Lonesome: The American Culture of Country Music*. Chapel Hill: University of North Carolina Press, 1994.

Townsend, Robert B. "News: History PhD Numbers Lowest in Almost a Decade as Job Listings Continue to Rise." *Perspectives on History: The News Magazine of the American Historical Association*, January 2007. https://www.historians.org/publications-and-directories/perspectives-on-history/january-2007/history-phd-numbers-lowest-in-almost-a-decade-as-job-listings-continue-to-rise.

Townsend, Robert B., and Julia Brookins. "The Troubled Academic Job Market for History." *Perspectives on History: The News Magazine of the American Historical Association*, February 2016. https://www.historians.org/publications-and-directories/perspectives-on-history/february-2016/the-troubled-academic-job-market-for-history#.

Trefzer, Annette. "Indian Literature." In *The New Encyclopedia of Southern Culture*, vol. 9, *Literature*, edited by M. Thomas Inge and Charles Reagan Wilson, 92–96. Chapel Hill: University of North Carolina Press, 2008.

Tudor, Andrew. "Why Horror? The Peculiar Pleasures of a Popular Genre." *Cultural Studies* 13, no. 3 (1997): 443–63.

Tullos, Allen. *Alabama Getaway: The Political Imaginary and the Heart of Dixie*. Athens: University of Georgia Press, 2011.

Turner, Daniel Cross. "From Blue Ridge to Blue Sea: On Teaching a Southern Literature and History Travel Immersion Course." *James Dickey Review* 28, no. 2 (2012): 8–19.

———. *Southern Crossings: Poetry, Memory, and the Transcultural South*. Knoxville: University of Tennessee Press, 2012.

TuSmith, Bonnie. "Out on a Limb: Race and the Evaluation of Frontline Teaching." In TuSmith and Reddy, eds., *Race in the College Classroom*, 112–25.

TuSmith, Bonnie, and Maureen T. Reddy, eds. *Race in the College Classroom: Pedagogy and Politics*. New Brunswick, N.J.: Rutgers University Press, 2002.

Tweed, Thomas. "Our Lady of Guadalupe Visits the Confederate Memorial." *Southern Cultures* 8 (Summer 2002): 72–93.

United States Census Bureau. "State and County Quick Facts." http://quickfacts.census.gov/qfd/index.html.

United States Department of Education. White House Initiative on Historically Black Colleges and Universities. "HBCUs and 2020 Goal." http://sites.ed.gov/whhbcu.

Valentine, Charles. *Culture and Poverty: Critique and Counter-Proposals*. Chicago: University of Chicago Press, 1968.

Varsanyi, M. W., ed. *Taking Local Control: Immigration Policy Activism in U.S. Cities and States*. Stanford, Calif.: Stanford University Press, 2010.

Von Doviak, Scott. *Hick Flicks: The Rise and Fall of Redneck Cinema*. Jefferson, N.C.: McFarland, 2005.

Wakelyn, Jon. *Biographical Dictionary of the Confederacy*. Westport, Conn.: Greenwood Press, 1977.

Wald, Elijah. *Escaping the Delta: Robert Johnson and the Invention of the Blues*. New York: Amistad Press, 2004.

Waldrep, Christopher. *African Americans Confront Lynching: Strategies of Resistance from the Civil War to the Civil Rights Era*. Lanham, Md.: Rowman and Littlefield, 2009.

Wallach, Jennifer Jansen, ed. *Dethroning the Deceitful Pork Chop: Rethinking African American Foodways from Slavery to Obama*. Fayetteville: University of Arkansas Press, 2015.

Wallerstein, Immanuel. *The Modern World-System II: Mercantilism and the Consolidation of the European World-Economy, 1600–1750*. Berkeley: University of California Press, 2011.

———. *World Systems Analysis: An Introduction*. Durham, N.C.: Duke University Press, 2004.

Walton, Becca. "Center Director Ted Ownby on Current Efforts to Remove Confederate Symbols." Center for the Study of Southern Culture, June 24, 2015. http://southernstudies.olemiss.edu/center-director-ted-ownby-on-history-and-inclusiveness-in-current-efforts-to-remove-confederate-symbols.

Wang, Ning. "Rethinking Authenticity in Tourism Experience." *Annals of Tourism Research* 26 (April 1999): 349–70.

Ward, Brian. "Forum: What's New in Southern Studies—and Why Should We Care?" *Journal of American Studies* 48, no. 3 (2014): 691–733.

Ward, Brian, Martyn Bone, and William Link, eds. *The American South and the Atlantic World*. Gainesville: University of Florida Press, 2013.

Warf, Barney. "From Surfaces to Networks." In *The Spatial Turn: Interdisciplinary Perspectives*, edited by Barney Warf and Santa Arias, 59–76. New York: Routledge, 2009.

Warner, John. "On Being Afraid of Students." *Inside Higher Ed*, June 2, 2016. https://www.insidehighered.com/blogs/just-visiting/being-afraid-students.

Warnes, Andrew. "Edgeland Terroir: Authenticity and Invention in New Southern Foodways Strategy." In Edge, Englehardt, and Ownby, *The Larder: Food Studies Methods from the American South*, 345–62.

Washington, James. *Frustrated Fellowship: The Black Baptist Quest for Social Power*. Macon, Ga.: Mercer University Press, 1986.

Watson, Jay. "Body." In *The New Encyclopedia of Southern Culture*, vol. 4, *Myth, Manners, and Memory*, edited by Charles Reagan Wilson, 30–33. Chapel Hill: University of North Carolina Press, 2006.

———. *Reading for the Body: The Recalcitrant Materiality of Southern Fiction, 1893–1985*. Athens: University of Georgia Press, 2012.

Wekker, Gloria. *The Politics of Passion: Women's Sexual Culture in the Afro-Surinamese Diaspora*. New York: Columbia University Press, 2006.

Welty, Eudora. *The Eye of the Story: Selected Essays and Reviews*. New York: Random House, 1977.

"What Is Southern Studies." Mercer University Southern Studies Center. https://cla.mercer.edu/southern-studies/what-is-ss.

White, Deborah Gray. *Ar'n't I a Woman: Female Slaves in the Plantation South*. New York: W. W. Norton, 1985.

———, ed. *Telling Histories: Black Women Historians in the Ivory Tower*. Chapel Hill: University of North Carolina Press, 2008.

———. *Too Heavy a Load: Black Women in Defense of Themselves, 1894–1994*. New York: W. W. Norton, 1999.

White, Derrick E. *The Challenge of Blackness: The Institute of the Black World and Political Activism in the 1970s*. Gainesville: University Press of Florida, 2011.

White, J. Hebert. *Up from a Cotton Patch: J. H. White and the Development of Mississippi Valley State College*. Itta Bena, Miss., 1979.

Whitney, Frank P. "The Six-Year High School in Cleveland." *School Review* 37, no. 4 (1929): 267–71.

Wickman, Patricia R. *Osceola's Legacy*. Tuscaloosa: University of Alabama Press, 2006.

Williams, Chad. "#CharlestonSyllabus and the Work of African American History." African American Intellectual History Society blog, June 23, 2015. http://aaihs.org/charlestonsyllabus-and-the-work-of-african-american-history.

———. "Why I Founded #CharlestonSyllabus after the Charleston Shooting." *PBS Newshour*, July 9, 2015. http://www.pbs.org/newshour/updates/founded-charlestonsyllabus-charleston-shooting.

Williams, Rhonda Y. *The Politics of Public Housing: Black Women's Struggles against Urban Inequality*. New York: Oxford University Press, 2004.

Williamson, J. W. *Hillbillyland: What the Movies Did to the Mountains and the Mountains Did to the Movies*. Chapel Hill: University of North Carolina Press, 1995.

Wilson, Carlton. "Viewpoints: Minority Students Pursuing History PhDs." *Perspectives on History: The News Magazine of the American Historical Association*. December 2002. http://www.historians.org/publications-and-directories/perspectives-on-history/december-2002/minority-students-pursuing-history-phds.

Wilson, Charles Reagan. *Flashes of a Southern Spirit: Meanings of the Spirit in the U.S. South*. Athens: University of Georgia Press, 2011.

———. "Sense of Place." In *The New Encyclopedia of Southern Culture*, vol. 4, *Myth, Manners, and Memory*, 253–55. Chapel Hill: University of North Carolina Press, 2006.

Wilson, Charles Reagan, and Mark Silk, eds. *Religion and Public Life in the South: In the Evangelical Mode*. Walnut Creek, Calif.: AltaMira Press, 2005.

Wilson, Darlene. "The Felicitous Convergence of Mythmaking and Capital Accumulation: John Fox Jr. and the Formation of An(Other) Almost-White American Underclass." *Journal of Appalachian Studies* 1 (Fall 1995): 5–44.

Wilson, Jeff. *Dixie Dharma: Inside a Buddhist Temple in the American South*. Athens: University of Georgia Press, 2012.

Winders, Jaime. "Changing Politics of Race and Region: Latino Migration to the U.S. South." *Progress in Human Geography* 29, no. 6 (December 2005): 683–99.

Wise, Benjamin. *William Alexander Percy: The Curious Life of a Mississippi Planter and Freethinker*. Chapel Hill: University of North Carolina Press, 2012.

Wood, Amy Louise. *Lynching and Spectacle: Witnessing Racial Violence in America, 1890–1940*. Chapel Hill: University of North Carolina Press, 2007.

Wood, Robin. *Hollywood from Vietnam to Reagan . . . and Beyond*. New York: Columbia University Press, 2003.

Woodward, C. Vann. *The Strange Career of Jim Crow*. New York: Oxford University Press, 1957.

———. "What Happened to the Civil Rights Movement." In *The Burden of Southern History*, 167–86. Baton Rouge: Louisiana State University Press, 2008. First published 1968.

Working Group on Evaluating Public History Scholarship. "Tenure, Promotion, and the Publicly Engaged Academic Historian." *Perspectives on History: The Newsmagazine of the American Historical Association*, September 2010. https://www.historians.org/publications-and-directories/perspectives-on-history/september-2010/tenure-promotion-and-the-publicly-engaged-academic-historian-a-report#.

Wray, Matt. *Not Quite White: White Trash and the Boundaries of Whiteness*. Durham, N.C.: Duke University Press, 2006.

Wright, Charles. *The Southern Cross*. New York: Random House, 1981.

Yaeger, Patricia. *Dirt and Desire: Reconstructing Southern Women's Writing, 1930–1990*. Chicago: University of Chicago Press, 2000.

———, ed. *The Geography of Identity*. Ann Arbor: University of Michigan Press, 1996.

Zarchi, Meir. *I Spit on Your Grave*. DVD. Troy, Mich.: Anchor Bay Entertainment, 1978.

Žižek, Slavoj. *For They Know Not What They Do: Enjoyment as a Political Factor*. 2nd ed. New York: Verso, 2008.

CONTRIBUTORS

ALIX CHAPMAN is a visiting professor in women and gender studies at Spelman College. His areas of interest include performance ethnography, black queer studies, and the intersections of African diasporas in U.S. and global South contexts. His dissertation addressed the ways in which home, heritage, and bodies are reconceptualized in the wake of crises. Through a combination of performance ethnography and historical and literary critique, Chapman explores Sissy Bounce, a local genre of hip-hop that expresses meanings of black queer people's lives and struggles. He looks at how these cultural productions intersect a public sphere in which socioeconomic disaster and reconstruction determine the life chances of all black people. His recent research appears in *Cultural Dynamics*.

RICO D. CHAPMAN is associate professor and interim assistant chair of the Department of History and Philosophy at Jackson State University. He is also academic director at the Fannie Lou Hamer Institute @ COFO. His areas of interest include the struggle for justice by students throughout the African diaspora, particularly in Mississippi and South Africa, where he studied and taught museum studies and historic preservation.

MICHELE GRIGSBY COFFEY is an instructor of history at the University of Memphis. Her areas of specialization are U.S. history, African American history, and women's and gender history, with an emphasis on political mobilization in the American South. Her article "*The State of Louisiana v. Charles Guerand*: Interracial Sexual Mores, Rape Rhetoric, and Respectability in 1930s New Orleans" in *Louisiana History* won the President's Memorial award for the best article published in that journal in 2013. Coffey is also interested in critical pedagogy and is author of a high school leadership curriculum approved for use in Texas public schools.

KIRSTEN DELLINGER is chair and professor of sociology in the Department of Sociology and Anthropology at the University of Mississippi. Her areas of specialization are gender, sexuality, work, and qualitative methodology. Dellinger is coauthor of numerous articles and essays, including several examining the American South. She is part of the interdisciplinary Faculty Working Group on the Global South at the University of Mississippi, and as part of that group she has coauthored "The Catfish Industry and Spatial Justice in the Mississippi Delta: A Global South Reading of Steve Yarbrough's *The Oxygen Man*" (*Southern Spaces*, August 2013) and "Interdisciplinary Perspectives on the Global South and the Global North," the latter published in Gregory Hooks, ed., *The Sociology of Development Handbook* (University of California Press, 2016).

LEIGH ANNE DUCK is associate professor in the Department of English at the University of Mississippi. Her published work concentrates on literary and visual representations of the U.S. South as well as comparative approaches to Jim Crow segregation and South African apartheid. She is the author of *The Nation's Region: Southern Modernism, Seg-*

regation, and U.S. Nationalism (University of Georgia Press, 2006) and edits the journal *The Global South*. Her current book project is tentatively titled *Hollywood South: Starring as Itself*.

GWENDOLYN FERRETI is a PhD candidate in anthropology at the University of Texas. Her research and activism focuses on the intersection between community formation within the growing Latino communities in the American South and state regulations that impact this population. She has twice been recognized for her work with Latino communities in Alabama. In 2013 she received the Billy Jack Gaither Humanitarian Award from Equality Alabama, and in 2012 she received the Realizing the Dream Horizon Award from the Martin Luther King, Jr. Realizing the Dream Committee. Ferreti has also published in the American Anthropological Association's *Anthropology News* and has delivered numerous presentations and invited lectures in addition to providing source material to reporters from National Public Radio, *Politico*, the *Guardian*, *USA Today*, and other media outlets.

KATHRYN GREEN is an associate professor in the Social Sciences Department at Mississippi Valley State University. She is the coordinator of the history program, through which she oversees a student alumni oral history interview initiative. Her areas of interest include African American, African, Islamic, and Middle East histories, digital humanities, historic preservation, and public history. Her research appears in the *African Studies Review* and *African Arts*. Her current research focuses on historical memory in American culture surrounding the Emmett Till murder and on convict labor in Mississippi following a federal court case that led to a restructuring of Parchman Farm (Mississippi State Penitentiary).

ROBERT GREENE II is a PhD student in the History Department at the University of South Carolina. His fields of specialization are U.S. political history, with an emphasis on the American South, African American history, and American intellectual history. He has presented on the relationship between the national press and the Black Power movement at the Association for the Study of African American Life and History conference and the Media and Civil Rights Symposium at the University of South Carolina. Greene is also a weekly contributor to the blog of the Society for U.S. Intellectual History (s-usih.org).

JOHN HAYES is an assistant professor of history at Augusta University. With a PhD in history and master's degree in theology, his field of specialization is religious history, with an emphasis on the South. His recent writing is featured in Michael Pasquier, ed., *Gods of the Mississippi* (Indiana University Press, 2013) and Charles E. May, ed., *Flannery O'Connor* (Salem Press, 2012), and appears in *Perspectives in Religious Studies* and the *Journal of Southern Religion*. His current book project *Hard, Hard Religion: The Other World of the Poor South* weaves together folklore, music, oral history, photography, and material culture to reconstruct the history of folk Christians in the New South era.

JEFFREY T. JACKSON is an associate professor of sociology at the University of Mississippi, specializing in globalization, international development, race and ethnicity, and sociological theory. He is coauthor of several essays and articles, including "Volunteer

Voices: Making Sense of Our Trip to the Mississippi Gulf Coast after Katrina," published in Danielle A. Hidalgo and Kristen Barber, eds., *Narrating the Storm: Sociological Stories of Hurricane Katrina* (Cambridge Scholars Publishing, 2007). Jackson also wrote *The Globalizers: Development Workers in Action* (Johns Hopkins University Press, 2005). His latest work, *The Rise of the Globalizers: The Brief Global History of Nation Building*, is under consideration by the Johns Hopkins University Press. He is also part of the interdisciplinary Faculty Working Group on the Global South at the University of Mississippi.

ANNE LEWIS is senior lecturer in the Radio-Television-Film Department at the University of Texas at Austin and an independent documentary maker associated with Appalshop Films, a media arts and cultural center located in Whitesburg, Kentucky, in the heart of the Central Appalachian coalfields. She is the producer, director, and editor of several important documentaries examining the modern South, including *Anne Braden: Southern Patriot* (2012), *Morristown: In the Air and Sun* (2007), *Texas Majority Minority* (2004), and *Ready for Harvest: Clearcutting in the Southern Appalachians* (1993). She is also the associate director of the Academy Award–winning documentary *Harlan County, USA* (1975). Her current works in progress include "Austin Beloved Community," a multimedia website based on *Anne Braden: Southern Patriot* that pulls together Austin-based social justice organizations with funding from the City of Austin cultural contracts program.

KATIE B. MCKEE is the McMullan Associate Professor of Southern Studies and English at the University of Mississippi. She co-edited the two-part special issues of the *Mississippi Quarterly*, "Postcolonial Theory, the US South and the New World Studies" (Fall 2003 and Winter 2003–2004). She also co-edited *American Cinema and the Southern Imaginary* (University of Georgia Press, 2011) and "Global Contexts, Local Literatures: The New Southern Studies," a special issue of *American Literature* (2006). McKee is also part of the interdisciplinary Faculty Working Group on the Global South at the University of Mississippi.

KATHRYN RADISHOFSKI is a PhD student in ethnomusicology at Columbia University. Her master's thesis examined the impact of blues tourism on Clarksdale, Mississippi, and won the Lucille and Motee Daniels Award for the best thesis in southern studies in 2013. She has authored pieces in the *Southern Register* and *The New Encyclopedia of Southern Culture*, and she has presented her work at multiple symposia. She also served as the graduate student editorial assistant for the *Global South* at the Center for the Study of Southern Culture.

EMILY SATTERWHITE is an associate professor in the Department of Religion and Culture at Virginia Tech, specializing in popular culture and the American South. Her book *Dear Appalachia: Readers, Identity and Popular Fiction since 1878* (University Press of Kentucky, 2011) won the Weatherford Award for the best nonfiction book about Appalachia from the Appalachian Studies Association and the Berea College Loyal Jones Appalachian Center in 2012. She is also the author of "Objecting to Insider/Outsider Politics and the Uncritical Celebration of Appalachia," in the *Appalachian Journal* (2010), and "Romancing Whiteness: Popular Appalachian Fiction and the Imperialist Imagination at the Turns of Two Centuries," in La Vinia Delois Jennings, ed., *At Home and Abroad:*

Historicizing Twentieth-Century Whiteness in Literature and Performance (University of Tennessee Press, 2009).

JODI SKIPPER is an assistant professor of anthropology and southern studies at the University of Mississippi. She specializes in historical archaeology, African diaspora studies, heritage tourism, museum studies, and public history, with more specific research interests in heritage politics and the cultural representation of black southerners in tourism spaces. Her recent research appears in *Black Scholar*, the *Journal of Community Archaeology and Heritage*, and the *Southern Quarterly*.

JON SMITH is an associate professor in the Department of English at Simon Frasier University. His research focuses primarily on the southern United States from postcolonial and cultural-studies perspectives. His essays have been published in *American Literary History*, *American Literature*, *Contemporary Literature*, the *Global South*, and *Modern Fiction Studies*. He co-edited *Look Away! The U.S. South in New World Studies* (Duke University Press, 2004) and authored *Finding Purple America: The South and the Future of American Cultural Studies* (University of Georgia Press, 2013). Additionally, Smith is co-editor of the New Southern Studies series of the University of Georgia Press.

MELANIE BENSON TAYLOR is associate professor and chair of the Program in Native American Studies at Dartmouth College. She is a literary critic specializing in southern studies. She is author of *Disturbing Calculations: The Economics of Identity in Postcolonial Southern Literature, 1912–2002* (University of Georgia Press, 2008) and *Reconstructing the Native South: American Indian Literature and the Lost Cause* (2012). Her recent research has been featured in Eric Gary Anderson, Taylor Hagood, and Daniel Cross Turner, eds., *Undead Souths* (Louisiana State University Press, 2015) and David A. Davis and Tara Powell, eds., *Writing in the Kitchen: Southern Foodways and Southern Literature* (University Press of Mississippi, 2014). She is currently working on two book projects examining the effects of economic anxiety on the construction of cultural identity and borders.

ANNETTE TREFZER is an associate professor of English at the University of Mississippi, specializing in American literature and literary theory. She has been co-editor of several collections published by the University Press of Mississippi examining the works of William Faulkner (2009, 2010, 2012, and 2014) and is author of *Disturbing Indians: The Archaeology of Southern Fiction* (University of Alabama Press, 2007). She was also co-editor of the influential "Global Contexts, Local Literatures: The New Southern Studies" special issue of *American Literature* (2006) and is part of the interdisciplinary Faculty Working Group on the Global South at the University of Mississippi.

DANIEL CROSS TURNER is an associate professor in the English Department at Coastal Carolina University, where he is also the founder and advisor of the southern studies minor. His primary research interests include the literature and culture of the American South, poetics, film, and genre studies. He is author of *Southern Crossings: Poetry, Memory and the Transcultural South* (University of Tennessee Press, 2012) and recently co-edited *Undead Souths: The Gothic and Beyond in Southern Literature and Culture* (Louisiana State University Press, 2015). His research appears in several other outlets, including *Mosaic, Genre, Southern Quarterly, Mississippi Quarterly,* and the *Southern Literary Journal.* He is currently co-editing a poetry anthology entitled *Hard Lines: Rough South Poetry* for the University of South Carolina Press. His book in progress, *Regions of the Dead: Resurrecting Death in Contemporary Southern Literature,* is under contract with the University of Tennessee Press.

CHARLES REAGAN WILSON is the recently retired Kelly Gene Cook Sr. Chair of History and professor of southern studies as well as the former director of the southern studies program at the University of Mississippi. He is the author of *Baptized in the Blood: The Religion of the Lost Cause* (University of Georgia Press, 1980), *Judgment and Grace in Dixie: Southern Faiths from Faulkner to Elvis* (University of Georgia Press, 1995), and *Flashes of a Southern Spirit: Meanings of the Spirit in the U.S. South* (University of Georgia Press, 2011). He is co-editor of *The Encyclopedia of Southern Culture* (University of North Carolina Press, 1989), which won the Dartmouth Prize from the American Library Association as the best reference book of the year, and is also general editor of the twenty-four-volume *New Encyclopedia of Southern Culture* (University of North Carolina Press, 2006–2013). Additionally, he is co-editor of *Religion and the American Civil War* (Oxford University Press, 1998), *The New Regionalism* (University Press of Mississippi, 1998), and *Religion in the South: Essays* (University Press of Mississippi, 1985).

INDEX

16th Street Baptist Church, Birmingham, Ala., 97

Aaker, David A., 256, 263n28
abolition, 62–63
Absalom, Absalom! (Faulkner), 40, 46
Addams, Jane, 61
Affordable Care Act, 90, 99n5
African American history. *See* history, African American
African American Intellectual History Society, 131
African Americans: and activism, 62, 127, 129; and black exceptionalism, 31, 79; and Black Lives Matter, 133n18, 198–99, 260; and blackness, 31, 81, 217–18, 218–19; and community engagement, 106, 118–19; and cotton, 111–13; and higher education, 103, 106, 107, 109, 116–17; and identity, 11, 31–32, 39, 173–74, 179n15–16, 222; and the police, 115, 128–29; and political office, 124, 127; and public history, 101–22; social experiences of, 215; and southern studies, inclusion in, 23, 26, 31–32, 33–34, 39; violence against, 124, 128, 129, 260. *See also* African American studies; Africana studies; African diaspora studies; African Methodist Episcopal (AME) Church; blackness; civil rights movement; cotton; Emanuel African Methodist Episcopal (AME) Church; history, African American; history, intellectual; plantations; race; sharecropping; slavery
African American studies, 29, 31, 38–39, 104, 116, 118, 127, 255
Africana studies, 113–14
African diaspora studies, 6, 8, 73–75, 103, 107, 118, 158
African Methodist Episcopal (AME) Church, 63. *See also* Emanuel African Methodist Episcopal (AME) Church; evangelicalism; Methodism

After Redemption: Transformation of African American Religion in the Delta, 1875-1915 (Giggie), 35, 53n32
Alabama Black Caucus, 97
Alabama Coalition for Immigrant Justice, 95, 97
Alabama Getaway (Tullos), 48–49
Alcorn State, 108–9. *See also* historically black colleges and universities; Mississippi
Alfred, Taiaiake, 258, 260, 263n35
Allen, Jafari, 76, 83n6, 84n19, 84n22
American Baptist Home Missionary Society, 115
American Cinema and the Southern Imaginary (McKee and Barker), 47–48
American Film Institute (AFI), 194
American Historical Association, 101, 117, 120n5. *See also* Southern Historical Association
American Literature, 23, 26
American Mediterranean (Guterl), 40
American Mercury (Mencken), 58
American Missionary Association, 63
Americanization of Dixie, The (Egerton), 123
"American Wedding" (Hemphill), 83
Anchor Bay Entertainment, 235, 244n38
Anne Braden: Southern Patriot, 10, 182, 186–89, 197
Anniston (Ala.) Star, 92–93
antebellum era, 40, 58, 64, 104–6, 124–25, 163, 171, 225–26n6; and pastoral narratives, 167–68
anthropology, 1, 3, 8, 17n12, 30, 33, 38, 42, 74–75, 90, 102, 104, 107, 117–18, 137–38, 155–56, 185, 198n3, 216, 219, 222, 227, 241n2, 249
Anti-Saloon League, 61
Appalachia, 140; and class, 196; and coal, 37, 190–91, 196–97, 200n53; cultural studies of, 148, 182, 190, 227; cultural transformations of, 140, 190; and ethnicity, 146–47; in fiction, 9, 139, 141–42, 145–46; in film, 11, 12, 182–200, 227–45; and methamphetamine

299

Appalachia (*continued*)
usage, 142–45; and "New Appalachia," 148–49; otherness of, 140–41; Scots-Irish settlement in, 146; and space, 190, 194–95; and stereotypes, 141, 142, 227–28; in transregional context, 145–46. *See also* hillbilly horror; Lewis, Anne; Satterwhite, Emily; Turner, Daniel Cross; *Wrong Turn 2*

Appalshop, 182, 185, 189, 190, 194. *See also* documentary film; Lewis, Anne

Army Corps of Engineers, 208

Army of Northern Virginia, 136

Atlanta, Ga., 34, 68, 91, 127, 141, 143

Atlanta Constitution, 187

Atlantic, The, 131

Austin, Texas (ATX), Declaration on Southern Documentary Film (Lewis), 183

authenticity: in blues music, 216–18, 222, 223, 224, 225n16; in southern studies, 251. *See also* indigeneity

Avery, Goren "Red Dog," 258–60

Away Down South: A History of the Southern Identity (Cobb), 41, 52, 133n10

Ayer, Charles, 115

Ayer Hall, 115, 116

Ayers, Edward, 16–17n10, 34

Bains, Lee, III, 257

Baker, Houston, Jr., 5, 16n5, 23–24, 26, 31, 47

Baltimore, Md., 116, 128

Baptist and neo-evangelical culture, 67, 69; northern, 62–63; southern, 58, 59–60, 61, 62, 64, 65. *See also* Bible Belt; evangelicalism

Barker, Deborah, 47–48

Barret, Elizabeth, 190

"Battle Hymn of the Republic," 63

BBC Radio, 130

Beason, Scott, 87, 92, 95

Beason-Hammon Alabama Taxpayer and Citizen Protection Act (HB56) 7, 99n9; and attrition, 90–94, 100n21; defined, 87–88; immigrant resistance to, 94–97

Behind the Big House (BTBH) education program, 104, 105, 106, 107, 110, 111, 118. *See also* plantations; race; slavery; tourism

Beloved (Morrison), 46

Benjamin, Walter, 230

Bevel, James, 127

Bible Belt, the, 6, 57, 58–59, 62, 65, 66, 69, 136. *See also* African Methodist Episcopal (AME) Church; Baptist and neo-evangelical culture; Catholicism; Church of Christ; Disciples of Christ; Emanuel African Methodist Episcopal (AME) Church; Episcopalians; evangelicalism; fundamentalism; Holiness-Pentecostal Churches; Judaism; Lutherans; Methodism; Methodist Episcopal Church, South; National Association of Evangelicals; Presbyterians; Southern Baptist Convention

Birmingham, Ala., 28, 89, 126, 186–88, 258–59

Birth of a Nation, The, 61

Bischof, Libby, 111–12, 121n36

Bitter Southerner, 129, 250, 257

Black Codes, 190, 215

black exceptionalism, 31, 79. *See also* African Americans

Black Lives Matter, 11, 129, 133n18, 134n22, 197, 199n17, 260. *See also* African Americans; violence; white supremacism

blackness, 27, 31–32, 76, 81–82, 133n16, 163, 173–74, 217–19. *See also* African Americans; race

Black Power movement, 116, 123, 127, 133n1. *See also* civil rights movement

black queer theory, 6–7, 73, 75–76, 78–79, 82–88. *See also* gender studies; intersectionality; queer theory

black studies, 29, 31, 38–39, 104, 116, 118, 127, 255

Blair Witch Project, The, 230, 242n13

Bland, Sandra, 128. *See also* African Americans; Black Lives Matter

blues, 31–32, 42–43, 46, 257; and authenticity, 216–17, 223; and blues tourism, 11, 104, 120n16, 214–26; country blues, 219; R&B, 219; soul blues, 219. *See also* music

Bohanek, Jennifer, 169–72, 174. *See also* psychology

Boles, John, 65

Bond, Julian, 126, 128. *See also* civil rights movement

Bone, Martyn, vii, 2, 15n2, 16n5, 37, 53n36, 53n38

Bonilla-Silva, Eduardo, 93, 100n14, 216, 225n15, 225n24. *See also* race; racism

Booker's Place, 113
bounce music, 76. *See also* music
Bourdieu, Pierre, 43, 74
Bowen, J. W. E., 64
Braden, Anne, 10, 186–89, 197
Brandeis University, 131
Breaking Bad, 144
Bridging Southern Cultures (Lowe), 2, 15n4, 26, 52n11, 53n17
Brinkmeyer, Robert H., Jr., vii, 141, 150n9, 241; *Fourth Ghost*, 38, 53n42
Brown, Alton, 251, 262n9
Brown, Michael, 128
Brown v. Board of Education, 123, 133n1
Brundage, W. Fitzhugh, 36, 52, 121n32, 252, 262n10
Burden of Southern History, The (Woodward), 127
Burning Bright (Rash), 142–44, 146, 150n14, 150n16, 150n26
Burton, Vernon, 136
Bush, George W., 58, 66–67, 124, 133–34n18
Butler, Judith, 48, 74, 83n10

capitalism, 37, 40, 163, 184; colonialized, 202–3; consumer, 145–46, 209, 234; critiques of, 187, 198–99n17, 228–29, 234, 235, 236, 237, 239, 241n6; disaster, 75; in film, 228, 230, 232, 235–36; global, 22, 155–57, 163, 193, 202; indigenous, 207; industrial, 204, 228–29, 232, 235, in literature, 201, 205–6, 209; market, 235–36; and postcolonialism, 160–61; U.S. model of, modern, 37, 142–43; white elite, 239. *See also* economy; globalization; *Swamplandia!*; *Wrong Turn 2*
Carter, Chelius, 105, 120n18
Carter, Jimmy, 126
Cartwright, Keith, 147, 150n29
Case, Neko, 28
"Case for Reparations, The" (Coates), 259
Cash, Johnny, 28, 46
Cash, W. J., 33, 38, 64, 71n27
Castells, Manuel, 157, 165n9
Catholicism, 47, 59, 62, 64–65, 67–69, 71n36; and Latinos, 46, 51, 91, 94; in literature, 207. *See also* Bible Belt; Louisiana
Census of Religious Bodies (1926), 59
Center for Immigration Studies, 94
Center for the Study of Southern Culture (CSSC), 3, 5, 14, 24, 32, 104, 131, 149n5; faculty, 1–2, 3, 4, 5, 32, 44, 149n5; and public history, 104; and southern studies, 249, 251. *See also* Ownby, Ted; Southern Foodways Alliance; Transforming New South Identities Symposium; Wilson, Charles Reagan
Chanan, Michael, 193–94, 199n44, 200n46
Chapman, Alix, 6–7, 83n7, 172
Chapman, Rico D., 8, 102, 107; and public history work, 114–17
Charbonneau, Stephen Michael, 194, 200n47
Charleston, S.C., 63, 110, 128, 130–31, 134n24–26, 136, 260. *See also* Confederacy; Emanuel African Methodist Episcopal (AME) Church
#CharlestonSyllabus, 131, 134n28, 134n30–31. *See also* Confederacy; Emanuel African Methodist Episcopal (AME) Church; public intellectuals; Roof, Dylan; violence; white supremacism
Chatelain, Marcia, 131
Chavez, Leo, 93–94, 100n16
Childs, Becky, 148, 150n31
Ching, Barbara, 43, 54n58–59
Christian Century, 67
Christianity Today, 67
Church, David, 228, 241n9
Church of Christ, 60. *See also* Bible Belt; evangelicalism
cinema verité, 10, 183–84, 185, 189, 192, 198n3. *See also* documentary film
Civil Rights Congress, 188
civil rights movement, 27, 33–36, 51, 104, 114–16, 122n43, 123–26, 132, 133n1, 133n6, 133n9; and collective identity, 197, 199n17; documented, in film, 186, 198n17; and Latino immigrant activism, 97; opposition to, 136, 146. *See also* documentary film; history, intellectual; Jackson, Miss.
Civil War, 33, 40, 51, 62–63, 65, 68, 109, 128, 145, 197, 257; memory, 36, 74, 131. *See also* slavery
Civilian Conservation Corps (CCC), 208
Clarksdale, Miss., and blues tourism, 11, 120n16, 122n43, 214–26. *See also* Coahoma County, Miss.; Mississippi Delta
classism, 164, 227, 231

Cleveland, Ohio, 128
Clinton, Bill, 40
Coahoma County, Miss., 214. *See also*
    Clarksdale, Miss.; Mississippi Delta
coal, 10, 37, 49, 182, 190–91, 195–97, 200n53, 201.
    See also Appalachia; capitalism; *Justice in the Coalfields*; Lewis, Anne
Coates, Ta-Nehisi, 130–31, 134n27, 259
Cobb, James C., 41, 52, 52n4, 52n11, 133n10, 224–25n6
Cody, Iron Eyes, 202
Coffey, Michele Grigsby, 10, 178n3, 182, 241, 249, 262. *See also* Center for the Study of Southern Culture; Transforming New South Identities Symposium
Cohn, Deborah, 16n5, 52n4, 52n11, 53n46, 54n77, 157–59, 165n10, 165n13
"Collectors, The" (McAdams), 210–11, 213n13
colonialism, 158–61; critique of, 198–99n17; in literature, 207
Combs, Barbara Harris, vii, 178n2
Confederacy: leaders of, 64; memorials of, 16–17n10, 51, 54n80, 134n33; and religion, 65; and white identity, 26, 74, 129, 146
Confederate flag, 51, 110, 125, 136–37, 146, 149n2, 240, 262: debate about, 130–31, 134n27, 134n32, 203, 212–13n7. *See also* Emanuel African Methodist Episcopal (AME) Church; Roof, Dylan; South Carolina Statehouse
Cooper, Roy, 145
Cooper Owens, Deirdre, vii
Corbett, Katharine T., 111, 121n34
cotton, 104, 109, 111–13, 121n28, 137, 156, 217–18. *See also* capitalism; economy; plantations; sharecropping; slavery
Cotton Picker of America Monument, 109
country cosmopolitanism, 31–32
country music, 34, 43, 46, 54n58. *See also* music
Cowie, Elizabeth, 184, 198n6, 199n19
Cox, Karen, 132, 134n34
Cravey, Altha, 90–91, 99n7
Creation of Confederate Nationalism, The (Faust), 65
creolization, 30, 40, 42, 46, 50, 51; in Louisiana, 173–74, 179n15–16. *See also* Louisiana; race
Crespino, Joseph, 54n77, 133n2, 163, 250, 262n3
Crisis of the Negro Intellectual (Cruse), 127

Critical Regionalism (Powell), 47
critical theory, 13, 25, 37, 47–49, 173, 177, 178n2, 181n31, 216, 241
Crosby, Fanny, 61
Cruse, Harold, 127
cultural citizenship, 95–96, 100n20
culture, popular, 229, 242n11; and the American South, 139–40, 141–42, 144; and cultural anxieties, 140. *See also* blues; film studies; hillbilly horror; music
Cunningham, Rodger, 140–41, 150n7

Daughters of Mother Jones, 196, 200n54. *See also* labor
Davis, Thadious M., 38–39
Davis Plantation, Holly Springs, Miss., 105. *See also* Behind the Big House; Mississippi; plantations; slavery
Dear Appalachia (Satterwhite), 148, 245n49
Dees, Morris, 128
Deferred Action for Childhood Arrivals (DACA), 90, 99n5
Delany, Samuel, 80–82, 84n29, 84n32
Deliverance, 238
Dellinger, Kirsten, vii, 9–10
Delta Blues Museum, 222–23
Delta State University, 108–14, 180n29
Democratic Party, 123–25, 133n11. *See also* Mississippi Freedom Democratic Party
Desai, Gaurav, 156–57, 165n5
Development, Relief, and Education for Alien Minors (DREAM) Act, 96, 100n22. *See also* immigration
Dickey, James, 238
Dirt and Desire (Yaeger), 53n35, 249
Disciples of Christ, 60. *See also* Bible Belt; evangelicalism
Dissent, 129, 131
Disturbing Calculations (Taylor), 184, 198n9
documentary film, 3, 10–11, 44, 104, 182–84, 197n1, 199n19, 251–53; and activism, 186, 191, 192–93, 196–97; approaches to, 182–85, 189, 198n3; and cognitive mapping, 193–95, 200n52; ethnographic, 189; and marginalized communities, 29, 82, 185, 194, 198n11; and transformation, 187, 188–91, 196
Dominguez, Virginia, 173–74, 179n15, 179n18
Donaldson, Susan, 23, 41, 54n50

Doty, Roxanne L., 94, 100n17
Douglass, Frederick, 62. *See also* African Americans: activism
DREAM (Development, Relief, and Education for Alien Minors) Act, 96, 100n22. *See also* immigration
Duck, Leigh Anne, vii, 10, 16n5, 17n17, 27, 34–35, 52, 53n14, 53n30, 54n81, 141, 144–45, 150n10, 150n20, 212n6, 241
Duke, Marshall P., 169–72, 174, 178n4, 179n6–9, 179n11. *See also* psychology
Durham, N.C., 110, 116, 126
dystopia, rural, 229–30, 242n11. *See also* hillbilly horror

economy: of Mississippi Delta, 214–15; representations of, in film, 228; southern, post–Civil War, 62, 63–64; transregional, 142, 143, 145. *See also* capitalism; coal; cotton; globalization; New South; plantations; sharecropping; tourism
Edelman, Lee, 76, 84n20
Eden, Don, 176, 180n26
Edge, John T., 2, 54n62–66, 251, 257–61, 262n5, 263n31, 263n36–37, 263n39–42, 264n44–46, 264n48; *The Larder*, 2, 44, 54n62, 251; Southern Foodways Alliance 44, 149n5, 251, 257, 258, 259; *Southern Foodways Alliance Community Cookbook*, 251. *See also* Center for the Study of Southern Culture; foodways, southern
Edible South, The (Ferris), 257–58, 263n32
Edmondson, Amy, 174, 179n20
Egerton, John, 123
Eggleston, Jenifer, 105
Eighteenth Amendment, 61
El Día del Niño (The Day of the Child), 94–95
Emanuel African Methodist Episcopal (AME) Church, 110, 128–30, 132, 134n23, 213n7, 260–61; Emanuel Nine, 136–37, 146. *See also* African Americans; African Methodist Episcopal (AME) Church; race; violence; white supremacism
Emory University, 169
emotional labor. *See* pedagogy: emotional labor in
Encyclopedia of Southern Culture, 24, 29. *See also* Center for the Study of Southern Culture

Endowment for the Future of the South, vii, 14. *See also* Center for the Study of Southern Culture; Transforming New South Identities Symposium
Englehardt, Elizabeth S. S., 2, 16–17n10, 45, 54n62
Episcopalians, 59–60, 65. *See also* Bible Belt; evangelicalism
Equal Rights Amendment, 124
Escaping the Delta (Wald), 42, 54n54, 225n19
Eskew, Glenn, 42–43, 54n57
ethnographic studies, 5–7, 30–31, 44, 50, 52, 84n23–24, 90–91, 98, 138, 216; and blues tourism, 214–26; and co-performance, 6, 76, 83; and cultural biography, 76–81; and film, 189, 227–40, 241n8
Ethridge, Robbie, vii, 29, 53n19
evangelicalism, 61, 65–67; and African Americans, 69; and cultural politics, 66; neo-evangelicalism, 65–67, 69; northern evangelical Protestantism, 62–63; southern evangelical Protestantism, 45–47, 57–59, 61–62, 64–66. *See also* African Methodist Episcopal (AME) Church; Baptist and neo-evangelical culture; Bible Belt; Church of Christ; Disciples of Christ; Methodists
E-Verify, 88, 98n2. *See also* immigration
Evers, Medgar, 115. *See also* civil rights movement; Mississippi
Explo '72, 67

Falwell, Jerry, 68–69. *See also* evangelicalism; Religious Right
Family Narratives Project, 169–70. *See also* pedagogy; psychology
Fannie Lou Hamer Institute @ Council of Federated Organizations (COFO), 114–15. *See also* Jackson State University
Farish Street Historic District, 115
Faulkner, William, 28, 35, 38, 40, 46, 157
Faust, Drew, 65
Feagin, Joe, 165n2, 216, 225n12
Federal Emergency Management Agency (FEMA), 80
feminism: black, 16n9, 75, 84n18, 84n25, 134n29; and feminist theory, 33, 41–42, 45, 227; postcolonial, 161; third-wave, 16n9; transnational feminist model and

feminism (*continued*)
  scholarship, 155, 161–62. *See also* black queer theory; gender studies; queer theory
Ferguson, Mo., 128, 260
#FergusonSyllabus, 131. *See also* Black Lives Matter; Brown, Michael
Ferreti, Gwendolyn, 7–8, 17n11
Ferris, Marcie Cohen, 257–58, 263n32. *See also* foodways, southern
film studies, 25, 29, 33, 47–48, 82; documentary, 10–11, 182–200. *See also* documentary film; hillbilly horror
Finding Purple America (Smith), 16n5, 27–28, 49, 53n16, 150n28, 252, 261, 262n11
Fisher, Stephen L., 190, 199n32, 199n34
Fivush, Robyn, 169–72, 174. *See also* psychology
Flashes of a Southern Spirit (Wilson), 46
Florida International University, 103
Florida Museum of Natural History, 210
Flynt, Wayne, 66
foodways, southern: and new southern studies, 255, 257–58; and Southern Foodways Alliance, 44, 104, 149n5, 251, 257, 262n9; and southern studies scholarship, 2, 44–45, 149n5, 250–54, 257–59; and whiteness, 249, 256–57, 258, 260–62. *See also* Edge, John T.; *Edible South, The*; Englehardt, Elizabeth; Ferris, Marcie Cohen; *Larder, The*; *Mess of Greens*; Ownby, Ted; Romine, Scott; Warnes, Andrew
"For 'the Children' Dancing the Beloved Community" (Allen), 76, 83n6, 84n19, 84n22
Fourth Ghost (Brinkmeyer), 38, 53n42
Frankenberg, Ruth, 174, 179n17
Frankl, Viktor E., 167, 176–77, 180n27–28. *See also* psychology
Frederickson, Mary, 50
Freedomways, 127
Freeman, Elizabeth, 74, 84n11
fundamentalism, 61, 66–67. *See also* evangelicalism
Fundamentals, the, 61

Gaines, Jane, 189, 199n31
Garden and Gun, 250
Garner, Eric, 128–29
gender studies, 8, 13–14, 16n9, 25–27, 31–33, 41–42, 45, 48, 50, 74–78, 81–82, 83n10, 99n6, 124, 137–39, 161–62, 164, 166n23, 168, 171–72, 177, 178nn2–3, 231, 261. *See also* feminism; intersectionality; queer theory
Gentry, Gail, 197
geography, 3, 29, 44, 54n75, 61–62, 69, 90, 138, 156, 163, 227–29, 239–40, 241n2; imagined, 194, 228; racialized, 259
Giardina, Denise, 196
Gibbs, Phillip Lafayette, 115, 116, 122n44
Gibbs-Green Memorial, 115, 116
Giggie, John, 35–36, 53n32
Giroux, Henry, 177, 178n2, 181n31. *See also* pedagogy
globalization, 17, 22–23, 25–28, 30, 37–39, 43, 49–50, 52n4, 53n32, 53n39, 53n41, 137, 140, 153, 155–56, 160, 182, 190–95, 202. *See also* capitalism; economy
Global North, 22, 155, 158, 194
Global South, 3, 5, 9–11, 26–28, 32, 36, 39, 43, 49–50, 52n10, 54n76, 111, 127, 140, 142, 191, 215, 224, 254, 258; and American exceptionalism, 159; Caribbean and Latin America, 22, 39–40, 53n43, 157, 194; comparative hemispheric model, 26, 155, 157–59, 162; and decentered interlocality, 154, 162–64; and decoloniality, 160; and domain assumptions of theory, 154; and First World, 162; geopolitical model, 155, 159–61, 162; and globalism, 38, 53n32, 53n39, 53n41, 137, 149n3, 165n4; and Global North, 22, 155, 158, 194; India, 22; inflow-outflow model, 155–57, 160, 162; and institutionalized oppression, 161, 164; and interdisciplinary studies, 153–54, 155, 162, 163, 164, 165n3; and literary studies, 154; and postcolonial studies, 155; and regional exceptionalism, 38, 52, 159; and southern exceptionalism, 163; as term, 153–54; and Third World, 161; and transnational feminist model, 155, 161–62, 164; and the U.S. South, 157, 160, 191
Global South, 159
"Going Deeper with Red Dog" (Edge), 258–60
gospel songs, 59, 61. *See also* music
Gouldner, Alvin, 154
"Governing through Meth" (Linnemann), 144

Gracing the Table (GTT), 105–6, 116, 118. *See also* Holly Springs, Miss.
Grady, Henry, 10, 187, 191, 199n23. *See also* New South
Graham, Billy, 67
Granik, Debra, 144
Grant, Adam, 174, 179n19
Gray, Freddie, 128. *See also* Black Lives Matter
Gray, Richard, 23, 51, 54n79
Great Depression, 145. *See also* capitalism; economy; Roosevelt, Franklin
Great Revival (Boles), 65
Green, James, 115–16, 122n44
Green, Kathryn, 8, 102, 107; public history work, 108–14, 117, 118
Greene, Robert, II, 8–9, 14, 130, 134n20–21, 134n26, 134n32
Greensboro Massacre of 1979, 126–27
Greenwood, Miss., 113. *See also* Mississippi Delta
Griffin, Larry J., 254–55
Ground Zero Blues Club, 217, 222, 226n44. *See also* Clarksdale, Miss.
Grounded Globalism (Peacock), 37–38, 52n4, 53n32, 53n39, 53n41, 137, 149n3, 155–56, 165n4
Grundy, Saida, 132. *See also* public intellectuals
Gussow, Adam, 42, 54n55
Guterl, Matthew, 40, 163, 166n27
Gutierrez, Luis, 89

Hagood, Taylor, 15n2, 147–48, 149n6, 150n30
Haiti, 40, 159; Haitian Revolution, 163. *See also* Global South
Haley, Nikki, 131, 137. *See also* South Carolina Statehouse
Hall, Jacquelyn Dowd, 35, 133n1
Hall, Stuart, 214, 216, 241n7
Hammon, Mickey, 87, 95, 99n12
Handley, George, 157–58, 165n11
"Handshake with Alabama," 92
Hansberry, Lorraine, 127
Harber, Kent, 176, 180n24
Harding, Vincent, 127, 133n14
Harlan County USA (Lewis), 185, 191, 195
Harvey, David, 37
Harvey, Paul, 46–47, 53n36, 54n69, 54n72, 57–58, 70n2, 70n8, 70n21, 71n30

Hasty, J. Daniel, 148, 150n31
Haunted Bodies (Jones and Donaldson), 41, 54n50
Hayes, John, 6, 71n30
Haygood, Atticus, 63–64, 70n23
Helena, Ark., and blues tourism, 220, 224n3, 225n11, 225n33
Hemphill, Essex, 72, 83
Henninger, Katherine, 41–42, 54n53
Herberg, Will, 68, 71n36
Herzog, Werner, 183–85, 197n2, 198n3, 198n8, 198n10–11. *See also* film studies
Heyrman, Christine, 57, 65, 70n26
Highlands Bar and Grill, 258–59, 260
Hill, Samuel, 57–58, 65
hillbilly horror, 12, 227–45; and capitalism, 228–30, 232–36, 239; and drug use, 144; and environmentalism, 228, 230, 232, 234–35; and gender, 227, 231, 239; and interdisciplinary studies, 227; and politics, 227–29, 235, 239–40; and race, 227, 229, 236–40; and tropes of the south, 141. *See also* Appalachia; film studies
Hillcoat, John, 140
hip-hop, 31–32, 257. *See also* music
historically black colleges and universities (HBCUs), 108, 120n16, 257; and collaborations with historically white academic institutions, 103, 106, 118. *See also* Alcorn State; Jackson State University; Mississippi Valley State University; Morgan State University; North Carolina Central University; Rust College
history, African American, 48–50, 52, 73–75, 104–7, 109, 111–17, 124–28, 130–31, 168, 178n3, 179n14–16, 186–89, 217–18, 221–22; and social media, 131
history, intellectual, 23, 129, 133n15; and African Americans, 127, 132; African American Intellectual History blog, 131; the Black Power Movement, 127; and civil rights movement, 123–24, 126; and media, 129–32; Society for U.S. Intellectual History blog, 129, 134n19; and southern studies, 8–9, 124; and white-black relations, 124
history, public, 15n1, 104, 105; and community engagement, 106, 111; and

history, public (*continued*)
diversity, 101–2, 106–8, 117, 119n4, 119–20n5; institutionalization of, 104–19; interdisciplinary nature of, 103, 118, 120n12; and southern studies, 8, 11, 102–3; and sustainability, 112; and underrepresented groups, 107, 108, 110
History and Memory in the Two Souths (Cohn), 157, 165n10
Hobson, Fred, 23, 52n6, 70n13
Holiness-Pentecostal churches, 60. *See also* Bible Belt; evangelicalism
Holly Springs, Miss., 104–8, 111, 116
Holly Springs Garden Club, 105
Holocaust, 177
House, Son, 213, 217
"How Do We Get There? Racial and Ethnic Diversity in the Public History Profession," 101
Howard University, 116, 120n15, 122n45
Howe, LeeAnne, 29
Hurricane Katrina, 6, 181n31, 197; and discourse of criminality, 80; increased birth rates following, 72–83; and levee breaks, 72, 79
Hurricane Rita, 197

I'll Take My Stand, 22
Image of the City, The (Lynch), 193
imaginary, southern, 27, 47–48
immigration, 50, 59, 62, 65, 140, 156, 160, 190, 208, 257; and xenophobia, 229, 240. *See also* globalization; race
immigration, Latino, 124, 129, 133–34n18, 192; and anti-immigrant movement, 7, 93–94, 98n2; and attrition via enforcement, 87–88, 93–94, 97, 99n10; and concept of family; 96–97; criminalization of, 87, 91–93, 98; and immigrant justice movement, 7, 89, 94–96, 98, 100n19; and self-deportation, 87–88, 93; and southern studies, 7, 17n12, 50; undocumented, 73, 87–90, 94, 99n4–5, 100n22–23, 133–34n18, 193. *See also* Development, Relief, and Education for Alien Minors (DREAM) Act; globalization; Latinx community; race
Immigration and Customs Enforcement Agency (ICE), 88, 99n10

Immigration Reform and Control Act (1986), 124
Indian Country Diaries, 29, 53n19
Indianola, Miss., 109. *See also* Mississippi Delta
indigeneity, 11, 90, 99n6, 159–60, 201–2, 206, 208, 210–12, 258; and capitalism, 207; and memory, 204; and tourism, 213n9
Institute of Southern Studies, 126
Institute of the Black World (IBW), 127
Interpreting the Texas Past, 104
intersectionality, 6, 7, 16n9, 31, 161, 168. *See also* black queer theory; feminism; gender studies; queer theory
"In the South" (Rushdie), 21, 22
Into the Abyss, 184–85, 198n11
Isaac, Rhys, 65
Israeli Defense Forces, 176
Itta Bena, Miss., 108–9. *See also* Mississippi Delta

Jackson, Jeffrey T., vii, 9–10
Jackson, Miss., 102, 113; and civil rights activity, 114–17. *See also* civil rights movement
Jackson State University, 102, 109, 122n42, 122n44; history of, 114–15; and Natchez, Miss., 115; and public history, 114–18. *See also* historically black colleges and universities
Jacobs, Henry P., 114–15
Jacobson, Lenore, 175–76, 180n23
Jacobson, Mathew Frye, 179n14
Jameson, Fredric, 193–94, 199n45, 200n52
Jefferson, Thomas, 21
Jim Crow, 26, 33–39, 43, 53n25, 94, 104, 108, 110, 112, 126, 163–64, 215, 224–25n6; desegregation, 108, 187; and politics, 126; and sharecropping system, 112–13, 117. *See also* race; segregation; sharecropping
John R. Lynch Street Historic District, 115–16, 122n43. *See also* Jackson, Miss.
Johnson, Robert, 42, 214, 217. *See also* blues
Jones, Anne Goodwyn, 41
Jones, Edward P., 46
Jones, Rhonda, 110
Journal of American Studies, 125
Journal of Southern History, 52. *See also* Southern Historical Association

Journal of Southern Religion, 46
Judaism, 60, 62, 68, 71n36. *See also* Bible Belt
Jumpin' Jim Crow (ed. Dailey, Gilmore, and Simon), 33
Jussim, Lee, 176, 180n24. *See also* psychology
Justice in the Coalfields, 10, 182, 196–97, 200n55. *See also* capitalism; coal; documentary film; labor; Lewis, Anne

Khafre, Inc., 109, 118, 121n29
Kim-Puri, H. J., 161–62, 166n23
King, Martin Luther, Jr., 127, 186. *See also* civil rights movement
King, Stephen A., 220–21
kinship: as networks of choice, 78–82; queer, 73–75, 79, 82; and reproduction, 74–76; white, heteronormative, 6, 73, 75. *See also* black queer theory; queer theory
Kipling, Rudyard, 61
Kirby, Jack Temple, 32–33, 53n23
Kirkman, Robert, 139
Knight, Barbara, 191
Known World, The (Jones), 46
Koch Foods, 192
Kopple, Barbara, 185
Kreyling, Michael, 23, 26, 52n6, 52n9
Ku Klux Klan, 97, 126, 136. *See also* race; violence; white supremacism
Kumar, R. Sreevalsa, 176, 180n25
Kwon, Miwon, 28

Labode, Modupe, 101, 119n3, 120n8, 121n40
labor, 28, 37, 50, 63–64, 135, 207–8, 215–18; cultural, 78, 82; enslaved, 40, 64, 105–6, 109–11, 156, 163, 190, 215; intellectual, 112, 135, 164–65n1, 168–69, 179n12; organized, 35–36, 50, 158, 190–97; racialization of, 40, 88, 90, 93, 105–6, 109–11, 178n3, 190–91, 215, 221–23. *See also* capitalism; economy; globalization; immigration; immigration, Latino; race; sharecropping; slavery
Lacan, Jacques, 27, 199n19, 250, 253, 260. *See also* psychology; southern studies, new
Ladd, Barbara, 51, 54n78, 254, 263n21
Larder, The, 2, 44, 54n62, 251. *See also* foodways, southern
Lassiter, Matthew D., 54n77, 124, 163, 250, 262n3

Latinx community, 7–8, 17n12, 51, 82, 88–94, 98, 99n8, 119n4, 119–20n5, 125, 147, 184, 198n11; and activism, 7, 94–97; and indigeneity, 89–90, 99n6. *See also* immigration, Latino; race
Laymon, Kiese, 259–61, 264n47
Lazarus, Amber, 169–72, 174
Lee, Calinda, 101, 119n3
"Letter from Birmingham Jail" (King), 186. *See also* civil rights movement; race
Levander, Caroline, 159–60, 164, 165n17, 165n19, 165n20, 166n28
Levine, Robert S., 160, 165n19
Lewis, Anne, 10–11, 17n17, 182–200, 241; *Anne Braden: Southern Patriot*, 10, 182, 186–89, 197; Appalshop, 182, 185, 189, 190, 194; Austin, Texas (ATX), Declaration on Southern Documentary Film, 183; *Harlan County, USA*, 185, 191, 195; *Justice in the Coalfields*, 10, 182, 196–97, 200n55; *Morristown: In the Air and Sun*, 10, 182, 190–93. *See also* documentary film
Lewis, John, 46. *See also* civil rights movement; race
LGBTQ rights, 74–75, 186
LGBTQ studies, 43–46, 74, 76. *See also* black queer theory; intersectionality; queer theory
Life, 67
Linnemann, Travis, 144, 145
literary studies, 9, 135, 138–39; and film, 12, 47–48, 227, 241n4; and food studies, 44–45, 149n5, 253; and gender studies, 41–42, 45; and the Global South, 26–27, 39–40, 49, 154–58, 165n17; and modernism, 22–23, 27, 34–35; and music studies, 42, and Native American studies, 11, 29, 201–13, 213n9; and new southern studies, 12–13, 23, 26, 49, 149n5, 158–59, 212n5, 212n6, 249; and postmodernism, 23–24, 33, 37, 253; and sexuality, 43–44; and social engagement, 9, 139, 141, 147–49, 149n5, 238, 240, 242n11; and southern studies, 2, 9, 11–13, 26, 36–39, 249, 252–55, 261, 262–63n13, 263n21; and transdisciplinarity, 29–30, 32, 44, 46–47, 105, 139, 147, 149n6, 165n3, 211, 241n2. *See also* blues; foodways, southern; gender studies; memory studies; Native American studies

INDEX 307

Livingston, Jenny, 82, 83n6, 84n33
Lomax, Alan, 214, 224n2
Look Away! The U.S. South in New World Studies (Smith), 16n5, 26, 52n4, 52n11, 53n46, 54n77, 158, 165n13. *See also* Smith, Jon
Looking South (Frederickson), 50
Lopez, Richard, 184–85
Lost Cause ideology, 63, 146, 172, 176–77
Louisiana: and Catholicism, 59–60; in film, 199n29; and migrations, 77–78; and race, 173–74, 178n3, 179n15, 179n16, 179n18. *See also* Bible Belt; creolization; Hurricane Katrina; New Orleans; race
Lovell, Jarrett S., 97, 100n26
Lowe, John, 2, 6, 9, 15n4, 28–29, 52n11, 53n17
Luckett, Robert, 114
Lutherans, 59–60. *See also* Bible Belt; evangelicalism
lynching, 26–27, 41–43, 46–47, 54n52, 178n3, 188–89, 215; religious roots of, 46. *See also* Ku Klux Klan; race; violence; white supremacism
Lynching and Spectacle (Wood), 41, 54n52

Madison, D. Soyini, 76, 84n23
Malcolm X, 94, 100n18
Mallinson, Christine, 148, 150n31
Man's Search for Meaning (Frankl), 167, 176–77, 180n27–28
Margaret Walker Center (MWC), 114–16
Márquez, Gabriel García, 40, 157
Martin, Trayvon, 197
Marty, Martin, 66, 71n29
Massey, Doreen, 189–90, 194–95, 199n28, 199n35
Mathews, Donald, 46, 54n72, 57, 70n3–4
Mayfield, Julian, 127
McAdams, Janet, 210–11, 213n13
McCall, Sophie, 258, 263n34–35
McCarthy, Cormac, 140
McDannell, Colleen, 59, 70n14
McGee, Willie, 188–89
McKee, Kathryn, vii, 9–10, 26, 47–48, 52n10
McLeod, Alisea Williams, 105–6, 118
McPherson, Aimee Semple, 61
McPherson, Tara, 25–26, 44, 49, 54n74
memory, 26, 36; and the Global South, 26–27, 157–58, 165n10; and the Lost Cause, 131; and Native Americans, 202–4, 206–7; and race, 36, 128–31, 133n1; and southern studies, 11, 27, 32, 135–36, 147–48, 254. *See also* Confederacy; literary studies; Lost Cause ideology; race
Memphis, Tenn., 26–27, 30–32, 53n20, 252
Mencken, H. L., 58–59, 65–66, 70n9–10, 70n12
Mercer, Johnny, 42–43, 54n57
Mercer University, 255–56, 257
Mess of Greens (Englehardt), 45. *See also* foodways, southern
methamphetamines, 9, 139, 141–46, 150n19, 150n21, 150n22
Methland (Reding), 144
Methodism, 60–65, 67, 69. *See also* African Methodist Episcopal (AME) Church; Bible Belt; Emanuel African Methodist Episcopal (AME) Church; evangelicalism
Methodist Episcopal Church, South, 63. *See also* Bible Belt; slavery
Mignolo, Walter, 159–60, 164, 165n17, 165n18, 166n28
Milanich, Jerald T., 210, 213n12
Miller, Howard S., 111, 121n34
Miller, Karl, 43, 54n60
Minnesota Historical Society, 106–7
minstrelsy, 43, 223. *See also* race
Mississippi, 10, 102, 103, 104; and the Global South, 153–54, 159, 162, 164; Hill Country, 102, 104–8, 117
Mississippi Delta, 40, 111, 114; and blues tourism, 11, 214–26; and cotton production, 109; and education, 108–9; and poverty, 112, 217–18; and religion, 64. *See also* capitalism; Clarksdale, Miss.; cotton; economy; Greenwood, Miss.; Itta Bena, Miss.; plantations; sharecropping; slavery
Mississippi Department of Archives and History (MDAH), 113–16
Mississippi Freedom Democratic Party, 122n43
Mississippi Museum of Art, 115
Mississippi Valley State University, 102, 108–14, 121n28. *See also* historically black colleges and universities
Mockingbird Song (Kirby), 32, 53n23
Mohanty, Chandra, 161–62, 165n21, 166n26
Montgomery, Ala., 95

308 INDEX

Montgomery, Isaiah, 109
Moody, Dwight, 61
Moreton, Bethany, 65
Morgan State University, 116. *See also* historically black colleges and universities
Morrison, Toni, 46
Morristown, Tenn., 182, 190–93
Morristown: In the Air and Sun (Lewis), 10, 182, 190–93. *See also* economy; globalization; immigration, Latino
Moses, Jesus, and the Trickster in the Evangelical South (Harvey), 46–47, 54n69
Moses, Robert, 127
Mound Bayou, Miss., 109. *See also* Mississippi Delta; race
Moynihan, Daniel Patrick, 78, 84n17
Muñoz, Jose, 76, 84n21
Murphy, Bernice, 229, 241n2, 241n6
Murray, Albert, 26
Museum of the Mississippi Delta, 113
music, 250, 252; and authenticity, 216–17, 223; blues, 31–32, 42–43, 46, 219, 257; and blues tourism, 11, 104, 120n16, 214–26; bounce, 76; country, 34, 43, 46, 54n58; gospel, 59, 61; hip-hop, 31–32, 257; R&B, 219. *See also* blues
Myth of Southern Exceptionalism, The (Lassiter and Crespino), 54n77, 163, 262n3

Nation's Region (Duck), 16n5, 34–35, 53n30, 141
National Association of Evangelicals (NAE), 66–67. *See also* evangelicalism
National Council on Public History (NCPH), 101–2, 106, 114, 118, 120n11, 121n39
National Precursor Log Exchange, 145
Native Americans: and colonial-capitalism, 202, 203; and the Confederacy, 212n7; and Indian alterity, 202–3; and industrial-capitalism, 204; in literature, 11, 17n21, 201–2, 204–12; and removal, 109; and rhetorics of rebellion, 203; and violence, 203. *See also* indigeneity; race
Native American studies, 11, 29, 201–13, 213n9. *See also* literary studies; memory
Native South, 29
Negro Family, The (Moynihan), 78, 84n17
Nelson, Dana D., 5, 16n5, 23–26, 31, 47, 52n7, 54n51, 54n73

New Deal, 66, 68, 124–25, 128. *See also* capitalism; economy; Roosevelt, Franklin
New Encyclopedia of Southern Culture, The, 24, 29. *See also* Center for the Study of Southern Culture
New Mind of the South, The (Thompson), 123
New Orleans, La., 6, 72–83, 109. *See also* Hurricane Katrina; Louisiana
New South, 10, 53n27, 59–64, 126, 187, 191–92; rhetoric, 8, 127, 197. *See also* economy; Grady, Henry
"New South" (Haygood), 63–64
new southern studies. *See* southern studies, new
New York Times, 142, 201
Nichols, Bill, 184, 198n3, 198n5
Niebuhr, Reinhold, 64
Night of the Living Dead, 235
Nixon, Richard, 123
No Future (Edelman), 76, 84n20
North Carolina Central University (NCCU), 110, 116–17, 122n46. *See also* historically black colleges and universities
Nothing Gold Can Stay (Rash), 142–44, 150n15, 150n17, 150n18
NPR, 136, 142

O'Brien, Michael, 127, 253, 255, 263n14, 263n26
O Brother, Where Art Thou?, 33
Obama, Barack, 2, 8, 16n10, 99n5, 124, 128, 261
Obama, Michelle, 134n29
"Oceans Connect: The Indian Ocean and African Identities" (Desai), 156, 165n5,
O'Connor, Flannery, 59, 68, 70n15, 71n35
Odum, Howard, 59–60, 70n16, 252
Old Capitol Museum, 113, 115
Old South, 16–17n10, 40, 187, 203. *See also* antebellum era; Lost Cause ideology; New South; plantations
Oliver, Donna, 109
Oliviera, D. France, 219, 225n28
On Critical Pedagogy (Giroux), 177, 181n31
One Place after Another (Kwon), 28
Ordering the Façade (Henninger), 41–42, 54n53
Orthodox immigrants, 62
Osceola, 207–8, 210–11, 213n11. *See also* Native Americans

Ownby, Ted, vii; as director of the Center for the Study of Southern Culture, 32, 53n21, 131, 134n33, 249–54, 257, 262n1, 263n18, 263n29, 263n33; and foodways, 2, 44–45, 54n62, 149n5, 251, 262n7; *The Larder*, 2, 44, 54n62, 251; and religious history, 65; *Subduing Satan*, 65. *See also* Center for the Study of Southern Culture; foodways, southern

Oxford, Miss., 1, 168, 177. *See also* Center for the Study of Southern Culture; Mississippi; University of Mississippi

Oxford American, 128, 250, 258–59

Paden, Red, 222
Page, Hélan E., 219, 225n28
Palleres, Amalia, 96
Paris Is Burning, 82, 83n6, 84n33
Patterson, William, 188
Payne, Daniel, 63, 70n21
Peacock, James, 38, 52n4, 53n32, 53n39, 53n41, 137, 149n3, 155–56, 165n4
pedagogy, 4, 8–10, 12–13, 105–8, 252; emotional labor in, 13, 112, 119, 132, 167–68, 177, 178n2, 179n18, 258–59, 260–61, 264n47, 264n49; and faculty professors of color, 167–68, 175, 178n2, 179n12, 179n21, 262; and female faculty, 168, 178n2, 179n12, 179n21; and intellectual intergenerational self, 10, 169–70, 171–75, 177; and international students and southern studies, 174; and psychological safety, 174–75; and psychology research, 169, 174, 175, 175–76; and student performance, 175–76, 177; and students of color, 101–2, 106–8, 173, 174, 178n2, 262; and white faculty professors, 168, 175, 179n21; and white students, 167–68, 171–74, 176, 256–57; and white supremacism, 168, 171–73, 174, 175

Percy, Walker, 67, 71n33
Percy, William Alexander, 44, 54n61
Pew Research Center, 67, 93
Phillips, U. B., 36
philosophy, 114, 149–50n6, 164–65n1, 227, 241n3
photography, 41–42, 190–91, 220, 251, 253. *See also* Center for the Study of Southern Culture; documentary film; lynching; tourism: blues
Pickering, Mimi, 186

Pinckney, Clem, 136
place, sense of, 157, 250, 251; and Native American literature, 29; postsouthern, 37, 38; and U.S. South, 23, 28, 30, 36–37, 49, 147, 195
"Place and the Past in the Global South" (Smith), 49
plantations, 25, 41, 105–6, 109, 204; and the Global South, 22, 39–40, 157–59; as metaphor, 262, 264n49. *See also* cotton; Davis Plantation; economy; Global South; Lost Cause ideology; Mound Bayou; Old South; sharecropping; slavery
Politico, 130
postcolonial studies, 27, 39–40, 155, 158, 160–61, 225n28
postmodernism, 24, 26, 28, 30, 32–34, 52n6, 53n36, 53n37, 53n38, 156–57, 193–94, 199n45, 200n52, 253. *See also* documentary film; literary studies
Postslavery Literatures in the Americas (Handley), 157, 165n11
poststructuralist theory, 24–25, 34
Powell, Douglas Reichert, 47, 241n2. *See also* documentary film
Presbyterians, 58–60, 65. *See also* Bible Belt; evangelicalism
Preserve Marshall County and Holly Springs (PMCHS), Inc., 105, 108. *See also* Holly Springs, Miss.; Mississippi
Presley, Elvis, 257
Prohibition Act, 61. *See also* Eighteenth Amendment
Promise of a New South (Ayers), 34, 53n27, 53n29
Protestant, Catholic, Jew (Herberg), 68, 71n36
psychoanalysis, 252
psychology: educational, 10, 169–72, 174–76, 178n4, 179n6–9, 179n11, 180n23, 180n24, 180n25; empirical, 252; Lacanianism, 27, 199n19, 250, 253, 260; logotherapy, 176–77, 180n27, 180n28. *See also* Bohanek, Jennifer; Duke, Marshall P.; Edmondson, Amy; Fivush, Robyn; Frankl, Viktor; Grant, Adam; Harber, Kent; Jacobson, Lenore; Jussim, Lee; Kumar, R. Sreevalsa; Lacan, Jacques; Lazarus, Amber; pedagogy; Rosenthal, Robert; Teklu, Fiseha
public intellectuals, 8, 14, 17n14, 131–32, 134n29

queer theory, 6–7, 16n9, 73–76, 78–79, 82–88, 227. *See also* black queer theory; feminism; gender theory; intersectionality; kinship; LGBTQ studies

race, 11–12, 215, 224, 260; in American society, 124–30, 163; and class, 12, 144, 146–48, 188, 195, 228–29, 231; economic power, 11–12, 33–35, 50, 90–91, 106–7, 109, 111–12, 157–60, 190–93, 196–97, 210–12, 214–15, 219–23; in film, 11, 47–48, 231; and gender, 6–7, 25, 41, 42, 75, 168, 173–74, 252–53; in a global context, 39–40, 50, 155, 157–60, 163–64; and higher education, 8, 10, 12–13, 101–2, 106, 108–10, 112–19, 132, 167–68, 171–77, 251–57, 261–62; and immigration, 7, 88–98, 93; and intellectual history, 123–25, 127; and politics, 8, 33–35, 48–49, 82–83, 87–98, 123–27, 194, 240; and reconciliation, 11–12, 105–6, 116, 126, 164, 216, 219–20, 224, 258–61; and religion, 45–46, 58, 62–64, 69; and representation, 29, 31–32, 42, 51, 105, 130–31, 136–37, 146, 171–72, 183, 201–4, 214, 217–19, 256; and sexuality, 6–7, 43–44, 73–83, 239; in southern narratives, 23, 25, 26, 29, 32, 38–39, 73–74, 201; and violence, 41, 46, 87, 126, 128–31, 136–37, 178n3, 186, 188, 197, 260–61; and white supremacism, 7, 10, 17, 33, 36, 74, 89, 93–94, 98, 127, 130, 132, 136, 146, 168, 171–72, 174–75, 186–89, 193, 224, 229, 239–40, 260–61. *See also* African Americans; black queer theory; intersectionality; Latinx community; Native Americans

racism, 31, 40, 61, 82–83, 93, 123–25, 127–28, 130, 132, 225n25, 227; color-blind, 93, 216–19, 224, 225n16, 242n11, 256; in film, 231, 236–39; intellectual, 101–2; and power dynamics, 10–11, 163–64, 216; structural, 34–35, 73, 94, 98, 155, 161–62, 164, 259. *See also* Jim Crow; segregation; violence; white supremacism

"Racism Can't Destroy This Charleston Church" (Greene), 130, 134n26. *See also* Emanuel African Methodist Episcopal (AME) Church; Roof, Dylan

Radishofski, Kathryn, 11, 120n16, 225n25

Rash, Ron, 9, 139, 141–47

Ray, Celeste, 30

Reagan, Ronald, 123

Real South, The (Romine), 16n5, 27, 52, 52n12, 53n14, 53n15, 54n81, 250, 263n17

reception studies, 12, 148, 227–45

Reconstructing Dixie, 25–26, 54n74

Reconstruction, 35–36, 50, 62–63, 65, 124–25, 188–90, 197, 257; "Second Reconstruction," 125, 133n6, 133n12

Reding, Nick, 144–45

Red's Lounge, 222

Reece, Florence, 191, 195

Reed, John Shelton, 24

Regeneration through Violence (Slotkin), 229

Regents of the University of California v. Bakke, 126–27. *See also* race

regionalism, critical, 47–49, 241n2. *See also* southern studies, new

Reid-Pharr, Robert, 262, 264n49

Reinhart, Shirley, 191–92

religion, in the South. *See* African Methodist Episcopal (AME) Church; Baptist and neo-evangelical culture; Bible Belt; Catholicism; Church of Christ; Disciples of Christ; Emanuel African Methodist Episcopal (AME) Church; Episcopalians; evangelicalism; fundamentalism; Holiness-Pentecostal churches; *Journal of Southern Religion*; Judaism; Lutherans; Methodism; Methodist Episcopal Church, South; National Association of Evangelicals; Presbyterians; Southern Baptist Convention

Religious Right, 68–69

religious studies, southern, 6, 45–47, 57, 61

Republican Party, 66, 125, 133–34n18, 183, 257; of Alabama, 87, 92; political dominance of, 58; and "Southern Strategy," 123–24

Rice, Tamir, 128

Richardson, Bonham, 39, 53n44

Ring, Natalie J., 125, 127, 133n5, 254–55

Rivlin, Elizabeth, 142, 150n13

Road, The (McCarthy), 140

Roberts, Cecil, 197

Robeson, Paul, 127

Robinson, Zandria F., vii, 31–32, 132, 134n34, 134n35, 241, 242n10, 242n11, 245n52, 245n56

Romero, Cameron, 235

Romero, George, 230, 235

Romine, Scott, 15n3, 16n5, 27, 44, 52, 149n5, 212n6, 250, 253, 255, 259, 263n17, 263n38. *See also* foodways, southern

Rony, Fatima Tobing, 189, 199n29

Roof, Dylan, 130–31, 136. *See also* Confederate flag; Emanuel African Methodist Episcopal (AME) Church; race; violence; white supremacism

Roosevelt, Franklin, 62. *See also* New Deal

Roots/Heritage Tourism in Africa and the African Diaspora (conference), 103–4. *See also* tourism

Rosenthal, Robert, 175–76, 180n23. *See also* psychology

Rubin, Louis, Jr., 23, 36, 52n5

Ruby, Jay, 185, 198n14

Rural Gothic in American Popular Culture, The (Murphy), 229

Rushdie, Salman, 21, 22

Rushing, Wanda, 30, 31, 159

Russell, Karen, 11, 201, 204–5, 206, 207, 208–11

Rust College, 105, 106, 118. *See also* Behind the Big House; historically black colleges and universities; Holly Springs, Miss.; Mississippi

"Sahara of the Bozart, The" (Mencken), 58–59

Sandlin, David, 139–40

Sankey, Ira, 61

Satterwhite, Emily, 12, 148, 245n49

Scalawag, 129

Schweiger, Beth Barton, 57–58

Scopes, John T., trial of, 58

Second Coming, The (Percy), 67

Secure Communities, 88, 92

Segregating Sound (Miller), 43

segregation, 33, 34–35, 37–39, 43, 94, 108, 117, 164, 170, 187, 220; Jim Crow, 163. *See also* economy; Jim Crow; race; white supremacism

Serena (Rash), 142

Shack-Up Inn, 217

sharecropping, 44, 105, 109, 111, 112, 117, 171, 217. *See also* capitalism; cotton; economy; plantations; race; Reconstruction

Sheheen, Vincent, 137

Silent Majority, The (Lassiter), 124

Simon, Scott, 142

Skipper, Jodi, 8, 241, 249, 262. *See also* Center for the Study of Southern Culture; Transforming New South Identities Symposium

slavery, 25, 26, 40, 62, 63–64, 75, 94, 158–59, 184, 187, 188, 210, 215, 242n11; and Baptist-Methodist Christianity, 64–65; as collective identity, 196–97; and globalization, 156, 163–64; and public history, 105–6, 111, 117. *See also* capitalism; Civil War; cotton; economy; labor; Methodist Episcopal Church, South; plantations; race; sharecropping; white supremacism

Slotkin, Richard, 229

Smith, Barbara Ellen, 49, 190

Smith, Henry Nash, 256–57

Smith, Jeromey, 195

Smith, Jon, 8, 12–13, 147, 149n5, 168, 212n6; *Finding Purple America*, 16n5, 27–28, 49, 53n16, 150n28, 252, 261, 262n11; *Look Away! The U.S. South in New World Studies*, 16n5, 26, 52n4, 52n11, 53n46, 54n77, 158, 165n13. *See also* southern studies, new

Smith, Laurajane, 108

social activism, 7–8, 49–50

social theory, 37, 48, 189, 193

Society for U.S. Intellectual History, 8, 129, 134n19

sociology, 9, 16n9, 30, 37, 227; feminist, 161

Soja, Edward, 37, 39, 53n37

Soles, Carter, 232, 241n2

#solidarityisforwhitewomen, 258

Somos Tuskaloosa, 96–97

South Carolina Statehouse, 136–37. *See also* Confederate flag

South Magazine, 126

South: Modern Southern Literature in Its Cultural Setting (ed. Rubin and Jacobs), 23

South to a New Place (Jones and Monteith), 26, 52n4, 52n11, 54n77

South to a Very Old Place (Murray), 26

Southern Agrarians, 22, 36, 37, 38

Southern Baptist Convention, 63. *See also* Baptist and neo-evangelical culture; evangelicalism; fundamentalism; National Association of Evangelicals

Southern Christian Leadership Conference (SCLC), 97. *See also* civil rights movement; King, Martin Luther, Jr.

"Southern Cross, The" (Wright), 136, 146
Southern Cross (Heyrman), 57, 65, 70n26
Southern Crossings (Turner), 135–36
Southern Cultures, 250
Southern Exposure, 126, 127
Southern Focus Polls, 257
Southern Foodways Alliance, 44, 149n5, 251, 257, 258, 259; and public history, 104. *See also* Center for the Study of Southern Culture; Edge, John T.; foodways, southern; University of Mississippi
Southern Foodways Alliance Community Cookbook, 251
Southern Heritage on Display (Ray), 30
Southern Historical Association, 66
Southern Literary Renaissance, 38
Southern Past, The (Brundage), 36, 52
Southern Poverty Law Center, 128, 180n22
Southern Regional Council, 126
Southern Regions of the United States (Odum), 59–60
Southern Renascence, 23
Southern Spaces, 37, 197n1, 262
"Southern Strategy," 123. *See also* Nixon, Richard; race
southern studies, new, 22, 23–25, 40–41, 50–51, 52, 147, 249–50, 253; and American studies, 250; and critical regionalism, 47; and cultural and literary studies, 24–29, 34–35, 38–39; and cultural heritage studies, 30; and foodways, 44–45, 57–58, 149n5; and globalization, 37–38, 39–40; and historians, 252–53, 254–55; and LGBTQ studies, 43–44; and literary scholars, 254; sense of place, 36–37; and social activism, 49–50; and social scientists, 254; sociological studies, 30–32; and southern bodies, 41–42; southern history, 32–34, 36; and the southern imaginary, 47–49; and southern music, 42–43; and southern studies students, 253–54, 255; and spirituality, 45–47
Southern Voices, 126
southscape, 39
Southscapes (Davis), 38
spatial theory, 38
Staten Island, N.Y., 128
Staunton Hill, 227–28, 229, 230–31, 235–38, 242n14, 242n17. *See also* hillbilly horror

STEM (science, technology, engineering and mathematics) disciplines: and African Americans, 110, 112, 117; and southern studies, 138
Stitt, Frank, 258–59
Stitt, Pardis, 259
Storming Heaven (Giardina), 196
Strangers and Kin, 194
Stranger with a Camera, 190
Subduing Satan (Ownby), 65
Sunday, Billy, 61
Swamp Preacher, 139–40
Swamplandia! (Russell), 11, 201, 204–9, 211–12
Sweat Equity Investment in the Cotton Kingdom Symposium, 109–10, 111, 113. *See also* cotton; economy; plantations; slavery; sharecropping

Taylor, Cheryl, 113
Taylor, Chris, 106, 110
Taylor, Melanie Benson, 11, 17n21; *Disturbing Calculations*, 184, 198n9
Teklu, Fiseha, 176
Texas Chain Saw Massacre, The, 228, 230, 235, 236, 243n29, 245n43, 245n47
This Ain't Chicago (Robinson), 31–32, 134n34, 242n11
Thompson, Ashley B. 254, 255
Thompson, Tracy, 123
Thorpe, Angela, 102, 103, 117; diversity and public history, 106–7, 108, 110–11; and University of North Carolina at Greensboro, 101
To Serve God and Wal-Mart (Moreton), 65
tourism, 104–5; and African American heritage, 117; and African American studies, 103–5; blues, 11–12, 104, 120n16, 214–26; as field of study, 104, 120n16; industry of, 117; Native American, 213n9
traditionalism, southern, 21, 36
Transformation of Virginia, The (Isaac), 65
Transforming New South Identities Symposium, 3–5, 10, 12–14, 167, 177, 180n29, 182, 185, 249, 251–52, 254, 263n21. *See also* Center for the Study of Southern Culture; Coffey, Michele Grigsby; Skipper, Jodi
Trefzer, Annette, 9–10, 17n21, 26, 29
Tresca, Michael J., 233–34, 244n34
Troy, Bill, 193

True Blood, 139
Truth and Reconciliation Commission (Canada), 258
Tullos, Allen, 48
Turner, Daniel Cross, 9, 15n2, 135–36; *Southern Crossings*, 135–36; *Undead Souths*, 141, 144, 149n6
Turner, Linda, 105
Turnipseed, Cassie Sade, 109, 110, 111, 112, 118
Tuscaloosa, Ala., 88, 90–91, 94–97, 99n6
Twentieth Century, The, 185. See also documentary film
Twitter, 130–32, 133n18

undead, 9, 149n6, 210; as concept, 140, 150n6; in fiction, 142–46; in popular culture, 139–40, 141
Undead Souths (ed. Anderson, Hagood, and Turner), 141, 144, 149n6
United Food and Commercial Workers, 192
United Mine Workers of America (UMWA), 197, 200n53
United Nations, 153
University of Georgia Press, 16n5, 26, 44, 149n5
University of Memphis, 132, 179n18. See also Memphis, Tenn.
University of Mississippi, 4, 9, 102, 149n5, 249, 252, 257; faculty of, 167; and Global South, 153–54, 159, 164; and Global South Working Group, 9–10; and pedagogy, 167, 171, 179n13; and public history, 104, 106–7, 114, 118; symbols, 16n10. See also Center for the Study of Southern Culture; Oxford, Miss.; Southern Foodways Alliance; Transforming New South Identities Symposium
University of North Carolina at Chapel Hill, 45, 17n10, 121n32, 252, 253, 257
University of North Carolina at Greensboro, 101
University of North Carolina Press, 26
University of South Carolina, 167, 257, 263n30
University of Texas at Austin, 23, 45, 104, 167, 180n29
U.S. Civil Rights Commission, 89
U.S. District Court for the Middle District of Alabama, 93
U.S. Office of Economic Opportunity (OEO), 194

Valentine, Charles, 222
Vanderbilt Agrarians, 22, 36, 37, 38
Vesey, Denmark, 136
Vicksburg National Military Park, 113
Vietnam War, 125, 188
violence, 34, 48, 81, 99n4, 126, 211, 229, 260; Civil War, 63; in film, 183n10, 231, 239; and Native Americans, 203, 253; police, 81, 115, 124, 128, 129, 186; racial, 41, 42, 82–83, 245n56, 260; religious, 46; and whiteness, 174, 238. See also Ku Klux Klan; lynching
Volstead, Andrew, 61
Voting Rights Act of 1965, 8, 123, 133n1, 198n17

Wald, Elijah, 42
Walker, Margaret, 116
Walking Dead, The, 139, 141
Wallerstein, Immanuel, 39–40, 165n1
Ward, Brian, 2, 252, 262n13
Warf, Barney, 156–57
Warnes, Andrew, 44, 251
War on Poverty, 190
Washington Post, 130
Watson, Jay, 41
Wekker, Gloria, 74, 75
Welty, Eudora, 36
Wey, Tunde, 259
Wharton Business School, 174
"Which Side Are You On?" (Reese), 191, 195
"White Man's Burden, The" (Kipling), 61
white power, 33, 240, 261
whiteness, 32, 107, 146–47, 148, 158, 174, 229, 239–40; and southern studies students, 171–72. See also foodways, southern; race; violence; *Wrong Turn 2*
white privilege, 171, 240, 260; and blues tourism, 224; and southern studies faculty, 168
white supremacism, 33, 36, 74, 89, 93, 98; and anti-white supremacist thought, 132; in film, 10, 186, 229, 240; gendered dynamics of, 178n3; and international context, 127; and labor, 193; and Minuteman Project, 94; and racial oppression, 7, 187, 215, 224, 261; and southern studies pedagogy, 10, 168, 171–73, 175; and symbolism, 17n10, 136, 146; and violence, 130; and white privilege, 224
Williams, Chad, 131

Williams, Juan, 128
Wilson, Charles Reagan, 5, 7–8, 16n5, 16n7, 17n21, 58; *Flashes of a Southern Spirit*, 46. *See also* Center for the Study of Southern Culture
Winders, Jamie, 89
Winter's Bone, 144
WNYC, 130
Women's Christian Temperance Union, 61
Women's Museum in Dallas, 104
women's studies, 29, 32. *See also* feminism; gender studies; intersectionality
Wood, Amy Louise, 41
Woodrell, Daniel, 144
Woodward, C. Vann, 33, 34, 127, 133n6
Works Progress Administration (WPA), 208. *See also* New Deal

World War II, 50, 66, 68, 133n8, 187, 242n11
Wright, Charles, 136, 146, 147
Wrong Turn 2, 228–29; and Appalachian stereotypes, 229–31; and consumer capitalism, 234; and industrial capitalism, 232–35; political uses of, 239–40; and whiteness, 239–40, 242n14, 242n17, 243n23, 243n29. *See also* hillbilly horror

Yaeger, Patricia, 23, 36, 49; *Dirt and Desire*, 53n35, 249
YMCA, 61

Zimmerman, George, 197
Žižek, Slavoj, 260

The New Southern Studies

The Nation's Region: Southern Modernism, Segregation, and U.S. Nationalism
    by Leigh Anne Duck
Black Masculinity and the U.S. South: From Uncle Tom to Gangsta
    by Riché Richardson
Grounded Globalism: How the U.S. South Embraces the World
    by James L. Peacock
*Disturbing Calculations: The Economics of Identity in
Postcolonial Southern Literature, 1912–2002*
    by Melanie R. Benson
American Cinema and the Southern Imaginary
    edited by Deborah E. Barker and Kathryn McKee
Southern Civil Religions: Imagining the Good Society in the Post-Reconstruction Era
    by Arthur Remillard
Reconstructing the Native South: American Indian Literature and the Lost Cause
    by Melanie Benson Taylor
Apples and Ashes: Literature, Nationalism, and the Confederate States of America
    by Coleman Hutchison
Reading for the Body: The Recalcitrant Materiality of Southern Fiction, 1893–1985
    by Jay Watson
Latining America: Black-Brown Passages and the Coloring of Latino/a Studies
    by Claudia Milian
Finding Purple America: The South and the Future of American Cultural Studies
    by Jon Smith
The Signifying Eye: Seeing Faulkner's Art
    by Candace Waid
*Sacral Grooves, Limbo Gateways: Travels in Deep Southern Time,
Circum-Caribbean Space, Afro-creole Authority*
    by Keith Cartwright
Jim Crow, Literature, and the Legacy of Sutton E. Griggs
    edited by Tess Chakkalakal and Kenneth W. Warren
Sounding the Color Line: Music and Race in the Southern Imagination
    by Erich Nunn
Borges's Poe: The Influence and Reinvention of Edgar Allan Poe in Spanish America
    by Emron Esplin
Eudora Welty's Fiction and Photography: The Body of the Other Woman
    by Harriet Pollack
Keywords for Southern Studies
    edited by Scott Romine and Jennifer Rae Greeson
Navigating Souths: Transdisciplinary Explorations of a U.S. Region
    edited by Michele Grigsby Coffey and Jodi Skipper
The Southern Hospitality Myth: Ethics, Politics, Race, and American Memory
    by Anthony Szczesiul

Where the New World Is: Literature about the U.S. South at Global Scales
    by Martyn Bone
Red States: Indigeneity, Settler Colonialism, and Southern Studies
    by Gina Caison
The Whole Machinery: The Rural Modern in Cultures of the U.S. South, 1890–1946
    by Benjamin S. Child

Printed in the USA
CPSIA information can be obtained
at www.ICGtesting.com
CBHW011412251124
17967CB00010B/394